Education as
My Agenda

D1564396

Palgrave Studies in Oral History

Series Editors: Linda Shopes and Bruce M. Stave

Education as My Agenda

Gertrude Williams, Race, and the Baltimore Public Schools

Gertrude S. Williams

with

Jo Ann Ooiman Robinson

EDUCATION AS MY AGENDA
© Gertrude S. Williams and Jo Ann Ooiman Robinson, 2005.

First published in 2005 by
PALGRAVE MACMILLAN™
175 Fifth Avenue, New York, N.Y. 10010 and
Houndmills, Basingstoke, Hampshire, England RG21 6XS
Companies and representatives throughout the world.

PALGRAVE MACMILLAN is the global academic imprint of the Palgrave Macmillan division of St. Martin's Press, LLC and of Palgrave Macmillan Ltd. Macmillan® is a registered trademark in the United States, United Kingdom and other countries. Palgrave is a registered trademark in the European Union and other countries.

ISBN 0–312–29542–1
ISBN 0–312–29543–X

Library of Congress Cataloging-in-Publication Data

Williams, Gertrude S., 1927–
    Education as my agenda : Gertrude Williams, race, and the Baltimore
Public Schools / Gertrude S. Williams with Jo Ann Ooiman Robinson.
        p. cm.—(Palgrave studies in oral history)
    ISBN 0–312–29542–1 (alk. paper)
    ISBN 0–312–29543–X (pbk. : alk. paper)
    1. Williams, Gertrude S., 1927–. 2. School principals—United States—
Biography. 3. African American school principals—Biography. 4. Public
schools—Maryland—Baltimore—History—20th century. 5. United
States— Race relations—History—20th century—Sources. I. Robinson,
Jo Ann, 1942–. II. Title. III. Series.

LA2317.W5132A3 2005
371′.01′09752′6—dc22   2005047619

A catalogue record for this book is available from the British Library.

Design by Newgen Imaging Systems (P) Ltd., Chennai, India.

First edition: October 2005

10 9 8 7 6 5 4 3 2 1

Printed in the United States of America.

This book is dedicated to the memory of
Mamie Wallace Williams
and her faith in education as the key to freedom

Contents

Series Editors' Foreword

Oral historians enjoy a particular relationship with the subjects of our inquiry. Like all historians, we investigate topics that interest us. But in addition, we frequently interview people we admire, people whose personal histories we believe deserve wider recognition and whom we want to represent well to others. Moreover, the intimacy that often develops in an interview can serve to heighten our regard for the narrator, as we come to a fuller appreciation of the complex human being with whom we are speaking. Yet the positive relationship we have with narrators has its drawbacks too: it can inhibit critical inquiry, prevent us from asking the hard questions, and lead us to represent interviewees as heroes rather than historical actors.

Jo Ann Ooiman Robinson's oral biography of African American educator Gertrude Williams is notable, therefore, for the skill with which it has negotiated the Scylla of admiration and Charybdis of historical inquiry. This balancing act is all the more remarkable because Robinson herself is an actor in Williams's story, which embraces much of the history of public schooling in Baltimore during the last half century. She played a leadership role in parent organizations at Baltimore's Barclay School during Williams's tenure as principal and joined her in numerous struggles to improve the quality of education at the school. Yet with the discipline and dispassion of the historian, Robinson has prodded Williams to give a full historical account, pointed out those (few) places where this account differs from the extant record, and provided informed context for Williams's narrative.

Of course, it is not just Robinson's skill as a historian that accounts for the sophistication and depth of *Education as My Agenda*. Gertrude Williams herself is an articulate and self-assured narrator, a woman with a sharp memory, firm point of view, and keen awareness of the historical significance of her story. She began her career in 1949 as a third grade teacher in Baltimore's segregated school system and retired in 1998 as principal of an integrated elementary and middle school. During those 49 years, she was both witness to and participant in the enormous changes, many of them racially inflected, convulsing urban education during the latter half of the twentieth century. Coming of age at a time when teachers enjoyed the highest regard in the African American community, Williams retained a profound sense of vocation throughout her career, rooted in a passionate belief in every child's right to an excellent public education. During the latter half of her career especially, this belief led her to become an education activist in Baltimore City: she advanced innovative programs at Barclay School, cultivated networks of support within the school community, and goaded an unresponsive bureaucracy into action.

For both the significance of the story and the skill with which it is rendered, we are pleased to include *Education as My Agenda* in *Palgrave's Studies in Oral History* series, designed to bring oral history interviews out of the archives and into the hands of students, educators, scholars, and the reading public. Volumes in the series are deeply grounded in interviews and also present those interviews in ways that aid readers to more fully appreciate their historical significance and cultural meaning. The series also includes work that approaches oral history more theoretically, as a point of departure for an exploration of broad questions of cultural production and representation.

Linda Shopes
Pennsylvania Historical & Museum Commission

Bruce M. Stave
University of Connecticut

Acknowledgments

Gertrude Williams and I owe a debt of gratitude to the many individuals and institutions that supported and helped us as we have worked on *Education as My Agenda*. Her sisters, Sarah Jewett and Lottie Child, and her niece and nephew, Joan and Harley Spry, helped us recover family history and find family photos. The memories of Mrs. Jewett, along with those of Gertrude's classmates, Eva Flynt and Leroy Williams contributed to our reconstruction of life at Germantown High School in the 1940s. Similarly, her college roommate, Clara Jones, shared and confirmed memories of Cheyney State Teachers College in the era immediately following World War II. One of my college roommates, Jane Campbell, lent her genealogical expertise and enthusiasm to our search for Williams family data in U.S. Census records.

We received expert and gracious assistance from librarians and archivists at the following institutions: the Orange County Historical Society and Orange County Court House in Virginia; the Germantown Historical Society, the Conwellana-Templana Collection of the Temple University Library, the Enon Tabernacle Baptist Church and Grace Baptist Church, all in Philadelphia; the Alan Mason Chesney Medical Archives of the Johns Hopkins Hospital and the Ferdinand Hamburger Jr. Archives at the Johns Hopkins University (Homewood Campus, Baltimore); the Maryland Room, the African American Special Collection Department, as well as the Social Science and Periodicals Departments of the Central Branch of the Enoch Pratt Free Library in Baltimore; the Baltimore City Archives; the Special Collections Department, Langsdale Library, University of Baltimore; and the Reference Department and Beulah Davis Special Collections of the Morris Soper Library at Morgan State University.

Graduate students currently enrolled in the Department of History and Geography at Morgan State who deserve thanks for assisting with research are Amy Tillerson, who traveled to the Orange County Court House to check land records, and Medrika Law-Womack, who performed yeowoman's service in indexing most of the audiotaped interviews, helping to organize the bibliography, and tracking down a number of elusive facts. Before he graduated, student assistant Mario Nisbett began the task of indexing the interviews. We also called on alumni of the Morgan History Graduate program. Dr. Donna Hollie and Dr. Gloria Warren helped us resolve a number of research quandaries. Anthony Ratcliff, as he was packing to leave for a doctoral program at the University of Massachusetts, found time to assist me at long-distance when I was on sabbatical leave and writing in the north woods of Minnesota. Thanks are due to Morgan State University for that sabbatical.

To historian Vincent P. Franklin, retired Baltimore City Public Schools administrator Lewis Richardson, retired Barclay School kindergarten teacher Janice French, Esther Bonnet, Barclay's most loyal volunteer, and all of the individuals named in the "Interviews" section of the bibliography we extend gratitude for their time and patience in responding to our questions. We are indebted to veteran (and now retired) journalist, Mike Bowler, for the rich store of data on city schools that he compiled as education reporter and editor of the *Baltimore Sun*. We thank everyone at Palgrave Macmillan and Newgen Imaging Systems who had a part in shepherding our book through the process of publication, especially the three individuals who worked most closely with us, Palgrave Editor Alessandra Bastagli, Editorial Assistant Petrina Crockford, and Newgen copy-editor, Maran Elancheran. Finally, a special word of appreciation for our editors, Bruce Stave and Linda Shopes. They believed in *Education as My Agenda* when it was still in a quite rough stage and proffered encouragement that urged us on. Linda's meticulous and trenchant editing was invaluable.

We could not have composed the history that follows without the support of all who are named here. At the same time, any errors, sins of omission, or other infelicities are totally our responsibility.

Jo Ann Ooiman Robinson

Introduction

"Tonight we are witnessing the beginning of a new era" declared former Baltimore Mayor, Thomas J. D'Alesandro III on December 10, 1987, as he opened the inaugural ceremonies for the city's first elected black mayor, Kurt L. Schmoke.[1] The young and earnest mayor-elect was stepping into a role that, as the *Baltimore Sun* observed, "has . . . for decades been occupied by mainline politicians and . . . since 1971 has been dominated by William Donald Schaefer, now governor." A cheering throng of 13,000 constituents warmly applauded Schmoke's pledge to make "a great city greater." No one in that crowd responded more enthusiastically than Gertrude Williams when Schmoke revealed his vision for the future:

> Of all the things I might be able to accomplish as mayor of our city, it would make me proudest if one day it could be said of Baltimore that this is the city that reads. . . . And this is the city whose citizens, businesses, industries, and institutions joined together to make education work for all who were willing to work for an education.

Gertrude, the principal of public school #54, The Barclay School, had brought nearly 200 students with her to the inaugural ceremony. When a reporter asked one of them, Patricia Cuffie, why she was there, the eight-year old replied, "to honor the mayor . . . I know he could really make a change," she added. "He's really nice and he could do something."[2]

Parents, educators, and the business community shared Patricia's hope that Schmoke would lead a revival of the Baltimore public schools, which, like most urban school systems, were struggling to meet the needs of increasing numbers of needy students with resources that were ever shrinking. However, among political observers, the young mayor's vision of school reform provoked skepticism. Pointing to failed mayoral efforts at school improvement in Detroit, New York, San Francisco, Chicago, and Philadelphia, *Baltimore Sun* journalist, Michael Ollove, concluded that "the history of American mayors thrusting themselves into educational affairs has not been a happy or successful one." Ollove quoted Johns Hopkins political scientist, Paul Peterson: "The basic problem is that we don't know how to make the schools better. It's not like filling a pothole."[3]

Gertrude Williams could not have disagreed more. In 1987 she was a 38-year veteran of the Baltimore school system. Having begun as a teacher in the Colored School District, she worked as a counselor in the early days of desegregation, and in 1969 was assigned to Barclay as an assistant principal. After four years, she was one of the first appointments made by Baltimore's first black superintendent, Roland Patterson, who named her principal of Barclay School. Her reputation for candor and feistiness had attracted the attention of former mayor Schaefer, who called on her to serve on a community task force dealing with racial tensions and later on the board of the Fund for Educational Excellence, a belated school reform initiative of the Schaefer administration.

Now, at the dawn of the Schmoke era, Gertrude had a plan for improving student performance at Barclay. She saw this plan as a pilot project that might well point the way to higher achievement for other city schools. Since Schmoke had placed education at the top of his priorities list, and since her plan was so straightforward, clearly conceived, and economically viable, she expected to gain his blessing.

In Baltimore, as in many urban centers, public education was the focus of widespread dissatisfaction. Employers lamented the poor skills and shoddy work habits that public school graduates brought to the workplace. College faculties expressed similar dismay over how poorly the products of public schooling were prepared for college level work. Political leaders issued ominous warnings that the United States' standing in the world was at risk as students from other countries out-performed ours in critical subject areas of science and technology. Students themselves demonstrated their disaffection from education by being truant and dropping-out at astounding rates. Magnifying such signs of distress was the factor of race. Throughout the country black and impoverished student populations lagged behind white and middle-class youth by every common measure of achievement, including course-work grades, standardized tests, rates of graduation, and employability. The profile of large numbers of black students in Baltimore was no different.[4]

Researchers and commentators produced a litany of causes for this education malaise, including badly prepared teachers, low student self-esteem, flawed curricula, inadequate and inequitable funding, and dysfunctional school bureaucracies. As a principal, Gertrude grappled on a daily basis with these and a multitude of other problems endemic to urban public schools. At the same time, however, she communicated by word, and even more by compelling example, her deep belief in the importance and potential of the American public school as a meeting ground for all the races, nationalities, creeds, customs, and socioeconomic classes of a democratic society.

As principal and author Deborah Meier has written, "for many children and their families schools are one of the few institutions that can provide the experience of membership in an enlarged common community . . ."[5] Gertrude labored joyfully at creating and sustaining such a community at Barclay. She engaged teachers, families, and various community institutions in an ongoing collaborative endeavor to empower every Barclay student with the knowledge, social skills, and habits of mind that a free society requires of its citizens and that its citizens must employ if they are to keep their society free.

At the time of Schmoke's inauguration, this endeavor took the form of a plan for Barclay teachers and students to adopt the time-tested, traditional curriculum of the prestigious Calvert School, a private institution a few blocks north of Barclay. Setting perfection as the standard for the work they required of students, teachers trained in Calvert methods were satisfied with nothing less than developing the full potential of every child. Gertrude felt certain that these methods would work just as well for her mostly black and poor students as they did for the wealthy and mostly white children attending Calvert.

Her confidence was bolstered by knowing that once the school system approved the plan, the Abell Foundation, a major philanthropic organization in the city, was prepared to fund it. All she needed was that approval, and Schmoke's concern about the quality of public education gave her hope that the approval would be forthcoming. Her dismay was boundless when—a few months into the new mayoral administration—Schmoke's new superintendent, Richard Hunter, told her "no." The school board upheld his decision and the mayor went along with them both.

A year and a half later, exhausted in body, bruised in spirit, but still battling for the Barclay–Calvert program, Gertrude took advantage of a public forum to confront Kurt Schmoke. June 3, 1989, on a hot Saturday in a recreation center crowded with several hundred citizens, the five-foot Gertrude, wearing a surgical collar to ease the pain of an arthritic spine, stepped to the microphone. "Over thirty years ago," she declared, "I took education as my agenda, as you did when you ran for election. It is a tough and demanding agenda, but it is rewarding." By the time she finished speaking and answering his questions, Gertrude had Mayor Schmoke on her side.

Another year of negotiating and the ouster of Superintendent Hunter would occur before the school board agreed to the Calvert plan for Barclay. With signed agreement in hand, in the spring of 1990, Gertrude went forward into the most dramatic chapter in her already distinctive and ambitious life as an educator. Bringing the Barclay–Calvert partnership to fruition, she would watch her teaching staff come alive as never before and would rejoice as students excelled beyond all expectations. Their success was broadcast by the national media, and Gertrude and the Barclay School community found themselves in the national spotlight. They were able to sustain the demanding Calvert program in the chaotic public school system for only a short time, but in that time Gertrude was more than vindicated in her conviction that poverty and kindred disadvantages need not prevent inner city public school students from attaining the same knowledge, skills, and self-esteem as children in private schools coming from wealthy and privileged backgrounds.

Although establishing the Calvert curriculum at Barclay was the most distinguished achievement of her 49-year career, that career was notable in many respects. Her individual agenda intersected with a myriad of agendas grafted onto, and frequently sloughed off by, public education: desegregation, standardized testing, innovations in funding, curriculum, teacher education, school management, ad infinitum. In some cases the intersections were harmonious, or at least unremarkable. Sometimes—and particularly as she gained stature as Barclay's principal—Gertrude challenged the prevailing "system" and clashed with the public education bureaucracy.

She fought intrepidly for the financial and material resources that she deemed essential for her students and faculty. Working with staff and parents, she adjusted the school schedule, set up classes and teaching assignments in innovative ways, initiated policies and programs—all according to what would best meet student needs, irregardless of central office mandates. An intrinsic element of her clashes with the authors of such mandates was her collaboration with parents and members of the community. Gertrude and her "Barclay Raiders," as some parents jokingly called themselves, were known in school district offices and at City Hall as a force to be reckoned with.

When she retired in 1998, the *Baltimore Sun* called Gertrude "the most powerful of principals" who "tangled with two superintendents and beat them both."[6] In this memoir, she identifies what she is convinced are the essential elements of sound education and describes the battles she waged to try to secure those elements. She also describes her own education—growing up black in largely white Germantown, Pennsylvania; studying black history and culture for the first time at Cheyney State Teachers College; and meeting the rigorous demands of that teacher training program, from which she graduated in 1949. In retracing her career, Gertrude examines the highs and lows of urban public education since World War II. Never for a moment has Gertrude doubted that children can be well served by public schools. She is at once an outspoken critic and spirited advocate of the system to which she has devoted her life.

Unofficially, Gertrude's and my collaboration on this book extends back to 1976, the year we met, when I entrusted my first born to kindergarten at Barclay School. By the time his younger sister followed him into Barclay in 1979, I was hopelessly entangled in public school politics, drawn in by Gertrude, who seemed to live at the school (some children believed that she actually did!) and to never sleep. Her passion for her job was the most powerful example of *vocation*, in the original sense of *being called*, that I had ever encountered. Thirty-four years old, with a doctorate in history and a position on a university faculty, I thought that my days of being inspired by great teachers and mentors were over. Instead, I found the most inspiring teacher-mentor of all in my kids' principal.

As I witnessed and often participated in many of the struggles that Gertrude describes in this book, I found myself thinking—and telling her—that she ought to record her experiences, for she has not just lived through the transformations of public education wrought by major demographic, cultural, social, and political changes. She has wrestled with them and forcefully challenged policy makers when she found their adaptations to such changes unacceptable.

Officially, the process that produced this book began on February 5, 1999. Between then and June 17, Gertrude and I met 12 times to record her experiences on audiotape. Each session lasted from 90 to 150 minutes, with most running 2 hours. We worked from a schedule of questions that I composed and that was organized chronologically, from childhood through the years at Barclay. However, as the processes of memory and reflection proceeded, there were many departures from the chronology and a considerable amount of movement back and forth between the various life stages.

Over the next year and a half, I transcribed the tapes from the 1999 sessions and submitted transcripts to Gertrude for her review. In five meetings during February and March of 2001 and a later session in mid-June 2001, we reviewed the transcripts together, taping additional thoughts and recollections as well as correcting facts and spellings. Though tedious, this process enhanced the material in the original tapings with richer detail.

Between July and November 2001, while enjoying a half-year sabbatical from teaching, I pieced together the narrative chapters that constitute the main body of *Education as My Agenda*, using the corrected transcripts of the 1999 interviews and the tapes from the 2001 sessions.[7] In an intensive series of ten meetings between November 30 and December 20, 2001, we read chapter-drafts and made changes according to her observations and wishes. When she added new information, or when we discussed some aspect of the narrative in detail, we taped those additions and discussions. In a three-hour session on January 20, 2004 we reviewed and responded to queries and suggested revisions from editors Linda Shopes and Bruce Stave. Again, when an editorial issue elicited extensive discussion we recorded those discussions on tape. Finally, we met for two to three hours several times between late April and early May 2005 to read the copy-edited version of the manuscript together word for word.

Throughout the editing process I strove to remain faithful to Gertrude's language and meaning. However, the narrative presented here is not a verbatim record of her taped words. I frequently supplied words and phrases to bridge gaps between incomplete thoughts and sentences. I regularly combined passages from one transcript or tape with passages from another transcript or tape that addressed the same subject. Nonetheless, the narrative is Gertrude's in that she reviewed, amended, and approved the final manuscript. Although it reflects her memories, understandings, and points of view, I am responsible for the contents of the footnotes, the essays preceding the chapters, the book's conclusion, and this introduction. In these sections, I offer background information, context, and interpretive comments.

When we began this project, Gertrude did not want to do an autobiography. She insisted that our focus should be on "the story of Barclay School," on the "pro-education community" surrounding the school, and on how she and that community empowered each other to innovate, take risks, and "battle" (her favorite verb) so that every student would have the opportunity to realize his/her full potential. However, as she responded in the first interviews to general questions about family background and her formative years, both of us began to feel the importance of this early history as a prime source of the beliefs and values that informed her adult life and guided her career as an educator. So we widened our scope and began trying to capture as much as we could of her life and work before Barclay.

For me this meant delving into census records, asking to see family papers (which proved to be very sparse), consulting city directories, school board minutes, newspapers, and other such sources and combing relevant secondary literature for data and imagery that would help bring alive the environs in which Gertrude lived and matured before she arrived at Barclay. Similarly, I consulted a plethora of primary and secondary sources to document and contextualize her years at Barclay. While this process could be frustrating and disappointing when I failed to find all of the evidence we needed, it was also heartening. Consistently, the material that was available corroborated Gertrude's memory. Her recall of names and her descriptions of places and people were rarely contradicted by the written record. The major exception to this pattern was her initial failure to mention the segregation and other racist features of the Philadelphia area in which she grew up, a matter that I take up in chapter one.

Although I found no reason to doubt her powers of recall, I did have to be watchful where chronology was concerned. While Gertrude was generally accurate in placing experiences within their actual time frames, she sometimes blurred the sequence of events within a given period. I made a point of having on hand for our recording sessions a chronology, based on newspaper reports, minutes of school meetings and similar documents to which we could refer when we needed to be specific about dates. Gertrude was always definite in her interpretations of major controversies in the city school system or unpleasant conflicts at Barclay and was unfazed by documentation that ran contrary to her view. This was notably true regarding her assessment of Roland Patterson's term and ouster as school superintendent (1971–1975) and her account of how the partnership between Barclay School and Calvert School came to an end in 1996. As the reader finds, her accounts stand as she gave them in her narrative, for this is fundamentally her story. Nonetheless, note is taken of the other points of view in footnotes and/or my commentary that introduces each chapter.

Throughout her recollections, Gertrude sets forth encounters with other individuals in the form of dialogue between them and her, as though she has a mental transcript of exactly what they said to one another. I have set down, within quotation marks, these remembered conversations, because—although they cannot possibly be verbatim accounts, they are so intrinsic to her way of telling a story that summarizing or otherwise tampering with them would do violence to the tone and quality of her narrative.

In the first four chapters of *Education as My Agenda*, Gertrude tells her story chronologically, bringing her to the point of her appointment as the vice principal at Barclay. Beginning with chapter five her narrative becomes thematic, centered around her relationships with the children and staff of Barclay School, as well as the children's families and other community residents who became her partners and advocates in instructional and curricular reform campaigns. I composed, introduced, and annotated chapters one through four by following the standard guidelines for research and documentation—guidelines emphasizing the value of "objectivity." That Gertrude and I have been friends for a quarter of a century undoubtedly predisposed me to believe and sympathize with what she said. But in these early chapters we were dealing with subject matter that bore no direct relationship to me. I could scrutinize it in the light of other sources and present it in a balanced fashion. As noted earlier in the chapter I could identify discrepancies between the written record and her descriptions and not hesitate to probe them. For her part Gertrude, for all her certainty, showed no signs of resenting such challenges.

The Barclay chapters, on the other hand, posed several dilemmas. First, I had participated substantively in most of the experiences that Gertrude recorded. In the course of our taped conversations she occasionally addressed me directly, as "Jo Ann," noting my role in the events she was describing. She and I had relived and dissected some of these experiences many times before we began this book. Was it possible to stand back now and take a fresh look, as opposed to rehearsing the old stories one more time? Second, I was fervidly on Gertrude's side in nearly every battle that she described. How balanced could her accounts, contextualized and documented by me, possibly be? Third, my basement—jammed with file drawers, cartons, and suitcases full to overflowing with correspondence, fliers, newspaper clippings, copies of petitions, task force and commission reports, and multiple other artifacts from Barclay and the city school system—served as the "archive" from which I drew most of the primary sources for these final chapters. Were these materials sufficiently comprehensive? Fourth, some of these sources (for example, Parent–Teacher Organization [PTO] minutes) were written by me. How acceptable can it be to quote myself?

If ever there were a case that seemed to fit what oral historian Valerie Yow has warned of—the danger of a researcher being "too much invested in [a] topic, too closely identifying with a person or a cause"—this could certainly be it. As Gertrude and I set to work, I was keenly aware of the pitfalls in having such a close relationship to her. Just as Yow had cautioned, in our early interview sessions I felt disinclined to press Gertrude on sensitive topics. I experienced what interviewer/author Karen Fields, reflecting on her experience with interviewing her grandmother, has described as the discomfort that arises when applying "the methodological distrust required by objectivity" to the account of someone who is an important part of my life. What is more, I knew I had to apply that same distrust to my own memories and perceptions.[8]

If *Education as My Agenda* has escaped at least a measure of the polemics, nostalgia, and self-celebration that my personal involvement could easily burden it with, it is because I have tried to remain self-conscious of the perils of subjectivity. Gertrude and I both very much want to make an honest and substantive contribution to oral history and to the history of public education generally. We have sought to publish a book that is frank without being self-righteous and has a clear point of view without being offensively opinionated. Having our work dissected by the eagle eyes and tough love of our editors, Linda Shopes and Bruce Stave, went a good way toward helping us achieve that objective.

We have sought out others who figured prominently in Gertrude's account (and especially in the chapters that are focused on Barclay) and whenever possible we have included voices and viewpoints that differ from ours. We welcomed the editorial challenges from Linda and Bruce and revisited points of weakness that they high-lighted and that we then documented more adequately or, failing that, deleted. What is perhaps most interesting is how through several successive sets of interviews the uneasiness attached to the probing of sensitive issues and my hesitancy to press Gertrude concerning discrepancies between the written record and her account began to dissipate. The oral history process encourages those who rigorously partici-pate in it to step back and assess critically the experiences they are trying to recapture. Certainly, the process had that effect on Gertrude and me.

All that said, it is still true that—to use a metaphor from Karen Fields—I have run a few "methodological red lights."[9] I *do* quote myself when a memo or minutes that I wrote in the past help to illuminate an issue about which we had scant other evidence. Throughout the interviews on the Barclay years, I walked a fine line between facilitating Gertrude's remembering and reflecting and applauding the choices she made and relishing the feisty style in which she made them. I will not claim that I never fell into cheerleading territory. Still, I argue that the scholarly disadvantages inherent in being so close to the subject of this book were finally, if not outweighed, at least balanced to a significant degree, by the advantages.

In the same article where she warns of getting too close to one's subject Valerie Yow quotes historian Alice Kessler Harris:

> I think that to become emotionally involved, while it's true that it violates the first canon of the historian, which is objectivity, nevertheless, puts you intimately into a situation and thus enables you to understand it in a way, I think, you can't understand it if you remain outside the situation.[10]

Not only do I share Harris's view, I admit to emulating (at least for purposes of this book) the "new type of historian" identified by French scholar Pierre Nora. This new breed, he has observed,

> is ready to confess the intimate relation he maintains to his subject. Better still, he is ready to proclaim it, deepen it, make of it not the obstacle but the means of his understanding.[11]

Having been a participant-observer at Barclay was of immeasurable value in the interview process and in organizing, clarifying, and translating into readable narrative form the memories, commentaries, gossip, arguments, accusations, and adulation that informed the interviews. Since historical record-keeping had not been a priority for Gertrude or for the school system, my basement archive, however biased in content for having been collected by me, was an indispensable source of documentation. In the final stages of manuscript preparation, I contacted and was able to visit retired Deputy Superintendent Lewis Richardson who generously shared Baltimore school system documents from his own library, which provided additional background on events discussed by Gertrude.

All of the raw materials that have gone into *Education as My Agenda*—including audiotapes, transcripts, and basement-archive data—will be deposited at the University of Baltimore's Langsdale Library in the Special Collections Department.

Jo Ann Ooiman Robinson

Beginnings

In 1930, 70 percent of the black residents of Philadelphia were migrants, and the largest number of them (18.9 percent) had come from Virginia.[1] Among them were Gertrude Williams's father, Horace Williams, her mother, Mamie Wallace Williams, and six of her siblings. Gertrude made seven; an eighth child would be born in Philadelphia. Horace's youngest sister, Emma, also came with them. Their exact reasons for leaving Orange County, Virginia we do not know. But even a cursory examination of that locale's history, social structure, and economy is suggestive.

Lying in the Virginia Piedmont, below the Blue Ridge Mountains, about 85 miles from Richmond, Orange County was home to farmers raising tobacco, grains, legumes, alfalfa, and some livestock—particularly fine horses and fat hogs. The "Orange cured ham" was a product of special local pride.[2] The county also boasted of producing heroes for the American Revolution and the Civil War, as well as two U.S. presidents, James Monroe and Zachary Taylor.

In his history of the county, W.W. Scott noted that, in 1860, 6,111 slaves resided there. He did not provide the details on their lives but devoted several pages to graphic accounts of the brutal punishments visited on those who resisted enslavement.[3] Of most significance to Scott was that the 6,111 enslaved souls represented "one million and a half dollars, nearly double the value of all other personal property." With the Union victory, he lamented, the wealth "was wiped out as with a sponge."[4]

Quite possibly, the grandparents of both Horace and Mamie Williams were among those whose status as chattel was wiped away by the "sponge" of emancipation. Census data indicate that Mamie's maternal grandmother, Julia, was 10-years old in 1865, and her maternal grandfather, Caesar Wallace, was then 45, the same age as Horace's paternal grandmother, Grace Williams.[5]

Neither Scott's account nor other discussions of Orange County history ask, let alone try to answer, how Julia, Caesar, Grace, and their neighbors and kin experienced

Reconstruction and its aftermath. The histories do note the Virginia Constitution of 1869 that established the state's first free public schools. As soon as a superintendent of public instruction was appointed, he segregated the new system.[6] The 1869 constitution also required counties to divide into townships for taxation and voting purposes. Scott explained how Orange County whites handled this:

> As they [African Americans] had already flocked in numbers to Gordonsville and Orange, the two principal villages in the County, it was deemed essential that these precincts should be in the same township, so that the white people might maintain political ascendancy in the other three . . . [7]

Thus, even before Reconstruction ended on the national level in 1876, the whites of Orange County had the upper hand in matters of governance and finance. In 1902, the 1869 constitution was replaced. The new version instituted voting requirements, including a poll tax, that few black residents would be able to meet.[8] With obvious satisfaction, Scott reported in 1907 that to that date:

> [T]here has never been a negro [sic] supervisor in the County, nor any negro [sic] elected to office, and rarely has there been a negro [sic] jury.[9]

This was the case in a county where, according to the 1900 census, 40 percent of the population was black.[10]

Living conditions for large portions of the Orange County population were substandard. A health survey sponsored by the federal government in 1914 found that 25 percent of the county's white children and 38 percent of the black children were malnourished, diagnosed with hookworm and a variety of other intestinal parasites.[11] Works Progress Administration (WPA) researchers reported in the 1930s that blacks in rural Virginia suffered from poor health in significantly greater degree than whites. While the white death rate was declining in the period from 1920 to 1930 (from 10.7 deaths per thousand to 9.9), the death rate for blacks was increasing (from 15.9 to 16.6).[12] Nor were educational opportunities improving. The 26.5 percent of Virginia's high school student population that was black was crowded into 13 percent of the rooms available for high school instruction. The overflow was taught in church basements and other makeshift spaces.[13]

The impact of World War I on Orange County was partly reflected in a sharp population decrease from 1910 to 1920, attributed by scholars to black as well as "foreign born" out-migration.[14] In the next decade the proportion of black to white in rural Virginia had decreased from 35.4 percent to 31 percent, the black out-migration was continuing, and the income of black farmers was declining.[15]

Gertrude's parents came of age in this period. Extant sources on their formative years are sketchy. As she relates later in the chapter, her great grandmother, Julia Wallace, was the central figure in the upbringing of her mother, Mamie Wallace, and

Mamie's sister, Mattie Wallace. Their mother, Gertrude's grandmother Charlotta Wallace,[16] reportedly moved permanently to Philadelphia when they were still toddlers. Their father's identity is not known. Land records verify that Julia owned her house and land. By what means she had accomplished this has not been discovered.

The records also show that Julia's land was near the land of Douglas and Margaret Clark Williams, the parents of Gertrude's father and 13 other children. The two families attended the same Baptist church, Mount Holy in Unionville, founded in 1866. Its members held services in a log cabin until 1871. The edifice where the Wallace and Williams families worshiped had been built in 1885, replacing an earlier structure destroyed by fire. Reverend Adolphus Hobbs, who pastored the Mount Holy congregation from 1902 to 1912, migrated to Germantown, Pennsylvania sometime thereafter. His presence there as the pastor of Enon Tabernacle Baptist Church would be one of the factors that would encourage Mamie and Horace to resettle there.[17]

In their youth Gertrude's parents appear to have gone to Sunday School together and were both instructed by the local black schoolmaster, "Uncle William" Taliaferro (pronounced "Tolliver"), who was the brother of Horace's mother. Family lore depicts Taliaferro as very light skinned and related in some way to a wealthy white family through whom he had acquired financial resources that set him apart as "well-off" in a community where most people were struggling to survive. Some of the Williams's land had been purchased by Douglas Williams in partnership with William Taliaferro's brother, Gilbert Taliaferro, and some Douglas had purchased independently.[18]

Both the Wallaces's and Williams's owning land suggests that striving for economic independence was a part of the upbringing of Gertrude's parents. Having William Taliaferro as his uncle appears to have been another significant influence for Horace, who—according to stories passed down to Gertrude's generation—sent Horace to Manassas Training Institute where he earned a certificate in carpentry.[19]

Horace Williams and Mamie Wallace were married in 1916 in upstate New York, where their marriage certificate shows them both residing. In their first years together as husband and wife, Horace and Mamie were somewhat nomadic. At the time of their marriage, Horace's parents and most of his siblings were dead and the land that his father had owned had been lost. The 1920 census places Mamie and Horace back in Orange County living as renters with their first three children and Horace's youngest sister, Emma.[20] Gertrude recalls stories of a period that she cannot date, except to say it was before her birth, when her parents lived in Pittsburgh. Although Mamie was in Orange County when Gertrude was born in 1927, Gertrude believes her parents were settled in Philadelphia by then, and her arrival occurred when Mamie was visiting her sister Mattie. The first documentation we have of the Williamses in Philadelphia is the 1935 city directory. They are listed as renting 13 Good Street, the house that Gertrude remembers as her first home.[21]

The concepts of "push" and "pull" that historian Joe Trotter has attached to black migration from rural to urban areas, and from north to south, may be applicable to the Williams's decision to put down roots in Philadelphia.[22] The oppressive laws and customs, poor health conditions, meager economic opportunities, and thoroughly racist political system that oppressed all blacks in rural Virginia had very likely taken their toll on the Horace Williams family. According to a story passed down to Gertrude from her mother, Horace at that time had a temper that could flare quickly and was particularly dangerous in confrontations with whites. Failure, for whatever reason, to maintain the family tradition of land ownership, may have contributed to the urge to start afresh in a different setting. Among the factors that may have pulled the Williams family to settle permanently in the Germantown section of Philadelphia was the presence of kin and, as noted earlier, their former pastor, who had preceded them to that area.

Their characteristics as a family partly conform to the profile of black migrants compiled by scholars and partly diverge from it. According to that profile, most of the migrants who moved to Philadelphia (by 1930 the third largest city in the United States) were young adults. Those who were married tended to have small families. They were largely unskilled laborers, "the working poor" in the rural areas from where they had come. The earnings of every family member who could work comprised their family income. In the Depression years, many were unemployed and relied on public assistance.[23] Most were affiliated with a church.[24]

When they settled in Germantown, Horace and Mamie Williams were relatively young—in their early thirties—but their family of seven, soon to be eight, children was not small. If Horace did possess a carpentry certificate from Manassas Training Institute (and it is likely that he did), it would probably qualify him as a skilled laborer and perhaps gave him a leg up in the Depression era job market. Although he was never unemployed, his wages alone could not sustain the family, and were supplemented by Emma's and Mamie's earnings doing days work, as well as by Mamie's taking in laundry, and jobs that Gertrude and her siblings took as soon as they were old enough. With this pooling of resources and Mamie's superlative frugality the Williams never had to turn to public or private charity. In keeping with the migrant profile, church membership and religious faithfulness were central parts of their family life.

What most sets the Williamses apart from the majority of blacks who exchanged a rural way of life for the urban environs of Philadelphia is that they relocated to a section of the city that was largely white while also including a stable black population.[25] Originally settled by Dutch and German weavers in the late 1600s, Germantown was incorporated into Philadelphia in 1854. By 1890, it was home to a prosperous white upper-middle class living in large Victorian homes, and a black servant class in more modest dwellings near the homes of their employers. By the time the Williamses arrived, Germantown was known as a community where the "better class of Negroes settled."[26]

However, this community had an ambiguous racial history. In some respects, Germantown could be identified with social justice and humanitarian pursuits.

An impressive historical marker at Germantown Avenue and Wister Street claims that corner as the site of "the first protest against slavery in North America," a declaration composed by Quaker residents in 1688. Another Quaker-related landmark, the Johnson House on Germantown Avenue and Washington Lane, was a stop on the underground railroad—which lends irony to Gertrude's memory in this chapter that she and other African American students at Germantown High School did not attend the social functions that were held at the Johnson House, because that facility, which had become the Women's Club of Germantown, was not open to blacks.[27]

In other respects, Germantown partook of the same racism that poisoned so much of American society. A Ku Klux Klan (KKK) cross burning occurred in 1929 in the backyard of one of the community's most prominent African Americans— businessman and church leader William Byrd. Oral histories of other black Germantown residents describe a generally segregated social environment, where most public accommodations were for "whites only" while entertainment venues, such as movie houses and theaters, relegated blacks to balconies or other restricted areas.[28]

The street on which Gertrude grew up—West Duval Street—was an exception to the dominant housing pattern in Germantown. While most black houses were clustered together and set apart from white housing, on West Duval Street residents were both black and white and in several instances black and white lived next door to one another. In addition, West Duval could boast of a number of black homeowners, making the street especially attractive to black families.[29] Unlike the crowded ghettos where most black migrants landed, different from other predominantly white areas that were demonstrably hostile to black incursions,[30] and as Gertrude experienced it on Duval Street in the 1930s and 1940s, Germantown was relatively spacious, diverse, and tolerant.[31]

If Germantown provided a relatively secure home for blacks, Philadelphia's relationship to its black citizens was more problematic, as the memories of other blacks of her generation and the findings of historians demonstrate. Richard Taylor's study of the activist clergyman Milton Galamison depicted "appalling incidents . . . of racial bigotry" in his childhood. Tracing the history of her Philadelphia family, Kathryn Morgan evoked the city in the late 1930s as a place where "de facto segregation had become a way of life." Allen Ballard's reconstruction of his ancestors' experiences in Philadelphia, after moving from South Carolina in roughly the same time period, also made clear that Jim Crow had good friends in the City of Brotherly Love.[32]

Historians note that Philadelphia, while technically a northern city, was still very close to the Mason–Dixon Line, and reflected southern influence in that many public accommodations were segregated. The black migrants who swelled the city's population seeking jobs created by World War I found themselves on the unemployment rolls when Philadelphia's manufacturing sector went into a long and steep decline at war's end, and the city experienced the racial tensions that often accompany economic hard times. In Philadelphia during the 1930s and 1940s there also occurred numerous outbreaks of violence directed at blacks, and the city's political and socioeconomic systems were intertwined with and pervaded by discrimination and injustice.[33]

Black migration to the city contributed to increased segregation of the Philadelphia public schools. Every school district in Pennsylvania was governed by a state law enacted in 1881 prohibiting compulsory segregation by city and county governments but not preventing school districts from operating segregated facilities. Nonetheless, until migration swelled the black population in Philadelphia, racially segregated schools were the exception rather than the rule.[34]

As early as 1928 researcher W.A. Daniels noted segregated seating in mixed-race public schools. By 1940, almost half of black junior and senior high school students were assigned to a handful of segregated schools.[35] At the same time, the public school teaching staff was entirely segregated. Black teachers could work only in all-black elementary schools; they were barred from junior and senior high schools. The system maintained two eligibility lists for certified teachers—one black, one white. Even when organized black opposition forced the school system to dispense with the dual lists in 1937, black teachers were not appointed to other than all-black schools (which meant only elementary schools) until 1942. When the lists were merged, black candidates who may have been relatively high on the old list were ranked low on the new one.[36]

The evidence from historian Vincent P. Franklin and others is strong that instruction in the Philadelphia school system was governed by a well-rooted and pervasive belief in the inferiority of blacks. Prominent academics had published studies that buttressed that belief, such as the 1907 work by Byron A. Phillips, positing that "retardation" was much more prevalent among the black children of Philadelphia than among their white counterparts. In his 1928 study, W.A. Daniels reported as "common knowledge" that white principals "deal with Negroes of whatever age, as if they were children," including their students' parents. That such views still prevailed in 1940 was indicated by more than 500 black secondary and college students who were interviewed by researchers for the state of Pennsylvania. The students attested to "numerous instances of prejudice" in the Philadelphia public schools. The same researchers investigated textbooks and found derogatory references to "other racial and cultural groups."[37]

Gertrude did not once mention these negative themes in Philadelphia history in the first 20 hours of oral history interviewing that began our work on this book. When I asked about them directly during the second round of taping, she readily described how she and her friends and family were forced to sit in Jim Crow balconies in the downtown movie houses, were excluded from various recreational and entertainment facilities, and seldom shopped without encountering intentional rudeness on the part of white sales clerks. She also recalled being frightened by the presence of armed soldiers, state militiamen called in to keep order during the 1944 public transit strike in Philadelphia. The strike was sparked by white transit workers who opposed the city's hiring of blacks to drive trolleys and buses.[38] However, as she told it, so caught up was she in getting an education, helping at home, and working at part-time jobs that she had no time or energy to expend on racial resentments or rebellions. Similarly, in the first round of interviews, when she noted that her parents chose not to send her and her siblings to all-black schools and that, with the exception of one student teacher, all of her teachers were white, she recalled encountering prejudice in only one of those teachers during her entire experience in the public schools, from 1934–1945.[39] In the second round, in response to my probing, she identified a few other episodes in which she may have experienced discrimination; and she reflected on the memories of her best friend, Cozy, and her younger sister, Sarah, both of whom were keenly conscious of a racial caste system at work at Germantown High School. Still, Gertrude concluded that she was well served by the public schools of Philadelphia, because they effectively prepared her for college.

As the first chapter of her narrative relates, Gertrude provided clues to the discrepancy between her positive recall of her formative years and the negative evidence regarding the experience of blacks in Philadelphia during the same period. She observed how family and friends helped to insulate her from the impact of discrimination. And she suggested that she might have "compartmentalized"—shunted aside and ignored negative situations—in order to concentrate on her goals of attending college and avoiding a life of menial labor.

Such compartmentalizing was not unique. Historian Stephanie Felix found the same practice among the African American women that she interviewed, women of Gertrude's generation. She concluded that her subjects were "not negating segregation," they were "explaining Blacks' coping mechanisms."[40] Gertrude made the same point in noting that growing up black had involved "learning how to read people in order to survive and learning how to choose your battles." What oral historian Karen Fields observed about her grandmother's account of her life as a black woman in segregated South Carolina, might be said of Gertrude's recollections as well. The story, wrote Fields,

> was not about the racist system that partly enclosed it. Matters of race and color are a permanent presence without being her principal subject. They are constituent to life, but they do not define life. . . . [M]atters of race and color . . . are there in the way Mt. Kilimanjaro is there in Africa . . . hardly to be missed yet hardly to be noticed, at once native and alien to the life around it.[41]

Other factors that may have affected Gertrude's outlook were the harmony she seems to have felt between her household and their white neighbors; the perception that the white employers of her parents, her aunt, and herself were decent and generous people; and her appreciation of most of her white public school teachers. The sense of security that she recalled may be similar to that attributed to Texas Congresswoman Barbara Jordan by her biographer:

> [Jordan] had grown up in a supportive—if strict—home. She had the sense of being cared for, and being taken care of, in a fundamental way. She developed a belief that if she worked hard and did her part, everything would turn out okay, because it

always had. She had no sense of urgency about social or political problems. They were not personal. . . . She knew the larger system was wrong, but she was managing quite nicely within the smaller system that was her county. . . . [She] had a remarkable sense of responsibility for her own self-development, but little for society as a whole. Personal change was possible and could be immediate. Society's change was desirable, but distant.[42]

Gertrude was the first of Horace and Mamie Williams's eight children to graduate from high school; the first to enter college; the path-breaker for her younger sister, Sarah, and for the nieces and nephews of the generation to come. Assuming such a role took intense effort and powerful concentration. It required the strong sense of identity that her family, particularly her mother, had long nurtured in her. Only the most egregious attack on that identity could cause her to break stride and engage in battle. As she relates in the pages that follow, one high school history teacher launched such an attack, and in the young Gertrude's response one can glimpse the out-spoken, combative woman that she would later become. The reader may find other signs of that woman in the making, but the most important development in this first chapter of Gertrude Williams's story is her acceptance of the importance of formal learning. Faith in education is one of the strongest themes (along with religious faith) running through African American history. Sociologist Hortense Powdermaker summarized it: education "was viewed as the gateway to equal opportunity, the threshold of a new and better life." The transmission from her parents to Gertrude of this belief in the power of education, laid the foundation for her life's agenda.[43]

* * *

I was born October 1, 1927 in Orange County, Virginia. When I arrived, Mom was staying with her sister, who was ill. Mom and Pop both grew up in Virginia, where their great grandparents and grandparents had been slaves. My maternal great grandmother, Grandma Julie (Julia Wallace) had several children, including a daughter, Charlotta, who had two children—my mother, Mamie, and her sister, Mattie. Mom was born by a midwife. When she reached the age to apply for Social Security, we realized that she did not have a birth certificate. I had to send to Richmond, and the record they sent back read something like this: "When the census was taken in 1910 there were two girls living in Julia Wallace's house—Mamie, who was the approximate age of 12; and Mattie who was the approximate age of, or was reported to be, the age of 15 . . ." They never had birth certificates. Only white people got birth certificates, not colored people. When they took the census, that's how they judged her age.[44]

Mamie and Mattie were raised by their grandmother, Julie. According to family stories, their mother, Charlotta, moved to Philadelphia and became the cook for a white family. I have a picture of Charlotta. Mom did not know her father's name;

neither did Aunt Mattie. Each of them may have had different fathers. Mom told of seeing her father one time, when he came past Grandma Julie's house. She said he looked just like an Indian. (Aunt Mattie, who is dead now, looked Indian and so does Mattie's daughter, Willie May, who is a retired teacher living in Baltimore.) There are family stories that during the Civil War, Grandma Julie hid injured northern soldiers and helped get them well. I was very small when she died, but I remember visiting her and her coming once to stay with us when my mother was sick. Her grave is beside Mount Holy Baptist Church, there in Unionville, Virginia. At that time in black communities, when the parishioners died they were buried beside the church.

I never met my father's parents. His mother, Margaret Clark Williams, was a slave. She married Grandpa Douglas Williams from Unionville, Virginia. They had 14 children. Living conditions were hard for them. My father remembered hunting for muskrat and possum and eating them. He said they either ate that or they starved.

It was said that Grandpa Doug's brother-in-law, Uncle William Taliaferro, had a white father who left him a lot of money. Uncle William could have passed for white. My father's sister, Emma, used to talk about the family belief that in some way Uncle William and Thomas Jefferson's slave (and probably mistress), Sally Hemings, were related. Monticello was not that far away from our family's part of Virginia. Uncle William lived in a lovely house there, but he was said to be rather mean sometimes. He was a schoolteacher. He taught my mother in the regular school and in Sunday School. He also paid for my father to attend Manassas Training School to learn his trade. Pop became a carpenter.[45]

My parents were married in New York State on August 2, 1916. I do not know why they were married in that location, except that my mother had relatives living there. She was 18 and he was 20. It appears that their first child, my oldest sister, Elizabeth, was born a year earlier.[46] Not long after they were married an epidemic went through and wiped out most of my father's family, except for his older sister, Lucy, his brothers Arthur and Charles who had left home, and the youngest child, my Aunt Emma. My mother and father took Emma in. She lived with our family until she died.[47]

My father was usually quiet, and he loved to laugh, but when he got angry—watch out! When people called him "boy" or something like that, his reaction could be violent. I get some of my anger off of him. My mother told the story of an episode that happened when they were still in Virginia.[48] My father had helped to build a house for this white gentleman. The man didn't pay him the money he was due and brought up something about slaves. My father went off and let him know that he wasn't a slave. He got so angry that he threatened to kill the man. So, according to Mom, my parents moved to Pittsburgh and stayed there for a while.

While he was in Pittsburgh my father worked around horses. He used to work with the trotters and would groom them for the horse races. When things got better they moved back to Virginia. For a while my father worked for a white undertaker, Mr. Johnson. He was one of the few who would accept black bodies, and he held funerals for blacks. In fact, he later funeralized my Aunt Mattie. But my mother wouldn't let my father get in the bed when he had worked on dead bodies.

Sometimes my parents and Aunt Emma would talk about how the law in those times wasn't fair, and how if blacks were accused of anything they would get lynched. My relatives saw people who were hung. They believed in self-defense. My father's mother, Grandma Margaret, always kept a musket. She would shoot at anybody who came there who didn't look right. My father said she was a sharpshooter. Women who came up in those hard times were as strong as men. My mother rode horses. My father used to talk about how she could ride faster than any man. She'd get mad, jump on a horse and she was gone.

When I was born my mother named me after a German woman that she worked for—Gertrude Luck. She named me "Gertrude Susan Williams." She went to register my birth so that I could get a birth certificate. The registrar put down "Susie." First they put "Susie Gertrude." "No," my mother said, "Gertrude Susan." And then they put "Gertrude Susie," and they left "Susie" in there and wouldn't change it. At that time you were called "cousin," "Susie,"—any thing that sort of had a racial overtone. My mother tried, but she couldn't change it. They also misspelled my father's name. Instead of Horace, they put "Horris." So I write my name "Gertrude S. Williams." My birth certificate says "Susie." I guess I could have gotten it changed later in life to "Susan." But it just shows the past—what happened at that time to those who were then called Negroes; black people now.

In Philadelphia our family settled in Germantown. I do not know the exact date. It was the late 1920s or the early 1930s. My parents probably chose this area because we had relatives from Virginia who were already living there. They attended Enon Baptist Church. The pastor of Enon, Reverend Adolphus Hobbs, had been the preacher at Mount Holy in Orange County. The Enon Baptist congregation took up special collections for Mount Holy and sent money to help the church back home. My father became a deacon at Enon Baptist. When we didn't call him Pop we called him Deac.[49]

The first house my parents rented in Germantown was at 13 Good Street. It was a two-story house with a big backyard. But it didn't have enough rooms for our big family. There were eleven of us—eight children and three adults—my mother, Mamie, my father, Horace, and his sister, Emma. The oldest child was Elizabeth; then Lottie. Charles and Marjorie were next. After Marjorie was Horace, then Moses, then me, then Sarah. Within a short time we moved to a bigger house at 44 Good Street that also had a big yard. When I was about ten years old we moved again, to 249 Duval Street. This house had three floors, a nice front porch and a big backyard. My parents bought this house—or at least they thought they were buying it. Years later, after I had become a teacher in Baltimore, they were informed that the deed had never been recorded in their name. I had to take out a loan to purchase the house for them.[50]

With so many people living in the house I always had somebody to talk to, but I never felt that our home was crowded. None of us children had a single room.

Aunt Emma had her own room and our parents had their room. Sarah and I always shared a room; Elizabeth and Lottie shared; our three brothers had a room and a half on the second floor in the back. They wore sneakers that were very smelly, and they would hang them on a pole out the back window!

Because there were so many children, we younger ones had to wear the hand-me-down clothes. The only times for new clothes were Easter and Christmas. When we got new clothes, Mom dressed Sarah and me alike. I hated that because Sarah was nicely shaped and I was straight up and down. She always looked so much better in her clothes. The one thing that we got new that I loved was black patent leather shoes with buttons. They were the joy of my life. On Sunday we wore those.

Mom baked cinnamon buns on Saturday night. She would make rolls and buns, and the house smelled so good. Deac built a separate section on the back of the house, because in the regular kitchen we had an electric stove, but Mom wanted her wood stove, like she had in Virginia. So she bought one, and we stayed back there most of the time, because it was always so yummy. We also had a potbellied stove in the living room. We had a cousin who worked for a coal company and could get us coal at a reduced price. In the winter we kept the potbellied stove stoked with coal and that, along with Mom's woodstove in the kitchen, kept the house very toasty.

During my early years we would go back and forth to Virginia, especially in the summertime. Mom would later talk about those trips. She'd remember how we'd be on the road and I'd say, "Why can't we stop and eat?" And then she would say, "because, you know, we cannot eat in those places." There were "For White Only" signs all along the way. Upper Marlboro in Maryland was one of the worst places. So Mom carried everything we needed in the car.

My father always had great big cars—he would buy Packards and cars like that. Now I see why. The whole family could fit in the car and it held a lot of gas, so we didn't have to stop very often. Even though these things happened and my parents probably resented them, they never said anything. It was a different world then. Even if they resented segregation they took for granted that that was the way it was, and they knew that those who crossed the line got hurt or killed.

We made these trips to attend the town meetings at my parents' old church. A town meeting—and it's usually held in the south—is where people who have left the area go back to their churches. They come back to see not only the minister but the other relatives and friends and all those they hadn't seen maybe in one or two years. Ministers who had moved to other places also came back. Some people would go every year. We did. My parents would take us down in the third week in July and the third week in August.[51]

It was an exciting time because we would see our other relatives. They would come from Philadelphia, Boston, New York, wherever they lived. And we'd see cars all over. Everybody was our cousin or our aunt. Aunt Mattie was usually my only real aunt there. But I remember that at least once my father's brother, Uncle Arthur, and their sister, Aunt Lucy, attended. Still, everybody else was also called "my aunt" or "my cousin." That was the way that was brought to the blacks, not using the name of the black person, Mrs. or Miss. They would say "Aunt Susie," "Aunt Flossie." And we just kept those titles. There were a lot of habits that were pressed upon us during slavery that were just passed down family to family.

At the town meetings the people who still lived in Virginia would prepare meals and set up tables. All the people would gather and talk, and the preacher would preach, and the kids would do terrible things. We would peak in the window while the church service was going on. Then we'd mimic the preacher and when members of the congregation started "getting happy" we'd mimic and make fun of them. We really liked to watch one person in the congregation—Aunt Alberta. She wore two pocketbooks around her neck and when she got happy those pocket books would just fly!

Then we would eat. Sing and eat! Eat pie! Some people made the best pie. But there were always some people there who couldn't cook. My mother would let us know who that person was and we would avoid her dish. It was a really exciting time. Town meetings still go on. Our family doesn't go back any more, but I know people who do go back to their home churches every summer.

When we went for the town meeting, we stayed with my Aunt Mattie on a farm.[52] I didn't like it much because it got so dark at night. And to get mail you had to walk through all these fields. It was such a long walk, because the mailboxes were on the main road, where the whites lived. The black farms were on little plots far off the main road. Mom would say, "You have to go to the mailbox." I hated that, because I had to walk through those fields. Then, there were snakes. I never came up on one, but my father used to say that—because they had cornfields taller than me—if you went through the corn you'd find black snakes.

Except to get the mail, blacks went near the whites' homes only when they were summoned to do work. Sometimes a white man or white woman would drive up and call out for "Aunt Mattie" or her husband, "Uncle James." They'd talk and come to an agreement about work to be done.

Life in the country could be scary and there were many hardships. But my relatives and their neighbors were secure within themselves. They raised their own food, had their own chickens and pigs, and were able to take care of themselves and one another. They relied on each other. When it was time to kill the hogs, for example, they all came together to do the slaughtering and the curing. My parents were raised this way, and they held on to many of the country ways. When we were growing up, they never tried to have us afraid of white people. But they taught us to be wise. Back then there were some things that you couldn't change by a direct challenge, so we learned to know our rights, but not to do foolish things. They also told us always to be respectful.

Religion was a very important thing as we grew up. Sunday was a whole day in church. When we lived on Good Street we children attended church services at Grace Baptist, which was on Sharpnack Street, in walking distance of our house and easier for us to reach than Enon Baptist. The pastor at Grace Baptist was Reverend Patrick Hughes.[53] He lived right on our street. He was extremely tall, had a big booming voice, a beard and crinkly hair that came down to his neck. If we did anything wrong he would spank us. I don't think I ever got a spanking, but the boys did. Reverend Hughes had classes to prepare us for baptism and then he baptized us. I thought I was going to drown!

When we were little, other adults could correct us and then our parents would correct us again. They gave others the right to discipline us. The minister of the church was like godfather. Reverend Hughes would take us into his house if we did something wrong. He would have us sit down and he would preach a sermon. And we had better not laugh. On Sunday morning we'd walk right on up to church behind him.

Religion influenced the whole way we lived and were brought up. Although neither my mother or father went that far in school, they knew the Bible, and they studied the Bible. They took literally the biblical passages about the "woman will obey thy husband." You just would do what your husband said you should do. Mom took care of Deac, just as according to the Bible she was supposed to take care of him. He never helped around the house. I once watched while Aunt Em was carrying out a big load of trash, and I asked why he wasn't helping her. "Men don't do house work," he informed me. He never learned to cook. At one time, when Mom was hospitalized, he made soup by filling a big pot of water and putting in a couple of little potatoes and some salt. It tasted horrible, but he told us, "eat it!" We called it stone soup.

Mom got up at five every morning to fix him a full breakfast and pack him a big lunch. He always had homemade bread. Mom made hoecake, like she had done in the country. She would make up a batch of dough that she would put on top of the wood stove in a skillet greased with bacon fat. When it browned on one side she would turn it to brown on the other, meanwhile it was also cooking inside. She'd slit that hoecake, the way we open pita bread, and fill it with whatever she was cooking, beef or pork and make a big hearty sandwich for Deac's lunch pail. She also packed a thermos of coffee and sometimes a thermos of soup. She took good care of him.

She would talk back to him sometimes, but in that generation the man was the head of the household. He'd come in from work and sit down and wait for dinner to be ready, even though she had worked, too. It wasn't a matter of him ordering her around. She wasn't submissive. She just felt it was the woman's responsibility to please the man, and it was even greater in the black race than it was in the white race. I think white women really started seeing the light sooner and said, "Wait a minute. We're working, too." But in the black race the woman served her man. That was the tradition, starting in Africa.

At night we learned Bible verses and had to read passages from the Bible. My mother or father—most of the time it was my mother—discussed what those verses meant, how they affected our lives, why it was important to be a Christian. But we were always told that you had to respect everyone's religion. I attended catechism classes with my best friend, Eva Jones Flynt, whom we called Cozy, and who was Catholic. I really enjoyed those classes.

When we moved to Duval Street everyone attended Sunday services at Enon Baptist. We went to Sunday School and then to church and then back to Baptist Evening Fellowship. The young people sat in the back rows, and one Sunday we were laughing and talking back there. All of a sudden here comes Deac. He hooks his finger, and oh! I was so upset! I walked all the way down to the Deacons's Bench with my head down, and I just sat there. I *never* talked in church again. He was steaming! But he never said a word. He just looked at me. I guess I was punished enough sitting on that bench.[54]

Whenever it was Deac's turn to pray in church he would pray the longest prayers! Mom would say to him, "Horace, why do you have to pray so long?" He'd say, "Mamie, don't tell me how to pray!" Often he would arrive at church before her. Just as they would be leaving the house she would decide she had to change her hat or that she needed to wear something different. So he would go on without her. One morning, when she and I went together, we found several people waiting at the top of the church steps, outside the door. When someone is praying or reading the Bible you're not supposed to go in. One of those waiting peeked into the door and said, "Oh, Lord! There's Deacon Williams. We'll never get in." Mom was upset at that, but I said, "You know she's right." Mom didn't stay ruffled very long.

In later years—around the time I went off to college—Deac joined the Masons. He was sponsored by another Deacon at Enon Baptist. He took his Masonic obligations seriously, just as he was very conscientious about his position in the church. He went to lodge meetings and funerals and participated in the Masonic rituals.[55]

Whatever good that's in us came from the beliefs that were developed through my mother and father. I used to get very excited when it was time to have tests or time to do this or that, and my mother said to me, "Now, I want you to say the Twenty Third Psalm." I do this even today. Before I go into anything I say the Twenty Third Psalm, and it calms me down. It has always given me that strength to say, "You can do it." Religion is just a part of my life.

As far as education was concerned, my mother was a zealot. There were certain expectations of us, going to school every day, doing our work. When we came in from school we sat down to our homework. When we finished, Mom wanted to see what we had done. She did not finish high school—I guess she finished the equivalent of sixth or seventh grade. But she wanted us to go further. My father was strict about education, too. But I wasn't afraid of my father the way I was afraid of my mother. I did not disobey her. As was true in most families at that time, Mom was the one who did the correcting, went to school, did the checking. She'd tell us, "You have to fear something, so you'll fear God and Mamie."

My aunt, who lived in the house with us and came up from Virginia with us, would help us with our homework. She had very little education. We used to say, "If Emma had a chance to get her education, she would be the president of a college or a bank," because she was just that sharp. If she hadn't been poor and black she could have done anything. It's just a shame that she never reached her full potential. We'd be doing algebra or geometry and she could figure it out. She didn't have that in school, but she could figure it out. She read a lot. All the children, and later the grandchildren, and even the kids in the neighborhood, all loved her dearly. She just had a way of knowing what to do to make you happy. She had the kindest heart. I got some of the things that I would later do with kids from Em.

I started in Emlen School, which was an elementary school in Germantown.[56] It was close to our house on Good Street, but such a long walk from Duval Street—about two miles. Hill School, which was all black, was closer, but my mother did not want to send us there. She believed that it was not as good a school as Emlen and that some of the children who went there were not well behaved.[57] There were no buses. My father walked me and Sarah to school. When we had a big snow—and at that time we had some unbelievable snows!—getting to school was a big challenge. We had to start early, bundled up in snowsuits, and we would walk behind Pop, in his footprints. Some of the snow banks would come up to our hips. We would fall down and scramble back up to catch up with him. We had to wear long stockings, and as soon as we got to school we would roll them down.

We had black and white students at Emlen. But the teaching population in Philadelphia was segregated, and all the teachers at Emlen were white.[58] In fact, I never had a black teacher until I went to college. Once we did have a black student teacher whose name was "White." I remember Patrick, a little blond-haired white boy who was driven to school by a chauffeur. We had to write letters home telling what we did that day and anything exciting about class. He wrote, "We have a new teacher. Her name is Miss White. She should be named Miss Black." Everyone clapped; nobody got upset. Well, the student teacher got upset, and I wondered, "Why is she mad?" Because, you know, she was not white.[59]

I went to Emlen from kindergarten to grade six. I only stayed in kindergarten a few weeks because my older sisters had taught me how to read; so I went on into first grade. Then from seventh to ninth I was at Roosevelt Junior High School. I was always a good student, but in those early years I was shy. There were so few blacks in every class, but I don't think that's why I was shy. Mom warned us not to talk in school. "You go there to be taught, not to teach!" she said. So I did not talk out in the classroom. When I was in seventh grade at the end of the year, when we got our papers back and were about to get our grades, our history teacher, Mrs. Coil, said, "If you think you deserve an 'E' (for 'excellent') come up here." Then that group went up to the front of the room. And she called for those who thought they deserved a "G" (for "good"), and so forth. I just sat there. Then she said, "I have a right to select," and she called me up for an "E." I was stunned. I quietly went up and she said, "Did you do your work well?" I said "Yes." "Did you earn Es?" "Yes." Then she asked me why I hadn't come up and I couldn't answer her. I guess I had been conditioned not to brag. And I lacked self-confidence.

At Emlen and Roosevelt I always had several black classmates, and the teachers were generally fair in their treatment of us. They made learning interesting and made us want to go to school. In eighth grade we took regional examinations, which decided the high school we could go to. I had the choice of attending Germantown or Girls' High, which was an all-girls' college prep school. Those who went to Girls' High had added prestige. They just automatically got into the good colleges. But I could not reach Girls' High without taking the trolley, and we couldn't afford the fare. So I went to Germantown High School, which was also an excellent school. You had to have a certain grade point average to attend Germantown, and very few black students were enrolled there. When I graduated in 1945 there were only 10 black students in a class of 400. The teachers and administrators were all white. I don't think that even the cleaning man was black.[60]

Sarah, who is two years younger than I, hated Germantown and the prejudice she met there. She is probably the brightest of all of my parents' children. She was studious and just naturally got "A"s. But she was very conscious of racial biases and was unhappy all the time she was there. The black student population was increasing every year, and it may be that the racial climate grew worse as she went on. When she was a senior, the school counselor told her that she was to receive an award from a bank downtown. Then a man from the bank came to school and they sent for her to come to the office. When he saw that she was black there was all this talking with the counselor, who finally told her that instead of being awarded first place she would receive another award. They gave the main prize to a white student. Sarah said this was just the last straw. She wanted to quit school. Mom and I talked to her, begged her to finish. We promised that if she would graduate we would send her to college, and we did. She went to the Chicago Institute of Fine Arts.

My best friend, Cozy, also hated Germantown. She and I had somewhat different experiences. There were three tracks—commercial, mechanic arts, and academic. She took the commercial courses and I took the academic courses.[61] I always had in the back of my mind the idea that if I didn't make it into college I could become an executive secretary with the academic background. Cozy said students in her classes were "clannish." Whites and blacks never mixed. There weren't enough black students in my classes for there to be clannishness. Often I was the only black in the room. I didn't expect to be accepted into the whites' groups. They were always polite to me; some white students seemed friendly, but most patronized us. Many of them came from wealthy homes in Chestnut Hill or Upper Mount Airy. The really rich children were much nicer than some of the pseudo-rich ones.[62]

Cozy was outgoing and liked to socialize. She saw the little slights that went on. When I looked back in my yearbook recently I saw that there *were* many clubs and groups that didn't have any blacks in them. Even though several of us were in the academic course, the Honor Society was all white. Membership in the Honor Society required a high number of A grades, a recommendation from a teacher, and the approval of the principal, Dr. Charles Nichols. We black students all knew that if you earned an A you often got a B. And sometimes if you earned a B the teacher would give you a C+. This was irking but very hard to do anything about. And then, it just wasn't likely that Dr. Nichols would ever sign off on an honor society membership for a black student.

We were also excluded from social activities. A lot of the places they used for dances and other gatherings were off limits to us. For example, the yearbook describes a "Gala Move-Up Hop" in January 1945 held at the Germantown Women's Club. Blacks could not go in the Women's Club. We did attend the proms, but they were about the only large functions that included us. Black students played on some athletic teams—mostly cross-country and track.

In any case, Cozy and Sarah were right, and they had good reasons for being angry. But while they allowed the slights from teachers and counselors and students to get next to them, I saw that anger was not going to change the situation. Mom always used to say to us, "You don't have to eat with whites, you don't have to sleep with them, and you don't have to go to their houses. You just have to get that work." I accepted that, but not everyone did. My brother Charlie would fight all the time with the kids and argue with the teachers, until he dropped out. But I was there to get my lessons. My thought was, you go to school to learn. You don't go there to be the most popular person. I guess that's what kept me in good stead, except for one time.

Mr. Gelman (I'll never forget him!)[63] was teaching a history class at Germantown High School. He was talking about the Civil War. Then he began on how blacks were inferior and not capable of dealing with things and that's why they weren't as good in school, and so forth. I was the only black sitting in the classroom. When he started talking that way I felt like two cents, and before I knew it, off I went. I said, "No, that's not true. We're just as intelligent as you are." I just went on and on about how blacks are just as bright as white people, and you can't say that about black people. Then it was "colored" people. You can't say that about colored people, because we have a right; and I'm in this class, too, aren't I? I went on—just like I do now when something gets next to me. I remember standing there, looking at him, defiant. And then the kids started clapping. He put me out—sent a note that I was being disrespectful to him and sent me down to the office of Dr. Nichols. I didn't care. I grabbed my books and went on down there, and if he had said something to me he would have gotten it, too.

Dr. Nichols sent me home. That's the only time in my life I was sent home. I said to myself, "Mom is just going to have to beat me. If she beats me I'll never speak to her again." I knew that in Mamie Williams's family you didn't talk back to adults. If an adult said it, it was true—whether it was true or not, you just didn't talk back to them. If an adult did something to me that was wrong, it was my business to tell her or Deac so they could deal with the adult. You didn't have the right to be rude to an adult. We all knew that you got punished if you talked back to an adult.

It must have been the way that I walked up and handed Mom the note from Dr. Nichols. Usually when I handed her a note I ducked, because she would hit me if she thought I had misbehaved. But this time I just stood there, and she must have known that I didn't care whether I got popped or not. She read it and asked me to tell her what had happened. When I told her, she said, "Finish your homework. I'll go to school with you tomorrow." I did not sleep well that night. I just knew she was going to embarrass me and say that I had no right to say what I had said.

The next morning my mother took me to the principal's office. She listened to him. Then she said, "I teach my children to respect you, their teachers, and all adults, but I never brought up any of my children to bow their heads or shuffle their feet. So Gertrude is going to apologize for being rude, but she's not going to apologize for what she said." I could have hugged her. It was unusual for a black parent to stand up like that to a white principal, especially Dr. Nichols who did not like blacks at all.

Dr. Nichols let me back in school. Mr. Gelman was always distant after that. He really didn't want me back in the classroom. I did my work and made sure everything was in. He gave me a "B" instead of the "A" that I believed I deserved. Mom said, "Don't worry about it; just move on." That episode taught me that sometimes it was best to just do what was necessary to get out of a situation that was hostile to me because I was an African American.

The only "D" I ever got was from another history teacher, Mr. Green.[64] I took his class after I had the experience with Mr. Gellman. Once again I was the only black student in the classroom, and I was determined to get everything right. I was answering every question, popping up every time, so one day he said, in the very clipped way he talked, "Gertrude is shining like a light." That is one of those things you don't say to a black person. It was a phrase that was used by the black race that meant you were greasy and looked oily, and I didn't like it. I clammed up and wouldn't answer any more questions.

Finally one day, Sarah and I were walking up Germantown Avenue, coming home from school, and there came Mr. Green: "Gertrude, get under my umbrella!" It was one of those days where it was raining on this side of the street, and the sun was shining on the other side. I said to Sarah, "I'm not getting under there." She said, "You'd better!" He went on to ask, talking in that funny little way, had some one offended me? What had happened? I was doing so well, but I had stopped working. I could not tell him what had happened, and he gave me a "D" at the end of that quarter.

My father exploded. I said to him, "Look at the boys' grades! They get 'Ds' and worse." (That was true, except for Horace who did well.) Pop said to me, "That's what they usually do, but that's not what you do, and you're not going to start now." I wanted to say to him, "Why are you doing this? You don't usually get it in our school business!" But he would have really laid into me then, so I didn't say it. He kept me in the house for two months. I never told him why I had shut down. The only person I told was Sarah. I brought the grade back up by the end of the year. After Mr. Green talked to me, I realized that he wasn't being rude. He was just saying to me that I was doing well. In every race you have little words that will set you off. People aren't aware of these buzzwords. Mr. Green wasn't like Mr. Gelman. Mr. Gelman was probably the only teacher I ever had who was out and out prejudiced.

My experiences with school—elementary, junior high, and high school—were very good, basically. I learned a lot and was prepared for college when I came out. The teachers were exacting but helpful. They knew what they were doing. They were prepared and made sure that we were prepared. They never watered down the curriculum; we had to reach for it. So I enjoyed school. I really did.

Just as we went to school with white students and teachers, we lived in a neighborhood that was mixed. For a period we were the only black family in our block on our side of Duval Street. The people were nice. They came up and introduced themselves. We went to an all-black church, and when my parents went out to socialize they would go out to black friends. But they'd sit on the porch and they'd laugh and talk with the white neighbors in the evening. We had little white friends that we played with on the street.

One family we called "the reds" because the mother and the children all had red hair. The mother was really nice, but we thought the father was strange-acting. But one time we had a leak in our roof and he heard us talking about it. The next day he came up and asked my father if he could help with it. My father said he didn't have the money to pay for getting the roof done. He said, "Well, you're a neighbor," and he fixed the roof and wouldn't take any money. After that he and my father became friends, because my father shared, helping to fix things for him. It wasn't that the man didn't want us in the neighborhood. He just didn't talk much.

As a carpenter my father worked for The Richmond Brothers who owned a large ice cream company and also an auto parts yard. Deac worked in that yard and also handled repairs at their stores and even their homes. They were very good to our family. They brought us turkeys and holiday baskets every year. Deac earned a steady salary working for them.

But then he ventured out to be a contractor. He never knew how to bid. He always won the bid because his was the lowest, and he always worked hard; but after he had to pay the people who worked for him he had almost no money left to bring home. He gave Mom a weekly allowance of $25.00. She said even if he made a million dollars, he would just give her the same $25.00. Mom knew how to stretch money, but we couldn't live on that. So the rest of the family had to help.

Aunt Em would add money in. She worked for a white family, the Masons. Mrs. Mason was a teacher and Mr. Mason was an insurance broker. Later, when I started teaching, Mrs. Mason gave me a lot of things that she had. Emma worked for them from the time she was 16-years old until she became ill when she was in her seventies. When she died they paid for all the funeral expenses and they gave money to the church in her name. The Masons's two sons used to come to our house to play. Em gave Mom some of the money she earned from the Masons.

Mom also worked for a white family, the Burkes on Gowens Avenue. They had a son, Jimmy. She used to take my brothers Horace, Charles, and Moses to work with her sometimes. One time she found Jimmy washing and washing his hair. And she asked him, "What are you trying to do?" He said, "I want those curls like your boys!" "Oh," Mom said, "you'll never get those." She was so tickled.

For a long time Mom also took in laundry. People would bring it to the house in big wicker baskets and she would wash and iron for them. At first she used an old wringer washing machine, which I got my arm caught in once. Later she bought a more modern machine. I had to help her iron. Sometimes we worked late into the night. I never minded the other jobs I had outside the house. But I really hated ironing. That iron was so heavy! I used to say, "I know there is something better in this world." Mom overheard me say that to Sarah. "Yes," she told me, "there is, but you have to get your education. These are the things you do when you're not educated."

I saw that this was true with my older sisters, Elizabeth and Lottie, neither of whom had finished high school. They would look in the newspaper for jobs. Because they hadn't finished school they didn't meet the qualifications in most of the ads. Many of the "colored" jobs specified "light skinned," and they didn't meet that standard either. So they would end up as domestics working for white families. Soon they would be fed up and they would quit. Then they sent Sarah and me to pick up their pay. We never wanted to go. It was terrible to walk up to that door and say that we'd come for our sister's money. The people would say, "Well, your sister didn't finish her work." I didn't want to hear that. Sarah would run, but I'd stand there and say, "Just give me her money." I'd get it and then *I'd* run.

When I was about ten, I went to work for a white family who lived nearby, the Brays. In the evenings I washed the dishes. On Saturdays, I cleaned the kitchen and scrubbed the bathroom. Then, around the age of 13, I started working on weekends at Penn Fruit, a grocery store on Germantown Avenue and Wayne Street. I wasn't old enough to get a permit. My mother had to sign a special form. I bagged and then I became a cashier.

During high school I had a job with a black lady who owned a shop on Germantown Avenue, Mrs. Ruth Deane.[65] It was what we would call a boutique today. I don't know if her customers realized that she was black. She was really a lady! I would look in her windows and sometimes lay by some little things that I bought by paying a little at a time. One day she said, "Would you like to work here?" So I did. I helped behind the counter and answered the telephone. I cleaned the shop— whatever she needed done. I worked there until she closed, when her husband became ill. The money I earned in these jobs—except from Mrs. Deane, which I used to buy little things from her shop—all went to the family.[66] Holding these jobs and having to help at home, I couldn't take part in activities after school. So the cliques and exclusion that bothered Cozy so much didn't bother me. I didn't have time to notice them.

Even though we all had to help financially, we weren't destitute. Poverty makes people either very slovenly or very crafty. Mom made thrift into an art. Because of her skill we didn't realize how poor we were. We always had someone in the house when we came home. We had someone who took care of us, looked out for us. We didn't have the latest fads, but we had clothes that we needed. We always had food. Mamie was a good cook and knew how to spread her money.

She used to get the big bags of flour, which came in different colors like floral blue and yellow and red. When the flour was used up she would make a dress. Then from the white ones she would make our little panties with little ruffles. She sewed by hand for awhile and then Deac brought home this sewing machine, the kind you pedal. Mom would wash and iron late at night. She had one of those irons that you put on the stove. We were always crisp going to school. My mother said, "You don't have much, but you're going to be clean."

She would order things from the neighborhood grocer. We called him Whitey, not because he was white but because he had ash blond hair. He would add little extras to the order, and Mom knew how to stretch that extra food. There was a bakery that sold discounted bread that had come back on the delivery truck. Gloria Kennedy, the white girl who lived across the street from us, and Sarah and I would take our wagons and pick up our families' grocery orders from the store and get the bread from the bakery.

In the summertime Mom always had a garden. Even when we were on Good Street she had a little garden in the backyard and raised cabbage, collard greens, kale, tomatoes, rhubarb, sage. Then when we moved on the 200 block of Duval Street there was a vacant lot in the 100 block. Mom and several other women on the street got permission to plant their gardens down there—like the victory gardens later. There she grew enough vegetables that she could can them to last us all year. I had to help with the canning. She did most of it on the wood stove. We had the backdoor open; it was *so* hot. Water would be pouring off of us. But she could can!

We would go out to the roadside stands and get peaches. Then we had to peel those peaches and halve them, until our hands were worn out. Then we'd snap the beans. She even made dandelion wine like they did in Virginia. We would go out and pick dandelions for her and she would make wine from them. She stopped that after my brothers got in it and then added water. Mom knew how to spread her money, but she always had a dollar, if you needed it. In later years she went back to school and earned a certificate as a practical nurse. Then she was assigned to various hospitals to care for patients who were critically ill.

When we were little, and we disobeyed, Mom sent us down to the end of the yard to this bush to get a switch. If it wasn't keen enough—because it was those thin ones that would really make us dance when she worked on our legs—she'd send us back to get another one. So we'd get a real thin switch and then we would dance all over the place, because Mom would tear our legs up. And she'd dare us to cry! But we didn't disobey for a long time after that.

As we got older, when we started junior high school, she would punish us by waiting until Saturday. If she had told us to clean the bathroom or this or that, and we had ignored her, on Saturday there we'd be, at home cleaning, while everybody else went off to the movies. Though Mom would get angry sometimes, I rarely saw my father get angry. He would look at us and we would understand what he meant. My parents never argued in front of us. I knew they had disagreements, because I was nosey and I heard them. But they showed us a united front. We couldn't trick them. If we asked Mom could we do something she would say, "what did your father say?" And if he had said "no" then her answer was "no," too. So my parents were strict, but we learned to understand what "yes" means and what "no" means and to complete the tasks that we were supposed to complete.

I learned from them that just because a child is poor, she doesn't have to miss learning right from wrong and having certain standards. Many children today don't have that kind of structure. We are living in times when many children are allowed to get their own way. They are too much influenced by the television and movies. Their parents allow them to be disrespectful to adults, even to the parents themselves. When their children get in trouble some of these parents will lie for them. Often such parents are in to drugs. Others seem to want to be as young as their children. Because of this in some cases, and because in other cases both parents are working and have little time for parenting, children are raising themselves and their brothers and sisters.

When I was little my father started calling me "Guts." Why he did, I am not sure. Maybe it was because I was gutsy and would take no stuff. I would just respond back, and my parents used to get after me so much about that. If someone said something that I didn't think was right, I'd let them have it, and then I'd get it. I was also an inquisitive child. My parents believed that "children should be seen and not heard," but I was always asking questions. This would get me in trouble, especially when we had company. Once a friend with one arm came to visit and I asked him what had happened to his arm. My parents were horrified, but I just wanted to know.

As I grew up Deac and I became rogues together. We would listen to Joe Louis's fights and really enjoy ourselves. Mom didn't like sports. I love sports. I was never a good athlete, but I love to watch sports events. After we got a television, Deac and I would watch the midget wrestlers. He would send me to the store on Germantown Avenue to get a pound of hot peanuts and we'd sit there and eat them and laugh while the midgets threw each other through the ropes. My father had a loud, hearty laugh. Mom would get so mad. She'd tell us, "People can hear you all over the city." I was closest to my father, but as far as stick-to-itiveness, I got that from my mother. She was the one who insisted that we do what we were supposed to do.

Most of the time we got along in our family. But we would squabble. My brother, Moses (we called him Larry), would do anything for you. Even though the boys did not have to do chores and the girls did, he would help us when we had to scrub and cook. But he was also a wayward spirit. One time Larry found this dead mouse. I have always been deathly afraid of mice. He kept me in the bathroom all day long. I'd peep out the door, and he'd be sitting on the step with that mouse. When my mother came home, I was in terrible shape! He got a good spanking. Another time all the other kids had mumps, but I never got them. I would take pickles and eat them outside their windows. I didn't realize until later how painful that was to them. These are the kinds of things people do in big families.

I worshiped my brother Horace and followed him all over. One time when he jumped over a wrought iron fence at the end of our street I decided to jump over that fence, too. I hit my face on the fence and broke my tooth. Mom wanted to beat me, but my lip was already swollen, so she let me alone. Horace was my buddy. I thought the world of him. We had a lot of fun in our family. On Sunday afternoons Deac would pile us all into his Packard and drive us out into the country. We'd go all around looking at how the rich folks lived. We never know what impression various experiences make on us, but I wonder if those Sunday rides didn't influence me to want to live a different kind of life.

One of our main entertainments was the Saturday movies. Cartoons and westerns played all day. We would pack our lunches and stay until the time Mom told us we had to come home. The movie houses were all segregated. At the Upsal Theater on Germantown Avenue blacks sat on one side and whites on the other. There was no balcony. At the Rialto on Germantown Avenue blacks sat in the balcony or in the far back on the ground floor. Sometimes, if the "colored" area became crowded, a few blacks would move over with the whites. Then the manager would come and make them get up and leave. Once in awhile we went to live shows downtown on Broad Street where we always had to sit in the balcony. We didn't like the segregation. But we didn't raise Cain about it. We were always in a group, with our friends, and we had a good time.

Another source of recreation was the Germantown YWCA. Our "Y" was a nice facility, and it was all black. We went there for dances and shows. There was an excellent tennis program there. My future house-mother at Cheyney State Teachers College, Butch Dudley, worked at that "Y." Mom told her to "take care of her little girl," and she ribbed me about that from the time that I got to the campus until I graduated.[67]

In 1944 a transit strike broke out in Philadelphia. White transit workers were protesting blacks being hired to drive trolleys and buses. I remember being scared to death riding the trolleys with soldiers who had guns. Many people were afraid to use the public buses and trolleys at that time, because they didn't know what might happen. Bricks were thrown into the trolleys, and the threat of violence was so great that the state militia was called in.[68] Everyone was concerned about it, but at home we didn't discuss it. Deac probably talked to some of the neighbor men about it out on the porch. But he didn't sit down and have discussions with us about things like that. He and mom came up in a generation where children did not ask questions about such topics.

As time passed, my older sisters got married and my brothers went to the Second World War. Charles had dropped out of school and married. He was drafted. The draft took Horace out of school and Larry, who was also still in school, lied about his age and enlisted. That really upset Mom.[69] He and Horace were in the navy. Charles was in an all black army infantry unit with a white leader. He was trained at Parris

Island, and he said it was brutal. It was awful to hear of some of the things he had to go through. He was so angry when he came out of the service. He thought that America was horrible in the way they treated black fighting men.

Horace hated it, too. When his unit got to England, the people would stare at them, looking for tails, because they had been told that all blacks had tails. Something seemed to have happened to Horace in the war. When he came home he acted odd; sometimes he wouldn't talk. None of my brothers could get jobs right away when they got back.

Finally, Horace became a welder. He married and had two sons. He died suddenly of a cerebral brain hemorrhage in 1968 at the age of 45. I was home visiting and answered the phone when his wife called to ask for help because he had fallen unconscious. I went right over but he was gone by the time the ambulance arrived. My father (for whom Horace was named) recently had a stroke, and I was afraid to tell him that Horace had died. But he reacted quietly. Mom, on the other hand, fainted when I told her, and for a long time after she was beside herself. She would put on two aprons and do other things that showed how distracted and distraught she was. I went through a major shutdown myself. I couldn't eat, couldn't even keep water on my stomach. He was such a fine man, and he and I had been so close. His was the first death in our immediate family.

Charles had moved away by then. We didn't know where he was. Mom held up Horace's funeral, hoping we could notify Charles. We didn't find him until the police contacted Mom in 1972. He was found dead in an apartment in Florida. He was 57. Because he had been in the service they had records that they could use to find his family. We had his body returned to Philadelphia and held a funeral there. We never knew the cause of death.

Larry, who was like Deac—he could make anything, do anything—lived with my parents after the war. One night in 1954 Larry was jumped by hoodlums. We never found out who they were. They left him for dead. He was in a coma for several months. When Mom called me in Baltimore with this news I took leave from my job and was with the family for three weeks. When the school year ended I spent the entire summer break in Philadelphia, taking turns with Mom, sitting by Larry in Germantown Hospital, talking to him, not knowing if he heard. When he finally started coming around he didn't know anybody. He was permanently brain damaged. He recognized Mom and me, because we were with him so much; but he didn't really know us. He had to learn the names of all the other family members. One night my oldest sister Elizabeth came to dinner. She had put on some weight. Larry asked Mom, "Who's that fat lady sitting there?" He had to relearn everything. He didn't know about himself or his past.

He lived with Mom until she went into assisted living and he into a veterans' home. She died in 1992 at age 94 and he at age 70 in 1996. He became compulsive about keeping the house neat. He would smooth out the seat of a chair as soon as a person got up from sitting. If someone moved a paper from where he had placed it he would move it back. He cleaned all the time, ran the poor vacuum cleaner to death.

Of my seven siblings, two sisters are now still living—Sarah and Lottie. All of my sisters married and raised families. Sarah has four daughters, all of whom went through college. Lottie, who worked at Penn Fruit until she retired, had a son who died and a daughter who became a teacher. My oldest sister, Elizabeth died in the year 2000. She had five sons, two of whom are still living. Marjorie died two years later. Her daughter is disabled by multiple sclerosis and her son became an electrician.

I was the first person in my immediate family to go to college. My mother would have worked to send my older brothers and sisters, but they seemed to feel that there was no reason to go on in school. We didn't have many role models who had earned college degrees. And our parents' financial struggles may have discouraged their older children.

Elizabeth completed junior high at Roosevelt and then just stopped going to school, and apparently the school authorities never attempted to draw her back. Lottie also completed junior high school and took night school courses later on. Marjorie attended high school but never graduated, dropping out to go to work. World War II diverted my brothers, none of whom tried to continue their schooling after the war.

I, on the other hand, always knew that I wanted a college education. I read a lot, and I knew there was something else to do in life besides washing and ironing clothes and scrubbing floors. There's nothing wrong with that work; it puts food on the table. But I wanted something more. I also didn't want to always work in a store like Penn Fruit. I wanted to become independent. In the generation after mine we would have many college graduates. My sister Sarah and I were the beginning of a new family pattern.

I really wanted to go away, to Morgan State in Baltimore. I wanted to get that distance away from home and to grow up. As a girl in a house like ours, with old-fashioned parents, I could never grow up totally. No matter how old I was, all my goings and comings were timed. My mother would say, "I never tell you what to do," and then she would say, "If I were doing it . . ." However, my father said he couldn't afford to pay for Morgan. Cheyney was a state teacher's college, so I got a full scholarship there.

Even so, there were other expenses. For one thing, I needed clothes. Marion Bray—the white woman that I had worked for—bought some of my outfits. Mom also bought some, and I could pay for a few. I wore those clothes the whole time I was there. Now and then I would get something new. Sarah had gotten a job, and she bought me a little short navy blue coat that I kept until just the other year. My mother, instead of buying the new winter coat that she needed, wore a spring coat padded with sweaters, so that she could help me through Cheyney.

Growing up, and throughout my life, so many people have done so many good things for me. I grew up in a loving family where I was cared for and protected.

My mother especially was tough. She would have fought anybody, would have gone to battle with anyone, who harmed her children, just as she went to school and stood up to Dr. Nichols. Along with being strong, she could accept people for who they were. Many people had been good to her, too. She took in laundry and all, but the people she worked for did a lot for us, especially for Sarah and me.

Many white people were kind to me—Mrs. Coil in seventh grade calling me up for an "excellent"; Mrs. Bray buying my college outfits; Mrs. Mason, sending me things she knew I would need for teaching; and Mr. Mason, who sent me fruit every year until he died. In later years when there was a problem with the deed on my parents' house a white lawyer, Mr. Wolfe, worked out a way I could clear the house, and he didn't charge me. I learned not to paint all white people with the same brush.

It's true that we had to deal with segregation. When my parents used to take us to Virginia and we couldn't eat or drink in certain places, we had our food in the car, and our water, so it didn't impact upon me that much. When I grew older and had to sit in balconies and deal with prejudiced store clerks I learned to move on in spite of the discrimination. I realized that there were schools where blacks couldn't go; and there was a question of how far any black could go—that it was expected that if you were black you would do only certain jobs, and go certain places, but I never became bitter. Maybe I compartmentalized, ignoring what I couldn't change.

I didn't grow up with my head in a hole. But I didn't grow up, either, in a world where if one person was mean to you, you took it out on every other person. I was brought up to respect people for who they are and not for their color.

Teacher Training at Cheyney

In the fall of 1945, Gertrude left her large family in Germantown and moved 25 miles southwest to the campus of the State Teachers College at Cheyney, a historically black school with an enrollment of close to 300 students in Cheyney, Pennsylvania. In some respects her new surroundings were not that different from home and high school. College administration and staff maintained a firm rule of *in loco parentis*. They enforced high standards of personal deportment and academic performance. Religion held a central place in campus life. To make economic ends meet many students, including Gertrude, held jobs. At the same time, Cheyney—administered and staffed entirely by African Americans—opened up new vistas for its black student population. The institutional mission and curriculum incorporated a special emphasis on the history and place of African Americans in contemporary society.

At the time Gertrude entered Cheyney, it had been educating African Americans for 93 years, first as the private, Quaker-funded Institute for Colored Youth (ICY, 1852–1913), then as the Cheyney Training School for Teachers, still Quaker-funded until 1921, when it became part of the state college system as Cheyney Normal School. In 1933, 12 years before Gertrude arrived, Cheyney attained the status of a full-fledged college and became the State Teachers College at Cheyney.[1]

From the outset Cheyney's character was defined by three strong features: African American educators of superior intellect and attainment implemented the curriculum; they maintained (except for a brief period) a curricular balance between academic and vocational instruction; their rigorously trained graduates transmitted the standards, skills, and values of excellence to rising generations.

In its formative years the school operated under a Quaker Board of Managers, whose members generally doubted the intellectual capabilities of blacks. One outstanding exception on that board was Alfred Cope. Quite wealthy and a progressive thinker, Cope was assertive and held sway over his fellow Managers. He staunchly supported the black faculty as they developed courses of study in mathematics, science, languages, natural philosophy, and—in keeping with its original mission, and to meet the post–Civil War demand for black teachers—pedagogy.[2] After Cope died in 1875 the black educators and the Quaker board were frequently at odds, but the faculty and a succession of dedicated administrators became increasingly adept at raising funds independently for projects to which they were committed. Fanny Jackson Coppin, whose tenure as principal extended from 1865 to 1902, was especially gifted and effective in nurturing ties between the school and the black community, as well as inspiring substantial contributions from white sources beyond the board.

"Quaker beneficence had made the physical existence of the Institute possible," historian Linda Marie Perkins concluded, "but the black leaders of the Institute and in the community molded and shaped its direction and developed the school into one of the most outstanding black educational institutions of the nineteenth century."[3] When Cheyney came under state control in 1921, the college's administration and faculty continued to take the initiative in curriculum development and fund-raising while meeting state standards, as enforced by an all-white Board of Trustees.

With excellent credentials, frequently from elite white colleges and universities, the all-black faculty were demanding taskmasters. In 1905, Evangeline Rachel Hall, the third African American to graduate from Radcliffe College, joined them as math and English teacher. A presence at Cheyney for 42 years, as a classroom instructor and especially as supervisor of student teaching, she left the imprint of her "lofty standards" on generations of students, including the generation to which Gertrude belonged. Hall was singled out in 1920 by the state supervisor of Normal schools who had inspected the campus to determine if Cheyney was eligible for state accreditation. He found her "unequaled in any Normal School that he had visited in the State for her ability and background." When the Board of Managers sought a new principal in 1913 Hall urged them to investigate the qualifications of Leslie Pinkney Hill, whom she had known when he was at Harvard, and who became the board's unanimous choice. By the time Gertrude reached Cheyney, Hall and her colleagues, under the leadership of Leslie Pinkney Hill, had raised the school to the status of a full-fledged Teachers College.[4]

Hill himself was at his professional peak when Gertrude lived under his watchful administration.[5] "Intimately concerned with the welfare of his students," he was a forceful deterrent to poor performance or undignified behavior. Sought after as a public speaker, in his lectures he celebrated self-respect, redemptive suffering, moral suasion, and humankind as one family. Calling himself a "liberal conservative" he rejected the politics of confrontation and direct action.

As Hill's biographer has observed, scholarly discussion of black education in the late nineteenth and early twentieth centuries has fixed on the opposing viewpoints of Booker T. Washington, who emphasized vocational education, and W.E.B. DuBois, who emphasized academics and has largely overlooked educators such as Hill who drew from both camps, while avoiding identification with either extreme. In order to attain state accreditation, Hill and the Cheyney staff had to moderate the stress on the industrial arts in their curriculum. But they never jettisoned it, and it remained an integral part of the college curriculum. While Hill succeeded in largely avoiding the ideological warfare of the Washington–DuBois debate, he could not so easily sidestep controversy regarding racial segregation. For a significant sector of the black community his role in promoting Cheyney as a center to train black teachers to serve black students, and establishing it as a state Normal school, amounted to racial treason. At a time when other black leaders and black parents were campaigning against segregated public schools, Hill, his detractors charged, was promoting state-sponsored segregation.[6]

Though his critics were harsh, voluble, and persistent, Hill stood his ground. Distinguishing between involuntary and self-imposed segregation, he championed the latter. He was certain that to adequately prepare the leaders who would bring their race into the mainstream of national and world societies, African Americans needed all-black schools. He wanted blacks to discard the assumption that "excellence is synonymous with white, . . . shake off this tyrannical white complex, and substitute for it a sturdy self-respect."

Hill interpreted black culture as "the enduring culture of the ages." In almost mystical terms he implied that this culture's transformative powers would eventually eradicate injustice and reveal the essential oneness of humanity.[7] He identified black families, black schools, and black churches as the guardians and transmitters of that culture and spotlighted the role of teachers. "Second only to the parent is the Negro teacher," he averred.

> We must have a new type of Negro teacher for Negro youth. That teacher must have the usual professional equipment, but he must also come to our children with that knowledge of the great traditions and accomplishments of our race by which we may be able to really inspire them to believe that there is no attainment, no character, no service that black boys and girls may not reach.[8]

Gertrude was profoundly moved by this vision of the new Negro teacher. In a historical period when few professions were open to African Americans, Hill invested her chosen field of teaching with dignity and nobility.

The faculty charged with producing Hill's new kind of teacher earned accolades from W.E.B. DuBois, who told readers of the National Association for the Advancement of Colored People (NAACP) *Crisis* magazine in 1923:

> I have seen schools in two continents and ten countries, and I have yet to see a finer group in character and service than the teachers of Cheyney.[9]

In addition to Evangeline Hall, several others among the faculty that DuBois had praised were still teaching when Gertrude's student cohort arrived. Fifty years after, she had clear memories of Hall; English teacher Katherine Robinson, a Wellesley College graduate; and science teacher Marie Gould who had earned her degree at Oberlin College. Gertrude's memories suggest continuity in the college mission from the time DuBois had written to her era.

For Cheyney students serious about pursuing a teaching career, Hill and his faculty provided a rich and supportive environment. Yet, in many respects the college was a conservative setting. The curriculum was traditional and its vocational courses might have been considered outmoded in some higher education circles. Student social life was carefully controlled. Though an earlier rule—which required written permission from a girl's parents if she were to be visited at school by a boy from outside the campus—had been lifted, the women of Gertrude's generation still could not visit with the opposite sex on campus unless a chaperone was present. Gertrude and her fellow students still had to operate under the careful scrutiny of President Hill, of whom it was known that "foremost among his personal taboos was the display of poor manners, social discourtesy and any perceived lack of self-initiative and self-respect amongst his students."[10]

Nor was Cheyney on the cutting edge of black politics. In an era when the NAACP was launching a major challenge to school segregation at all levels, and when A. Philip Randolph's March on Washington Movement (MOWM) and the Congress of Racial Equality (CORE) were calling for mass protest and direction action, Hill defended voluntary segregation and urged "adaptation and adjustment by cooperation."[11] His prescriptions were tools of survival, means of preserving life, limb and dignity amidst the dangerous and discouraging conditions under which African Americans had been living since the end of Reconstruction. Self-reliance, self-control, decorum and diligence, racial pride—with these values he armed his students to endure as necessary, and counter whenever possible, segregation, disfranchisement, systemic economic oppression, and the threats of violent reprisal for stepping out of one's "place" that underlay all such racist manifestations.

The NAACP, CORE, and MOWM foreshadowed a new era of direct attacks upon racist institutions, laws, and mores. As that era progressed, the values championed by Hill would be eclipsed by much bolder, more openly angry, insistent, and expansive demands for justice. For Gertrude, whose career paralleled all the major civil rights and Black Power struggles of the last half of the twentieth century, Hill's teachings and her Cheyney education were enduring touchstones. "Cheyney was the backbone of everything I have done in education," she said. A warm current of personal concern and affection suffused the racial consciousness, the lessons of self-respect and responsibility, and the strong academic and pedagogical preparations that characterized life at Cheyney. One feels it in Hill's reflections:

> Students say to me again and again that they find at Cheyney their first chance . . . to develop fully and freely without withering social embarrassment. . . . Education provides for the free and full expression in functioning human personality. They know that they are free at Cheyney because they are wanted and not merely taught and tolerated.[12]

Gertrude's future students, and those who would know her as counselor or principal, might well recognize in Leslie Hill's statement an apt description of the freedom they found under the tutelage of "Miss Williams," as well as a clue to why she would on occasion break ranks with what were the most popular views in the black community and march to a drummer of her own.

*   *   *

From 1945 to 1949 I was a student at Cheyney State Teachers College in Cheyney, Pennsylvania. Leslie Pinkney Hill was the president. He was a brilliant man, one of the first blacks to go to Harvard. He was a writer, a musician, an orator. We respected him for his brilliance and his dignity. He would walk across the campus, and everybody would know it. He was a gentleman. He always opened the door for women, and was courtly like that. Even though we were in college he kept in touch with our parents. If he didn't think that we were keeping up he would call them. No one wanted that, so we stayed on the straight and narrow.

I think that Dr. Hill was very angry inside about the treatment of blacks. Something serious must have happened to him. He was one of the first blacks to go to Harvard. What he must have suffered while he was there, breaking the color line, stuck with him. He was angry.[13] That's why he demanded so much out of us. He said, "You cannot allow people to see you being less than what you are." He held blacks accountable for their own growth, and I do too. I think we can understand what has happened—slavery and segregation and all. But we can't wallow in it. We just have to move on, and we must handle ourselves in such a manner that we can demand respect.

When the need for integrated schools became a national issue some black leaders started in on Cheyney. They said it was an example of forced segregation. They claimed that the Quakers established it to keep blacks from attending their schools. Cheyney students and alumni have always rejected that view. We believed with Dr. Hill that the college was meeting needs that no other institution was meeting, giving black students a good education and holding them to standards that they had to meet to overcome the effects of slavery. Those standards could best be established for blacks by blacks—a fact that remained true long after slavery.

When I became a principal I could take black students aside and talk to them in ways that a white principal could not. As for Cheyney forcing segregation—we attended Cheyney because we wanted to be there. No one was kept out of the college. If whites wanted to come they could.[14] At Cheyney I learned to understand my race and to be proud of my race.

At the same time, I learned more about prejudice at Cheyney than I had learned in Germantown High School. At Cheyney I discovered that there was more than prejudice between the black and white races. There was this really serious group of light-skinned black people who stuck together and looked down on people with darker skins. We had an instructor, William Menchan, who was also Dean of Men, who explained how during slavery fair-skinned slaves were kept to work in the house and the darker ones worked in the fields. I learned that the light-skinned blacks have their own societies in Washington, DC and Philadelphia and other places that are closed to blacks with dark skin. I had lived in Philadelphia, and I didn't know this! I found it unbelievable how many black people were prejudiced against other blacks.

I did not feel any personal rejection because of my dark skin. My campus big sister, Dorothy Bobo, was light and treated me warmly. Still, I could see in the Cheyney dining hall and in other campus activities how the light-skinned students tended to stick together. But I also noticed that some of the light-skinned girls liked the darker men. Dr. Hill called in women students with dark boyfriends and told them to stop dating them. He was very light skinned, and he was prejudiced. Families like his only married fair-skinned people, to keep the family line light.[15] Yet, whether we were dark skinned or light skinned, he held us all accountable. This was also true of the faculty, many of whom looked almost white. When it came to getting our work and being expected to perform, they treated us all the same. They all had high standards.

My first year at Cheyney there were only three male students on campus, those who were rejected for one reason or another by the military draft. However, Lincoln University was close to us, and there were boys there. We used to go to their campus and they would come to ours. The second year the boys came back to Cheyney, and what a life we had then! Still we could not sit with a male friend without a chaperone sitting there with us.[16]

I met my good friend, Clara Cobb Jones, at Cheyney. She was, and is, a character. She wore her hair in one braid down the back and always said what she felt like saying and did what she felt like doing. She was something! We have remained close over the years. We both became teachers in Baltimore. She has a heart of gold and will do anything for anybody. Another special friend at Cheyney was Marcus Foster. After the men were back, that second year, we were all assigned big brothers. Marcus was my big brother. He was such a great person. He would talk with me and advise me on my class work. We shared the same aspirations to find satisfying work and make a difference in the world.

Marcus went on to become a teacher and then a principal in Philadelphia where he was known for really turning around Gratz Senior High, one of the toughest high schools in Philadelphia. Eventually he became an associate superintendent and then took the job of superintendent of public schools in Oakland, California, where he was killed. That was a horrible thing. What a loss![17]

The Cheyney campus was small but gorgeous. The surrounding area was home to several quite wealthy families, including the Duponts. Some of them had fox hunts that we used to watch from campus. Dr. Hill and a number of faculty lived in cottages on the approach to the campus. The campus itself was a quadrangle with the women's dorm (Emlen Hall) at one end, the men's dorm (Burleigh Hall) at the other, and six other buildings, three on each side: Biddle (administration), Humphreys (classroom), and the cafeteria comprising one border; Brown (Home Economics), Penn Hall (auditorium), and the library making up the other. The "senior bench" sat between Penn and the library. That bench was a prized possession. It was just a little gray bench, but no one could sit on it except seniors.

Behind the cafeteria lay a field for tennis and other sports and a gymnasium. There were designated paths between buildings. We were not allowed to walk on the lawn; that was always beautiful. The knobs on the doors of the buildings always shined, because we had to shine them. The buildings were spotless inside. Now the campus has spread out in all directions and the quadrangle seems so small. But to us it was great. It was very peaceful, because it was off to itself. I loved to just sit out on the grass and read.

Since the women's dorm would not hold all of us, we were moved to Burleigh Hall. We took the top floors and when the boys returned, they were down on the bottom floors, with a housemother on the second floor. That lasted for one year. The boys raised so much Cain that Dr. Hill said, "No, this can't be," and he moved the boys up into Tanglewood, where they would have to walk back to get to class. At first the boys said they wouldn't move, but when Dr. Hill said "you move," they moved.[18]

Although we worked hard and usually conducted ourselves well, we did have our times when we were boisterous or just plain silly. When we were living in Burleigh Hall we found a small, black, speckled bird that we named "Harry T." (for H.T. Burleigh, the famous black composer that the dorm was named for). We kept him in our room, even though that upset the housemother. Then Harry T. died, and the word went out that we had to have a funeral. We built a little coffin and laid him out. At the appointed time we sneaked out of class. I'll never forget that day. We dressed up in black and put on veils. Clara was the preacher. The sun was shining and we were crying over Harry T. Burleigh. We prayed and sang old hymns and Clara moaned and groaned that "Harry is gone!!" We buried him, right there on the campus. Miss Napper, our housemother, gave us a fit for carrying on. We all were dormitory-bound for skipping class.

One day out of every year was "Cheyney Day." This was the day when the trustees came back to campus. A few days before they came every student was assigned a place to work. Dr. Hill walked around the campus while we scrubbed and cleaned. If he couldn't see his face in the surface we shined, we shined it over. We worked on that campus until it sparkled. On Cheyney Day we had to dress up and be on our best behavior. The trustees, who were all white men, inspected every building. The chorus sang and there were other activities to showcase student accomplishments. That was a special day.

I sang in the chorus at Cheyney. We traveled with Dr. Hill, went singing all over the New England states and were invited as well to other colleges and regions. He would take the chorus with him whenever he had to speak. He was an excellent,

excellent speaker. He was also a taskmaster. One day we acted up during practice. The next morning he came over to our building, got us up at 5:30, and we had to go practice at that hour of the morning. I complained then, but I know now that experiences like that make one a better person.

Because I needed pocket money I had a job in the campus office. Lottie Conway, a fair-skinned black woman who had light brown, almost blonde, hair was in charge. She was always very kind to me. She hired me because I knew how to type. I had to be bonded because I took students' fees and recorded their payments. Having this job meant that most people on campus knew me. I also worked every summer during college, back at Penn Fruit. In addition to the hours I put in at the store I babysat with the daughter of the store manager, Mr. Hassek.

The Cheyney curriculum included courses in home economics for women and industrial arts for men. The industrial arts course was set up especially for those who were going to teach that subject in high school. All of us were being prepared to become teachers in a certain area—elementary education; secondary education; industrial arts; or home economics. Girls weren't supposed to take industrial arts. Some boys went into home economics, but no girls in industrial arts.

I wanted to take that course. I thought it was my right and that it was prejudiced to limit what we could learn. I thought that girls needed to know how to build things just as well as boys. Most of all, I wanted to be in there because the instructor and others said I couldn't be! So I fought, and finally I got in. The fellows in the class were glad I had broken the barrier, and they helped me in the course. We learned how to put things together, how to measure. We had a lot of math. For my final project I made a bird house. The instructor was Wade Wilson, who became President of Cheyney in the late 1960s. After he heard my father call me "Guts," he called me that, too.[19]

I learned a lot of black history at Cheyney that had never been taught to me before. In high school and the lower grades we heard over and over about Phyllis Wheatley being bright and writing poems, Booker T. Washington sweeping that darned floor until it was so clean, and George Washington Carver and that peanut. Now we talked in detail about the lives of these people and began to understand their real importance. We learned about many other blacks of great influence. We also studied the African background of black Americans and the experience of slavery. Dean William McKinley Menchan emphasized that not all blacks had been slaves. He and my other history instructor, Estelle Scott Johnson, were great. They helped us understand the historical background of some of the problems that society faced in the present time.

Our English teacher, Mrs. Katherine Robinson, also Dean of Women, was extremely demanding. She would take ten points off from an essay if you left out a period. One of our science teachers, Mr. Talmadge Hayre, was a neat person but not much of a teacher. In his classes students could cheat and he wouldn't know what to do. They could talk and act up and he would say, "Okay, I know you're not listening," but he couldn't command respect, even though he was a very nice man. He knew his subject but he couldn't teach it.

Mrs. Marie Gould was another science teacher. She would take us on nature walks, where we had a list of items to identify. We'd be talking as we came out the door and she'd announce, "Number One!" We'd have to write it down, and we'd all be saying, "What? What?" "It just flew by," she'd say, meaning a bird that only she had seen. She'd point to a plant. We'd have to tell what it was, and smell it—like sassafras and different other plants—and write it down. All of us failed her walking tests. But we learned science. All of the instructors at Cheyney were tough and had high standards. Some students might carry on a little bit, but we were afraid to do too much because the wrath of Dr. Hill would come down on us.

Teacher training was the center of our education. Evangeline Hall was our supervisor. She taught us how to open a lesson, how to close, how to motivate. We learned how to deal with a student who was having difficulty and how to challenge students who were way ahead. Most of all, she insisted that we must be role models for the children. Miss Hall advised us to teach as if one-third of each class was blind, one third was deaf, and one third had difficulty speaking. Which meant that she wanted us to always teach so that we used the visual, auditory, and kinesthetic senses. A teacher can't assume that every child learns the same way as every other child. We had boxes of sand where children who relied on the sense of touch could write their letters. We used mirrors to work with children who had speech problems. She expected us to work with every child and not leave anyone behind.

In our sophomore year we went out for observation, to the demonstration school on campus. A path behind Burleigh Hall led to the little school building where we observed and then got our first chance at practice teaching. Years before, the demonstration school received students from an orphanage.[20] But by the time I was at Cheyney the demonstration students came from well-to-do families and were often the children of college faculty and staff. They were very bright, which gave us a skewed picture that was corrected when we went out to "real" public schools in our junior and senior years.

As juniors we went into Philadelphia for observation and participation. We had two three-week sessions, one in the primary grades and one in the intermediate grades. In the early part of each session we would observe and then we were assigned tasks: working with a small group of children, helping individual students while the teacher was teaching, serving somewhat like teachers' aides do now. This was to prepare us for student teaching. In our senior year we went to Philadelphia as student teachers. We would ride a bus from campus to Market Street and 13th Avenue, by City Hall. That's the coldest corner! Then we'd take the subway to our assignment and would return to Market Street at the end of the day, from where the bus would take us back.

We had to write lesson plans for Miss Hall to approve every week. I'd always pray, "Please don't let her find something wrong." But she almost always did. Then

I'd have to go back with the correction before I could teach. The rare times when she didn't find anything I would just skip out of her office, I'd be so relieved. She had us write out the questions we were going to ask, and the anticipated answers. She pointed out that if we could not answer one of our questions we could not expect a child to answer it and therefore it must not be a good question.

She had to first check whatever materials we were planning to use in a lesson. For example, if we were doing a unit on the weather and were going to have the children build weather stations to record the direction of the wind and so forth, we had to build a model and have her approve it before we could use it in class. Nothing was left to chance. When she got sick, we had to go to the hospital with our plans for her to look at before we could teach.[21] This training proved very useful when I began teaching in Baltimore. The requirements of my first supervisors were very much like those of Miss Hall.

For student teaching I was assigned to an elementary school on Wharton Street in Philadelphia, to the classroom of Ursula Curd. Miss Curd and most of the pupils were black, as was the neighborhood where the school was located. This was a different experience for me, having grown up in a predominantly white area and having gone to predominantly white schools until college. She asked me what subject I would like to teach least. Now, I did not know that Ursula Curd was a concert pianist, and I said, "music." She said, "Oh, well then, you will start with music." Oh, my Lord! I learned to teach it though. That's the kind of instruction we got at that time. There was nothing left unturned. Even our clothing was scrutinized. We had to wear stockings with the seam up the back. My legs have never been big, and it was *so* hard to get that seam straight. We also had to wear gloves and a little hat.

Facing students for the first time was frightening. I looked at them and they looked at me, and everything that I'd prepared—because I had to have every word written out; every question that I wanted to ask and every answer that I expected; I had to have all of that ready. I had sat up all night, gotten the pictures together and so on. Then I stood up in front of the class and my mind went blank. I just *stood* there. Miss Curd had my papers with everything that I was supposed to do, so she started me off, because I had frozen. Then I picked up and went on. I apologized to her afterwards. She said, "I did the same thing when I started teaching. There is something about meeting children for the first time and having them look at you like, 'what are you going to do?' " And that's the truth. They are going to size you up the minute you walk in that classroom and you're either going to be someone who's going to teach them and not have any foolishness or you're going to be a pushover.

They had a white mouse in Miss Curd's classroom. As I've mentioned, I am *so* afraid of mice I could almost die. Miss Curd knew how scared I was. I was helping a student, bending over, and one of the other students put that mouse on my shoulder. I almost went out! I couldn't scream; I couldn't utter a sound. She saw, and she went off on that child. But he said, "I was just playing! I was just playing!" That's a child for you. I should never have let him know I was afraid. You have to kind of puff up to be a teacher. I used to be afraid of thunderstorms until I started student teaching. One day we were in the classroom and it got really dark. Miss Curd saw me freezing. She walked up and said, "Continue. The storm will not come in." She saw me shaking. After that I got over it. I could deal with it.

When we graduated from Cheyney we had worked, and we came out ready to be good teachers. There was a lot demanded of us, and we knew the curriculum. Anyone who wasn't a good teacher was stopped after the sophomore year and had to leave. Today we have teachers who have gotten not only their BS but their Masters degrees and are illiterate. They go into classes and they regurgitate ignorance. In some of today's Masters programs nothing is taught. The Masters candidates just talk about some of the things they are doing in their schools. There is no way that some of the teachers who teach our children should have passed out of college.

I have gone into classrooms after school and read the blackboards and had to change spelling in the work on the board. Now, anyone can misspell something once in awhile. And when I was teaching I had children correct me if I misspelled something. I told them, "If you see a misspelled word and you catch me, you get points. If I catch you, I get points." But today we have teachers who don't know if their spelling is wrong. They just are not prepared to teach the children.

I also find that many of the leaders in the colleges and universities don't stand for much, and their institutions are failing to prepare teachers for the classroom. They are really part of the reason why there's such a breakdown in education today. Students today don't have parents who hold them accountable; and they don't have teachers or leaders who hold them accountable either.

My friends and I cried when we left Cheyney. Cheyney is the backbone of whatever I've done in education. And the example set by Leslie Pinkney Hill, Evangeline Hall, and other demanding instructors, has stayed with me. Every Cheyney student had to memorize a poem written by Dr. Hill titled "The Teacher." It really didn't have meaning for me until I started teaching. But then it meant—and means—a lot because, as teachers we're hypocritical sometimes. We don't always live what we teach. As a principal, on special occasions I used to quote "The Teacher."

THE TEACHER

Lord, who am I to teach the way
To little children day by day,
So prone myself to go astray?

I teach them *knowledge*, but I know
How faint they flicker and how low
The candles of my knowledge glow.

I teach them *power* to will and do,
But only now to learn anew
My own great weakness through and through.

I teach them *love* for all mankind

And all God's creatures, but I find
My love comes lagging far behind.

Lord, if their guide I still must be,
Oh, let the little children see
The teacher leaning hard on Thee.[22]

We took the National Teachers' Examination while we were at Cheyney.[23] We got the results back, and I had passed. Then we had to do the Locals. You would apply to places and take their local tests and be interviewed. I applied to Baltimore and Philadelphia. In Baltimore we went to the black Department of Education, across from where the black Providence Hospital used to be—a white wood building on a hill on Madison Street. Black teachers called it "Uncle Tom's Cabin." Dr. Elmer Henderson was the Superintendent of Colored Schools. There were other new teachers outside waiting when I arrived, and they asked me, "Where are you from? Where do you live?" When I said I came from Philadelphia they said, "Philadelphia? You came down *here* to take *this* test? Girl, it's going to be hard!"

I started to go home. But I went in and they had different people in different rooms. I walked through and would talk to one person on one subject and then go to the next and talk on different subjects, and I went on around. I had to wait for the letter telling whether or not I had passed. I really didn't want to teach in Philadelphia, so I was very upset when I heard from there first. But then I heard from Baltimore. I passed. Yippee! I later learned that some of those who had tried to scare me from taking the Baltimore test did not pass.

I had visited Baltimore several times, staying with my Aunt Sarah (the sister of my grandmother Charlotta), who lived on upper Emondson Avenue. I had liked it: the place with the white steps. Scrubbing those steps in the morning and evening. My parents were anxious for me to stay in Philadelphia. Men and women their age believed that unless a woman was married she should be with her parents. I was anxious to leave. That was the only way I could learn to be independent. Since we had relatives in Baltimore, and since it was close enough to Philadelphia that I could get home to see the family whenever I wanted or needed to, I finally got the okay from my mother and father, and I came to live in Baltimore.

THREE

Teacher at Charles Carroll
of Carrollton

When Gertrude moved to Baltimore in 1949, the city was home to more black residents than any other northeastern urban center. It retained a decidedly Southern social structure and climate. While a substantial black middle class lived and consolidated their resources in neighborhoods adjoining the black cultural mecca of Pennsylvania Avenue in West Baltimore, the majority were restricted to three severely crowded ghetto areas, with one of the worst tuberculosis rates in the nation. They were permitted to hold only certain jobs—principally the most menial, the dirtiest, the most dangerous, and the lowest paying. Most entertainment facilities barred them. The few that didn't relegated them to balconies. Only the most limited and shabby playgrounds and sports facilities were open to them. Most restaurants were out of bounds as were all hotels for black out of town visitors. African American children were assigned to dilapidated, segregated schools, and those who persevered and sought a college education were forced to enroll in a historically black college or look out of state, since higher education institutions in Maryland were "white only."[1]

Nonetheless, World War II had produced improved employment opportunities, as Baltimore became "an arsenal of defense" and the steel, ship-building, and aeronautics industries underwent rapid expansion. The Bethlehem-Fairchild shipyards alone took on 47,000 new workers between 1941 and 1945. The burgeoning job market triggered population growth of more than 10 percent during the 1940s; African Americans accounted for more than four-fifths of this growth. For the first time, black workers found jobs opening to them in the war industries and as fire fighters, policemen, bus drivers, and sales clerks. However, they still faced resistance from whites determined to maintain their historical monopoly on such work.[2]

The swelling black population made a heavy impact upon the separate and decidedly unequal Baltimore City public school systems. Before the war, enrollment in the "colored schools" constituted less than a third of the white school enrollment. Over the next decade black enrollments ballooned, placing a great strain on staff and physical plants.[3]

William H. Lemmel, who became Superintendent of Public Instruction in 1946, set up and chaired a School Plant Planning Committee that examined the physical condition and capacity of city school buildings. In June 1948, the year before Gertrude came to Baltimore, Lemmel announced the committee's findings, summarized by the *Baltimore Sun*: "Overcrowded classrooms, outmoded buildings, substandard plumbing and sanitation facilities." Examining the same issue two years later the city school board noted the disproportionate burden these conditions placed upon black students:

> The colored schools in the heart of the city have felt the impact of the steady growth in pupil population most severely. Most of the schools which have felt the burden heaviest are in buildings which have been scheduled for replacement since . . . 1922.[4]

Lemmel had also warned of a growing personnel shortage. He reported that to meet state standards the city was going to have to find 496 new elementary teachers and approximately 200 other staff such as librarians, art and music teachers, and health instructors.[5]

Since the onset of the war, staffing public school classrooms had become increasingly difficult. Lucrative jobs in defense production lured teachers away in alarmingly large numbers.[6]

Replacing thousands of departing teachers were wives of military personnel and other housewives and non-professionals who did not measure up to state certification standards. This influx of inexperienced and untrained individuals appears to have affected the white schools most, with the result that by 1953 black teachers in Baltimore City were reported to have "attained a higher level of education than white teachers" and black elementary and junior high teachers had more teaching experience than their counterparts.[7]

Gertrude's recollections of the rigorous supervision that she received as a probationary teacher at School #139, Charles Carroll of Carrollton, a part of the "colored" division of the school system, squares with other accounts of that system—from both black and white sources—in the late 1940s and the decade of the 1950s.[8] Her descriptions of the meager resources with which the #139 teachers had to make do is also borne out by the historical record.

The division was administered by a black assistant superintendent, Dr. Elmer Henderson, from a separate headquarters on Madison Avenue. While certification and performance standards were "identical" for black and white divisions, per pupil funding allocations were not, and neither were facilities, as Gertrude would discover when she took a new assignment in 1965 at a predominantly white school. The relegation of black children and their teachers to substandard—and in most cases, dangerous and unhealthy—buildings would be an unresolved issue throughout the years of Gertrude's career as an educator. In 1967 a fact-finding commission of the National Education Association (NEA) pointed out that 58 schools in Baltimore City were identified in 1921 as uninhabitable. In 1967, children were still attending school in 35 of those buildings, in 27 of which the students were more than 90 percent black.[9]

Ten years before Gertrude began teaching in Maryland, white teachers were paid almost one-third more than black teachers, who reportedly earned less than white janitors. By the time Gertrude started her career, Maryland paid black teachers on the same scale as white teachers, thanks to future Supreme Court justice, Thurgood Marshall, then a young National Association for the Advancement of Colored People (NAACP) lawyer. With a mother who taught in the Baltimore city schools, Marshall, according to biographer, Juan Williams, "took it personally that his mother's work was valued less than a white teacher's." After he won cases for salary equalization in Montgomery and Anne Arundel Counties, the state government passed a law establishing one standard for all teachers.[10] As a probationary teacher in 1949, Gertrude earned $1,600 per year Superintendent Lemmel advocated vigorously for the salary scale to be upgraded, and gradually it would be. By 1954, a year after his death, a Baltimore City teacher's salary was $3,200 per year.[11]

Lemmel was progressive in all policies related to race. He initiated interracial staff meetings, instituted a city-wide parent–teacher organization (PTO) that was integrated, and supported the 1952 petition of 16 African American students for admission to Baltimore Polytechnic Institute, Baltimore's magnet high school for science and engineering. The school board, in a vote of 5 to 3, approved the petition, and the students began their studies at Poly in September 1953, eight months before the Supreme Court mandated school desegregation in *Brown v. Board of Education*.[12]

Lemmel's efforts were valued by the local affiliate of the American Federation of Teachers (AFT), the Baltimore Teachers Union (BTU), which was campaigning for school integration at least a decade before the decisive federal court ruling on that issue. With its rival, the Public School Teachers Association (PSTA), an affiliate of the NEA, BTU prodded the school board to demand more funding for all the schools. BTU leaders worked amicably with Lemmel and his successor, John Fischer, on such issues as salary equalization and improved benefits and working conditions for teachers. They also began to press the school system to adopt collective bargaining.[13]

Gertrude recalls attending integrated staff meetings and representing School #139 on one of Lemmel's interracial committees. But these experiences seem to have been incidental to her life as a teacher. Nor did the landmark *Brown* decision, declaring school segregation to be unconstitutional, appear to have a direct effect upon her work at Charles Carroll of Carrollton, where she would remain for 16 years. In part, no doubt, this was because Baltimore's response to *Brown* was so cautious at first that the staff and students of many city schools were virtually unaffected. In the case of Gertrude and Charles Carroll of Carrollton, they were affected not at all in any official manner.[14]

In 1953, John Fischer succeeded Lemmel as Superintendent and, in response to *Brown*, presided over the first phase of desegregation. While many districts in the state and nation plotted resistance, the Baltimore school district adopted a "freedom of choice" policy. All parents were free to enroll their children in schools of their choosing until the school reached its capacity. In this way, Fischer explained, the city would "open the door of all our schools to all children without discrimination, but not . . . push or pull anyone through a door. We believed it was wrong to manipulate people to create a segregationist situation. We believe it equally wrong to manipulate people to create an integrated situation."[15] Negative white reactions to this policy were relatively few and short-lived. Baltimore's leaders congratulated themselves on how smoothly they put the new policy into effect, and the Baltimore "voluntary desegregation" method received highly favorable comment nationwide.[16]

Fischer and other white leaders in Baltimore operated within a public culture that prized order and good manners, and that fostered a paternalistic stance toward the public, black and white. They moved quickly to assure the federal government of their compliance with the Supreme Court, but the methods they chose to implement the court decision were designed more to avoid social disruption than to change the racial status quo. The results were that, in the immediate aftermath of the court decree, Baltimore stood out as a Mecca of tolerance in contrast to the "Massive Resistance" erupting in towns and cities throughout the Deep South.[17] In the long term, however, the city fathers had merely postponed the day of reckoning, and in as late as 1974 the public schools of Baltimore—amidst mounting racial discord— would still be out of compliance with federal desegregation guidelines.

Various factors account for why so little desegregation, and no true integration, took place in the Baltimore public schools between 1954 and 1974. The school board's "open door" policy was laissez faire to the point of being nearly meaningless. In the first year after *Brown*, 42 of Baltimore's 131 elementary schools remained all-white and 50 all-black. The degree of "mixing" in the remaining 38 schools was a matter of debate. For school officials the presence of both black and white students, whatever their relative proportions, signified desegregation, and the school board consistently published reports reflecting a steady decline in the number of schools that were all one race. However, for critics, who soon began to press for a more forceful policy, any school population that was made up of 90 percent or more of one race was still segregated, noting that in 1961—despite several years' effort to achieve racial balance—the great majority of both white and black students were still in segregated schools.[18] Residential segregation played a major part in this state of affairs, given the tradition of (and often the family preference for) sending children to their neighborhood school.[19] At the same time, African Americans, including school-age children, were moving into Baltimore in increasingly large numbers, and white families were relocating to the suburbs. When Fischer resigned in 1959 and his replacement, George Brain, assumed the superintendency later that year, the school system had become majority black.[20]

Until 1963, another factor that limited school desegregation in Baltimore City was "districting." Under this policy, a school could refuse new students if it was overcrowded. White communities pressed successfully to have their neighborhood schools districted, though in many cases they were really not overcrowded. Meanwhile, numerous black schools were forced to put their students on shifts because of severe overcrowding. When students were moved from these schools, they were sent to other black schools. Organized protest, spearheaded by black parents who took the name, "Group of 28 Parents," forced the end of districting, the adoption of busing students to schools outside their "districts," and the elimination of shifts.[21]

Still, the increasing imbalance between the growing black student-body and the shrinking white population made system-wide desegregation virtually impossible. During the 1960s the city lost 7,000 white students and gained 54,000 black students. Even those schools that experienced some racial change were destined for "resegregation" in the near future. The reality described by black associate superintendent, Houston Jackson, in 1961—that there were "more Negro children today in essentially segregated situations than we had when segregation was compulsory"—would persist.[22]

The same demographic revolution that was transforming a predominantly white to a mostly black school population was also working changes within the Baltimore school board and school administration. The nine-member Board of School Commissioners was appointed by the mayor. Traditionally, appointees were drawn from the civic elite and selected to be representative of the city's major religious and racial groups, as well as of the three largest institutions of higher education in the area—the University of Maryland, the Johns Hopkins University, and Morgan State University.

Social scientists who examined this tradition came to varying conclusions. From one perspective Baltimore was unique and fortunate to have such a school board, because the close connection between the board and leaders in the business and legal communities smoothed the way when decisions on sensitive issues such as race had to be made. From another perspective, the board could be described as overly cautious and insufficiently responsive to community demands for change. This perspective penetrated the veneer of urbanity and well-meaning worn by a majority of the board, as they repeatedly missed the growing anger among the city's black population over the failure of desegregation efforts to address mounting inequities within the under-funded and overcrowded schools of the inner city.[23]

According to research by the school system's own staff, the failure rate of children in these schools was 25 times as high as the failure rate of children in more prosperous areas of Baltimore. The school system was offering "Special Education"—individually prescribed instruction provided by specially trained teachers, in small groups, with as much individual attention as possible—to 12,000 students identified as "learning disabled." Superintendent Brain reported that "40,000 more" children needed such services.[24] Yet neither the school board nor the several superintendents who headed the school system in the years while Gertrude worked at School #139 aggressively pursued the financial resources that such a situation demanded.

Throughout her years of teaching at Charles Carroll of Carrollton, Gertrude's students were, without exception, African American. The policies and politics of desegregation would not directly affect her until she left School #139 in 1965 to accept a new assignment. Other developments within the school system and in the city also seem to have made little impression on Miss Williams, the teacher. When I asked during the oral interviews, about the Citizens School Advisory Committee, established by George Brain in 1961 and the source of an extremely thorough assessment of the Baltimore City Public Schools (BCPS) published in 1964, she did not recall the committee or their report.

Brain's Citizens' Committee is a historical monument to both the prodigious talent, energy, and goodwill of the citizens who produced it—including their chairman, journalist Clark Hobbs, and the coordinator assigned to them by the school system, Robert Lloyd—and to the capacity of a bureaucracy to absorb the most thoughtful and constructive of critiques and recommendations while remaining unaltered by them. While many of their recommendations—including smaller classes; more parent involvement; special programs for disruptive students; full-time social workers, counselors, nurses, and home visitors assigned to every school—would have improved conditions in her classroom, since they were not implemented there was little reason for Gertrude or any other teacher or building administrator to pay attention to them.[25]

While aware of the several forces agitating for change, such as the BTU, PSTA, and an array of civil rights advocates, Gertrude did not join them. At this point in her career she was intently occupied in mastering the art of teaching and meeting the needs of her students. If she was conscious of the politics of public education (an arena in which she would later become quite expert) she was not yet inclined to explore it. Only when she left Charles Carroll of Carrollton did her horizons begin to widen, and not until she became an administrator in 1969 and began to sit in on the school board meetings that were held at her newly assigned school, Barclay Elementary, would she begin to think in terms of "the system"—how to make it work for her students and how to fight it when necessary.

In Baltimore, as elsewhere, the struggle for school desegregation was part of a broader movement for human and civil rights after World War II. Baltimore's civil rights movement joined and, to some degree, pioneered the nation-wide black revolt. Well-established black organizations and institutions, including the *Baltimore Afro-American* newspaper, the local chapter of the NAACP the Interdenominational Ministerial Alliance, and the newer but highly visible chapter of the Congress of Racial Equality generated nonviolent direct action on numerous fronts: challenging segregated public parks, theaters, restaurants, and lunch counters (years before the famous 1960 student sit-ins in North Carolina); bringing pressure to bear on racist hiring practices in the private and the public sectors; and increasing the power of the black vote through voter registration and voter education campaigns.[26]

These initiatives helped to change the social climate in which Gertrude, her students, associates, and friends were living. As Douglas B. Sands, executive secretary of the Maryland Commission on Interracial Problems and Relations, observed in 1961:

> The idea of standing up and fussing is catching on. Negroes are less worried about the feelings of white people than they used to be. If they have an urge to crusade, they will.[27]

Amidst these portentous changes, Gertrude was maturing as a teacher and taking on leadership roles at her assigned school. Within its walls, the capacity for righteous indignation that she had first revealed in Mr. Gelman's Germantown High School history class was awakened periodically during the 16 years she spent at Charles Carroll of Carrollton: the confrontations that she describes in this chapter reveal a keen sense of justice, intolerance for arbitrary behavior, whether by colleagues or supervisors, and a temper whose sudden heated flashes she could not always control. Her memories also reflect a clear understanding of the importance of forging school–parent connections and a nascent sense of how school staff can tap into community resources. Above all, the woman who emerges from these recollections is passionately devoted to teaching and to improving the life-chances of her students.

*　*　*

In the fall of 1949 I began to teach in Baltimore at Charles Carroll of Carrolton, public school #139. But first I had to find a place to live. Through the YWCA I was directed to William and Rebecca Griggs, who were both teachers. Their home was in the 1500 block of Pulaski Street, in West Baltimore, and the whole block was made up of teachers. So the Griggs and I had common ground. When I first moved there I had a room, and I fed myself. But then I was sending my sister, Sarah, to college and pinching pennies and wasn't eating that well. I'd get a pound of hot dogs and eat one hot dog a night. I would pack one sandwich and carry it to school. So I started losing weight. Becky Griggs said, "Why not just eat with us? Because," she said, "you're just going to die right here." So I started eating with them. We sat around the round table and talked at dinner. In the morning all of us would be rushing to go to work, so I'd get a bowl of cereal and get out of there. Every weekend in the summer they went to Magothy Beach, a black resort on the Eastern Shore of Maryland, where they had a home and often I would go with them. They really looked out for me.

Even though I liked Baltimore a great deal, I was shocked by the segregation that was worse than in Philadelphia. There were still stores downtown where you couldn't try on dresses. I seldom shopped in Baltimore, except at a couple of stores that let you try on clothes. I did most of my shopping in Philadelphia. Even today the old attitudes still exist. You can feel the prejudice in the way people come up to you in a store. Some stores I just don't go in.

After I was settled at the Griggs's I began teaching on Central Avenue and Orleans Street in east Baltimore. At first I walked four blocks every morning to catch a bus to work. I had to transfer to a second bus to reach the school. I had to leave at the crack of dawn, carrying my shopping bags of supplies. (You can always spot a teacher by all the bags she carries!) I would get home at dusk and have the same four blocks to walk. At that time student teachers could ride for a reduced fare. Since I looked very young and I didn't have that much money, I just paid that fare. After awhile a neighbor, Cassius Mason, carried me in his car. He was the assistant principal at School #116 that backed onto Charles Carroll of Carrollton's playground. Then I met Laura Waller, who taught at Charles Carroll and also lived on Pulaski Street, and I began to ride with her. I was trying to save to buy my own car, but every time I came close to having enough there would be some need at home and I would have to use my money to help the family.

School #139 was a four-story building with an enrollment of 1,500 children. It was located in an area of factories. An industrial tram that carried coal and other products to these factories ran down the middle of Caroline Street, in front of the school. We could hear it in our classrooms when it rumbled by. We could also hear the glass popping in the Caplan Glass factory nearby, on Orleans Street. A few of the students at #139 lived in houses that were scattered on Orleans Street, but most came from housing projects, especially the all-black Douglass projects. Another set of projects on Central Avenue, the Latrobe Homes, housed white families whose children went to another school at a farther distance, even though they could have walked right up the street to #139.[28]

George Simms was principal at #139, and he was one of the best principals in the whole wide world. I was hired to take a sixth grade class, but when he saw that I weighed 85 pounds and was five feet tall he said, "Oh no, you cannot teach sixth grade"—because sixth grade children were very tall. In those days schools retained students in the grades they did not pass, no matter their age or size. Mr. Simms put me in third grade and told the other third grade teachers that each was to pull out some of the children to give to me to have a class.

Well, they cleaned out any kids that were potential problems and put them in my classroom. We had 1,500 children in that school then. So there were several third grade classes, and they held 40, 45, or sometimes 50 children. In my class I had about 35 students, but they included many children who were catalysts for other children, and I couldn't even start meeting their needs.

I was in a situation that none of my previous experiences had prepared me for. I was shocked to find that teachers had to be with the students from the minute we walked into our rooms until the time we sent them home. When they went to physical education, we went with them. When they went to music, we went with them. We even had to eat lunch with our children. I remembered when I went to Emlen Elementary. When the bell rang for lunch our teachers sent us out to the cafeteria if we were going to buy our lunch, or to the gymnasium if we brought a bag lunch.

After lunch we went outside to play, without supervision. When the bell rang we got in line. When the second bell rang we passed to our rooms, in the order of our classes, with the youngest students passing first. At School #139 the students were supervised every minute.

I came to realize the differences between Emlen when I was young and #139 in the late 1940s. Even though I came from a poor family, most of my schoolmates had parents who were well-off. Most of the parents, including mine, placed high value on education. They also stressed discipline and good behavior. My old elementary school was located in a quiet, well-kept neighborhood and was adequately funded.

Most of the Charles Carroll of Carrollton families were poor. Many of them had not fared well in school and had mixed feelings about education. Although there were some excellent parents who lived in the projects and whose children were great students, some had very weak parenting skills. School #139 was located in a noisy industrial area and was far from adequately funded. So the children needed all the attention—and discipline and structure—that we could give them.

I had learned the basics of teaching at Cheyney, but the children I dealt with there were also different from these children at Charles Carroll of Carrollton. The students in my practice teaching and student teaching classes had parents who had prepared them for school. They had been told stories and read nursery rhymes. They knew the sounds of the alphabet and were ready to learn phonics when they started school. Many of the #139 students were not that well prepared.

Two weeks after I began, I packed up my things and was ready to walk out the school door, with a dollar and a half in my pocketbook. But Mr. Simms caught me on my way out. I said to him, "I came here because I wanted to teach. I did not come here to lose my mind."[29] He came into the class. Then he met with all the third grade teachers, and he chewed them out. He had just expected other teachers to be fair to a new person, and he was shocked. "How could you do that?" he demanded.

So he decided, "I will design the class." He took all the top kids out of each class. That was heaven. I later had good friends at #139, but there at the start those teachers were haughty. They were very rude to me. They didn't want to be bothered helping me. Mr. Simms talked to me and said, "No, you can't let people do that to you. You've spent your time in school, and you're entitled to be treated fairly." I never forgot this and when I became a principal I always supervised the make-up of the classes for new teachers.

From then on, for my first two years—until I received my tenure—I had good classes. That was Mr. Simms's philosophy. When a teacher is learning how to do all the things she's supposed to do in the classroom, she should not have to deal with numerous problem students. Mr. Simms was going to do everything he could to make sure that new teachers succeeded—that the classes we got were teachable. He made sure that we had the materials and things we needed. Once a week he would sit down and talk with me: "How are things going? Are you keeping in touch with your parents?"

During that time my parents were about to lose their home because of a problem with the deed.[30] To get their property straight I needed to borrow money, and I asked Mr. Simms to co-sign the loan. He said, "I don't sign loans for anyone. But since you're helping your mother and father. . . ." So he signed.

As a new teacher my biggest concern was being prepared every day and learning how to manage large numbers of children who were working at several different levels. In the third grade I had some children who were still reading in primers. My class had about 35 students, and at first I was trying to teach them in five groups. That was too much to juggle. The assistant principal, Mabel Davis (who later married and became Mrs. Booker), came to my rescue.[31] She showed me how to integrate the groups and teach overall skills as general work to the whole class. Then, while the children were practicing those skills, I could identify students who needed work on specific parts of the lesson and work with them as a group. Instead of having fixed groups, I could pull children together according to who needed extra help with a given skill or concept.

Miss Davis taught me management skills that helped me move from day to day. For example, a new teacher will often speak too loudly. She would point this out. When a new teacher asks a question she may repeat it and repeat it. Miss Davis would say, "You ask the question once and make them listen. When they know you're going to ask it at least three times they won't listen until you ask it the third time." She taught me to have all board work ready before the children walk into the classroom; and to stand at the door, where I could see the class when they came in and see them when they were passing down the hall.

Other management tips involved walking with the children down the hall: the teacher should position herself near the end of the line so that she can see most of the students, and give the leader of the line specific directions: "Walk to the clock." Don't say, "Walk down the hall." And always have the hand of the wiggliest kid. Teachers now put those kids at the end of the line. They say, "I put him back there because he always carries on." Well, if the teacher's at the front of the line what is he going to do? He'll push that line to the end of the hall! The kids will be pushing and shoving each other and the teacher will ask, "What can I do?"

Miss Davis also demonstrated the right way to present class work. Be sure to go over the directions; have students read them silently; ask if there are any questions; and then have someone do the first example. She showed me that when children work in groups the teacher seats herself so that she can see the whole class. When all the children are working don't stand in the front of the room. Walk around, look at the papers. If someone is not getting it right, stop and help. But always walk the way that you can keep your eye on the class. After you grade papers and return them, always have the children go over the lesson again, and make sure that they understand all the answers, so if a child has gotten a wrong answer he can understand the right answer and will not keep compounding his mistake. Never ever give a child an assignment when the skills that are needed haven't been taught.

In these first years of teaching I was guided not only by Mr. Simms and Mrs. Davis-Booker but also by curriculum supervisors and specialists who closely observed, evaluated, and advised me. Their watch-word was "careful planning." All the time I was a teacher I had to make a long-range plan every year. I had to turn in a plan to the supervisor for what I was going to do every month. Then I had plans for each week and a skeletal plan on my door, so that anybody coming to the room would see what I was supposed to be teaching and when I would be teaching it. This is not done anymore. The unions and the system have cut it out. But it really should be reinstated. With formal planning the teacher is focused; she can gather all the materials she is going to need for the lessons; and the children and parents will know what to expect.

My first curriculum supervisor was Emma Bright. I admired her so much. She was smart and genteel, and I loved her clothes. She made everything she wore! I took lesson plans to her at Uncle Tom's Cabin every Wednesday. Before I could begin teaching those lessons on Monday, she had to go over my plans. She okayed them and made suggestions. The plans were based on the Baltimore City curriculum, which, at that time, was very comprehensive. It laid out what must be taught. The teacher's plans dealt with how the material would be covered. Emma Bright would also come and observe my teaching. If I had problems I could go to her.[32]

I had a little boy who was stealing, and I called her because I didn't know what to do. Her first response was always, "Talk with the child; he must be having problems." Usually children who steal are missing something somewhere. In this case it turned out that the boy was hungry. I went to his home and his mother had nothing. He was stealing lunches and any money that was sitting around. When the school stepped in and helped them, he stopped stealing. I never felt uncomfortable saying to Emma Bright, "I am having a problem." She never acted as though a person was stupid or incompetent. She would take us very seriously. "And if this doesn't work," she would say, "then try this or that." And she would follow up on it.

Dan Rochowiak was another supervisor who worked with me on classroom management and math instruction.[33] He taught me to set up a system of pals or buddies, so that children working in a group did not have to always come to me for help. They could go to any other person in the room who knew the answer. This worked well, and children were not shy about asking for help. One day when Dr. Rochowiak was observing my classroom a little girl tried to get his attention by banging on his leg. She didn't know it was a wooden leg, and at first he didn't notice her. I saw her and thought, "Oh, my God." But when he looked down and saw her he talked to her as though nothing was unusual. I said, "I'm sorry!" But he was unfazed and said, "She was just doing what you told her to do. And I was glad to help her."

Just as the students could help one another through the buddy system, they could participate in setting the rules that we followed in the classroom. I set up a big box and asked for suggestions on ways that could help us have a peaceful classroom. At one time the cloakroom that was part of our classroom space was a trouble spot.

Anytime children went for their coats there would be some kind of problem. I said to them, "We've got to solve this problem." We could not continue having them crying out, "Miss Williams! He did this; she did that!"

Then one of the children put in the box that we should have signs: "IN" on one side; "OUT" on the other. Someone else recommended that the boys should pass into the room first one week and the girls would go first the next week. The group going second would sit at their desks until it was their turn. We also had class monitors, and the children decided that a monitor would stand at each end of the cloakroom and help keep order. The students knew what was wrong and how to fix it. Having made the rules they proudly followed them.

The confidence that I steadily gained as a classroom teacher was put to a test one day when Emma Bright came to observe. Mr. Simms came in, too. There was a piece of paper on the floor next to a student's desk. As I walked past the child's desk I reached down and picked up the paper. Mr. Simms said to me, "You shouldn't have picked up that paper." I just looked at him and kept on and finished the class. But I was steaming! Afterwards, Emma Bright talked to me and then left; she had given me a nice rating. Then Mr. Simms asked me to step out into the hall.

George Simms was outstanding, but he would never let anything rest. "You should always make children accountable," he said. He had this little pad that he kept in his coat pocket, and he'd write down everything. He insisted, "The child should have picked up the paper." I said, "Why should the child pick up the paper? The child was working." So he took out that pad and wrote it down. I knew he was coming back if he wrote it on that pad. I said to him, "You take this damn class!" And I ran down the hall. I have a temper. I know I have a temper, but only when people push me to a point.

Margaret Wilson, another teacher, had a clothes closet in her classroom that was as big as a room. Mr. Simms sent Miss Davis to cover my class and looked for me all day long. Somebody must have tipped him off that I was in Margaret Wilson's closet. So he came in there and asked, "Is Miss Williams here?" And she goes, "Who?" So he knew I was there. Finally he came to the closet and said, "I need to talk to you." I answered (like a baby), "I'm not talking to you!" "Well," he said, "we need to talk." I said, "Only if I can talk as a woman and not a teacher." He agreed: "Well come on then." We got in his car and rode all around. I said to him, "You do things that are nerve-wracking. Why should I stop in the middle of a lesson, tap a kid on the arm to pick up the paper? Then he would lose his train of thought!" We argued. Finally he said, "Well, you're right," and he apologized. Then I went back to class. But I had been *so* angry.

Even if he got on my nerves sometimes, the fact was, Mr. Simms had an organized school. He knew what was happening in that school. He knew what teachers were supposed to be doing, and he could walk in any room and know if the teacher was teaching the lesson correctly. He demanded that his teachers do everything possible to meet the needs of every student. I found out what this could mean the first time

I recommended that a child, a student named Lawrence, be retained in the same grade for a second year.

Mr. Simms called me in and asked, "What didn't you do? What did you miss in teaching this child? What will another teacher do that you couldn't have done?" I was so frustrated. I was nearly in tears. I said, "I worked hard with Lawrence. I worked with him in class. I kept him after school. Lawrence's behavior just stops you from being able to help him." Mr. Simms looked at me and said, "I don't have a paper here that shows where you asked me to intercede with Lawrence." That was true. I should have told him that Lawrence was having a hard time. Although Lawrence didn't do his work, he usually stayed in his seat, and he wasn't enough of an annoyance that I thought to go to Mr. Simms about him. But I should have. He did accept my recommendation to retain Lawrence, and I was careful from then on to alert him whenever a child was falling behind despite all my best efforts.

Years later, when I had become a principal, I followed Mr. Simms's lead. I told teachers, "If you're having difficulty with a child, don't tell me in May that you need to send a letter to the parents that this child is failing. Come to me earlier. If I cannot do anything with the child, I need to seek help, bring in other services, and the parents need to know before May."

There were also times when Mr. Simms supported me. One day I kept a child in after school because she hadn't done her work. I sent a note with another child to tell the mother that I would walk her daughter home. The mother came up and went to Mr. Simms. She told him that I was too young and simple to be teaching. He replied, "Well, Miss Williams takes care of almost forty children every day, and now she's helping your child. Now, how many do you take care of?" That quieted the mother down, and she went home. After that, I started bringing her in and having her work with us in the classroom, and we didn't have any more trouble with her.

After I taught third grade for two years, I came up for tenure. I was visited not only by the supervisors from Uncle Tom's Cabin, including Romaine Jones, the Assistant Superintendent of Colored Schools. A white administrator also observed me. My tenure was approved.[34] When a first grade teacher left #139, Mr. Simms assigned me to replace her. Two years after I started with the first graders, Audrey Quarles, a niece of the famous historian Benjamin Quarles, came to Charles Carroll as a kindergarten teacher. She and I worked together on improving the transition between kindergarten and first grade. Sometimes, when the weather was bad, we would bring our classes together during the lunch hour and after we had eaten we would have songs and games in her room, which was huge. She made sure that her children learned the skills they would need when they came to me for first grade.

Audrey and I both thought that working with parents was very important. When the school had parent–teacher meetings it was very hard to get the parents to come out. I asked some of my students' parents why they didn't come. They said that they didn't have nice clothes, and that it made them feel bad to see teachers come in their fur coats. It was true that teachers would come to PTA meetings dressed to the hilt, because they were going to party afterwards. I told Mr. Simms that this was making the parents uncomfortable and he spoke to them. Though many teachers dressed up I can recall only two people—his assistant and another person—who actually wore furs. I didn't own one, and I doubt that most teachers did.

It wasn't very popular then for parents to be in schools. It was a time when schools really wanted parents to stay home. However, Audrey and I worked to bring in our students' parents. I had "parent parties" every Friday where I would teach them the skills I was going to be teaching the children in the coming week. At first only a few parents came, but then the word got around and most parents came, or, if they had to work, they sent another adult. They would come for the last half hour of the day and sit with their children. I would present the skills. They would ask questions. I started this because some of the parents complained that they were having trouble helping their children at home. Audrey also had programs for parents and once in awhile we had both groups of parents come for a discussion and some light refreshments. A few of the other teachers complained about our having the parents in. They were afraid that they might be made to do it. Mr. Simms told us to ignore them.

When teachers have high expectations students will rise to them, and sometimes they even surprise us. One year Mr. Simms decided that I should remain with my first graders as the second grade teacher. The opening day of that school year I overslept. I had worked hard and late the day before. That morning I looked at the clock: twenty-five after eight. I kept running around the bed and looking at the clock again. Finally I called the school and told the assistant principal. She said, "Wait a minute; I haven't heard anything from your classroom." She came back and said, "Just come in as fast as you can. Your students have taken over. They've had their opening exercises. Dvorak Maddox [a student] has passed out the paper for opening work." I said, "Thank you Jesus!" They went right on because that's what they were expected to do.

Because we had no planning period, we worked late at night and we'd come in early in the morning. Today the teachers' union would probably say that the long hours we worked were unacceptable. But when I was teaching joining the union was optional, and I never joined. I did not think that I needed to be in the union. I was doing my job, and I could speak up for myself when things came up that I didn't like. A lot of people didn't join the union early on.

I did meet teachers and administrators from all over the city when I was selected to represent Charles Carroll of Carrollton at school system meetings. As school representative, I had my first big school fight when William Lemmel died.[35] The school representatives were called to a meeting. I came back and reported that it was suggested that each teacher give money for the flowers for Dr. Lemmel's funeral. Some of the teachers at #139 rebelled; they didn't think that it was their responsibility to give money and said they should have a choice. I said, "How selfish can people be?" Dr. Lemmel had done well by the system. He had really given his life fighting for the teachers. After I went on enough, I got the money! At the same time, I saw another side of people who take for granted the things that are done for them, and who cannot go into their own pocketbook for even a small token of respect.

We struggled to get materials and supplies in that all-black school and had to fight to get just the basic things for the children. If their parents' electricity was cut off or there was some need like that, Mr. Simms could draw on the school benevolent fund to help them. The fund was set up by the staff social committee. We made monthly contributions to it. Mr. Simms also taught me how to call downtown to get help from various agencies for families in need.

We spent much of our own money to get materials and supplies. We weren't making big salaries, but we paid to get things for the children. We would go to the stores and beg for different leftovers, like little mats that the carpet stores had. We would ask for them so that the children would have mats to sit on the floor. Laverne French, who also taught at #139, and I were walking one day to see what was in the community. We found a factory where they made shoes, located near the school, close to Baltimore Street. So many kids did not have decent clothing, and we teachers would buy little shirts and things for them. We went into the shoe factory and told the man there about our school and he said, "Come back and tell me how many children need shoes and I'll give them to you for 25 cents a pair." And we got those shoes for a lot of children for 25 cents a pair. That's how we had to scrounge around.

I used to keep cigar boxes in the classroom. I'd put the children's names on them. Each box had a washcloth and a toothbrush and toothpaste. If the children came in without their faces being washed and without their teeth being cleaned, I'd just tell them to take their boxes. There were so many of them they didn't get embarrassed. They'd come and ask, "Can I have my box now?" I bought combs, so they could comb their hair. This was not being poor. Some of these children were less than poor. Their parents were not teaching them even the basic health rules.

I became sharply aware during these years in the classroom that there were so many children who needed so much. They were destitute. It wasn't like how I grew up. Even though we were poor, we always had food and our clothes, and we were always clean. We ate dinner around the table and talked, and we went places as a family. Many of the children at #139 had never sat around a table; they didn't eat as a family. I would look at them and say to myself "something has to happen here to give them a chance at a decent future." That's when I really knew that I wanted to stay with teaching. When I started I had said "I'll work ten years and then go into something else." But I discovered at #139 that I belonged in education.

It became my "calling" to work with children and their parents and help them to understand that without education they can't make it in this world. Without education they can't demand their rightful place in society. Without education they are never free. They are always dependent on someone else. When there are instructions to be read, a contract to be signed, a purchase to be made, a critical decision to be reached, the person without education is lost. He or she will lose out on the best parts of life. If we can light a spark in children in the earliest grades—if they love learning then and gain confidence in their abilities—nobody can take that away from them later on. That is what I have tried to do, and that is how education became my agenda.

Though working with children was always rewarding, there were times when it was very painful. One year when I was teaching first grade I had to be hospitalized. I went to my physician in Philadelphia for what was supposed to be a simple procedure. It became complicated when he discovered that I have the sickle cell trait. While I was away one of my students died. The teachers all swore not to tell me about her death while I was still sick. But when I came back to Baltimore and was recuperating, one of the custodians came to see me, and he told me that she had died. I thought I was going to die. I knew that she had been born with a hole in her heart. She was a lovely girl, a very sweet child, and had lived just those six years. I've only had two students die, and each was a wrenching experience.

While teaching took up the greatest part of my time, I was also occupied in other ways. I started having a lot of friends and went different places with them. On my twenty-second birthday some of my new acquaintances wanted to take me out. One of them was Sam Wilson, who headed the Arena Players.[36] He and the others took me to a nightspot where they wouldn't let me in, wouldn't believe I was 22. I guess it was because I was so short.

For a long time I saved to buy a car. Finally, in 1956, I did it. When I told the salesman how little I had to spend, he gave me a big rebate and wrote it up as though that was the down payment. I was able to get the rest of the money through the credit union. So now I owned a new brown and tan Chevrolet. I just needed to learn how to drive. I called Easy Method and began lessons. The instructor put a stack of pillows under me and more pillows at my back so that I could see over the steering wheel. He picked me up once a week and I practiced until it was time to take the driving test. The test then wasn't just in the lot of the motor vehicle office. It was all in the street, in real traffic. I don't know how I passed. I think I closed my eyes making some of the turns. But I got my license.

After about ten years living with the Griggs, I moved to my own apartment. When I told my father that I wanted a place of my own he told me "No." And I said, "Well, goodness! You raised me and I would hope you set up the standards for me to be able to live on my own." Finally my mother said, "You just go and get your apartment." So I rented this little tiny place on Rosalyn Avenue, about three miles from where I had been living. My neighbors were mostly professionals—doctors, lawyers, and other teachers. The apartment was so little that if I put a Christmas tree in the living room I had to take the furniture out. But it was my first apartment, and it was just perfect. I kept that about eight years.

A few years before I moved to Rosalyn Avenue I began working toward a Masters degree in reading from Temple University. I completed it in 1957. At that time black teachers could not do graduate work in Maryland. The city paid us to go out of state. I was shocked when I first realized this, but then I said, "Well, if they're going to pay, I might as well go on." We received money for tuition and room and board. I could stay with my parents and have money left over. I went up to Philadelphia every weekend and every summer. We would talk about how stupid they were to put out all this money rather than have blacks attending Maryland schools of higher learning.[37]

A lot of teachers went to New York University. But I wanted to study with Emmett Betts at Temple.[38] He was very well known and highly regarded. I often read about him in professional journals, and his name was always coming up in meetings and conferences about reading. He planned to retire from Temple the year after I started there, so I got special permission to take three courses from him that first year. He approached reading as a process and advocated the use of many different teaching methods and "differentiated instruction" tailored to the different skill-levels of students. Phonics had a place in his system as one of many learning aids. He didn't claim that any approach by itself was best. He taught a balanced use of various approaches. I loved reading and thought that after I finished my Masters I would move from the classroom and go into a Reading Center. At that time every Baltimore City school had such a center. They were for those students who needed additional help. For some children the phonics and the regular teaching in the classroom weren't enough. Some children were dyslexic or had other forms of reading disabilities. The Reading teachers were masters in skill development with these children.

While I was getting my Masters I would arrive home on Friday evening, attend class all day Saturday and on Saturday evening leave right away with a group of friends, including my high school buddy, Cozy, the brother of another friend, Lillian Miles—we called him Skeets—and Skeets's friends, Bill Cosby, and other basketball players on a local team from Mount Airy.[39] We would go over to New Jersey where the fellows played another local team there. The teams weren't officially sponsored, as I remember it; this was an informal competition. Bill Cosby wasn't famous then, but he used to crack jokes and keep the bus in stitches. We would laugh all the way over and all the way back. He wasn't a buddy of mine in the way that he was friends with some of the others. But I do remember how he made us laugh.

I would not get back from these Saturday night trips until late. My father expected me to get up early Sunday morning to go to church with him. When I would tell him I was too tired to go, he would get upset. One Sunday he started grumbling about "You have time to run all around but you don't have time to go to church." And then he said something like, "I'm just ashamed." I just looked at him and said, "Well, you had the pleasure of having me." When I said that it just shocked him, and he started toward me. I went up the steps backwards, got to the top of the steps and flew into my room and locked the door. He went on to church, and I packed my things, put them in the car and drove back to Baltimore.

My mother called me that evening. She said, "Don't ever do that again because you made your father so angry." But the words had just flipped out of my mouth. After all, I was a grown woman. But, then, he was an older Southern gentleman, and his view was that if you had time to "run around" you'd better get up on Sunday and go to church, no matter how late it was when you got in.

I continued to work at #139 and was there at the time of the famous Supreme Court decision on school desegregation, *Brown v. Board of Education*. Like almost every black in the land I was excited about it. In addition, Billy and Becky Griggs, where I stayed, were related somehow to Thurgood Marshall, so I had met him at their house. He had come by to see Billy Griggs's father, who was living with them then. They introduced me to him. He was a very striking man. There was so much of him! He was jolly that day, laughing and telling jokes.

Even though we were excited when Marshall won the *Brown* case, it didn't make any difference in Baltimore City. It was just a pronouncement. It caused changes in other places, and it made us know that the courts had said that the schools need to be equal, but our school system didn't try to enforce that equality. The school board just said that parents could send their children to whatever school they chose, and not many parents took up the offer. As far as I know no children left #139 for a white school. So the decision didn't impact me right then and there. I would understand its importance more when I left #139 to work in a school that was mostly white. As an African American I had learned not to expect much from the courts or the political system. I was used to the courts making pronouncements and nothing being done about it. So even though we were very proud of Thurgood Marshall, we knew there was so much more to be done. We were happy about it, but you can't do cartwheels until something really happens.

When George Simms left School #139 in 1959, Samuel Owings became my next principal.[40] This was not long after his wife was drowned. They had a boating accident near Wilmington, Delaware. It was said that he had held his wife's body up in the water until he was rescued. That seemed to do something to him mentally. He would corner us and start talking about the accident. We would try to duck him, but sometimes he would come right in the classroom while we were teaching and start talking. I don't think the school system realized how disturbed he was.[41]

Mr. Owings set up committees and required that we put our names down for at least two, and then we would end up on three. One time when the sign-up came around I only saw one committee that I wanted to get on, so I only put my name on one. Later I was coming up the steps with my class, and there he was at the top of the steps on the second floor. He said to me, "Williams, I don't like that! I don't like what you did." I said, "What's that?" He said, "I said two." I replied, "Well, I'm not doing two. I did one and that's it, because I don't want any other." And then he started raising his voice.

That brought Allegra Taylor out into the hall. She taught in a room right across from mine. I said, "Children, go in the room." I had a pile of books right by the door, on the front desk, that I was going to pass out to the students. Allegra saw me pick up one of those books, and she stepped in and said, "Put it down." She said, "Mr. Owings, I think you need to go downstairs." And he went down. "I know you," she said, "now just cool off." I said, "He can't yell at me like that!"

Then Allegra said, "Let me tell you something. Sometimes you can't tell people what you're not going to do. You just don't do it. And when they come back you say,

'Oh, didn't I do that? I thought it was okay.' Never just defy them." She was right. I do have that tendency to just say, "I'm not going to do it!" And "Don't tell me!" I've kept her philosophy. A lot of things we want to do, if we work on them and do them, when whoever's opposing us finds out, they're already done. Allegra's advice has been useful many times.[42]

Mr. Owings thought that I should be working with children who had problems, because I could handle them. One year he assigned a class to me that was *full* of children who had *serious* problems. One little boy would get up in the middle of a lesson and start singing. Another would suddenly go over and hit one of the other children. There was a dancer in the class, who acted like he was hearing music, and a girl who would scream and cry for no apparent reason. After I had worked myself to the verge of a breakdown trying to manage and teach this class, I finally said to myself, "It's not them. It's me. I am the atypical person in this room, and I'm fighting a losing battle."

These children were all in a program at Johns Hopkins Hospital. It was called the Children's Comprehensive Clinic.[43] The doctors running the program followed the children's progress from year to year and met with them regularly. The doctor of these children asked them, "Who is your teacher?" When over half of his group said "Miss Williams," he came to the school and told Mr. Owings that having that many clinically disturbed children in one class was not good. The children fed off of one another. Mr. Owings assured him that I could do it; I could handle them. When the doctor insisted that Mr. Owings move some of these children, my principal said he couldn't; he had no place to put them.

At that point the hospital began to send someone twice a week from the Hopkins staff to observe and help me work with that class. Eventually some of the children were put in special schools. I think of this experience when I hear that now our school system wants to close the special schools that serve physically and mentally disabled students. The parents and teachers of those special students are not the only ones who should be protesting that plan. Every teacher and every administrator should be saying, "No! Do not close those schools." Mainstreaming all those children will lead to many of them being suspended all the time, few of them learning anything, and probably some child getting hurt.

The students that I taught—and that Johns Hopkins was tracking in the late 1950s and early 1960s—were probably suffering from lead poisoning and/or Fetal Alcohol Syndrome. Drugs of the kind that we are battling today were not prevalent then. But the housing projects where many of those children lived had been painted with lead-based paint. In addition, we'd started having a generation of children whose parents were younger and running around. Some of them were drinking too much. Even children who did not suffer severe physical problems were showing the effects of having parents who did not know how to take care of them, who sent them to school but never followed up.

This is also when we started seeing the children with Attention Deficit Disorder (ADD), but it wasn't named that yet. We had children who could not read, who could not sit still, who were constantly ready to fight. Large parts of our teaching time had to be devoted to just trying to get students to focus and pay attention. It was because I wanted to understand these children better that I decided I should take some courses in guidance. I earned a counseling certificate in 1967 from Loyola College in Baltimore.

In 1961 Clarence Gittings was brought to #139 as principal. He had a bad heart and the school had four floors, so an elevator was installed for him. He stayed one year, and he turned the school around after it had begun to slide under Mr. Owings.[44] He was an excellent principal—so organized and super bright. He knew the curriculum, he knew the children, and he knew the teachers. Teachers who did not do well he moved out. That was good because it helped those of us who were working very hard. We knew that he was sincere about quality education. And at that time the school system still demanded quality and the teacher supervisors backed up the principal.

We still had to have our teaching plans laid out and we took them to our supervisor every week. My supervisor was now Rebecca Carroll.[45] She would examine that lesson and make sure that it followed along from the previous lesson. She would ask, "What skills have the children been taught up to now?" and I would have to prove that I knew what I was doing and why before I was allowed to teach that lesson. Although Dr. Carroll was demanding, she was never rude to me. Some used to say, "that's because you're both eentsy." (She and I were about the same height.) I had friends who would come out of her office in tears. After she had observed in the classroom of one of my friends at #139, Dr. Carroll told her, "They are still hiring at Social Security." Stories were told of Dr. Carroll marking through the work that a teacher had prepared on the black board or tearing up papers that they had planned to pass out to the children.

At that time administrators did not make excuses for people who couldn't teach. They automatically released teachers who did not receive their tenure after the third year. It helped that there was a waiting list of teachers wanting jobs. If a new teacher came in, and goofed around, and wasn't willing to be helped, Clarence Gittings would remove that teacher the first year; he wouldn't wait for three years. He had to request first that a specialist and the supervisor try to work with the new teacher. But if they wrote her up—that is, submitted a written report to the district director regarding their concerns about her performance—then she would go. By the time I became a principal, in the 1970s, getting rid of a poor teacher was harder, mainly because documenting the teacher's performance takes so much time, and we no longer had the supervisors and specialists with the time to work with us. There were too few of them, so their workloads were unreasonable and some of them were poorly trained themselves As I matured as a teacher and became proficient in the basics of classroom instruction I started to focus more on understanding my students and broadening my knowledge. I took courses at Loyola College and Morgan State College in such subjects as counseling, curriculum, science, and economics. These courses helped me function better in the classroom. Even with first and second graders, when we discussed shopping and the cost of items in their market baskets or talked about saving, I could use information from that economics course. Mostly I took courses because I wanted to keep growing. Any personal growth a teacher has will be good for her children.

Mr. Gittings designated me as a demonstration teacher for other teachers that the supervisors would bring in. One day I was giving a demonstration lesson for a large number of teachers and supervisors who were crowded in all around the room.[46] In front of all of them, a student named Henrietta came up to me and said, "Miss Williams! You have misspelled 'Brittany'!" I said to myself, "I'm going to die." But I replied to her "Really? Did I, Henrietta?" She said, "Yes maam!" I told her she knew what to do. She answered, "Oh, yes. I'll correct it," and she went to the board and added the "t" that I had left out. I thanked her and she strutted back to her seat. Everybody knew Henrietta. I imagine she's somebody's lawyer now.

Rebecca Carroll would come into the class before the scheduled demonstration lesson. She would single out any child who had problems and tell me to send that student home before the demonstration. She and I battled about that. I felt that new teachers will have problems; they will have students who may be driving them up a wall. They need to see how the demonstration teacher handles such students. So I never sent home my problem children.

After acting as a demonstration teacher I was named the "primary coordinator" for #139. That made me responsible for working with a team of teachers in the primary grades, helping them with their planning, advising them on any problems they were facing in their classrooms, developing teaching activities that would help tie the instructional program in one grade to what the children would be learning in the next grade. From that assignment I was moved into the role of "helping teacher." Any teacher at any level in the school could ask me to assist in resolving problems in her or his classroom.

Meanwhile, the principal at #139 had changed again. The new man was Reginald Watts.[47] I liked him as a person but I found him to be a poor principal. He was supposed to be in charge, but I did not have much respect for him, and I would lay him out all the time, because he would say things that I thought were just dumb. Audrey Quarles (who had married and become Audrey Hardin) and other teachers would tell me, "Now you know better. You should leave him alone." And my comeback was, "No, He doesn't leave me alone!"

One day early in 1965 Herbert Stern, who oversaw the school system's counselors, called me at school and said he would like to talk with me. I said, "Fine," and he asked if I could leave school early to meet him. When I told Mr. Watts that I had to go meet Dr. Stern, he said, "You're not going." I said, "Yes, I am." "He just wants to take you away from teaching," Mr. Watts complained. Well, I said I was going, and I went. Dr. Stern told me that they were starting counseling for children in the elementary grades, because they found that they had been waiting too late to try to help students. He asked if I would be willing to be on the counseling staff. I said no, I didn't want to leave my class.

I really enjoyed teaching. I loved the children. But then Mr. Watts kept worrying me, so I finally told Dr. Stern, "I will not leave my children now, but I will come at the end of the year." When he learned this, Watts carried on. One day I was with two other teachers in the hall and he came up saying, "Here she comes, the traitor." I had my lunch tray in my hand, and I slammed it on the floor and cursed at him: "I'm sick of your rabbit shit!" He flew! He had gotten on my nerves and was just grinding. He never reprimanded me for that. He knew better. He and the #139 staff even had a going-away party for me. I would never have gone into counseling if he hadn't bugged me and said I couldn't go.

Counselor at Mordecai Gist

By the time Gertrude left Charles Carroll of Carrollton, George Brain had retired from the superintendency to assume the deanship of the school of education at Washington State University in Pullman, Washington.[1] From January to July 1965 Edward Stein acted as interim superintendent. In time for the fall term the city school board hired Lawrence Paquin to take charge of the public school system. The *Baltimore News American* introduced him as a "frank and alert New Englander who quotes poetry profusely, reads voraciously (including mysteries) and delights in a challenge."[2] That he found delightful the challenges presented by Baltimore is unlikely.

Within two years Paquin was dead of cancer. In his brief tenure, student resegregation proceeded apace, his appeals for voluntary staff desegregation fell on deaf ears; and the first teachers' strike in the history of Maryland occurred in Baltimore—which also acquired the distinction of becoming the only major city to have sanctions brought against it by the National Education Association (NEA).

Paquin attempted to revamp the secondary schools to make them more demo-cratic. He wanted to end the tracking of students into curricula according to future goals (such as "college bound" and "vocational") and eliminate the practice of having the most talented students attend a few elite schools, while all other students were left with inferior programs. The alumni and parents of City College, the elite high school Paquin who were targeted first, blocked his proposal.[3]

Voluntary desegregation did not work any better as a method for changing the racial composition of school staffs than it did for changing the make-up of racially homogenous student bodies. Ten years after *Brown*, 61 of 151 elementary schools had "mixed" faculties. But in many cases (including Gertrude's new school, Mordecai Gist, #69), the mix amounted to one or two "other race" individuals in an otherwise single-race staff. Nonetheless, Paquin held to the philosophy of his predecessors and of the school board—that it was better to leave people with a choice than to force them into new situations. He refused to make compulsory staff transfers and tried instead to use friendly persuasion.

He promised that any white teacher who agreed to an appointment at a predominantly black school, or any black teacher who would accept assignment at a mostly white school, could return to his/her former position after two years. To teachers hoping to move into administrative positions, Paquin offered the incentive that "inner city school experience" would merit special consideration.[4] This latter incentive applied mostly to whites, not only because most black teachers were already teaching in the inner city, but because few African Americans were appointed to administrative posts. Black school board commissioner, Elizabeth Murphy Phillips (later Moss) repeatedly voted against all personnel recommendations brought before the board to protest the paucity of black principals and assistant principals.[5]

While school authorities and various activists and political factions wrestled with desegregation, teachers, counselors, and researchers were trying to address the challenge of a rapidly changing student body. According to the *Baltimore Sun*, the major difficulty, the socioeconomic profile of students coming into the system from West Virginia, Tennessee, North Carolina, and Georgia, children requiring "the most basic of instruction, from proper use of bathrooms to eating habits and hygiene." The same observers reported that enrollment in "mentally retarded classes" was sky-rocketing, and the transience of the new population left "some teachers scarcely knowing the composition of their classes week by week." The focus of instruction, they lamented, was on "slow learners," placing in jeopardy programs for advanced students.[6]

If class and cultural biases could be inferred from the *Sun* report, such biases were glaringly evident in an article by Ohio State University professors Charles Glatt and Arliss Roaden written for *The Maryland Teacher* in the fall of 1967. They observed an "exodus . . . of affluent whites" while "low income 'hillbillies' " and "a rapidly increasing, predominantly low income Negro population" were flooding into the city and its schools. Since these schools had been "designed for people whose biological, sociological, and psychological descendents are no longer the numerical mainstay of the city," Glatt and Roaden declared that new designs for school finance, administration, and instruction were now imperative. They stressed that "the newly emerging population" in Baltimore had different educational needs "The 'rich, mean-ingful experiences' advocated in a bygone era must become the 'enriching, appropri-ate experiences' that will translate the deprived child of today into the productive citizen of tomorrow."[7]

Glatt and Roaden were obviously trying to be diplomatic, but their educator audience was not likely to miss the implication that curriculum and instruction would have to be watered down and standards lowered to an "appropriate level" for the poor white and black children who were filling up the city's classrooms. Their analysis reflects the tone and content of discourse among professional educators in this era. At the practical level they were coming to terms with the need to adopt new measures to reach a new category of students. But no matter how well intentioned they were in pursuing this goal, their approach was tainted by faulty assumptions regarding race and class. Such assumptions appeared in the work of Baltimore's own research staff who reported that black students' IQ levels were dropping, while white students' IQs were rising. This divergence was attributed to blacks having inferior teachers. However, if the argument was referring to black teachers in schools that were still heavily black, it ignored the effects of ramshackle buildings and inferior and meager supplies. If it included those black students who were in predominantly white schools, with mostly white teachers, the prejudiced mind-sets that the black students may have encountered should have been, but was not, factored in.[8]

Whatever the diagnosis, the reality was that vast numbers of economically destitute children—the majority of them black—were floundering in the public schools of Baltimore city, as educators wrestled with how to address mushrooming student needs in the face of diminishing material and financial resources. Even the business community was beginning to take notice.

In December 1966, the assistant to the director of the Greater Baltimore Committee, an association of the city's top executives, briefed the members on conditions in the city schools. His conclusion was grim:

> Baltimore's past and present failure to meet its responsibility for educating the next generation, especially the children of already disadvantaged parents, could well lead to the demise of the city as the residential, business and cultural center of the region and the creation in its place of a physical and social jungle. . . . It would seem appropriate . . . to ask . . . what, if any contribution the Greater Baltimore Committee has to make to the resolution of this important and explosive issue.[9]

Responding to the increasing stresses on their schools, on May 11, 1967, members of the Baltimore Teachers Union (BTU) went on strike, making 35 demands, including higher funding, smaller classes, more resource teachers (such as speech therapists, art and music instructors), improved salary benefits, collective bargaining rights, and elimination of the National Teachers' Examination. Most of the strikers were secondary teachers. Only 15 elementary school faculties participated. Mordecai Gist's was not among them.[10]

Two months later, the NEA and its local affiliate the Public School Teachers' Association (PSTA), announced sanctions against the school system of Baltimore City. The sanctions were a means of alerting teachers throughout the country to the substandard conditions in Baltimore, and informing businesses and industries that might consider locating in Baltimore of the city's unfavorable education climate. The NEA based its action upon the findings of an investigative team that it sent to Baltimore in the summer of 1966.

The team, whose report had been released the same month as the BTU strike, fueling suspicions that rivalry between the unions was a major factor in both of their actions, found appalling disparities between a few exemplary, mostly white, schools and a large number of deteriorating buildings housing mostly poor black children.[11] Authors of the report laid down a challenge to the leaders of Baltimore City:

> They can supply the money and the creativity necessary to make the schools so good that white children will be retained or attracted back; or they can supply the money and creativity necessary to make the schools so good that it won't matter whether the white middle class children come back or not. Or, Baltimore can fail to provide the money and creativity necessary to enable the schools to meet the needs of children and pay the price in social consequences and wasted human lives.[12]

Although BTU and PSTA leaders denied that the strike and sanctions were part of a power struggle between them, most observers and nearly all school officials believed otherwise. In any case, BTU called off the strike as soon as the city agreed to hold an election to determine collective bargaining rights, and as soon as that election ended—with a very narrow margin of victory for BTU—the victor backed off from most of its strike demands. At the same time, PSTA/NEA ceased their advertising of sanctions.[13]

Lawrence Paquin died three months after the teachers' strike. An interim of October 1967 to July 1968 was filled by Thomas Goedke. Then the school board's selection for permanent superintendent, Thomas Sheldon, arrived from Hempstead, New York, where he, a white person, headed a predominantly black school district serving 5,300 students. Now, in Baltimore, he had 193,000 mostly black children in his charge.[14]

The assassination of civil rights leader, Martin Luther King Jr., and the racial uprising that followed it, had occurred just three months before Sheldon took the superintendent's post.[15] With wholehearted support from the mayor, Thomas D'Alesandro III, who had been instrumental in recruiting him, Sheldon moved quickly. He launched a school construction program of unprecedented magnitude, used federal funds to hire teachers' aides from the community, expanded the city's model schools program[16] begun on Goedke's watch, maintained and expanded the community schools under new black leadership, and proposed to reorganize the system by transforming one central office into a central office with regional branches throughout the city.[17]

Not only was Sheldon's reorganization proposal defeated by the school board, but despite his energetic and generally positive efforts, he was swamped by a rising feeling within the school bureaucracy, and in many quarters of the black community, that the time was at hand for an African American superintendent in Baltimore City. That feeling was also evident on the school board, which had been transformed in 1968 by Mayor Thomas D'Alesandro III. The mayor broke with the tradition of selecting older, well-established citizens as board members and of balancing board membership by race, religion, and representation from major schools of higher education. Announcing that the board must be representative of the city's population, D'Alesandro doubled its black membership and appointed several younger individuals, some with children in the public schools. Relations between Sheldon and that board went from edgy to hostile.

As these developments unfolded, Gertrude remained focused on counseling students at Mordecai Gist, a school that retained much of its predominantly middle-class character, including a modest number of students from black professional families, while seeking to accommodate growing numbers of black and white low-income children. In this setting, her upbringing, which emphasized "respect[ing] people for who they are and not for their color," served her well, as did the nonjudgmental approach that she took with children and their parents.

Her job as a counselor was to help children who were having social, emotional, and/or academic difficulties find solutions to their problems. To accomplish this she had to comprehend all dimensions of their lives. While comfortable and—given the eagerness of her supervisors to groom her for an administrative role—obviously effective at Gist, Gertrude found herself grappling with manifestations of racism that were new to her: the passing of racist values from parent to child; the fostering of gang-like behavior among children in densely crowded homes shared by multiple families; blatant segregation practiced by the principal of a neighboring school and so on.

What shocked and troubled her more than any other experience was the stark contrast between her new and former schools. She would remember School #69's superior physical plant and abundantly stocked storeroom when she became an administrator. She vowed that the school system would not short change the children of any school she ran the way she now realized her students at School #139 had been cheated. She was drawing these conclusions in a political and social climate that had been affected by more than a decade of national experience with the *Brown* decision, but during our interviews she was emphatic that she would have been stunned and angered by the disparate resources of Gist and Charles Carroll of Carrollton whether or not the *Brown* ruling had occurred. She did allow, however, that without the possibility of desegregation she would not have been assigned to Gist and may not have experienced the disparity in such a direct way.

Although through her years at Gist, Gertrude still did not involve herself in the politics of the city and the school system, her account holds many telling examples of how the city's half-hearted approach to desegregation, continuing racist practices, and changing student demographics played themselves out in one particular school.

*   *   *

My counseling assignment was at School #69, Mordecai Gist, in the 4000 block of Cold Spring Lane. Carolyn Motscheidler was principal and Stanley Curtain was vice principal.[18] I started there in 1965. By then desegregation had been the law of the land for over ten years, but there was really very little integration in the Baltimore schools. #139 was still all black. All the teachers were black, too. Mordecai Gist had been all white, but black families were moving in. This was happening in part because some landlords didn't care how they got their money. They would take a house that had been a single-family dwelling and, without dividing it into apartments, would rent it to several families who had moved from a low-rent area and pooled their money. These houses were referred to as "contract houses." In such overcrowded conditions the children of these families sometimes acted like a mini-gang.[19]

I was assigned to Mordecai Gist because the school system needed someone to deal with any problems that might occur as the children from these black families came into the school. Twelve years later, when the school was closed, #69 had become all black.[20]

Moving to #69 is when I learned how big the gap was between white and black schools. We never knew, when we struggled at #139 just to get the basic materials, that schools such as #69 were so well stocked. I was amazed. I told Carolyn that I needed certain things for my office, and she sent me to the storeroom. I couldn't believe all the materials and supplies that they had at that school. I said to Carolyn, "Do you know that they don't even have supplies like this at #139?" Her answer was, "Well, I don't know. We just send in our order and we get what we ask for." This was really the first time I realized that there was such a difference between the way "colored" and white students were being treated.

Charles Carroll, while it was in fairly good repair, had been a white sanitarium that had been ready to close down and was then turned into a black school. Mordecai Gist was a beautiful building. It had a lovely yard. I don't know why they later tore it down. Going from #139 to #69 I learned that there was a different ball game in the city for black children. That's why, when I later became the principal at School #54 (Barclay), I fought so hard for those children there to get what they deserved. I knew that some schools had musical instruments, the newest books, plenty of materials and supplies, and I knew that the system could give these to our children if we demanded it.

I was the fourth black person to join the staff at #69, but everyone thought that there were only two other blacks, because the third person, a physical education teacher, looked white. She was related to a very prominent white family in Baltimore. She said she "never bothered" to tell the people at Mordecai Gist that she was black. I found that a lot of teachers there had never been to college. The system had housewives without degrees working with children. The belief in the black community was that they hired these unqualified individuals to avoid hiring black teachers. At that time, an abundance of quality teachers was coming out of black colleges. It wasn't long before the Baltimore Teachers Union discovered this and demanded that untrained teachers either had to be rated "superior" to stay and become provisional teachers, or they had to be fired.

After 1954, when there were no longer separate colored and white systems, most people who were in supervisory positions were white. You could name the black supervisors in one breath—Emma Bright, Rebecca Carroll, Pearl Brackett, and Thelma Jackson. There were no black principals in junior high or high schools, except for School #130 for advanced black students and the black principals at the historically black high schools, Douglass and Dunbar. Promotional policies were still discriminatory.

I got along well at Mordecai Gist. Carolyn was a good principal, but she had some personal problems that interfered with her work, so frequently Stan and I ended up taking care of the school.[21] The student population was growing rapidly and we became extremely crowded. Students began coming in double shifts. Then Betty Getz, who was the area executive director, decided that since Fallstaff had space, some of our children would be sent there by bus—about a 25-minute ride.[22] We sent a letter to parents to ask if they wanted their children to stay at Mordecai Gist or be bused to Fallstaff. A number of parents, black and white, signed to send their children to Fallstaff.

We had a strong Parent Teacher Association at #69, and I was in charge of it.[23] Pretty soon some of the black parents who had signed for their children to go to Fallstaff began coming to me saying, "something's wrong." The Fallstaff principal had put all the black students into one class. At Moredecai Gist their children hadn't all been in the same class.

In the group of children who went to Fallstaff some were very able and some were average, so it was totally impossible that all the black students would be in the same class. They were just put together because they were the same color. All the Fallstaff children were white, and the white children from Mordecai Gist were placed with the other white students at their skill levels. The parents who were questioning this were middle-class and upper-middle-class blacks. They included Bill and Mildred Parrot. He was a principal and she was a teacher. Others who complained were Howard Marshall, a postal worker who would later serve on the school board; Jim Parker, a player with the Baltimore Colts football team; and Dr. Oakley Saunders, a prominent black physician. Their children were really bright, and these parents were very upset. When I told Carolyn, she said she didn't think the Fallstaff principal would do something that dumb, but when I asked if I could investigate, she said, "Sure."

One morning I followed the school bus to Fallstaff in my car and went in and asked the principal if I could see the children from #69, see how they were adjusting. "Oh, they're doing fine," she said. I again requested to see how they were doing. She hemmed and hawed, but I wasn't going to be put off, so I walked through the school. I saw the white children from #69 in different classes with other white children. Some of them waved at me. I wondered, "Where are the other children?" Then I saw this class of nothing but black students.

When they were passing in the hall I asked how they were doing, and they were upset, because they were all getting the same work. I went back to the principal and asked, "Is there a reason why all the children of color are in one class?" "Oh," she answered, "we tested them and they were on the same level." I asked to see the tests.

There were no tests. I was *so* upset. I told her I would report that the children were being segregated within that school. I went back and did just that. Carolyn drove up there and told the woman she was going to report her, and then she called Betty Getz. The Fallstaff principal was moved, right in the middle of the year. A new principal was assigned, and all the children were grouped according to their levels—reading level, math level, and so forth.[24]

It was a great experience to work with those parents at #69. They were like the parents I would later find in the Barclay community—pro-education and willing to do anything to help the school. I worked closely with them, and we did a lot of things together. Gist served families in different economic levels, including the lower economic brackets. Some of our children came from very poor families.

One little white boy named Jack lived with his mother. I had to talk with Jack frequently because he always seemed to be getting into trouble. One day after school (I'd be there after hours in case there was a need for me) there was a banging on my door. I opened it, and there was Jack running in. "Close it! Close it! Close the door!" And then he said, "Those niggers gonna' get me!" So I said, "Okay", and we closed the door. Then I said, "What is it?" "Those niggers are after me." He was still never looking at me. I asked, "What is a nigger, Jack?" He said, "Must be somethin' bad, 'cause my mother said when those niggers move on the block we're gonna' have some trouble!"

I went outside, and there was this group of boys, including Aubrey and his brother. Aubrey was one of the black children who lived in a contract house, with multiple families. When someone bullied him he'd get all the kids from the house together; they were like a gang. This day I asked Aubrey, "Why are you chasing Jack? What are you doing?" He said, "He calls us names." I said, "Okay. I'm going to get Jack to stop calling you bad names" (and he *was* calling them niggers), "and you're going to leave him alone." Then I talked to Jack, and I asked, "Where did you hear the word, nigger?" He said "my momma said, those niggers . . ." "But," I asked, "do you know that that word causes the boys to be angry?" He replied, "well, that's what my mother said." "Okay," I told him, "I'm going to go home with you."

His mother was really steaming when she saw this black woman come to her house. But I sat and talked with her, and I said, "You know what you're doing—when you start using that language, you're causing your son to be harmed. It was a good thing I was there at school, or they would have beaten him." Finally, she cried and said she was sorry They were very poor. The day I went there I noticed that they did-n't have electricity. I said, "We have a fund at school, so I'll see what we can do to help you, but you're going to have to start coming to school and helping us." And she did.

I got her to help in the school library, work as a lunch monitor, and be a chap-erone on school trips. We worked with her to get her electricity on, and we also got her a second-hand stove. I won't say that she became an angel, but she stopped using inflammatory language, and Jack stopped using that word. In fact, he got to be a pretty good little student. But that day he had looked right at me and never even figured out that I was the same race as Aubrey and the other boys. That's one of the first times I'd seen that kind of racism, passed from the parent to the child.

Working as a counselor, I learned to know children of all different persuasions. They came to me with their problems. I listened to them and talked with them and worked out ways in which I could help them. I had to see the whole child, understand his strengths and weaknesses, know his likes and dislikes, have some background on his parents. If a child's parents didn't come to school I'd go to his home, and we'd sit down and talk. I tried to speak to the children in their own language and help them to develop ways to solve their problems.

Sometimes the things that happened were not their fault. Maybe the teacher was off that day, or something bad had happened at home. Too often we don't believe children, and then we treat them in ways that are not only unfair, but that hurt them. Realizing that the child is not always wrong, and learning how to find out what has really happened, would be very important to me when I became a principal.

There are too many reports in the news these days of students who erupt and kill other students and their teachers. School staffs really have to be aware of what's happening with their children. If a child is being picked on or bullied, principals must deal not only with that child, but the whole group of children who are involved. When the whole group is brought together, almost always some of them will admit, "Well, they've been picking on him for a long time." We really have to be observant. Children who are repeatedly teased are either going to hurt themselves, or they will hurt somebody else.

When I was counseling, and when I became a principal, I used to walk out in the community to see what was going on. When parents called and said that there was a problem with their child and other children, I dealt with the issue immediately— would not let the children leave the school until we had gotten to the bottom of the conflict. At times I also had to get after the teachers. Some of them would tell the students, "Don't argue in the classroom. Finish it on your way out." Teachers must pay attention to what's happening in their classrooms and handle problems in the right way—alert the principal, involve the counselor. None of us—administrators, teachers, parents—should ignore students who are angry. Their anger will explode somewhere along the way.

I was part of a team at Mordecai Gist. The team approach was another tool I would later use as an administrator. Members of the team included the school nurse, the social worker, the counselor, and the principal and vice principal. When a child had a problem he knew he could always find one of us. I was in my office every day for both school shifts. Any teacher with a child in her classroom who was going off could send me a note, and then the child could just come in and sit in my room and become calm. In many cases I would not talk with him. He could talk to me, but I would not start a counseling session unless I was the case manager for him.

Each member of our team was responsible for specific children. I wouldn't deal with another case manager's child beyond providing the space for that child to calm down. I would let the child's case manager know what had happened. When the situation called for it, the case manager would follow-up and if that manager decided that our team should become involved, then the team would get together. We would talk with the student, bring the parents in, talk through the problem and work on how we could deal with it.

We began to use videotaping for teacher training and counseling. Edith Walker, Assistant Superintendent for Elementary Schools, wanted to introduce taping in the classroom—as a training tool, so that teachers could see themselves. She asked me if I would be willing to be a guinea pig. After obtaining written permission from the parents of the children I was going to meet with, they taped me all day long for several days in my counseling office. I had this big plant, and they put the microphone down in it, and the children couldn't see it. The camera and its operators were back where the children couldn't see them. It was an excellent tool, because we could see ourselves at work.

When I looked at my tapes I discovered that all the time I would say "Really?" Then I'd repeat it: "Really"? After several tapings, Dr. Walker wanted to take the tapes to the Board of School Commissioners. I said, "Dr. Walker, you can't use those!" But she said, "It's all right; it will give people a chance to understand. I'll explain that you picked out things that you saw yourself doing that you are going to correct."

The board approved the use of taping for various instructional and counseling purposes. The school system also sponsored TV spots that I helped with. They would show a vignette of some problem situation to children in their classrooms and ask the children to solve the problem. For instance, they would depict a child finding a purse while walking home from school. Students would discuss what the child should do. Another vignette might show a child being picked on. How should he respond? To whom should he go for help? That went on for about a year or so. Later I used video-taping with the teachers at Barclay. After they looked at themselves teaching I would sit down with them, and we'd talk about what they did well and how they could improve. Unfortunately, vandals broke into the school at one point and stole all of our video equipment.

During the time that I held the counseling position at Mordecai Gist I began to assist Inez Pearson, who was the supervisor in charge of elementary counselors. She took Herbert Stern's place. I worked with new counselors as they came in. They would observe my work with the students, and I would talk with them about counseling methods. In the summers—the system ran summer school every year—I would observe the new counselors and continue to help them. I received a stipend for the summer work, but during the regular school year I was not paid extra for this work. I saw myself as part of a team, and just wanted to help the new team members. It was the same when I was a demonstration teacher. I didn't receive extra money for that. I just did it.

The good feeling that we had in the counseling staff, and that also was present at Mordecai Gist, was not felt system-wide. In 1967, two years after I began at School

#69, Baltimore City had its first teachers' strike. The teachers at Mordecai Gist did not participate. Carolyn was a good principal, and Stanley was also a good administrator. The Gist staff did not want to participate in the walkout. After the strike, the teachers' union placed sanctions on the school system. They sent letters out to the whole country and said, "don't accept a job in Baltimore City." The union just declared war on the city, because, in comparison with other school districts in the state and the country Baltimore City teachers were at the bottom of the pay ladder. But the sanctions and all the turmoil of that time tore the system down, and it has never built up again.[25]

By this time my career plans were changing. I never got over my love for reading, and my reading Masters degree was useful later when I needed to help teachers and had to evaluate their teaching. But I gave up the idea of becoming a reading resource teacher. I had not intended to become a counselor, but once I got into it, I liked helping the children and working with them and their teachers and parents. And although I didn't realize it at the time, the counseling experience was also good preparation for becoming an administrator.[26]

One day Carolyn and Betty Getz asked to meet with me. They said, "We have looked at your record, and you haven't taken the administrative exam." I said I hadn't because I didn't want to. Mrs. Getz told me that I wouldn't have to take an administrative job if I didn't want it, but I should have in my record that I'd passed the test, just in case some job came up that I did want. What she neglected to add was that the top scorers on the test could automatically be made administrators.

They kept after me until I took the test. My score was the fourth highest, and Betty just pushed me into an assignment as vice principal. "Oh, my God!" I said. "I thought I could take the test without going into administration." "Just give us two years," they urged. "Just two years."[27] That was in 1969. My new assignment took me to Barclay Elementary School, #54, at the corner of Barclay and 29th Streets in Northeast Baltimore. I became principal there four years later, and continued working on that corner until I retired in 1998. Those two years that became twenty-nine years were always lively, sometimes stormy, and very worthwhile.

1 Charlotta Wallace, Gertrude's maternal grandmother

2   Mamie Wallace Williams, mother of Gertrude

3   Horace Williams, father of Gertrude

4   Gertrude Williams, age 17

5   Germantown High School, Germantown, Pennsylvania

6 Main buildings on the campus of the State Teachers College at Cheyney, Pennsylvania, as they were when Gertrude matriculated there in the fall of 1945

7 The present day Academic Hall of Sojourner-Douglass College in Baltimore was previously the location of Charles Carroll of Carrollton Elementary School (P.S. 139), where Gertrude was a teacher from 1949 to 1965. Photo by Tony "Mujahid" Veniey

8

9

8 and 9   Gertrude with students at Mordecai Gist Elementary School (P.S. 69) where she was a counselor from 1965 to 1969

10 "Jack," the student at Mordecai Gist Elementary School whom Gertrude had to counsel, along with his mother, against using the inflammatory "N-word"

Unless otherwise noted, all photographs are from the private collection of Gertrude S. Williams

Becoming Principal at Barclay School

Though no one knew then, the "real fireworks" that woke up the neighbors of the old Baltimore Oriole baseball park in the wee hours of July 4, 1944 cleared the way for the building of Barclay School in 1959. The assignment of Gertrude Williams as assistant principal there a decade later guaranteed that fireworks would erupt on that spot again and again. The spectacular, eight-alarm blaze in 1944 reduced the ballpark, in the 300 block of West 29th Street in northeast Baltimore, to rubble, sent the then minor league Orioles to an old stadium on 33rd Street that was later replaced by Memorial Stadium, and left for the local tots to teens crowd "a vacant lot ideal for fort construction or ball playing."[1]

In 1954, the Board of School Commissioners erected an elementary facility on what had been the area around third base of the old ball park and named it—with a notable lack of originality—after the street fronting the school, Barclay School (#54).[2]

With 656 black and 335 white students, School #54's population when Gertrude arrived was one of the most integrated in the city.[3] The children's scores on the Iowa Test of Basic Skills fell below national norms, while hovering close to citywide averages.[4] The staff was also reasonably integrated. Although, according to most reports, the white principal, Helen Nitkoski did not inspire a strong sense of community among staff, or between school and parents, when contrasted with the turmoil in the school system at large, Barclay seemed a relatively good place to be.[5]

Not that School #54 was isolated from the general tumult. The Board of School Commissioners regularly commandeered the school auditorium for public meetings. Since building administrators were expected to remain at their posts until the meetings were adjourned, the new assistant principal was exposed to the issues and conflicts that came before the board. From that time forward, and for the next three decades, Gertrude would rarely miss a school board meeting.

It was a heady and troubled period in which to expand one's political consciousness. With the national civil rights movement veering toward Black Power and the racial composition of the city shifting to a black majority, local school politics were becoming progressively racialized. This highly charged climate affected everyone involved in operating the school system, from the superintendent to the school custodians. Most certainly it magnified the dilemmas with which Sheldon's successor, Roland Patterson, would have to struggle. Likely also, it contributed to the difficulties that Principal Helen Nitkoski was encountering at Barclay when Gertrude arrived there. And for the new assistant principal these stormy political times offered abundant opportunity to apply her training, test her beliefs, and, more clearly, define her life's agenda.

In her second year as assistant principal, the school board convened to interview the top finalist in the search for Thomas Sheldon's replacement—a scholarly looking African American with a small, thin physique and a combative temperament, Dr. Roland Patterson from Seattle, Washington. The Pacific Coast school district that he oversaw as an assistant superintendent was about 28 times smaller than the Baltimore City public schools, and he had been on the job there for less than two years. He later admitted that he applied to Baltimore "as a means of securing an invaluable personal learning experience." He did not expect to make the short list, let alone be offered the job.[6]

With this outlook and his natural outspokenness, during the interview Patterson was generally unguarded. He made clear his commitment to involving parents and communities in their schools and to reorganizing the bureaucracy to make it more responsive to the school site staff and their students. Near the end of the interview, in response to a question about whether an improved educational system might lower the number of persons sentenced to the prison system, he replied that many black inmates were in prison "for no other reason than political reasons." For the Black Power advocates who turned out to hear Patterson that night, his declaration on political prisoners would have been "right on." But for audience members of more moderate persuasions—including Gertrude—it was shocking.[7]

The school board dispatched three of its white members to Seattle to examine first hand the work that Patterson was doing there. They returned to Baltimore reassured by the positive recommendations he received from most quarters. Eight of the board's nine members voted to hire him.[8] He remained in Seattle through the opening of the new school semester to see through an integration plan that he had initiated in partnership with the community, and began his tenure in Baltimore on Gertrude's forty-fourth birthday, October 1, 1971. An anonymous skeptic at his old job site had written on a chalkboard in Patterson's office, "Baltimore? And Bust." According to a *Baltimore Sun* reporter, "cynics give him two years at most to survive."[9]

Patterson bested the cynics, hanging on in Baltimore for the better part of four years, from October 1971 to July 1975. But he had a rough ride all the way. Although she recognized that Patterson was heavy handed and she opposed him on certain specific issues, Gertrude was among those who were deeply moved by his passion for educational justice for all children, and particularly for the black children who comprised a majority of the students in Baltimore City public schools.[10] In this regard, she joined the substantial body of poor and working-class black parents who would remain the majority of Patterson's supporters.[11]

Patterson was true to his word regarding parent and community involvement and reorganization of the bureaucracy. He held public forums on such issues as school funding, included parents in deliberations on other matters, including desegregation, and divided the school district into nine administrative regions.[12] Despite his unquestioned commitment to improved student performance, test scores did not rise during his administration, and efforts to improve curriculum and instruction tended to be lost in the controversies that he generated.

As for those controversies—Gertrude's recall of them does not always mirror the newspaper reports and other contemporary sources. Perhaps reflecting an insider's view, perhaps misinformation, she alludes to issues that are not mentioned by any of the other sources, insisting, for example, that Mayor William Donald Schaefer was angry with Patterson because the superintendent had used all available funds in one fiscal year to pay off bills, rather than following what Gertrude believes was a more usual course of allowing a portion of the school funds to go back into the city general fund. However, Gertrude's version of events does dovetail with others' on two points: (1) Patterson's actions alienated many school system veterans; and (2) his opponents found him to be arrogant to the point of insubordination. In a 1986 interview Patterson's administrative assistant E. Robert Umphrey detailed the reshuffling of school system personnel that occurred in the new administration. Facing the grim statistic that more than 70 percent of the city's public school students tested below national norms in the basic skills of reading and math, and finding that central office administrators were failing to respond effectively to school site problems and needs, Patterson "wanted new ideas," explained Umphrey. Apparently assuming that long-time members of the school bureaucracy were not the most likely source of innovative thinking, he passed over many of them when setting up his planning teams. When he established regional offices, he gave the regional superintendents authority that effectively reduced the influence of the assistant superintendents in the central office. Supervisors and coordinators, including individuals whom Gertrude greatly admired, were renamed "specialists." Even though their salaries did not change, they felt downgraded.[13]

Patterson filled critical positions with people new to the city, such as Howard White as head of personnel.[14] The resentment stirred up by these and similar changes created what Umphrey described as "an inward opposition" to every new policy that the superintendent put forward. At the same time, Patterson provoked lethal outward opposition by a near total lack of diplomacy in his dealings with the mayor and the school board. "He even refused," Umphrey said, "to attend the mayor's executive committee meetings"—considered mandatory by the mayor. This so enraged

Mayor William Donald Schaefer that when Umphrey appeared at the meetings as the superintendent's designee, "Schaefer put me out."[15]

When he left Seattle, Patterson had reflected on how he "had to step on a lot of toes here to accomplish change. But once change takes place," he added, "it takes a couple of years—then it's possible to move on."[16] He may well have thought that what worked in Seattle would work in Baltimore. However, the elected school board and community council that backed him on the West Coast were very different from the board appointed and controlled by the mayor that held him accountable in Charm City. The tight control that City Hall held over the school budget was also quite different from the Seattle system in which the voters annually approved a school levy. In a flash of insight that he should have held onto, Patterson had remarked in 1971 that it was "a bit frightening to think that getting off on the wrong track with one or two politicians can make all the difference in the world."[17]

Perhaps without so much hostility arrayed against him, Patterson could have weathered the back-to-back crises that rocked his administration in 1974—a month-long teachers' strike and a federal desegregation order that compelled him to make very unpopular student reassignments and staff transfers. The teachers who were striking cited frustration over salaries, class size, and working conditions. Patterson sympathized with these complaints and had often, from the time of his arrival in Baltimore, asserted that the school system was generally under-funded by both state and city governments. He charged that the city paid police and fire fighters on a scale that was competitive with surrounding counties but failed to remain competitive with teachers' salaries.[18] Such public criticism did nothing to endear him to William Donald Schaefer.

The striking teachers also cited high-handed administrative practices among their grievances. Into this category fell Patterson's mandate that every teacher in every subject in every school would teach reading. On the face of it, this was a reasonable proposal, especially in the light of students' abysmal reading scores on national tests. However, as Patterson himself observed, secondary teachers were accustomed to working within given academic disciplines and did not take kindly to having reading-instruction superimposed on those instructional areas. Additionally, poor scheduling in the introduction of the "Right to Read" initiative raised many more teachers' and principals' hackles than it raised reading scores. Gertrude was among those who bristled.[19]

To the dilemma of desegregation there was no satisfactory solution. The lenient "open enrollment" policy adopted by the school board 20 years earlier was no longer acceptable to the federal government. The civil rights crusade of the past two decades had intensified black expectations, created new social programs that channeled substantial amounts of federal funding into the public schools, and simultaneously generated new laws, including the Civil Rights Act of 1964, Title VI of which stipulated that any institution in receipt of such funding must comply with desegregation or lose those federal dollars. A 1971 ruling by the Second District Court of Washington, DC required the U.S. Department of Health, Education and

Welfare (HEW) to enforce Title VI and to take court action against jurisdictions that were not in compliance.[20]

The HEW's Office of Civil Rights found that Baltimore was not in compliance, observing that "most of the schools segregated prior to the 1954 *Brown* decision . . . were still racially identifiable; that open enrollment had not been effective in establishing a unitary non-racial school system; and that the teaching staff was still segregated."[21] For all that, "racial balance" in a student body that was 70 percent black was impossible. Staff and student transfers in the name of such balance were increasingly disruptive in places where residential segregation was deeply entrenched. Yet choosing to avoid such disruption would place the school system and the entire city government in violation of the law. The school system stood to lose 34 million federal dollars. "It's a kind of situation," Patterson said, "in which there is no positive answer so far as the superintendent is concerned."[22]

When his administration sought to pair elementary schools, moving children between the schools in each pair for maximum racial balance; change junior high school zoning patterns to channel more black children into schools with large white populations; and convert more high schools into magnet schools, on the order of City College, Western, Eastern, and Poly, white students and parents protested. Every attempt by city authorities to adjust the assignment of pupils to achieve integration provoked more hostility within the white middle class, thousands of whom fled the city schools in 1974 and 1975. A black middle-class exodus appears to have begun in this same period.[23]

By late summer of 1974, the word was out that Patterson's days were numbered. In the early morning hours before the school board's regularly scheduled meeting of August 8 (the same day that President Richard Nixon would announce his resignation) telephone lines in the black community began to hum. Patterson supporters testified to taking calls as early as 4 a.m. The rumor was that the board would fire the superintendent that night. Sure enough, before the restless throng that packed Cold Stream Park Elementary School's auditorium that evening (Barclay's auditorium was no longer large enough for board meetings), commissioner Robert Schaefer (white but no relation to the mayor) presented a resolution to suspend Roland Patterson, pending a hearing on the charges against him, which were included in the resolution and centered around alleged misuse of funds and failure to work and communicate effectively with the school commissioners.[24]

At that point the formal meeting spun out of control. Directed by the future U.S. congressman, Parren Mitchell, from the floor, and commissioner and Patterson-supporter, Larry Griffin, from the stage, audience members lined up to be heard. No longer in control of the microphone, school board president John Walton yelled, "Out of order!"—to which a member of the audience replied, "Everybody's out of order so we might as well be out of order, too."

The gathering continued until all the people had their say. A number of them fingered the mayor as the impetus behind the attack on Patterson. Others directed their animosity at Walton, such as the speaker who told him, "And J. Nixon Walton, remember that we just got rid of one in Washington tonight, and you don't have to be far behind." Some launched broadsides, as the man who denounced "three snakes—the Mayor snake, the Schaefer snake, and the Walton snake." Most, but not all, of the speakers were black. Not everyone was sure about what was occurring. For at least one participant, the meeting created "utter amazement, amusement and befuddlement as to what the issue is at hand."[25]

This collective outburst from an audience that was almost entirely black, directed toward a school board and political system controlled largely by whites, registered, first, angry warning that the black community was there to look out for its children and was conscious of how poorly these children were still being served. More than one parent warned the board that "there is not enough politics in the world to protect you when you start messing with my children." The speakers made clear that they saw Patterson as their advocate and believed that he was committed to fighting for the resources and reforms that would help their students.[26]

As chairman of the school board, Walton was a special target of the animosity expressed in this racially charged meeting. Although four of nine commissioners were black, not only was the position of chairman still held by a white man but that particular white man was perceived as failing to respect the authority of the black superintendent. The belief was strong that Patterson was under attack because white leaders could not tolerate the exercise of real authority and power on the part of a black person. Long-time black activist St. George Cross undoubtedly spoke for many when he opined that "if Roland Patterson wasn't black and wasn't making $50,000 nobody would be worried about his job."[27]

In the days that followed, the *Baltimore Sun* labeled the "city school system's crisis . . . a clear-cut racial issue." The city chapter of the League of Women Voters (LWV) chided the school board for using procedures that resulted in "racial polarization" and recommended mediation. The National Association for the Advancement of Colored People (NAACP), black Ministerial Alliance and other leading blacks rallied behind Patterson while calling for Walton's removal. The City Solicitor ruled that the resolution that triggered the August 8 uprising was indeed out of order, and Patterson continued to work.[28]

Over the next year, he tried to proceed with administrative reorganization of the school district. But his ability to lead was seriously compromised. According to Patterson's assistant, Robert Umphrey, the superintendent discovered during this time that his chief personnel officer, Howard White, was corrupt. After White's resignation, Umphrey recalled that Patterson "began to distrust nearly everyone." He was trying to run the whole system with the help of two or three people," driving himself and them relentlessly.[29] They did not make much progress.

Very little power had shifted to the regional offices, and the advisory councils that were to give citizens a voice in each region were in limbo. Patterson and the school board remained adversaries.[30]

Indeed, Patterson had retained a lawyer, former school board commissioner Larry Gibson, and was insisting on a formal hearing before the school board, to force the board to prove its alleged case against the superintendent. He and his counsel insisted on receiving the charges prior to the hearing. The board, headed by a new white president, lawyer Norman P. Ramsey, conducted the hearing in several sessions between May 9 and May 21, 1975. In June, the commissioners sent Patterson their evaluation, based on those hearings and followed the evaluation with a resolution to dismiss him. They asked for his resignation by June 24 in order to appoint a replacement in time to prepare for the fall term. When Patterson refused to resign, the board announced that a public dismissal hearing would be held. Following weeks of maneuvering on both sides, the hearing opened on July 2, 1975.[31]

For 60 hours, stretching over 11 days, Patterson's backers and detractors crowded into the auditorium of the War Memorial Building in downtown Baltimore for what Gertrude refers to as "the Patterson trial." Actually a hearing, presided over by the president of the school board, it took on the appearance of a trial, with Patterson represented by lawyer Gibson and both sides calling witnesses. Most members of the standing-room-only audience were on Patterson's side. They gave him a standing ovation when he arrived on the first day and at the end, when the board voted 7–2 to sustain his dismissal, and black commissioner W. Eugene Scott read the dismissal resolutions, they cried out, "Lies!" "Tom!" and "Judas!"[32]

Covering the hearing for the *Sun*, Mike Bowler observed that "although there were hints that the board would produce evidence that would be highly damaging to the Superintendent, very little was forthcoming."[33] The absence of substantive evidence of wrongdoing by the superintendent characterized the entire proceedings, as a federal judge later observed, when Patterson took his case to federal court. Though Patterson lost his bid for $1 million in damages for alleged violation of his freedom of speech, his integrity was affirmed by District Court Judge Joseph H. Young who found that the board's charges "were not supported by the evidence presented." In Young's view, however, the board was vested with the authority to "remove the Superintendent for any reason except an unconstitutional reason." They were under no requirement "that the removal be for good cause or any specific reason." On those grounds the judge upheld the board's dismissal, and the Patterson era in Baltimore was over.[34]

Robert Umphrey—like many other Patterson-admirers—never doubted that the embattled educator "was not seeking personal glory." His plans for making the bureaucracy more servicable for the schools and more responsive to the community; his vision of every child in the system becoming a proficient reader and achieving full potential; his quest for capable, creative, committed staff in all positions and at all levels in the school district—these were noble goals. Umphrey conjectured that "someone with a less uncompromising personality than Patterson's could have succeed with his basic ideas."[35] Gertrude expressed a similar sentiment. She believed that he was deeply committed to creating equal opportunity for every child, a commitment that she applauded and shared. At the same time, she saw his prickly, defiant style as counterproductive.

Roland Patterson was a pivotal force in Gertrude's career. He appointed her to the Barclay principalship. He assigned her to his advisory committee, bringing her into direct and regular contact with the top people in his administration. According to her recollections, he sought her out as someone that he could talk with and trust. His policies of outreach and decentralization empowered her to raise parent and community involvement at Barclay to new levels. And in his final months in Baltimore, when he was truly under siege, he fought back with a fierce pride that Gertrude would not forget, and that was not unlike some of the stances she would ultimately take.

The first public stand she took in her professional life was to openly identify herself with Patterson's supporters, once the school board and City Hall had made clear their determination to oust him. She was convinced that the attack on Patterson was unfair and generally without merit. Meeting at his home to discuss strategies for his defense, taking personal leave days to attend the hearings on his dismissal, testifying on his behalf at those hearings—these were all learning experiences that drew her deep into school politics and established independence as a central component of her professional identity. They were also acts of resistance against the city power structure that was united against Patterson. As her retelling of these events indicates, in the climate of those days she was taking a risk, and she seemed more than ready for it.

* * *

Betty Getz sent me to Barclay because the principal there, Helen Nitkoski, was having a hard time. Each year more than half of the teachers were asking for transfers, and the parents would not even go in the school. Betty had witnessed the parent program that I carried on at #69, and she thought I could help with the parents at #54. She and the area director, Vivian Cord (always called Vic),[36] wanted someone there who would work with Helen to get the teachers settled down and get the parents willing to come into the school. Vic told me, "It's a great community. The children are very good, but something is happening and the parents are not supporting the school."[37]

I found that Barclay had some of the brightest teachers in the system, but Helen would not even deal with them. She acted with a sense of "me and them," as if everyone wasn't part of a total school. Instead of sitting down in their classrooms to observe teachers, she used giving out the salary checks as a way to look into their rooms. If she had a complaint about the way a staff member was performing, she would take the complaint to Vic instead of first going directly to that person.

She used the same management style with the rest of the staff. One night, somehow, the cap was left off the radiator in the teachers' lounge. Mr. Johnson was the custodian then. Instead of asking him what happened to the cap and did he leave it off, she called his boss, who came over and chewed him out. Mr. Johnson stormed into the office and said to Helen, "You called my boss on me. You had no right!" Helen acted afraid of his anger, so I stepped in and said, "Wait a minute, Mr. Johnson. Come here. You can't talk to her like that. You need to apologize." At first he refused and I told him I wouldn't leave until he did. Finally he apologized. She really did not relate well. I think it was more a fear of people than anything else.

At that time there were three forms principals could use to evaluate teachers. The main sheet was white. It included a space to write about the teacher's performance. But then there were also a yellow sheet that the principal could use to write commendations for people who were outstanding, and a green sheet for people who were unsatisfactory. At the Department of Education the supervisors wouldn't look at the white sheets that just meant that the person was average. They would pull out the yellow and green sheets. It was important for teachers who hoped for a promotion, or who wanted to move into another field, to have yellow forms in their folders. And if a situation arose where a principal wanted to remove a teacher, it was important to have sent in green forms describing that teacher's unsatisfactory performance.

In a staff meeting at Barclay I said something about the yellow sheets. None of the teachers knew anything about them, because Helen had never used one for any Barclay teacher, even though that was a strong staff. She would make positive comments on the white sheets but never used a yellow form. She rated everyone as "average." The teachers were upset. I think I got on Helen's bad side by telling them about the evaluation system. Afterwards she talked to me and said she didn't think there were any excellent teachers on the staff. In fact, she had a great team of teachers, but they felt stifled. Helen seemed cold. When I said to her, "I like the staff," she looked at me and said, "That's a word I don't use." I asked, "What word?" She said, " 'Like'; I don't deal in feelings. I've been brought up that you just do your job."[38]

When her brother died she was sure that no one from the school would attend the funeral. I said, "Helen, give me the address." "They won't come," she said. I made those teachers get over there. Three carloads of us went. It was raining and we had to go back in a muddy area. She was surprised that we got there. Her family was very nice, and they were glad to see us. So I really tried to bring Helen and the teachers together. But she fought my efforts.

I also tried to help her with the parents. When I started at #54, some parents from the Hampden neighborhood—a white working-class section—stayed outside the school all day. They just stood there. I said, "Helen, why are these parents out there?" She told me that Hampden parents always did that; they thought they needed to protect their children. I would go out and meet them, talk with them and say, "Come in. Why are you out here? Let's go in and talk." It took a long time, but finally they would come in and we would talk and they began to trust the school enough to leave their kids there. There were other parents who just refused to deal with Helen. They would not walk into that school.

I decided to visit the homes in the community, so I went down to the different neighborhoods and just started talking with the families. Of course, Helen didn't like that. She said, "That's my responsibility." I told her, "Fine, Helen, but you have to have parents coming to the school." When parents did come in, they were usually angry about something. A couple of times I had to stand between her and a parent. I'd say to the parent, "You cannot talk to her like that. You have to leave." And Helen would whisper to me, "Oh, you can't do that; they'll take you downtown." Helen was really afraid of parents. I'd say, "Helen, you can't allow people to talk to you like that."[39]

In some of these conflicts there was a racial element. Barclay was one of the most integrated schools in the city, with white children from the Hampden and Charles Village neighborhoods and black children from the Harwood area and black and white children from the Remington area. The staff was also integrated. In the school we had very little conflict. Black and white tended to stay to themselves when socializing, but we all worked together. In the community, however, there were factions, and there was a racial undertone that sometimes flared up.

Right after I arrived at Barclay I looked out my window one afternoon and saw a black child hitting one of the white boys. I knocked on the window and then ran around and got them and brought them inside. I said to the first boy, "Why did you hit him? I was looking out the window and I didn't see him do anything to you." The hitter answered, "You don't know what he did to my grandfather!" I said, "Little boy, you don't even know your grandfather! You hit him again and you're going to be in a world of trouble!" So there was that underlying anger. But I didn't see many cases like that.

We did have two white families from Hampden that we called the Hatfields and the McCoys, because they fought among themselves so much. When one of the boys in the "Hatfield" family fell ill in school I drove him home. I noticed that all the windows were broken out of his house. So I said, "Oh, my! Your mother is going to have to get the windows fixed. All the heat is going to go out." He said, "There is no heat. It was turned off." "Well," I asked, "why are your windows broken?" He told me it was because the "McCoys" threw rocks through them. I called the "McCoy" children down the next day and asked why they were breaking the "Hatfields'" windows. They explained that they played this game. And I said, "What game is that?" They replied, "Niggahs." "How do you play 'Niggahs'?" I inquired. They described it for me. "We get up on the hill and when they come we say, 'Run, Niggah, Run,' and we throw rocks at them." Like Jack at Mordecai Gist, these Barclay children were unfazed, using "Niggah" while I was looking at them.

There was another time when one of the girls from a Hampden family told me that "six colors" were going to beat her up. "Colors?" I asked. "Do you mean crayons?" "No! six colors girls." I went out and there were six African American girls waiting for her. So we had to talk about that.

I had a good relationship with black and white at Barclay. But I had a poor relationship with Helen. She thought that I was trying to take her job. I really wasn't.

However, a number of parents had gone to the superintendent making waves about her. These were white parents. The black parents didn't like her much, but they weren't the ones making noise. It was the whites who complained. The staff had also started complaining.[40]

One day when I was working in my office Helen came in and said to me, "Let me tell you something. There can only be one principal here, and I'm that principal." "Why are you saying that?" I asked. "Because of what you do," she said. I told her that I was just doing what I was supposed to do, what the area director, Vic Cord, had told me to do. Things just got worse after that. I did not want to stay at Barclay any longer, and I asked Vic Cord to transfer me.

However, a group of parents, led by Lorraine King, a white parent who lived in Remington, had come to me and asked if I would be willing to be principal. I said, "No. I don't do things like that." I knew that the parents were trying to get rid of Helen, but I refused to undercut her. Nonetheless, they went on to talk to the super-intendent, who was Roland Patterson. He told me later that he asked them, "Why are you interested in having her?" and Mrs. King said, "She doesn't care whether you're green, purple or black. She's going to get you if you're wrong. But she's fair."[41]

Around this same time Vic Cord had met with Helen and me and told Helen that she did not have all the academic credits required for a principal and that she would have to go back and get those credits. Helen had agreed, but believed that someone else would be brought in to hold her place. Then Dr. Patterson called me in and said that some of the parents were requesting that I become principal, and that I had done a good job as vice principal. I told him, "No." I did not want to be principal. He just looked at me.

An acquaintance of one of the Barclay teachers saw me coming out of Patterson's office and called the teacher, who told Helen. Then we had a big stew. We met with Vic Cord who asked me if I had consciously or unconsciously done anything to sway the staff against Helen. I said "No." And I told Helen that I wasn't taking her job. "I don't want it," I said. "I don't even *like* this job." Actually, I *did* like the staff and the students. I just couldn't work with Helen. Then the staff began putting pressure on me.[42]

One night I had accidentally left my extension phone off the hook. I noticed it the next morning, hung it up, and went to work. When I got there people were saying "Congratulations." I said, "For what?" They said, "You're now the Principal of Barclay School." I said, "No I'm not! No I'm not!" Dr. Patterson had submitted my name even though I had said "No." And the school board had met the previous evening and approved it.[43] Then I did have problems.

Some of the other principals were very ugly. The principal of a neighboring school had put in for the position at Barclay and became very angry when I was appointed. People began saying ugly things. Some asked me who was I sleeping with in the Department of Education and other sly things like that. Finally, I called my mother and told her I wasn't going to take the job. "Yes you will," she said.

"You're not important unless people talk about you, and you have to put your money where your mouth is." She didn't give me any sympathy. She was sure this was something I was supposed to do, and she expected me to do it. So that's how I became a principal.

In the years that I was teaching, counseling, and serving as vice principal the school system had been led by several superintendents. Roland Patterson was the first superintendent with whom I had real interaction. When Patterson was a candidate for the job he was interviewed in the auditorium at Barclay School. At that time the school board held all of its public meetings at Barclay. Helen and I always stayed for those meetings. We were busy the night that Patterson spoke.

Attendance was high at that meeting. Patterson was one of three candidates, and he was the only black. Except for Stirling Keyes, who was interim superintendent after Sheldon, Baltimore City had never had a black superintendent. All the community groups were there to hear him, including the Black Panthers. Someone from the Black Panthers group tried to get into the school office to use the phone. He refused to talk to Helen and was very crude. When he told me that he was my brother I told him that I wasn't his sister and he could not use the phone. The way he carried on disturbed me. I didn't consider Helen a close friend, but I wasn't going to let him be rude to her. When he started saying that I was trying to act white I said, "Don't even try that," and finally he left.

Patterson was very angry that night. Every question the board asked him was given back with a feeling of anger that the black students were not being given what they deserved. He was really down on white people. He talked about all of the horrible things that whites had done against blacks and said that's why blacks have not been able to move ahead.[44] Helen and I both said, "Well, they're not going to take him. He's too radical." When we learned that they had selected Patterson, we were stunned. We knew that there was going to be a rocky road ahead, because the split between black and white in the city was growing, and Patterson could only make it worse. I think he was chosen just because he was a rebel. The board had told him that he had to get the system straight. So when he came in he was horrible. He was getting us all straight. Most people did not like him. After he'd called us to meetings and ranted at us, I wondered, "What is the matter with him?" He was short, my height, and people used to say that he wanted to make himself look big. He acted like he was on a mission. He reassigned top staff. For example, Rebecca Carroll who had long been assistant superintendent for Early Childhood Education, was moved from the central office to another building. Although Dr. Carroll stayed on, many of the senior people said they did not have to take his rough tactics, and they just quit. The system lost a lot of strength that way. Principals and specialists who would speak up and fight to keep a strong curriculum and high expectations just left.

When Patterson met with us for the first time he told us what we were *going* to do, and he said he would make sure we did it because he was going to be in our schools. He did visit the schools and go into the classrooms. He liked to talk about the day he went into a classroom and parents were there. Maybe it was American Education Week, or some event such as that. He sat with the parents. The children's performance was shakey. Apparently hoping to take the blame off of herself, the teacher stopped by him and said, referring to the children, "Oh, this is the slowest group." She got fired. He told about that because he said, "It could have been a child's father that the teacher was talking to." He insisted that instruction should be just as good for the slowest children as the fastest children in the school. He was right, and he did get parents involved and did focus on the rights of students. Basically he was smart. He knew about education. But at times he was just too heavy-handed.

After I became a principal I had one run-in with him. He and his administrative team wanted to bring some program into the schools—it may have been the "Right to Read" program—and they said all of us had to do it. I said, "No, we just can't change in the middle of the year." After we argued back and forth, he finally just looked at me and said, "Well, I'll forgive you because you're from Philadelphia." I didn't even know he knew I was from Philadelphia. But after that he would come by Barclay and we would talk. He saw me as a friend, maybe because I was short!

He changed his approach in the middle of the stream. He realized that most of the system hated him and that he was being used. He was chosen to shake loose those people who refused to go along with the system, who spoke up and angered the powers that be. When he realized what he'd done, then his whole tone changed. He wasn't nasty anymore. But it was too late. He tried to make some positive changes. In 1972, the year before he appointed me principal, he divided the school system into nine regions, with a regional superintendent over each one. In some ways this was helpful. Being responsible for a certain number of schools the regional superintendent (ours was Bill Murray) was more reachable. He came to the school often, was informed about what we were doing, and would respond when I called him. But in other ways this reorganization divided the system. We would go for months without seeing principals in the other regions.

After Patterson realized that he was in trouble, and that the system was more complicated than what he knew and what he could handle, he had the nine regional superintendents and a few principals form an administrative committee. I was put on that committee. He met with us the first night and talked about how intricate the system was, and how he needed to understand the problems of the system. It would be our role to bring to the committee (it was headed by Assistant Superintendent Lewis Richardson) problems that the schools were facing, and to help work out ways to deal with them.

We examined some big issues. One was the budget for each individual school. In January or February every year City Hall would freeze our budgets; whatever we hadn't spent by then would be held until June 30th—when it would go back into the city's general fund. Patterson decided to break this pattern by paying all the school system's bills by the first of the year. That made the mayor very angry. We raised other basic concerns, including special education (which was under-funded and operated with expectations for the children that were far too low); class size; and teacher training.

Patterson organized a parent group.[45] He had workshops where they were given the right to speak up for their children. He brought in good speakers and people to train parents on how to deal with their children, the schools, and the teachers. There were cases where students were thrown out of school without real justification and he would put them back in school. Parents, especially the low-income minority parents, felt comfortable with Dr. Patterson. He empowered them.

Desegregation was an issue that caused Patterson a lot of grief. It fell down on him after attempts at voluntary integration failed. He assigned John Crew, who was in the planning and research department, to work out a desegregation plan. Dr. Crew set up several committees. I was on one charged with laying out what needed to be done to implement desegregation. It was chaired by John Crew. Mayor Schaefer and the board were angry with Patterson by this time and didn't want to hear anything he had to say. Finally John Crew came out with a plan to reassign students. This is when families abandoned the city to escape integration. Some went to private schools, some to parochial schools. Some did home-teaching. Some went to Baltimore County, or some other suburban area outside the city. The system lost a large number of its middle-class students then.

Another setback for Patterson was the teachers' strike of 1974.[46] About 75 percent of the Barclay teachers participated, and some of the parents walked on the picket line with them. I promised the teachers that those who wanted to come in would not be stopped or harassed, and neither would anyone interfere with those who were striking. There was sympathy for the strike among the non-strikers, but some said, "I cannot strike on these children." During the strike Bill Murray, the school system supervisor for the district that included Barclay, came to the school door with the press. He wanted to show them how well the school could run despite the walkout. I wouldn't let them in. He insisted that the press had a right to enter. When I wouldn't allow it, he left in a huff. But I wasn't going to have the teachers outside betrayed.

The Baltimore Teachers Union had some good demands and some demands that didn't make sense, like opposing hall duty for teachers and having teachers go into the schoolyard with their children at recess, and accompanying their classes to art and music and physical education. These were asinine demands. Being with students throughout the day is part of the teachers' job. They need to supervise recess and know what their students are learning in the resource classes. In addition, the resource teachers need them there to maintain class discipline.[47] Among the good demands that the union put forward were better pay and limiting the number of meetings principals could call and also limiting the length of those meetings. Some principals were unreasonable in wanting teachers to meet several times a week and holding them for long periods.

When it was all over there were a lot of disheartened teachers. Some excellent teachers left the city then.[48] We did not lose any teachers from Barclay. As soon as the strike ended I called the staff together and told them, "We are a team, and we have to work together. If you have any concerns, let's talk about them now and then get on with working for the children." A couple of teachers stated concerns. Then we made plans for the rest of the year.

The strike was bad for Patterson. We knew from newspaper reports that he and Mayor Schaefer were no longer friendly. One report stated that the superintendent had misused funds, that there were other issues, and that the school board planned to fire him. So the teachers' strike gave still another reason to attack him. All the different community groups were getting involved for and against him. I remember one night the board met and they tried to pass a resolution to dismiss the superintendent. People in the audience started carrying on, going right up on the stage. One group took over the meeting—just took the gavel right out of the hand of the board president, John Walton.

Patterson decided to fight. He called me and asked if I could meet at his house. He had called a few of us, and we met with him and his wife. I was the only principal, but there were others from the school system, about six of us, and a couple of parents, and the lawyer, Larry Gibson. We had dinner and sat around and talked. He told us that he knew he had been quite rude in the beginning, and he realized that he started on the wrong foot. But he liked Baltimore. He had bought this gorgeous house on Benhurst Road, and he wanted to stay.

Then he told us why the mayor and board wanted him to leave. He said there were two reasons: money and the empowerment of parents. First, he had stood up against the mayor regarding Schaefer's policy of freezing school funds in the middle of the school year in order to have them revolve back into the general fund. Second, he had involved parents in fighting for good schools, especially the poor black parents. The board felt threatened by them. He said he might lose the battle, but he was going to fight and he was looking for support.[49] Several of us agreed that we would speak on his behalf.

Soon after, the announcement came that there was to be a trial: Roland Patterson versus the Board of School Commissioners.[50] Larry Gibson represented Patterson as his attorney. I was there every day, and the place was always packed. I made sure that I went by the school first and marked myself out on vacation days.[51] Then I went to the trial. I wore my jeans and baggy tops and sat with the parents. The board members did not realize at first that I was an administrator. But eventually Commissioner Sheila Sachs noticed me. Someone in the audience came over and asked, "Are you a principal?" I said "Yes." She said, "You know they [members of the school board] were talking about you back there." After that Commissioner David Sloan—one of the two friends Patterson had on the board[52]—would call me over from time to time and say "Keep the parents quiet today, because if there are any outbursts they plan to clear out the whole place." The parent supporters who were there loved Patterson, and some of them carried on whenever his opponents on the board attacked him.

The trial was a travesty. Talk about a kangaroo court! I couldn't believe the pettiness of what they were talking about. Sheila Sachs brought up a notice, a memorandum to the schools that Patterson was supposed to have sent out. Larry Gibson showed that she had two pages stuck together and the memo wasn't Patterson's at all. When he held it up and said, "This isn't Mr. Patterson's" the audience hooted.[53]

The first time I got into trouble as a principal was when I testified at Patterson's trial. I told the board that in four years we had had three superintendents and that our children were paying for this, because as soon as one person came in and learned the system and started working, he was sent out. I warned that we might not feel the effects of this turnover now, but we were going to feel it later. I also said that I felt Patterson had had a rocky start but that he cared about the children. He was a bright educator and he wanted to carry out the will of the parents. I said, "See how many parents are in here?" and I ended with "I wish you would reconsider and let him stay."

Not only did they not let him stay, they really railroaded the man. At the end Commissioner Sloan stood up and said "We have the right to fire him. But we don't have a right to do what we've done to this man. If we don't care to work with him, we can fire him. But we don't have to slander him."[54]

I believe that the school board made a serious mistake when they drove out Roland Patterson. I think he could have turned the city around. He was really focused on making life better for black students and parents. If he had continued we would have seen improvement in what the children were learning. Black *and* white parents would have been pleased that their children were learning and getting the best. He had learned from his mistakes, but when he saw the light it was too late. There was so much unrest that he was doomed.

After I testified for Patterson I was told that my name was added to a list kept by the Commissioner of Police, Donald Pomerleau. A friend who worked at the City Jail warned me that I was on the list, and that my phone was being tapped.[55] For awhile, community activists looked out for me. Vernon Dobson, the pastor of Union Baptist Church, and Parren Mitchell, then a sociology professor at Morgan State College and soon to be Maryland Congressman, would come by the school to check on how I was doing. They thought I might be fired.

I didn't experience any direct harassment, but now I was known as a trouble-maker. Of course, from the time I was a teacher I had been getting into battles. It just happened. It's not that I wanted to fight; it was just that if something wasn't right I had to say so. When I was appointed principal a colleague called me and said, "They think they're going to shut you up by making you principal. That is the biggest mistake in the world."

Principal at Barclay, Part One: "Barclay is Everybody's Business"

One of the hallmarks of Gertrude Williams's administration as principal at Barclay School was the expansive and intricate web of personal relationships that she cultivated with students, staff, students' families, the school's immediate neighbors, and friends of the school from far and wide. The school organizations that she describes in this chapter (the Parent–Teacher Organization [PTO], the Steering Committee, etc.) seldom had large active memberships. Most of the battles with the school bureaucracy that she recounts were waged with the support of a small core of activists. But at critical moments, or—as she put it—when they "needed to make thunder and lightening"—she could count on the close ties that she had with most families and staff and the respect with which she was regarded in the larger community to generate enough signatures on a petition or enough bodies at a meeting to win the day. How she acquired and made use of the loyalties and affections that bolstered her principalship for 25 years is a complex story. It begins with the history of Barclay before she arrived.

Parents who took an active interest in their children's school were part of Barclay's ethos from the time it opened in 1959. In an interview 35 years after his experience as Barclay's first Parent–Teacher Association (PTA) president, the Reverend Austin Schildwachter recalled the PTA as a "close and active organization." His recollections were seconded by Audrey and Donald Eastman who watched the construction of the school from their home across the alley and enrolled their children there on the first day of its operation—their daughter in kindergarten and their son in sixth grade. Both Eastmans were involved with the PTA. Donald served as president for several years while Audrey volunteered in many capacities, including long-term substitute teacher.

The Eastmans's neighbors, Jan and Francis (Gil) French were also Barclay parents, with three children at the school in the late 1960s and early 1970s. In the PTA, Jan took on numerous roles: membership chairman, treasurer, corresponding secretary and "a lot of volunteering—collecting funds, covering classes for meetings, etc." She remembered that the PTA "bought clocks for the classrooms, had the intercom installed, fought to get a traffic signal at 29th and Guilford, and held a bazaar each year in the spring for which people got together weekly from Christmas on to make things and prepare." Accredited as a teacher, Jan served as a long-term substitute for several years and in 1972 joined the faculty as a kindergarten teacher, retiring in 1999.[1]

By the late 1960s and slightly before Gertrude arrived at Barclay, the surrounding community had also established links with the school. One of its most prestigious neighbors, The Homewood Campus of the Johns Hopkins University, was the source of several community initiatives, thanks to Mrs. Lincoln Gordon, the wife of the university's president from 1967 to 1971, and Dea Andersen Kline, Hopkins's community relations director. With their encouragement and facilitation, the St. George's Garden Club, the Hopkins Women's Club, and Hopkins faculty were volunteering at Barclay before Gertrude took over as principal. Among the Hopkins women was Esther Bonnet whose service at Barclay began in 1968 as an outgrowth of an "urban interest group" that Mrs. Gordon had started among faculty wives. Mrs. Bonnet worked as a classroom aide with teacher Jennifer Kenney and found the school to be "a wonderful place to volunteer." She recalled that the principal and staff "accepted us as non-professionals with some talent to share." Similar sentiments were expressed by the women of the St. George's Garden Club whose environmental education projects at Barclay began in 1971.[2] The benefit of these school–community ties went both ways. Students and staff gained instructional resources while contributors were exposed to a welcoming and well-ordered learning environment that did not conform to the popular image of a public school populated mostly by children of color.

The impressions that Esther Bonnet and the women of the Garden Club held of Gertrude's predecessor as principal, Helen Nitkoski, were warm and favorable—in contrast to the image of Nitkoski that appeared in Gertrude's narrative in the previous chapter and the observations of others associated with the school during Nitkoski's time. This suggests that she worked well with people of her own race from the middle and upper classes but was not comfortable with a racially integrated staff or with working-class parents of either race. Myra Lunsford, who taught at Barclay under Nitkoski, observed that the principal "had some strong feelings of her own about how black and white teachers socialized." Describing weekly social outings involving teachers of both races, Lunsford concluded, "Helen Nitkoski couldn't accept that in her world."[3] In short it appears that Gertrude's predecessor was temperamentally unready for the challenge of interacting with either the racially mixed Barclay staff or the increasingly diverse and lively parent–community coming and going through the doors of Barclay School in the 1970s.

Barclay took in children from one of the largest "catchment areas" in the city. The school's student body came from six neighborhoods, some with boundaries overlapping each other. Charles Village claimed the largest territory and was dominated by middle-class and upper-middle-class, mostly white, professionals. Many Charles Villagers were renovators, restoring the run-down Edwardian three-story brick townhouses that lined the main throughways of "the village." Relatively few village residents sent their children to the public schools, but the Charles Village Civic Association (CVCA), representing the community, followed school developments. Its members contributed to special school projects and acted as advocates for Barclay and the other area public elementary school, Margaret Brent.

In the northeast corner of Charles Village, residents of more modest row houses dating from the era of World War I carved out their separate identity as the Abell community. In the 1970s, a number of Abell families—including those instrumental in establishing the Red Wagon Day Care Center to whom Gertrude refers in this chapter—enrolled their children at Barclay. They were mostly white and middle class. However, one street within Abell's borders—Barclay Street—was dominated by African American households.

East of Abell lay the racially mixed Waverly community. Most Waverly children attended Waverly Elementary School, but for those living in one corridor, Barclay was the assigned school. The population in this corridor was heavily black, working class and, as time went on, increasingly unemployed and struggling with a spreading drug culture.

To the west of Waverly lay the Harwood neighborhood, whose blue-collar African American residents were the primary source of Barclay's enrollment. This area, in the 1970s, was characterized by small, well-kept row houses, but by the 1990s it too was fighting the blights of poverty and drug dealing. Like Abell, Harwood fell within the boundaries of Charles Village but its residents maintained their own neighborhood identity.

The Homewood campus of the Johns Hopkins University, and university housing for Hopkins's students, covered the expanse just beyond Charles Village's northern most reaches. Children from this area also attended Barclay. Their parents included graduate students, postdoctoral students, and faculty at the university. Many of these families were from Asia, Africa, the Middle East, Europe, and the Caribbean, adding an international dimension to the Barclay student body. In some years, 20 or more languages were represented among the student population.

During the mid-1970s desegregation attempt, Barclay's zone was extended to include Remington, where the racial composition was mixed, and Hampden, an all-white working-class enclave. Both lay east of Charles Village and Hopkins/Homewood. With the exception of Hampden, whose alienation from Barclay was one of the first concerns Gertrude had addressed as assistant principal, the school's location near the intersection of white and black, lower-and middle-class neighborhoods naturally brought children of varied backgrounds, cultures, and colors together under the same roof.[4]

The disparate politics and ideologies of their parents and neighbors—particularly in the 1960s and 1970s—enlivened the school community even more. At the time that Gertrude became principal, the national political climate was volatile, and the residents of the area surrounding Barclay school included an unusually large number of current or recent political activists. She assumed the role of school leader in the era of Watergate, the Vietnam War, and the antiwar movement that it provoked. The once idealistic New Left that helped fuel that movement was splintering into various factions, some of them espousing terrorism. Feminist organizations were proliferating. Black Power challenged the nonviolent, integrationist character of the civil rights movement, and urban warfare was erupting, such as the armed conflicts between the Black Panther Party and the police.[5]

The Waverly and Charles Village neighborhoods were home to numerous participants in the upheavals of this period. Among the parents sending their children to Barclay School were followers of various Muslim sects, members of black radical groups; editors of one of the earliest feminist journals, *Women: A Journal of Liberation*; impassioned supporters of the guerrilla pacifist priests, Daniel and Philip Berrigan; denizens of urban communes; and founders of the People's Free Medical Clinic and Sam's Belly food cooperative, two alternative institutions in the neighborhood. The Red Wagon parents, recalled by Gertrude in this chapter, included the founders of that day care center in Waverly, a few of whose politics derived from the teachings of Leon Trotsky. Both the presidents of Barclay's parent–teacher groups whom Gertrude discusses had spent time in the Deep South helping to organize for civil rights. Other community activists who volunteered at Barclay were veterans of the Peace Corps. As time passed, the causes would change but activists continued to be numbered among Barclay parents and neighbors—including the head of the local chapter of the White Lung Association, various union organizers, and an advocate and exemplar of transgenderedness. These experienced organizers were drawn to Gertrude's activism. She tutored them in how the school system functioned and dysfunctioned, and they were glad to join her in challenging it. They were not large in numbers, nor—being mostly white and middle class—were they demographically representative of the majority of black working-class and unemployed families with children at Barclay. But the strong bonds of trust and respect that linked Gertrude to nearly every one of those families insured support for any activist campaign carrying her imprimatur.[6]

In addition to Barclay's parents, the umbrella organization that served as a forum and resource for all the neighborhood associations—the Greater Homewood Community Corporation (GHCC)—identified support for the neighborhood schools as a major objective.[7] Looking back to when he was Director of GHCC in the 1970s, Charles Village resident Dick Cook described the activists of that era as being determined "to create a Great Society here in the city." His wife Karen Cook concurred. "We were very, very committed . . . to improving the quality of life in our neighborhoods, which involved improving the schools. We were committed to public education and wanted to keep our kids in public school." The first PTA president of Gertrude's principalship, Karen (Whitman) Olson conveyed a similar picture of the activist mind-set of those times. "My husband and I were dedicated to public education out of our overall politics of racial and social justice," she recalled.[8]

The GHCC established an education committee which evolved into the independent Barclay Brent Education Corporation (BBEC), dedicated to supporting and enhancing Barclay and Margaret Brent Schools. Most BBEC members were Barclay or Brent parents, but they also included individuals who had young children not yet in school and some with no children at all.[9] Harnessing the raw energy flowing around and into Barclay from all of these sources, while harmonizing the multiple cultures, classes, and races in the school population was no small challenge.

Of course, a principal is responsible not only for the school and to the community surrounding it. She must also answer to the "system"—that byzantine maze of regions, divisions, departments, offices, boards, task forces, policies, regulations, and mandates that comprised Baltimore's Department of Education—all with their own impressively titled authorities directing or enforcing them. David Rogers, a careful student of the New York City school bureaucracy, argued that to obtain the maximum benefits that the bureaucracy has to offer, "It is absolutely essential [for a principal] to work within the system wherever and whenever possible." However, he added, it is "equally essential to sometimes work outside the system and in seeming conflict with it—on those issues where it has failed to be responsive."[10]

As a new principal, Gertrude learned her way around the bureaucracy by making friends, developing contacts, cultivating relationships with personnel in every division and department. In this way she definitely followed Rogers's stricture on the necessity of operating within—and learning how to use—the system. Repairs, installation of new equipment, acquisition of supplies, busses for school trips, discipline or matters requiring the assistance of the school security force—for these and a host of other administrative matters Gertrude learned whom to call, the best times to call them, how to phrase the request, how to endear herself to them—or, in some cases, threaten them—so that they would swiftly respond when she called again. The Barclay Appreciation Luncheons that she recalls, and which came to have something of a legendary reputation within the school system, were the *pièce de résistance* in her repertoire of system manipulation.

At the same time, Gertrude worked for the Superintendent of Public Instruction and had to report directly to a regional superintendent.[11] These officials, saddled with ever-mounting burdens—including chronic under-funding, rising rates of poverty and disability among city students, and complex federal mandates—were not always as adept at meeting the expectations of individual schools as school communities such as Barclay expected them to be. Rather frequently, as a result, Gertrude could be found following the second part of Roger's advice, opposing the bureaucracy and its leadership.

When Roland Patterson was fired in the summer of 1975, he was succeeded by John L. Crew, who had been Patterson's deputy superintendent for planning, research, and evaluation. Crew, an African American, struggled with budget shortfalls throughout his tenure. Repeatedly the budget requests that he submitted and that the school board approved were cut at City Hall, requiring him to announce lay-offs and reduce allocations for the services and supplies that every school was counting on. At the root of these financial crises was the fact that while Baltimore City was home to over 40 percent of all impoverished children in Maryland (a figure that would continue to rise) and about one in five children in the city public schools was designated as disabled, the city school district received less money than all but three other districts in the state. This was because school funding in Maryland—as in many states—is based on the taxable wealth of every school district. As the middle classes moved to the suburbs the tax base shrunk as the number of needy children rose.[12]

Despite these disruptive and enervating budget rituals, Crew shared his predecessor's longing to raise the achievement levels of the system's predominantly black student population. By the late 1970s standardized testing had become a national obsession that would prove to be long-lived.[13] Given his background in testing and measurement, it was natural for Crew to seize upon tests as instruments of improvement and to celebrate any rise in test scores as proof of success.

Baltimore joined numerous other cities in the late 1970s and early 1980s in reporting that public school students were testing above national norms. How much actual learning such data represented was open to question, however. Researchers observed that scores inevitably went up when a district used the same test year after year; that training children in the skills of test-taking also raised scores; and that such training promoted "lower thinking skills" at the expense of meaningful instruction.

In contrast to the ephemeral claims based on test scores, Crew's more substantive achievements included the launching of the School for the Arts, an institution that would identify and nurture many of Baltimore's most creative and talented children, attract students from other Maryland districts and other states, and produce world-class performers.[14] He also promoted and oversaw the transformation of City College High School into a well-respected coed liberal arts center to which parents from Barclay and four other elementary schools proposed to add a "lower school." Gertrude describes later in the chapter how this attempt to resolve dilemmas facing the elementary students when they matriculated into middle school met with steely opposition and how, that, in turn, led to the addition of grades seven and eight to Barclay.

Perhaps most importantly, Crew began to address the system's long-neglected and expanding Special Education population. Citizens with physical and mental disabilities and their families were organizing on a national basis and gaining political influence. The passage by Congress of Public Law 94–142 (The Education for All Handicapped Children Act of 1975) was one sign of their growing power. It lent force to Crew's efforts to upgrade services for disabled children and provided an effective tool for monitoring and evaluating those services—the Individual Education Plan (IEP).[15]

At the same time, Crew had received a mandate from the mayor and the school board to calm the political waters roiled by his predecessor and to maintain a semblance of system harmony. He made a point of attending all of the mayor's cabinet meetings, suggested that the system adopt a new slogan, "something like 'We're Making It Together;' " and observed, regarding parent involvement, that he "believed in it . . . but felt that parent demands could get out of hand unless monitored."[16] As Gertrude's narrative illustrates later, Crew personally interacted with her and Barclay parents to a notable extent. In sharp contrast to the school chiefs who would head the system in the 1990s, this superintendent's considerable forbearance helped to foster the Barclay school-community's reputation as aggressive advocates and encouraged—however unintentionally—Gertrude's propensity to be outspoken and insistent whenever she believed Barclay's interests were not being well served.

Alice Pinderhughes—Baltimore's first female school chief, and also an African American—ascended to the position of superintendent when Crew retired of his own volition in 1983. Coming from within the system's ranks, she was a veteran educator "who had worked her way through nearly every job in the system." Initially appointed as "Acting," she accepted the position on a permanent basis after school board negotiations with an out-of-state candidate fell through.[17]

Coinciding with Pinderhughes's promotion, the National Council on Excellence in Education published *A Nation At Risk*. The commission, working under the aegis of the U.S. Department of Education, surveyed schooling at all levels, both public and private, throughout the country, finding a "rising tide of mediocrity that threatens the very future of our Nation." In calling for "more rigorous and measurable standards and higher expectations for academic performance and student conduct," commission members appealed to every segment of American society to join an effort to shore up teaching, and learning in all the nation's schools. They linked the country's standing in the world of nations to this effort, warning that America's "once unchallenged preeminence in commerce, industry, science and technological innovation is being overtaken by competitors throughout the world."[18]

Nation at Risk was as much a political landmark as an educational assessment. While calling attention to numerous, real signs of trouble in the nation's schools, the report could also be viewed as one more warning sounded in a long history of jeremiads lamenting the failings of public education in the United States.[19] For many years to come federal and state politicians were guided by its alarmist tone as they mandated various measures to exact accountability from educators and students. The concept of "outcome-based" education, emphasizing test results over all other aspects of learning, became a central feature of the politics of school reform.

Pinderhughes was attuned to the power of public perception and worked throughout her tenure to highlight and project the strengths of city teachers and students. She appointed a task force to examine the system's public image and recommend ways to enhance it. When the Fund for Educational Excellence (an agency created by Mayor Schaefer who appointed Gertrude to its board) initiated a citywide public school fair, Pinderhughes was quick to get behind it. Annually, for several years, in a large downtown convention hall from Friday to Sunday, every school in the district displayed students' work and trumpeted their accomplishments as scholars and artists, athletes and musicians, future citizens and leaders. Gertrude and parent leaders at Barclay backed these initiatives. A Barclay parent sat on the public relations task force and the parents and staff worked together to mount a display at every education fair.

Pinderhughes also enlisted teachers, parents, university faculty, business experts, and representatives of various civic groups on a plethora of committees to examine the public school system in all its facets. Again, Barclay parents were represented on these panels. Her staff boiled down the findings from these multiple sources into "Focus on Individual Success, a Local Imperative." This was a skeletal plan for academic and administrative reform. Using P.L. 94–104 as a model, the authors of "Focus" proposed that IEPs be mandated for *every* student in the system. A second major recommendation was that the system adopt school-based management (sbm) as an organizational model, shifting more decision-making authority from the central office to principals, teachers, and parents at each school site. Impressed by the Barclay Steering Committee, and having attended one of the Barclay Priority meetings, both of which Gertrude elaborates on in her narrative, Pinderhughes appointed a Barclay parent to co-chair the task force that was to work out a strategy to implement sbm.[20] Neither these nor other aspects of the "Focus" proposal materialized as a result of bureaucratic inertia in the central office and resistance among overtaxed teachers and school building administrators to unproven reform measures.[21]

Like her predecessor, Pinderhughes came up against the hard facts of under-funding. She riled state and city politicians when, in the local election year of 1987, she was asked by the business community how much money would be required for children in the city public schools to receive the same level of financial support enjoyed by children in the public schools of neighboring Baltimore County. Her answer of 157 million dollars may have been staggering but, as Mike Bowler has noted, "it was accurate." The city tax base was continuing to shrivel while demands on the school system to meet the needs of impoverished and disabled students mounted.[22]

Recurring funding crises had a heavy impact on every Baltimore city public school, with Barclay as no exception. While well aware of the historical and political sources of the school system's budget burdens, Gertrude also blamed Crew and Pinderhughes for poor fiscal management. Annual budget short-falls, requisitions that were partially filled but fully charged against the school's account; staffing shortages; cut-backs in art, music, and physical education instruction; incoherent curriculum guides: she blamed the superintendents for these and a myriad of other flaws and glitches in the system. However, the regional superintendents usually took the brunt of her protests.

The double-whammy of a tirade by her, followed by a flood of calls or letters from Barclay parents and, sometimes, neighbors, could drive the regional head to distraction. The effectiveness of these tactics is indicated in Gertrude's remembrance of the impact that the PTA parents had on her first regional superintendent, William Murray. His successors in the Crew years—Samuel (Mickey) Sharrow from 1975 to 1980 and Kathleen Luchs until 1988 received similar treatment. The first time Gertrude threatened to have parents call Kathy Luchs about a budget issue, the then new district director innocently said, "Just let them call." The parents did, tying up the district office phones for an entire day and thereby reopening a dialogue that Luchs had declared to be closed.

For the most part, the issues raised by Barclay parents and their principal were complaints common to public school operations everywhere—protests against budget cuts and staff-down-sizing; campaigns for toilet paper, window shades or classroom supplies; petitions for new programs, including gifted and talented, all-day kindergarten, and prekindergarten. The energy, tenacity, and increasing sophistication with which Barclay folk pressed their case were perhaps not so common.

For authorities such as John Crew, who believed in "monitoring" parents and preventing them from "getting out of hand," Gertrude's alliance with the Barclay parents and the Barclay community was disturbing. Nor was Pinderhughes comfortable with it. And certainly the regional leaders—Murray, Sharrow, and Luchs—found it annoying. All of these figures, however, remained available to hear out the Barclay delegations, engage them in conversation, and not infrequently find a way to address their concerns—which were always well documented and well presented. Gertrude took pride in observing that before setting out their case, those who spoke for Barclay "always did our homework."

Researchers have identified various factors to account for principals' leadership styles, including gender, race, and college training.[23] While these undoubtedly contributed to Gertrude's persona as a principal, it's doubtful that any of them counted for more in determining that persona than the composition of the school community to which she was assigned. Principal and community were exceptionally well matched. They shared a strong sense of social responsibility and a fierce devotion to children. With exceptional skills and a certain delight in taking on the system, they stood ready for organized collective action whenever students' interests were at stake.[24]

* * *

When Roland Patterson named me principal I was technically not qualified. I had yet to complete the administrative course work required for certification as an administrator. From my conversations with Betty Getz, I expected to go back to counseling after two years and had felt no need to take courses in supervision. Now I enrolled right away and met the requirement by January. Even without courses, I felt ready to take on the job, because all the time that I was an assistant principal I and other new administrators had met weekly with our area director, Vic Cord. She provided excellent training.

She prepared us for every experience that we were going to encounter. She would give us assignments to do at school with the staff. For example, she would have us meet with the staff and ask them to change the way they presented instruction—instead of working independently, work in teams of two, get them to work cooperatively. Or she would have us identify a problem at the school, perhaps too many scuffles among children as they were leaving the school. We were to talk with the staff and work out a solution. Then we'd go back and she would ask, "What response did you get? How did it work out?" We'd examine what we did and how we could improve. I also had taken the course in School Law at Loyola, and Vic followed up on that. She would give us cases and we would have to decide how they should be handled. Then she would critique our decisions. Under her I grew strong.

Vic Cord was one of those who retired because of Patterson. She was the best administrative supervisor I ever had. She told us that our role as administrators was to support our teachers and that they should feel able to bring their needs and concerns to us. If we could not handle an issue it was our responsibility to go to her, and she took responsibility for either handling the matter herself or going to the next person on the management ladder. Whatever she told us that she was going to do she did, and whatever she told us to do, she would back us up. Some of the area executive officers who followed her would tell us to do something, but then if there was some question raised, they would back out and leave us hanging. With Vic Cord we did not have to battle the system. She battled for us and respected us.

Bill Murray became our regional superintendent under Patterson. I could not count on him for the kind of support that Vic Cord provided. In fact, he worked me to death. He put me on numerous committees—helping to set up regional program plans for the year; helping to plan and carry out regional monthly meetings; representing him on a city-wide committee set up by the superintendent to coordinate activities among the various schools; representing the region on state-wide committees. And then he was always using Barclay as an example of "what was happening" in his region. This added to the resentment that other principals felt toward me. I was a new principal and could not know as much as they did; yet I was singled out. Besides, having all that extra work to do was tiring. I was already working long hours at the school. When I complained Murray said he didn't care. "I have to use the people who are going to do the work the way it needs to be done", he said.

Along with Vic Cord's training I could also, as a new principal, draw on my experience as a counselor. I learned how I could use it in administration. When things happened to children I knew what to do. One morning a little boy came in who was just hysterical. No one could find out what was wrong. I was able to help him calm himself and talk with him until we learned that his dog had been hit by a car. The counseling background made me better as a principal, because I didn't stay in paper work. I spent most of my time with children and teachers, and I tried to help them settle their problems.

If two children fought, they and I would talk it over, and they would have to see how they could have handled their differences in a better way. It got to the point that when they'd come to the office, if I'd say, "Both of you sit there, and I'll be back," by the time I got back, they would have talked the whole situation over, and they would say, "We know what we should have done."

I also went into the classroom a lot. I taught for teachers who needed help, or if there were emergencies and we couldn't get a substitute. I would get into the classroom as much as I could. I never wanted to get away from the children. After I had been principal for awhile, I was offered other positions, central office positions in neighboring counties and other states. But I never wanted them. Dealing with children and their parents and teachers, helping them, was very rewarding. I didn't want any other job.

My workday as a principal was long and full. I tried to get to school early enough to have a few minutes to think and get myself together. But usually when I drove up a parent or child or staff member would be waiting, needing to see me right away. I would speak with them and check for messages. If a teacher had called in sick I would have to call a substitute right away. Finding competent substitutes was always a chore. Next I would walk around the school with the lead custodian. She and I would make a schedule of her jobs. If we had a broken window or some other problem with the building, we tried to call in the repair order at 7:30 a.m., as soon as the facilities department opened.

When the custodian and I finished our rounds it was time for the children to arrive. I'd greet them outside or in the lobby. I liked to be outside. If some of them stopped at the store down the street, I would be waiting to collect the goodies they would be bringing with them—candy, donuts, other sweets, sometimes little toys, all distractions from learning. They could retrieve them from me at the end of the school day. I tried to spot any child who was having a problem. Often children leave home with serious problems. Sometimes they're ready to fall apart crying; sometimes they're angry and ready to tear apart the next person who talks to them. I would call them aside and say, "Why don't you wait in my office?"

After the children entered the building I followed them upstairs so that I could greet the teachers. After I went through the halls and made sure that the teachers were at their doors and the children were moving into the classrooms, I'd go back down to the office and speak with the child who was upset—or the children, since sometimes there was more than one. Then I'd make morning announcements over the office intercom.

My agenda for the rest of the morning depended on what meetings had been scheduled, what teacher might be needing help, and any unexpected problems that might arise. If I had been unable to get a substitute who could come right away I had to find another staff member to cover the absentee teacher's class, or teach it myself.

Since the school nurse divided her time among several schools I often had to pinch hit for her. When I first started as principal we had a doctor who came to the school regularly and a dentist. But those services were withdrawn. So if a child came in crying with pain because he had an abscess, I would have to get after that parent to take the child to a clinic and would sometimes have to take the parent and child myself. All of this cut into my regular schedule and insured that I would be working late and probably on the weekend. Not having a full-time nurse and other medical services also meant that the keeping of children's health records would often fall to me. Every visit to the health suite had to be recorded: the time, the purpose, the action taken. We also had to keep immunization records up to date, and maintain files on children with special physical problems, such as asthma or diabetes.

Once a week I met with the school ARD (annual review and dismissal) team. This was made up of the ARD manager, the school psychologist, the nurse, the speech pathologist, and the social worker. We reviewed the progress of all children who required special help and made appointments for their parents to come in. I had to arrange to cover the classes of teachers who would be needed in the parent meetings. I often sat in on those meetings as well. At Barclay, the ARD children comprised between 7 and 8 percent of the students before we adopted the Calvert curriculum. When Calvert was in place that number dropped to between 3 and 4 percent.[25] I would also have individual conferences with staff, students, parents, or community members. Often there were visitors to show around. The morning passed quickly.

At lunch time, with the help of aides and parents, I supervised the children who came to the lunchroom in three shifts. (After we added a middle school, we had five shifts). After eating, each group would go to the playground or, in bad weather, back to their classrooms to play quiet games. Lunch supervision can consume a lot of energy, monitoring behavior, making sure that the children who are hyperkinetic are not drinking chocolate milk or eating other foods that will set them off. When students go out to the yard the adult supervisors must be vigilant, ready to intervene if children are playing too roughly or doing anything dangerous. If two children had a problem playing together they would have to meet with me before the day was out to settle that problem.

The staff and I also had to know how to handle emergencies. One day when I was the only adult with a group of students on the playground, a sixth grade student just slumped over. I knew he had a serious asthma condition and also a bad heart. I sent one child in to have the secretary call 911 and contact his parents and another child to bring the custodian to help me carry him. At the same time I had to keep the other children calm and instruct them to return quietly to their classrooms. An ambulance took the sixth grader to the hospital where it was found that his heart condition had caused him to collapse. He was able to return to school in about a week, but was carefully monitored after that.

After lunch I always hoped for a block of time to call parents that I needed conferences with and to deal with the mail and paperwork—such tasks as checking that the attendance had been sent in accurately, that the payroll was correct, requisitioning materials, perhaps arranging with another school to borrow or swap supplies that were out of stock in the central warehouse, and submitting reports on whatever the central office or the regional office was demanding data on that day. When fax machines were installed in every school these demands for instant feedback on usually insignificant matters became ridiculous. The faxes just piled up, even coming in on weekends. I ignored some of them, and sometimes I just made up a reply. They never knew the difference.

If I had a good secretary and a strong assistant principal I might be freed up to do this work and freed up from some of it. But in all the years at Barclay I had only three or four good secretaries. Few assistant principals were as strong as the second person who worked with me in that position, Joyce Kavanaugh. Many assistant principals were weak, and sometimes I had no assistant principal at all. The system had decided that we had to have a certain number of children in the school to qualify for an assistant principal. If the enrollment dipped a little we would lose that position, even though we still had the same problems and the same work that we had to do.[26]

I found very little time to do the work that other principals managed to do during school hours. I wasn't satisfied to spend a lot of time behind a desk. I went through the school two or three times every day, just to make sure that everything was perking and children were being dealt with properly. If I had an incompetent teacher on staff that I wanted to remove, the union rules required that I monitor that teacher closely and write a program that would help her to improve. When I was a teacher, principals could call in specialists who would observe and work with the weak teachers. But we didn't have those specialists by the time I got to Barclay. So I had to write up all the observations and conferences, document all the steps taken to try to help the teacher, and keep a detailed record of the teacher's performance. That took a lot of time. The same was true of working with new teachers. Many of them came from liberal arts colleges where they had not learned how to teach. Once again, without the kind of specialists who had worked with me as a new teacher, much of the training for these new teachers was left to me. I was also responsible for routine observations and evaluations of every staff member.

When school was dismissed I again stood outside and monitored the children's departures. We had an after school program, so I would check on its operations. Then would come staff and parent conferences and, on some days, administrative meetings at the regional or central office. I would return from these to tackle the paper work and perhaps meet with parents who worked late and couldn't get to school until 6 p.m. or later. At times we had a custodian shortage, and I would help clean the classrooms. I kept a pair of jeans at school for that purpose. Being responsible for the physical plant, I kept a close eye on the boiler room. Barclay's boiler was an antique, and I had to learn how to read it and keep it in safe repair. I also learned how to operate the sump pumps, since Barclay has serious water problems.

The day usually ended late. There were community meetings to attend, parent–teacher meetings every two or three months, and always paper work to catch up on. One night at about 8 p.m. I was working in my office when I heard a banging on the window. A policeman was outside. He scolded me: "Miss Williams, you have to stop being here so late. Do you know there was a robbery just up the street?" But I was never afraid. At least one custodian was always in the building with me, and we left at the same time. More than that, I was in a community that cared about its neighborhood school. The parents and other residents kept an eye on Barclay, and looked out for me. As the school slogan said, Barclay really was "everybody's business."

In the beginning many parents were very shy about coming to school or uttering their displeasure. A lot of them would come to parent meetings and just sit. They were angry because they thought, "They don't want us to say anything." Karen Whitman (later Olson) was one of the first PTA presidents I worked with at Barclay. She brought instructors from Dundalk Community College, where she taught history and anthropology, to hold workshops. Faculty and personnel from the guidance program at Dundalk addressed ways that parents could enhance their children's learning. She encouraged parents to be vocal, to speak up about their children. In the workshops they talked about what to question, how to question, and what to do if they didn't get satisfactory answers. Some principals are afraid to have parents as a vocal part in the school. But I always encouraged Barclay parents to speak their minds.

I made a point of letting parents know what was going on in the school. When a problem arose I told them about it. I soon had a major problem with teachers being transferred out of the school. We had excellent teachers, and once they had the opportunity to make suggestions and have a share in making decisions they just started blossoming. The regional superintendent, Bill Murray, and others in the system saw this and began pulling them out to strengthen the staffs of other schools and take positions such as master teacher. In a single school year in the mid-1970s 15 teachers had been transferred and the sixteenth was to be removed at the beginning of June. Their replacements were never their equals, and the school was being weakened. I had protested and told Bill Murray, "You can't just keep promoting these teachers out of the school." He only said, "Well, we need them. You can't have all of the top teachers."

I talked with Karen, and she set up a parent meeting with Murray. She held it in the teachers' lounge, and it was jammed with parents and teachers. Murray kept saying, "Well, I'll tell you . . ." Finally, Karen glared at him and said, "I don't want to hear any more of this mish-mush!" That scared him and inspired everybody else in the room to go after him. He promised that he would hold up on the sixteenth transfer. Karen and other parents then went to the school board and made the case that teachers should not be moved in the middle of the school year, that doing so hurts the students. At least for awhile the mid-year transfers stopped.[27]

Roland Patterson had told principals that we should empower the parents. I took him seriously. We were supposed to have parents on each committee in the school, and I saw to it that we did. Karen was on our budget committee. When she saw the budget and how pitiful it was, she sent off a letter to the superintendent asking, "How can this school manage with such an inadequate budget?" Soon I received a call from Patterson's assistant, Robert Umphrey. He reported receiving Karen's letter. "She's concerned about the budget," he said. "How does she know about the budget?" I replied, "Because you told us we were to put parents on the budget committee." "Well, yes," he responded, "but you don't have to show them the budget." "Okay," I said, "I'm going to tell parents that you don't want them to see the budget." "No, no!" he said, "That's all right." From that day on he never chastised me about what parents should know.

Karen encouraged parents to become involved in the school by having events that they enjoyed and could easily take part in. Potluck suppers were popular. At winter holidays time we would invite all of the city and state legislators to a potluck holiday dinner. Karen would have them tell us what they were going to do for the schools. Then she would say to all the parents, "Now if they don't keep their promises you know what we will do at the next election." The PTA also sponsored talent shows and involved the teachers. In one of them the assistant principal then, Mildred Chester, helped teachers make little tutu skirts and they had a dance performance. The kids loved it. They would cry, "Go Miss Chester!"

Another parent initiative was fix-up day. That was one of the first times that some of the Charles Village parents who had been put off by Helen actually came to the school. They worked all day, oiled all the chairs in the auditorium, painted the building, made a lot of repairs. Barclay was probably the only school in the city with a bright yellow front door. That's what one of the parents, Judy Schultz, an artist, thought it should be, so we got the yellow paint and we had a yellow door. Parents took a large share of the responsibility for running Barclay's Reading Is Fundamental program (RIF).[28] Parents and teachers raised matching funds, selected and ordered the books, and organized the book distributions. Often parents invited special guests to participate in the distributions. The guests might be neighbors who would come and read to the children, or it might be the mayor of the city who would talk about his favorite books. Shortly after I became principal Mrs. McNamara herself visited Barclay, with an entourage of local politicians. They wanted to see our library, where Mrs. McNamara looked at the slips pasted in the books for children to sign when they checked them out. She was impressed by the long lists of readers. Senator J. Glenn Beall told reporters, "We want to see Barclay schools all over the nation."[29]

Beyond voluntary parent activities, I recruited and trained parents to join the school staff. Some of our cafeteria workers were parents. We arranged to have classes for parents interested in becoming substitute teachers. This was a benefit on both sides: employment for them and a reliable supply of substitutes for us. A few parents became educational assistants.[30] One of them, Tanya Jackson, completed her college degree and became the prekindergarten teacher. Some of our parent liaisons, the name given to those who were hired with Federal funds to organize parent involvement programs, were from the community, and so were some attendance monitors and other office staff. Having parents integrated into the school staff strengthened the tie between school and community. It was important to the children who saw their relatives and neighbors giving their best for the school and expecting them to do likewise.[31]

In the spring after I became principal, Art Nilsen, a sixth grade teacher, started the teacher–student softball game. A team of teachers played a team of sixth grade students. It became a major school event with each group rooting for its team. The students beat their teachers most of the time, until we got more young teachers. This is a tradition that has continued, involving grades six, seven, and eight and bringing together students, teachers, and parents.

In the spring of 1976 a group of about ten parents from the Red Wagon Day Care Center visited Barclay School.[32] Meeting with them was refreshing. They were well focused and asked good questions—about curriculum, the playground, the school schedule, and other matters that would impact their children when they enrolled that fall. They didn't phrase their questions as "What is the school doing?" Instead they asked, "What can we parents do?" That September, they and their children, and several other children with very active parents joined forces with the existing parent–staff–community partnership.

We continued to be fortunate in our ties with community groups. Among the parents who enrolled their children in 1976 were a couple who attended the Homewood Friends Meeting, which was located just a few blocks from the school. When they saw the number of children we had with serious health problems and that we had no school nurse, they went to the Friends and told them of our plight.[33] The Friends explored various ways to address the problem and decided that the Meeting would pay the salary for a nurse. Through one of their members we were put in touch with Fay Menaker, a trained RN who was working on a doctorate and could work for us part-time. I called her Nursey. She did so much for the children. She was like a mini-doctor. She had a stethoscope and listened to their hearts and checked them out.[34]

Fay knew how to talk to parents. They would come up just to talk to her. She upgraded our record-keeping system so that we could access every child's medical history and know immediately any problems he had. She encountered some serious problems, such as heart conditions, diabetes, and asthma. She knew how to work with the child and the families to help them deal with the problem. One day she called me in and said, "Look in this little boy's ear." I looked and I could see letters, like "o" and "y"—it was a piece of crayon with the outer wrapper that spelled the brand name. He said that his little sister had put it in when he was asleep. Fay had to take the boy and his mother to the hospital to have this removed. It had been there so long that it damaged his hearing.

The Friends had deposited enough money with the school system to pay Fay's salary for the whole school year. But before the year ended we were told that the money had all been used. We went down to the school system's financial director who said they had been taking out a fee to process her checks. They said they charged everyone for this service. After we got on them they backed off, and we learned not to let the system get hold of money meant for our school. That is why, when the Abell Foundation funded our partnership with the Calvert School in the 1990s, Abell channeled its grant through Calvert and did not go through the school system.

When she finished the degree she moved away from Baltimore. The system promised us a nurse to replace her, and we usually did have someone one or two days a week after that. But they weren't the same caliber as Fay.

We also looked to the owners of businesses located near the school for support of various kinds. Many of them took ads in the Barclay School yearbooks, some contributed goods for school raffles and others, such as the Waverly Farmers' Market, made cash contributions to our library. Jerry Gordon, the owner of Eddie's Charles Village Supermarket, was always especially generous. I will never forget the super long submarine sandwich that he built for us as a fund-raiser. The proceeds from selling slices of the giant sub helped us buy a copy machine that we desperately needed.

I always had good rapport with the organizations and institutions in our school community. When we said "Barclay is everybody's business," we included them. From her position in charge of community affairs at Johns Hopkins, Dea Kline led the way in creating ties not just between Barclay and the university but with the larger community. She became very close to us. Whatever situation Barclay found itself in, she would be there to support us.

Dea started "Community Conversations," a monthly breakfast program on the Hopkins campus for leaders from the schools, churches, businesses, hospitals, and other institutions in the area. She brought in speakers of all types—politicians, educators, financial leaders, artists, scholars. We would eat and talk and listen to the speaker and have a discussion. It was exciting. I was able to acquaint many community leaders with Barclay and what we were trying to do. Some of them became involved with the school, and we had their backing in some of our later battles.

Dea also sent Hopkins students to teach three week and six week courses to our students, on topics like oceanography. Then she set up an ecology project and took Barclay students to the Hopkins campus where they examined all the trees and developed a curriculum about trees. We would go to the adjoining Wyman Park and climb all through the brush identifying the different plants. And that was just the beginning. Every spring when the university held its Fair, she would invite our children to be a part of it. Hopkins began a summer camp where each child had a physical exam, played several sports, made art and music, and received nutritional meals.[35]

Through Dea the Johns Hopkins Women's Club, whose members included faculty and some female staff of the university, formed a long-term connection with Barclay. First, Betty Pitt, the wife of a prominent surgeon, came to hold story sessions with the children. Soon, the Hopkins women took on the daunting job of reorganizing the neglected shelves, repairing hurt books, disposing of outdated volumes, and soliciting donations to upgrade the collection.

The first coordinator of these efforts was Holly Sunshine, president of the club and married to a university vice president. When the Sunshine family relocated, Sharon Sturch, a Hopkins staff member and retired children's librarian, took up the challenge, and her successors, long-time Barclay volunteer Esther Bonnet, whose late husband was a distinguished faculty member of the Hopkins School of Public Health, and Lynn Jones, also a vice president's wife, continue to guide the club's work at Barclay to this day, with strong support from Wendy Brody, wife of the current president of Johns Hopkins, William Brody. They and the volunteers that they recruit meet with classes for reading and storytelling sessions and keep track of books checked out. Some of the club members have begun tutoring individual children. Although Madelyn Daniels long ago left Baltimore, she has made generous donations to establish a collection of library books in the memory of her husband, Paul Daniels. Mrs. Daniels made a special trip to Barclay for the opening of the new collection.[36]

Another great community resource was the St. George's Garden Club. They were the finest ladies one could ever meet. Their president was Lee Packard. Not only did they landscape and keep our school surroundings looking good, with their white gloves and little rakes, but they also planted most of the trees around the school. They worked with small groups of students on various projects.[37] One holiday season they taught us how to decorate a tree without having to buy expensive ornaments.

I especially remember the day one of the club members, Kitty Baetjer, came. The teachers' strike was on. She took one of the groups of students and told them a story about "Narcissus," and she had Narcissus bulbs to give out at the end of the story. She was planning to just work with a few of the younger children and only had bulbs for them, but the older ones had been listening very intently. They went up to here and said, "I'd like to have one of those for my little sister." Of course, they wanted them for themselves. They were all enthralled with her. Another member, Ellie Johnson, was the aunt of an assistant director of the Baltimore Zoo. She saw to it that our children went to the zoo anytime they wanted to and went free. The club would get the buses to take them there.

BBEC—the Barclay Brent Education Corporation—was started by a small group of parents with children in Barclay School and Margaret Brent Elementary School (located a few blocks south of Barclay), and other community residents. They met in members' homes. I started attending their meetings when I was assistant principal, since Helen never wanted to go. I especially remember meeting at the home of Dr. John Neff, who was on the staff at Hopkins Hospital. The early meetings were really rap sessions about the parents' concerns, for example, funding for the schools, curriculum, and how they could impact the schools in a positive way. BBEC soon began annual Charles Village house tours and, later, garden walks, to raise money for the two schools.

They set up a mini-grant program for teachers that still operates. When a teacher wants to do a special project or enrich her lessons with extra materials, she can request funds from BBEC. Another exciting project was the setting up of "Discovery Rooms" at Barclay and Brent. Parents constructed "discovery boxes" on various themes and placed them in the rooms. There might be a box on some scientific subject, with specimens to examine and equipment to become acquainted with. Another box might have a historical theme, with evidence to interpret. Children loved to visit those special rooms, and the parents got as much pleasure from making the boxes as the children did from exploring them.[38]

I also welcomed close association with Greater Homewood Community Corporation, the umbrella group for all the neighborhood organizations in our area. In the seventies the schools were a main focus of Greater Homewood. Their staff came to our parent meetings and we went to their meetings, took our concerns and needs to them. They put together a booklet on how the school system worked, and they had workshops with our parents on how to deal with the system. They explained the function of each part—the school board, the superintendent, the different offices and divisions, and showed parents where to start and how to proceed with a question or a problem and how to make the system accountable.

My connections with groups outside the school sometimes went beyond our immediate neighborhood. William Donald Schaefer started a new organization that he named the Fund for Educational Excellence. He appointed me to the governing board of the fund. When I received the letter asking me to come to a meeting and instructing me to confirm my attendance by calling Marion Pines, the director of the city's Manpower Program, I called her and asked, "Do I have to come?" She said, "I would suggest if the mayor sends you a letter that you should come." When we got there only Saul Lausch, the principal of City College High School, Andrea Bowden who was in charge of science in the school system, and I were educators. The others were businessmen. The mayor talked about how businessmen were tired of giving money to the school system and having it go every place but into the classroom. He went around the table to say why he selected each of us for this new committee. When he got to me I wondered what he was going to say. He said, "I've asked you because you're your own person. You will not let anyone tell you what to do. But you're pretty agreeable."

The goal of the fund was to get money into the classroom and give it to the teachers, never to have it involved with the powers-that-be in the school system. If a teacher had a science project she wanted to set up in the classroom, she could apply to the fund. If she wanted to start a classroom reading library; if she had children who needed additional help for math—any kind of thing that was creative that a teacher wanted to do. The mayor wanted to improve the quality of teaching, and he made clear that the grants should supplement the classroom curriculum. We were not to pay for things that were already covered in the regular budget. He also insisted that the money should go directly into the classroom.[39]

I took no part in reviewing the grant requests that Barclay staff sent to the fund. But other members of the board approved several of them, including the outfitting of a new science lab, materials for the English as a Second Language program, and a program where our students studied astronomy at the Maryland Science Center and anthropology at Johns Hopkins University. For several years the board stayed within the guidelines set by the mayor. Then the practice started of inviting the superintendent, who at this point was Richard Hunter, to our meetings and asking, "How can we support you and help you carry out your program?" The next step was to start giving money to the superintendent. This was absolutely against the reason why the fund had been established. Several original members of the board left when this began. I started missing meetings until my term was up.

While Mayor Schaefer was seeking positive ways to impact the city schools, Barclay parents, spearheaded by the Red Wagon group, were impacting School #54 in many new ways. We withdrew from the national Parent–Teacher Association (PTA) and formed an independent Parent–Teacher Organization (PTO). At that time the parents felt that the school did not benefit enough from being associated with the city, state, and national PTA to justify paying dues to each of those units.

In 1980 we set up a PTO steering committee to try to be more inclusive.[40] Parents and staff were elected from every grade level. The committee met once a month. The meetings were open to everyone, but only members could vote. At the monthly meetings, subcommittees made up of members and volunteers reported on such topics as the budget, the curriculum, and any recent legislative developments or school board rulings. All faculty and staff received steering committee minutes, and we posted them where they were accessible to parents and the community.

The steering committee also produced a school newsletter, published quarterly and featuring students' work and reports on their activities. Every child took a copy home, and we sent copies to our elected officials and community leaders. *The Barclay Bugle* let everyone know what was happening at the school. Soon after the first *Bugle* appeared the schools' director of publications sent out a directive that anything a school published had to be approved by her. Our parents called this censorship and protested all the way to City Council and the Superintendent of Schools. The directive was withdrawn, and City Councilwoman Mary Pat Clarke dubbed the protest "the Battle of *The Bugle*."[41]

I think the steering committee was the best thing that ever happened to Barclay School. It gave the teachers, parents, and me a forum where we could discuss and work through any issue affecting any part of the school. It became the springboard for our most important innovations—the middle school and the Calvert curriculum. Even though the steering committee was open and inclusive, some staff were uncomfortable with being so involved in the decision-making process. They weren't ready to make changes, assume new roles, adopt new methods. The same was true of some parents. When it came down to the time-consuming details of planning, setting up for meetings, sending out information, keeping up with issues—that work was left to a staunch few—a small group of mostly middle-class parents who were mostly white. There were many reasons for this.

By the late 1970s the majority of Barclay students qualified for lunch at no cost. And many of them were eligible for other federally funded services mandated by Title I of the Elementary and Secondary Education Act of 1965. This same act mandated that the school must establish a School Advisory Council (SAC) for their parents. In schools where principals did not want parent involvement and where the whole school was eligible for Title I this was a benefit for the parents. But in a school such as Barclay it was rather divisive. The non-Title-I parents did not identify with the SAC and the Title-I parents in the SAC tended to ignore the PTO/steering committee. Parents from both groups came together in school-wide meetings and for such activities as our annual spring fair or when a crisis called for a united front. But they otherwise stayed within their separate groups.[42]

It was also true that many Barclay children came from homes where some of the parents were afraid to speak up and did not want to be part of any organization. They received welfare checks and believed that if they complained too much they would lose those checks. Some of them were involved with drugs and other illegal activities and did not want to call attention to themselves. In many cases parents did not respond to the steering committee because they just weren't trained to take part in formal discussions and planning and the other work that steering committee members did. They could have learned. We had training sessions and many did get involved as a result of those. But others lacked self-confidence. Some had been conditioned to stay back and keep quiet. Some were just happy to let others do the work. Another factor was that the middle-class parents could do many jobs so very well. Those who were less prepared may have felt that they just couldn't measure up.

Even so, when we needed to make thunder and lightening to get our students' needs properly met, Barclay parents, staff, and community always came out in force. Those who did not do much work also did not work against us. They came out when we really needed them. We never went forward with a change or a protest that we had not discussed with the entire school and the school's surrounding community and given everyone a chance to say aye or nay. The core of leaders who usually spoke for the school were effective because of their own talents, but also because they always knew that they had the rest of the school behind them.

Because the parent spokesmen for Barclay were often white I was sometimes accused—mostly by people in charge of the school system—of being too partial to white parents. A few black parents may have felt this way, but anyone who spent any time in Barclay knew that those white parents were fighting for all the children, and they always had black parents with them. I think that people in the central office complained about the white parents because they fought so hard for what was needed in the school. The people in charge would say to me, "You have all these white parents . . ."

It is a shame that still we have people who believe that a black person who fights for all people is biased toward whites. It's almost as bad as the statement that a lot of kids use on black children who work very hard to get good grades. They say, "you're trying to be white," as though you can't be black and get good grades. The same type of attitude is used toward a black principal who fights for black and white. She's thought of as trying to be white. It's more insidious than racial disharmony, because we have people within our own race trying to strike us down.

The only time I can recall a breakdown of communication within the school with racial repercussions was a conflict that broke out between a small group of staff and a small group of parents. I can no longer recall specifically what triggered the conflict; I know that two members of the steering committee, a teacher and parent, had words, and some of the teacher's colleagues sided with her while other parents went to the defense of the parent. Jo Ann Robinson and I called a meeting for everyone involved in the conflict to air the problem. During the meeting a white teacher made statements attacking the white parents and their children. She said that there were other children in the school besides those children of the white parents who were trying to run everything, and implied that she thought that the children of these particular white parents were little brats. Jo Ann and I sat there trying to figure out what was going on.

Though what was said in the meeting was not supposed to be discussed with anyone else, discussions did occur. So finally I called a full staff meeting. I needed to find out how widespread these feelings against the white parents were within the staff. It turned out that they were not widespread at all. Only that little group of three or four teachers had a problem. The rest of the staff expressed the feeling that the whole situation was idiotic. We talked about how the white parents worked for *every* child. None of those parents ever asked for special favors for their children. They just wanted to help children, period.

This little tempest did not end right away. The parents and teachers having the conflict were supposed to work together on the Reading Is Fundamental Program. One of the parents wrote an angry note to the teacher who had attacked them, telling her that since the parents were not "representative" of the racial majority in the school, the teachers should set up their own representative RIF committee. This kept the bad feeling alive awhile longer. But in the end everyone cared enough about Barclay School that they stopped bickering. Though some of the parents always resented those few teachers, they continued to help with RIF and to support Barclay in many ways.[43]

There's no question but that public schools are stronger when the middle class uses them. When the middle-class parents—white and black—leave the system the expectation level is lowered because many of the parents who fight and push for high expectations have gone. The people who run the system then begin to blame poor performance on poverty. They water down the curriculum and say that poor children can't meet high standards. This is a terrible mistake, because brain power has nothing to do with economics. At Barclay we kept our expectations high for every child.

One method we used to build school unity was the convening of priorities meetings. We held two, one in 1981 and the second in 1987. Ann and Fred Leonard, whose two daughters went to Barclay, introduced the idea. These meetings were very important to me as a principal. In each case we spent a whole Saturday. We went back over our school history and then decided what our priorities would be for the next five years. This gave us a sense of direction. We knew what we were working toward, and we would set all our energies toward that. When we began to fight for a new program we were prepared, because we had really focused on our goals.[44]

By the time the steering committee took on its biggest challenges its members had a lot of experience with fighting the system. When school buses stranded a whole pack of students and our assistant principal, Joyce Kavanaugh, at the Baltimore Civic Center after an Ice Follies performance in the late 1970s, parent leaders joined me in taking to task the school transportation director, John Branch. Their memo impressed him so much that he came to the school and apologized in person. From that day on, until he passed away many years later, he would help us any way he could, even providing free buses a few times. He told me that he thought a lot of our school and the parents who stood up for it.[45]

In most situations parents and sometimes other community residents and I battled side by side, or steering committee members spoke for the school and were careful to avoid any action that might cause me or any other staff person to lose our jobs. But once in a while I had to take action without waiting for anyone else. This was true the day in 1979 when a contractor building the Barclay Recreation Center onto the school wanted to cut a hole in the wall of the school gym, where the doorway between the school and the new center was to be located, before bricking up windows and installing security gates to protect the school from intruders.

We didn't want the recreation center located there in the first place. It destroyed our plans to expand the school with an early childhood center.[46] So I was determined that if they had to build it there they were going to do it right, and they weren't going to risk the security of the school. We had already had a break-in right after the construction began. That is when we lost thousands of dollars of video equipment. Now I told this contractor that they weren't coming in through that wall until the school could be secured. He talked as if he had been drinking and he started to holler at me. He said that if he was my boss he'd fire me, that I was costing him a hundred dollars an hour, and that he was going to have me arrested.

Jo Ann Robinson had just dropped her child off at the school and came looking for me to talk about some steering committee matter. When she heard the contractor threaten to have me arrested she ran to the telephone and called several other parents and neighbors. They rushed over. Some were carrying morning coffee cups. Some still had their hair in rollers. There were about six of them, and they made a circle around me and backed up everything I was telling the contractor. The man knew that he was going to lose this battle, so he left and called my supervisor, Mickey Sharrow. When Mickey came he had to admit that we had been promised the necessary security measures. He soon got the windows bricked up and a metal gate installed that would prevent anyone who came into the construction area from getting into the main part of the school. District directors like Mickey Sharrow also came to respect the steering committee and its representatives, though Mickey sometimes complained that Barclay caused him to have bad headaches.

John Crew, who became superintendent after Roland Patterson, put Barclay's parent support to the test in 1980. The parents sent him a letter criticizing the way the school budget was handled. The school system would claim that we received so many dollars for every child. But a lot of money never got to the child. The central office would print school system publications, pay for meetings, and decide that all students must participate in certain activities (for several years we had to take the children downtown to frog races), and they would deduct the cost of these kinds of things from our per-pupil allocation. I explained this to the parents on the steering committee and on behalf of the parents Jo Ann Robinson wrote to Dr. Crew and complained. He wrote back that I had misinformed them and invited the PTO president to call him to discuss this problem of how the parents were being misled by me. He sent me a copy of that letter. I think that was one of the biggest shocks I've ever had. And I remember it like it was yesterday.[47]

Esther Jeffries was the school secretary then, and she always gave me my mail. We were having a fifth grade assembly. As I walked through the office on my way to the assembly Esther said to me, "Well, Miss Williams, you don't need your mail right now." That made my ears perk up and I said, "Why don't I need my mail?" I took Dr. Crew's letter from her and read it. She was just looking at me. I kept reading it, reading about how I had lied and misinformed the parents, and then I said, "That bastard!" Esther gasped.

I went into my room and dialed the superintendent. I said to his secretary, "You tell John Crew that as soon as I pack up my things—at the end of this day he can have this job." The next voice I heard was John Crew's. He called me "Gertie"—"No, no Gertie," he said. "No, don't be hasty." And I said, "You bastard, why would you write something like that?" "No, now, wait a minute." And then he asked would I be willing to come down and meet with him and Jo Ann—he not knowing that she was in the nurse's room also trying to get him on the telephone, because she had just picked up her letter. What had he been thinking? If he really wanted to divide the parents and me, why did he send me a copy of that letter?

The next day Jo Ann and I went down to the Department of Education. When we walked in all the secretaries who were typing stopped. They just watched us as we walked through to meet him. His secretary offered us coffee. "No, I want nothing! Nothing!" Dr. Crew came in and took us over to another room. He was nervous, because he knew he had done something that was really vicious. Jo Ann started questioning him about his letter. He would say, "No, no." He could not prove any of it. Then he said, "Gertie's my friend. I like Gertie." She said to him, "If you like her, I would hate to see when you dislike someone." By this time he was really nervous.

Then he said, "Gertie is so goddamned stubborn!" I don't remember all the other discussion. But I remember him saying, "I was *so* mad at Gertie—I just *wrote* that letter and sent it on." But he made a copy! He made a copy for me, and he had sent copies to the school board president and to my supervisor, Mickey Sharrow. He did a lot of sputtering in that meeting, and he backed off and promised to write me a letter of apology. It was awhile before I received it, but he did send the apology letter. Someone in the Department of Education once said to me, "If Dr. Crew knew how afraid of mice you were he would carry them in his pocket and throw them at you every time you got smart!"[48]

Through the 1980s we had one battle after another with the school system. For example, in 1981 the school board voted to eliminate "senior teachers" from the city schools. Teachers did not have strong supervisors like I had with Emma Bright and Rebecca Carroll. But senior teachers were assigned to each school. At Barclay two senior teachers, Joyce Hughes and Verna Chase, monitored instruction, helped teachers with classroom management problems, and held workshops to inform parents about the curriculum. Their work was important and we were outraged when it was announced that they were to be cut out.

The steering committee asked Michael Hrybyck, a parent with graduate training in statistics, to look at the study that, according to the school board, proved that senior teachers were ineffective. Mike tore the study to shreds. No one ever replied to his arguments; they tried to discredit them instead, calling his criticisms "libelous and slanderous."[49]

In the spring of 1982 Mayor Schaefer announced that the city budget had to be cut and teachers would be laid off. Two Barclay teachers received pink slips. Their students sent letters to the mayor. The *Baltimore News American* printed one of them on the front page. A troop of parents and students picketed City Hall and sang to the mayor. One of their songs was to the tune of "My Bonny Lies Over the Ocean" and played off of the mayor's pet project, the Baltimore Aquarium and the city nickname, "Charm City": "A school without teachers is nothing; It's like an aquarium without fish/ A City with bad schools isn't charming/ No matter what the mayor may wish." Refrain: "Bring back, bring back, O' bring back our teachers to us . . ." Other schools and organizations also protested the cuts, and the teachers were not fired after all.[50]

Because Barclay was such a lively place, being principal took up nearly all of my time. Still, I did stay active in my church—Provident Baptist Church—for many years. I was superintendent of the Sunday School, sang in the church choir and worked in the missionary society, helping the elderly, visiting the sick and reaching out to others in need. But I finally had to cut back on even that.

For many years my social life included the companionship of John Bacon, who was a guard at the City Jail. I met him while I was teaching at School #139 and we were a couple until we broke up in the 1970s. He married shortly after. Someone asked me one time, "What do you have against marriage?" I said, "Nothing! I think it's a fine institution." But I know me. When I get involved in something, I just throw myself in it, and no husband would have stayed long when I pulled the hours that I did when I was a principal. I went in to school early and came home late. Sometimes

I'd eat a sandwich for dinner or a bowl of cereal and go to bed. Some people can handle both a job and marriage well. I knew that I couldn't.

I went to parties and cultural events once in awhile. Occasionally I would get to New York to see a play. But often I would be invited to places and something would come up and I would have to stay at school to meet a parent at 6:30 or 7:00 p.m. I would be expected at the event by 7:30, and I would just give up. It was more important to meet that parent. I did often go to the opera, usually with Mary Jane Beneze, who taught third and fourth grades at Barclay, and sometimes with students. Title-I funds would pay for the tickets and for a time the parents of our music teacher paid for busses.

I found that even in the summer it was hard to get away. There was so much to do to get ready for the next school year. And it really wasn't a good idea to leave town very long, because when principals were away the central office could make changes in our budgets and staffs, and when we came back we would be shocked to discover the cuts that had been made without our input. I kept up with school board meetings during the summer and fought many a summer battle with 25th Street or later, North Avenue, over such issues as enrollment projections and personnel assignments.[51]

I usually did go home to Philadelphia for a short while when school was not in session. There were always things that Mom would be waiting for me to help with. And before I retired I did manage to take two real trips—a week in Jamaica in 1983 and a week at Disney Land in August of 1988.

Many of my colleagues belonged to fraternities and sororities but I did not. When I was at Cheyney we did not have Greek societies on the campus. I would not have been able to pledge anyway, because that costs a lot of money. In addition, some of the sororities asked only fair-skinned people to join. In later years I was invited to join a couple of sororities, but by that time I had no interest in them. I know that there are many fine people in such organizations, but some of them are not my cup of tea.

Baltimore Sun reporter, Will Englund, was on to something when he wrote an article on the influence that fraternities and sororities had in the city school system.[52] Much of the system ran according to who knew whom. This is not so much the case today, but for a long time to be promoted it really helped to be in a certain sorority or in a certain family or a certain color. I remember one light-skinned woman who was so anxious to be in the elite that she introduced her mother—who was darker—as her babysitter. I went to an affair where this happened, and when we left a friend told me that the darker woman was really the mother. I couldn't believe it. But my friend said, "She introduces her mother that way because she doesn't want any of her itty ditty friends to know that her mother is dark skinned."

These attitudes are not as bad today as they once were. But they still exist in some cases. I seldom go out with administrators to social affairs. Some administrators care more about their image and status than their responsibility for improving students' education. Some administrators have attitudes, and I just don't speak their language.

However, I mustn't leave the impression that I had no friends in the school system. There were many people who would come and help whenever I called. This was true from the day I started as principal. I would call and say, "Look, I'm new; I don't know how to do this. Would you please help me?" They always would. Barclay had many, many friends in every division, from physical plant to payroll, from secretaries and repairmen to division heads.

In talking to the staff one day I said, "You know, people have been so good to us. I mean the little people, not the people who run the top shop, but the people who come out and do the work. They need to be thanked in some way." I suggested, "What if we just all made our favorite dish and invited the people?" That's what we did; we had the people in for an "appreciation luncheon." They were so excited, and the food was good, because the staff went to town on cooking. Then we had it again the next year, and even went a little further and had the little children sing and recite. We expanded the guest list to include parent and community supporters. We also invited the dignitaries and often had the superintendent and members of the superintendent's cabinet, and the mayor and elected officials from the state and, occasionally, Washington DC.

One of the guests, Walt Robbins, who worked in the budget division, said to me, "Listen, you know black folks come. Why don't you have some chitterlings?" I told him, "Yes, Walt." So I called my mother and asked how to cook them. I thought, "Oh, this will be fine," and got ten pounds and ended up with a tiny little dish. Of course, that amount was eaten up, and so I promised the next year I'd do better. It got up to where I was cooking eighty pounds of chitterlings. Eighty pounds! I usually stayed up all night fixing them. But they ate them. I didn't eat them myself, but they always disappeared.

The Barclay appreciation luncheon became the party of the year. People would wait for their invitations. The staff always came through with wonderful food. For many years Evelyn Wallace, an educational assistant, coordinated the preparations, and she and her assistants became pros. We even published a Barclay cookbook with all the recipes of the favorite dishes from the luncheon. This was a great hit. People were asking for those books for years after we had run out of them. We had luncheons for 25 consecutive years. Since I've retired I still have people stop me to ask, "Why did you stop those parties?" People would tell me, "Whatever your school asks us to do, we will help, because you say 'thank you' in the nicest way."[53]

I have said many times that I was fortunate to become a principal in such a pro-education community. It was really exciting to have parents and staff willing to change when we saw the need. This gave me the chance to take risks, because I knew I would not be left out on a limb by myself. It made the staff more willing to try new approaches and make changes. We knew we could also count on the university and Greater Homewood and the other community groups to back us up.

In return, I knew that if parents and community were all willing to fight for the children, I had to be ready to step forward, too. I couldn't sit back and let them fight for us. I had to be with them. I have always felt that I must be ready and able to do any task that I might ask others to do. Any assignment I would give a teacher or a custodian or anyone who worked in that school, I would be able to do also. My belief is that the administrator's role is to be right there working with them, and, when need be, fighting with them. In the beginning we didn't know how often we were going to fight. We never imagined going through the battles that we had to go through just to improve the quality of the school.

Principal at Barclay, Part Two: "To Learn as Fast as They Can and as Slow as They Must"

For the first 15 years that Gertrude presided over Barclay School (1971–1986), William Donald Schaefer presided over Baltimore (1971–1986). In a 1983 portrait of the mayor, *The Baltimore Evening Sun* described his "ferocious, stubborn hold on all levels and details of the city government . . . his demanding standards, his fostering of new ideas, his unrelenting dedication to the city, his fierce criticism and his massive temper."[1] In only slightly qualified form, that same description might be applied to the Barclay principal.

If not ferocious, she certainly proved to be tenacious. As Superintendent John Crew is said to have noted, she was "so goddamned stubborn." And her control of the school extended over all levels and details. When she wasn't checking on classrooms in person she frequently reminded everyone of her presence through the intercom. She was a demanding leader, a fount of new ideas, and unrelentingly dedicated to the children. No one enjoyed being on the receiving end of her criticism, and no one who witnessed one of her tantrums—whether of the "real" or the "contrived" variety— would soon forget it.[2]

At the same time, she could be gracious and diplomatic. When groundskeepers were cutting the grass in extreme heat she made sure that they all had sodas to drink. "She was so good with people," declared former curriculum coordinator, Margaret (Peg) Licht. "She just kept such a wonderful attitude throughout that school." She was the driving force in launching the Barclay staff into major instructional and curricular changes. Gertrude's successor, David Clapp, recalled the feeling that her decisions represented what was "best for the kids." He described her as conveying the message that "I'm not the leader to tell people what to do; I'm the leader because I want to do things for the school." As a result, according to Clapp, she always had "teacher-buy-in" when she introduced innovative programs.[3]

Gertrude also inspired loyalty from her staff by championing their interests and being ever ready to go to bat for them, whether to facilitate a desired promotion, stop an unwanted transfer, run interference when red tape hindered their pursuit of some tool of professional advancement, or intervene to insure fairness in a conflict with a colleague, parent, or student. "She was our protector," said Evelyn Wallace, who served as an educational assistant throughout Gertrude's tenure as principal. Wallace also stressed Gertrude's competence:

> Anything in the building that went on, we knew she would take care of it. Ripping and running and fighting. If something happened in the middle of the day Miss Williams went right on and dealt with it. [She'd] go to North Avenue: "I'm on my way" [she'd announce over the intercom].[4]

Gertrude's way of commanding respect and exercising authority left a deep impression on her staff. First grade teacher Dorothea Rawlings recalled chaperoning a class to a program in the Barclay auditorium when she was still assigned to another school. Students were talking, laughing, and cutting up when they entered the auditorium but shortly thereafter Gertrude walked in, ordered them in her distinctive, somewhat raspy voice to "Freeze!" and the auditorium became instantly, totally still. "All the way back to my other school I said, 'Wooo, I want to be in that school. . . . That Miss Williams, she is really something!!' " Truemella Horne observed that when people first talked to Gertrude on the phone they had no idea that she was only five feet tall and were always shocked when they later came to the school and met her. She "commanded and demanded so much respect" Horne avowed. Barclay staff members saw Gertrude's exercise of authority as part of her exceptional "people skills." "She knew how to work through a situation and not blow it out of proportion," commented Tanya Jackson, who started at Barclay as a parent volunteer, became an educational assistant, and is now the prekindergarten teacher there.[5]

As described in the previous chapter, Gertrude took soundings of collective sentiment in the priorities meetings and in the steering committee, though the priorities sessions were not heavily attended and the steering committee fell short of being as representative as it was meant to be. She talked over new projects in staff meetings and entertained concerns and opposing views. Since the latter were usually few in number, "the majority ruled," and if she did not rule the majority, she strongly influenced it. When all was said and done, Gertrude, like Mayor Schaefer, led by dint of personal force. She labored against the backdrop of an aging, troubled city, while he battled to save that city and reinvigorate it.

The author of and booster behind major downtown renovations, the crowning glory of which was a glittering new Inner Harbor of shops, eateries, water taxis, and promenades, Schaefer was the primary architect of a nationally acclaimed "Baltimore Renaissance."[6] That renaissance did not extend to the public schools, however, just as the mayor's "demanding standards . . . new ideas . . . unrelenting dedication" seemed not to apply to the Department of Education. "He never had a strong attachment for the schools," a Schaefer supporter told the *Evening Sun*. The mayor—famous for promoting "creative financing" and other maneuvers around established policies and laws—piously invoked the limits that the city charter placed upon him when it came to matters of education. As he chose to read the charter, once he appointed the school board his responsibility for the schools was limited by their autonomy. The schools were their problem.

Political scientists Jeffrey Henig and colleagues have suggested that Schaefer—a white leader in a majority black city—used the school system for black patronage, appointing black superintendents, who in turn appointed deputies, assistants, and principals who were Schaefer supporters. Having observed the racial pyrotechnics that surrounded the departures of superintendents Thomas Sheldon and Roland Patterson, Schaefer wanted to avoid such episodes in the future. As one of Henig's informants stated, about the potential for racial conflict in the school system, Schaefer "didn't want to mess with it."[7]

In the final election campaign of his mayoral career (1983), Schaefer was challenged in the Democratic primary by black lawyer William (Billy) Murphy, who called the school system "atrocious" and attacked the mayor for not caring about the city's children. Though he won handily over his opponent, Schaefer appeared to take to heart criticisms about his schools policy (or lack thereof). At his primary victory celebration he presented himself as "a mayor who's going to take much more interest in education. . . . We're going to be in the schools . . ."[8] Shortly after winning the regular election the mayor established the Fund for Educational Excellence, appointing Gertrude to the first board of directors,[9] and began to show a more active interest in school issues. But these efforts were "too little, too late."

In 1986, as Schaefer moved from City Hall to the Maryland governor's office, an urban analyst placed Charm City under his academic magnifying glass and found "rot beneath the glitter," with the school system manifesting some of the worst of that rot. Commissioned by the Morris Goldseker Foundation, one of the most prestigious philanthropic bodies in Baltimore, Peter L. Szanton, former president of the New York RAND Institute and director of his own consulting firm in Washington, DC, laid out the prospects for the city's future in a document titled, *Baltimore 2000*. With population losses, a shrinking tax base, declining employment opportunities, and increasing poverty, Szanton included "a weakened school system" among the harbingers of trouble.

Like *A Nation At Risk* and other such commentaries on public education, *Baltimore 2000* presented a somewhat skewed view of city schools, spotlighting failure while impervious to the existence of schools such as Barclay with creative leadership and dedicated teachers and parents, eliding the meaningful teaching and learning that occurred—and still occurs—everyday across the Baltimore school system. But in Baltimore, as in the nation, the failures were real and troubling, rooted in chronic under-funding, manifest in glaring inequities both within the school district and between it and its wealthier suburban counterparts.

In 1985, the city's median household income was $16,7000, compared with $31,000 in the five counties comprising the metropolitan region. The overall "economic well-being" of Baltimore's black community which included the majority of the city's population, was ranked fortieth among forty-eight black communities in the United States.[10]

With the highest teen pregnancy rate in the nation and a cancerous spreading of drug and alcohol addiction across the city, the financially stressed city schools were inundated with children whose parents were themselves children and with "crack babies" and victims of fetal alcohol syndrome, and those who had ingested lead paint. These children presented volatile behaviors that demanded the expertise of school psychologists, social workers, nurses whose numbers were never adequate to meet the demand, and whose jobs inevitably were flagged when City Hall announced the latest budget cuts.

One factor that the report did not address was the use of addictive substances. By the 1970s an epidemic of addiction and violence was spreading throughout the city and into the suburbs. Whereas earlier addicts mostly used tactics short of violence to raise money to support their habits—such as con games, shoplifting, and petty larceny, by the 1970s they had adopted knives, guns and other measures of brutal force. The infusion of drugs into black neighborhoods that were already poor had lethal effects. As one addict observed, "It soon reached the point where human life didn't have much value. Guys were taking contracts on people, killing one another over $10 or $15."

The drug epidemic also had a debilitating impact on the family structure. In the words of another addict:

> When these people were using drugs, they couldn't earn a living, most of them, so they went on welfare. And their kids after them is on welfare, too, because they don't know how to do anything. They're intertwined, drugs and welfare, a part of each other.[11]

Between 1960 and 1970 the number of Baltimore families on welfare increased five times, "from 5,281 families with almost 18,000 kids to 26,666 families with 77,000 kids." An increasing number of those kids attended Barclay School.

They were subject to shocking neglect and abuse. In some cases, drug dealers in their families employed them as peddlers because the police would be less likely to pay attention to a child. This extracurricular employment played havoc with a child's academic performance. But students did not need to be directly involved in the drug trade to be affected by it. Drug-related robberies and shootings touched many of the children's lives and caused Gertrude to become cautious about making home visits in areas where trafficking was heavy.

Gertrude and her staff were aggressive and creative in addressing the needs of these children, marshalling all the social services and psychological and counseling resources that were available while at the same time fashioning an effective academic program. In the mid-1970s, the Barclay staff were among those city educators who had already recognized the urgency of working with children in their formative years. They lobbied for, and won, a prekindergarten program and on their own initiative began to offer all-day kindergarten. Only a few schools already had pre-Ks. Labeling them, a "luxury of the poor," a *Baltimore Sun* reporter found 21 such programs in 1971, as well as a "Model Early Childhood Learning Program" for three- and four-year olds in five other poor neighborhood schools.[12] All-day kindergarten was virtually unheard of. Indeed, in the year 2000 the State Board of Education was still debating its merits.[13]

Academic instruction remained the central mission of the schools. Guiding and encouraging every child to work to his/her full potential was the responsibility of every teacher in every classroom, whether they were working with students in Special Education, students who were "average" or those identified as "gifted." However, as Gertrude's account of her work at Barclay illustrates, the material resources needed to fulfill this responsibility were seldom adequate; recurring staff shortages and lay-offs undermined instructional planning and disrupted classroom teaching, while many of the directives from central office staff regarding curriculum and pedagogy lacked coherence. These were the kinds of frustrations that Szanton summarized by concluding that the school system was "widely condemned as ineffective, undisciplined and dangerous."[14]

Gertrude determinedly countered these great challenges. For each child to "learn as fast as he can and as slow as he must" became her mantra. Reflecting her respect for the individual student, it led directly to converting traditional classes into "nongraded" groupings. Research in child development indicates wide ranges of ability among students of the same age, particularly in the elementary school years, and differing abilities within the same child (reading well above the traditional "grade level," for instance, but performing in math below that level). Grouping children according to their actual stages of development and permitting them to move at their own pace is the essence of "nongradedness." Children were not locked into a given group but could move from one to another as their individual growth dictated.[15]

Baltimore had instituted the nongraded approach in five elementary schools in 1959. Principals of two of them, Kathryn Wilhelm and Dorothy Wilkerson, explained the approach to the school board in the following terms:

> The non-graded program differs from the traditional program in a variety of ways. Grade titles disappear and children are not considered to be in first grade, second grade, etc.

Instead, they work in groups based on their characteristics, level of maturity and needs. There is a total change in vocabulary of all those involved in the education process. . . . The terms "passing," "failing," "promotion," and "grade levels" are not used. The educational program seeks to provide appropriately for each child, not for a class as a mass group. It is hoped that such an organization will help remove the pressures children often feel when they are forced in learning tasks beyond their abilities . . ."[16]

Despite these endorsements, elementary educators monitoring the city's five nongraded schools noted three "concerns." First, transient students (whose numbers were growing) did not remain long enough in any one school to be evaluated and assigned to an appropriate grouping. Second, teachers who transferred frequently or who were "unqualified or disinterested" [sic] could undermine a nongraded program. Finally, nongradedness would not work in overcrowded classrooms. The "intensive study of children" that it required and the "individual growth" that it aimed for could only take place in relatively small groups.[17] Nonetheless, the report judged that the advantages of nongraded programs outweighed these concerns.

In a series of school visits ten years later, a city journalist came upon versions of such programs still functioning at four Baltimore elementary schools. In most cases, only two or three grades were folded into a nongraded sector of the school. Apparently, by the time Barclay's program was in place in the mid-to-late 1970s school officials had determined that the "concerns" associated with nongraded classes now overshadowed their advantages, and they no longer approved it as an option for a city public school.[18] With characteristic resiliency, when she was forbidden to continue the nongraded organization, Gertrude pursued the theme of "as fast as they can, as slow as they must" by a series of other innovations, intended to address the wide range of Barclay students' capabilities and needs, including sending students to different teachers for different subjects (departmentalization) and ultimately the adoption of a challenging private school curriculum.

Many students were deeply affected by Gertrude's unstinting efforts to provide them with the academic programs and opportunities that called forth their full potential. They were also moved by the care and concern with which she enveloped them. Her successor, David Clapp, who taught at Barclay several years before becoming an administrator, recalled how much she enjoyed the students and how "she spent a lot of time with them in the hallways, on the playground, in the cafeteria, popping in the classrooms asking them how they were doing." "She was incredible with the children," curriculum coordinator, Peg Licht, averred. "She knew them. She knew what they were thinking. She knew their parents. She knew everything about every single one of them."[19]

For many parents Gertrude was a godsend. Darice Claude, who sent three children through Barclay, identified the principal as "friend, confidant, motivator, counselor, preacher, doctor, lawyer, Goodwill ambassador to and for the parents."

"That woman knew things about me that I didn't know about myself," exclaimed Joanne Giza, whose son and two daughters attended School #54. Recapping, in 1983, 13 years of navigating "the tricky and deep waters of . . . public education" as the father of a recent public school graduate whose elementary education had begun at Barclay, Grenville Whitman dubbed Gertrude "the most spectacular person I encountered . . . Without fear or favor," he declared, she "stood up for her students, her parents, her school and her neighborhoods."[20]

However, the same forceful personality that endeared Gertrude to many could alienate others. Karen Olson observed that "over the years there were some parents who got into snits with" the Barclay principal. While she was genuinely open to hearing concerns and suggestions about school programs and policies and often adopted ideas proposed by parents, teachers, or others in the community, she did not always welcome direct challenges to her opinions and authority. She might retort sharply, could be very abrupt, and, as Barclay staff have recalled, could dig in her heels "even when she was wrong. . . . Sometimes she would make up some . . . rule on the spot in the office, give some reason why" she could not honor the request at hand "and somehow it would hold." But the parent or other person against whom she had invoked the specious rule would be infuriated. "All of us got angry with her," admitted educational assistant Evelyn Wallace. "I told her, 'sometimes I could shake you!' "[21] In the last analysis, though, Gertrude inspired a feeling of family unity among all who were associated with Barclay, and the weight of parent opinion about her fell heavily on the side of those who echoed Joanne Giza's declaration that "my children were very fortunate to have gone to this school. A lot of who they are today is because of Miss Williams and Barclay."[22]

Consequently, it was not surprising that Gertrude was the first person that Barclay graduates and their parents turned to in the mid-1970s when they met with a hostile reception at Robert Poole Junior High School. Until then, as she explains in this chapter, sixth graders from School #54 attended one of two junior highs just north of Barclay. When a federal order forced school officials to redistribute school populations for purposes of desegregation, they redirected Barclay's largely black student body to Robert Poole in the all-white Hampden neighborhood.

The then insular character of Hampden combined with racial antagonism to make life miserable and dangerous for black students who were subjected to verbal and physical attacks as they walked through the neighborhood and, in a few instances, while they were attending classes. The situation presented a classic example of how desegregation in the name of correcting historically racist school policies exacerbated racial tensions.

Rising to a new level of boldness—reaching beyond curriculum innovation, experiments with teaching methods, and programs of cultural and instructional enrichment—Gertrude and the Barclay parents determined that their children should have a new middle school. At first they worked in coalition with like-minded principals and parents of four other elementary schools in the immediate area.

However that coalition effort—which centered around establishing a "lower school" in the newly refurbished and still partially vacant City College—collapsed in the face of powerful and adamant opposition from City College administration, parents, and alumni. Thwarted but persistent, the Barclay forces regrouped and launched an independent, protracted, and ultimately successful campaign to house grades seven and eight within their own school building. By so doing they augmented both their own confidence in their collective ability to fight for their children and their reputation as a school community that always got its own way.

* * *

At Barclay we were always moving, trying new ideas, making changes. There was never a dull moment. To be bored at Barclay you would have to be dead.[23] Our main goal was to meet the needs of all the children in the school. Barclay drew most of its students from Harwood, a neighborhood just south of the school. When I first arrived at Barclay, Harwood was a solid, blue-collar, black community where residents took pride in their homes. The parents cared about the school. Their kids did their work, and most of them did well. We always had Harwood parents involved with the PTA or PTO and the steering committee. As time went on, however, the drug culture spreading throughout Baltimore slowly gained a hold in Harwood. This brought difficult problems that the long-time residents are still struggling with today. For Barclay it brought parents who moved in and out, children without food, without clothes, all kinds of abuse on children. We worked every angle to protect and help these children and their families—networking with city agencies, soliciting help from community businesses and institutions, going into our own pockets to help the students and—when necessary—calling the police.

From the days of the "New Frontier" and the "Great Society" we had certain federal programs that targeted "children at risk." The biggest of these was Title I of the Elementary and Secondary Education Act (ESEA).[24] Any school where 70 percent of the children qualified for lunch at no cost might be eligible for Title-I funding. That funding targeted the lower grades. Depending on how the school was categorized, these might be grades K through three or grades K through five. Any child in those grades whose standardized test scores fell into the "severe" range would become eligible for Title-I services, whether or not that child qualified for lunch at no cost. These services included individualized instruction on top of regular classroom lessons in subject areas where they were falling behind.

How Barclay became a Title-I school in the mid-seventies is an interesting story, because at that time the percentage of children eligible for lunch at no cost was less than 70 percent. After Title I was enacted, the federal lawmakers expected to see children in Title-I schools improve on standardized tests. The schools in Baltimore City were not making progress, and the federal government had given Baltimore two years to raise test scores, or else Title-I funds would be withdrawn. Roland Patterson had every regional superintendent select two high performing schools in his region and make them Title-I schools. Bill Murray had selected Barclay, but did not tell me.

When school opened in September I found all these new women in the building. They said they were assigned to Barclay by the regional office as Title-I children's aides. "But," I said, "We're not a Title-I school." I called Bill Murray, who told me that we had been selected because we had enough children who fell below the poverty level to qualify as Title I. Even though we didn't, I said, "Oh! Great!"

He told me that I could use the aides as I wanted. This was wonderful. I decided that they would become "educational assistants." In most schools they would have been "children's aides," helping with lunch, walking children to the lavatory or to the nurse, taking them to the office if they were misbehaving, and sometimes playing the role of "sergeant at arms"—handling the discipline that should have been handled by the teacher and the administrator.

I assigned the Barclay aides to classrooms to work with children who were having trouble keeping up. I made it clear that they were not there just to run errands or to be the disciplinarians, although there would be times when they would correct a student or be asked to walk a child downstairs. Mostly, I expected them to plan and work with the teacher, to help with instruction. They might work with individual children who needed extra help, or with a small group of students on a specific skill. They would not introduce new skills. That was the teacher's responsibility. But when the teacher was instructing the whole group, the assistant might walk around the room, making sure that students were on task. To be hired as aides they had to have a high school diploma, a successful interview with an administrator in the Title-I program, and receive training by the school system. I felt that this prepared them adequately to help with the instructional program.

The assistants were happy with this. They went to a meeting where they told Alice Pinderhughes, who was then in charge of the Title-I schools, that they were educational assistants. "No," she said, "You are children's aides." The Barclay assistants wouldn't back down, and they came back to the school very indignant. By then someone in the system had given the label of "educational assistant" to some other category of helping teachers. When Alice and I talked about it, I argued that the Barclay assistants were doing the same kinds of things that the other group was doing. Finally, Alice just let it go. The change in title gave the assistants new status. They carried themselves better, took great interest in instruction, and learned a lot about teaching. In some cases it was hard for a visitor to identify who was the teacher and who was the assistant in a classroom. With the assistants' extra help our students' test scores rose.[25]

At a meeting that Alice Pinderhughes called for principals later that year, she discussed the Title-I budget for the following year, and named every principal but me. I raised my hand and asked for my budget for Barclay. She told me that I was on the borderline. From the back of the room another principal called out, "Hey, Trudy! You didn't realize that you're supposed to keep 'em dumb!" That made Alice very angry, but my fellow-principal was right.

Several times we were in danger of losing our Title I status, because as soon as students who had tested as "severe" (working far below grade level) improved and began testing as "moderate" (working only slightly below grade level), they would be pulled out of Title I, and we would lose the funding for them. In some cases the difference between "severe" and "moderate" was only five points, and the students who moved up were not really on solid ground yet. They still needed extra help to become average students and to continue to develop. We could be in the middle of a semester, and administrators in the central office would take part of the staff away. This was the doing of the local school district, not a requirement of the federal law. Just as Bill Murray, doing the bidding of the Patterson administration, had given us Title-I status when we were not yet eligible, later Alice Pinderhughes, administering elementary programs for the Crew administration, was ready to take funds away from students who still needed them.

The Title-I rules required us to use Title-I funds to work just with the students who were performing at the very lowest levels. Eventually the law was amended to include "school wide" status for schools with more than 90 percent of their children qualifying for lunch at no cost. "School wide" status permitted us to work with all children in grades K through five who needed extra assistance, but we had to write out individualized programs for them. We did not receive school-wide status until the 1990s. The year we got that status I worked late several nights in a row, calling parents to urge them to send in their children's lunch applications, until we reached the 90 percent mark.[26]

Title I funded "high intensity" reading laboratories and math laboratories ("High-I labs"), which operated much like the old "reading centers" from when I was a teacher. They were the best resource for children who needed intensive training in reading and math. We had two very good teachers and two very good educational assistants—Sandra Brown assisted by Margaret Shanklen; and Jennifer Kenney with Evelyn Wallace as her assistant. They had those labs ordered so that each student's work was individualized by what skills that student needed to master. Children who tested "severe" on the standardized Comprehensive Test of Basic Skills (CTBS) would go to the lab where the regular lesson would be taught and supplemented by individualized instruction.

When the Barclay labs first opened, the materials that we were sent were mostly too difficult for the slower moving students. We had to adapt other materials for them to use. Meanwhile, there we were, with thousands of dollars of materials not being used. We decided to try these materials with our brightest kindergartners and first-graders. They loved the labs! One day we had surprise visitors from the Maryland Department of Education. They walked into the reading lab when the kindergartners were there. They were startled to see these small students using the lab materials. One of the visitors asked a little boy, "How old are you?" In a gruff voice the child replied, "Five." He questioned the boy to see if he knew what he was doing, and he certainly did. Later, the visitors asked me if those were really children or were we using midgets in our labs? When I told him that we couldn't stand to have all of that expensive material just sit there, and that it worked beautifully with the fast-moving younger students, he said, "Good," and added that we should be able to use the material as we needed. After a few years the funding for the High-I labs was discontinued, but with some juggling of the budget we were able to maintain ours for several more years.[27]

Another Title-I program, which I did not welcome, was the free breakfast program. Lewis Richardson, who was an assistant superintendent, and I got in a battle about that. I said, "I am not going to have it. I'm not! Next you're going to ask me to put children to bed. I think that parents should be made to do something. They can give them cereal or something. If we have breakfast, that's another add-on to my workload that will take me away from instruction and curriculum."

When Lew said he would send the free breakfast material anyway, I told him that it would just sit in the lobby. Finally, they put aides in the school to work with the breakfast program, and then I accepted it. After a year they pulled the aides out, and I continued the program. I saw its value and how much some of the children looked forward to it every morning. Nonetheless, I still believe that public schools should deal with instruction—not just reading, writing, and arithmetic; but also art, music, physical education. And because the children are with us all day, we should have arrangements for lunch. When it comes to adding in breakfast and other noninstructional services—these should be funded to include staff to carry them out and not be piled onto the principal's back.

One of the most exciting programs that we were able to add to Barclay because of Title I was prekindergarten. We were concerned that many of the kindergarten children were coming to school knowledgable about the TV soap operas, but they couldn't identify the colors, didn't recognize the numbers, didn't know any of the fairy tales and nursery rhymes. Our kindergarten teachers were concerned about how poorly prepared some of the children were. Title I funded a parent liaison. Our first was Vernetta Lynch, who was soon joined by Thelma White. Vernetta and I went through the community to find out how many children would be ready for preschool. We came back with 85 names. During the second semester of 1975 we presented this information to Alice Pinderhughes, who was then the assistant superintendent for early childhood education, and we told her, "We need a preschool."

We didn't hear anything until just before school was to open the next fall. We were sent a preschool teacher, Frances Crosby. We weren't prepared, but we hurried, made space, and got new flooring put down. We had to get teaching materials together, because when they sent us the program they didn't send us the money to go with it. So the teachers brought in things to help set up the room, and Mrs. Crosby brought materials that she had. The way she was welcomed was typical of the Barclay staff. They all came down to see her new room and helped her get acquainted with the school. The new preschool was packed, and we had a waiting list.[28]

For students to learn "as fast as they can and as slow as they must" was the guiding principle behind the nongraded system that we followed for several years, beginning in the mid-1970s. We didn't advertise our departure from standard procedures. We discussed it as a staff, and with the parents, and decided that this was the way we were going to proceed. It was hard to get some administrators to understand that children learn in different ways, so we didn't try to make them understand. We just moved on with our nongradedness.

The children moved according to levels. We kept a chart showing where each child was. When he or she was ready to move to another level we would call the parents and explain the move. It worked well. Those children who needed to take more time than others did not feel bad, because they were not labeled as being in a certain grade and made to think that they failed. They were just moving at their pace. And the faster moving children were able to move at *their* pace. We could also identify individual strengths and weaknesses. A student might be reading at a fourth grade level but be ready for math at a sixth grade level. Children were not locked in.

Our nongraded arrangement worked well. It gave the slower moving children a chance to catch up. And some did catch up and then kept moving. Some just had to move slower than others all along. It was also exciting for the faster moving children who could keep on going without being stopped by artificial grade blockades. I have always believed in moving children when they are ready and not as a whole bloc. However, we had to end nongradedness when visitors from the central administration discovered it and became upset. They were concerned that replacing grades with levels would disadvantage the children when they reached junior high and high school.

In place of nongradedness we started departmentalization. This allowed each teacher to teach to her strength. Elementary teachers are supposed to be masters of every subject, and most of them aren't. Some teachers are excellent in teaching reading skills. Some are excellent in teaching math skills. Some are great in teaching science. Our most outstanding science teacher was horrible in reading. We had another teacher who loved teaching reading skills and taught them all day, shortchanging children in all their content subjects.

Our departmentalization began with first grade and continued through sixth, except for the special education children who remained in self-contained classrooms with one teacher. Even for the special education children there were times when some would leave the self-contained rooms and join other students for reading, math, physical education, or art. The special education children went on school trips with the rest of the students.

There was some concern that young children would be overwhelmed by departmentalization. But the students loved going from teacher to teacher, looking forward to something new in each classroom. If a child had one poor teacher he could still have three good ones. Children benefit from working with teachers who work in their specialties.

While we went about the nongraded and departmentalization methods quietly, we had to campaign to get a program in the school for our gifted students. Dr. Patterson had instituted a school for very able students. They were called the GATE—gifted and talented—students. But there was only one GATE school in the city. Space was limited and every school was given just so many slots. If Barclay had ten children who were qualified and only seven slots, three of our children would be left behind. The other problem was that the children who went there lost contact with their friends at their home school. We decided that we needed a GATE program in our own building.[29]

The school counselor at that time was Gail Levy, whose services we would lose the following year, thanks to budget cuts. She went to the Department of Education in Washington, DC and discovered that the GATE program was covered by ESEA. It was considered a part of special education, which meant that there should be gifted programs in every school, just as there were special education programs for the slow-moving children. Gail and some of the parents of gifted students got together and prepared a presentation.

We set up a meeting with Rebecca Carroll, who you'll recall was Patterson's associate superintendent in charge of curriculum, and all the people in positions where they could make a difference. We knew that we could make people happy by having food. So we cooked these delicious dishes and fed them first. Then Gail and the parents showed slides that they had made—how many children were cut out each year, the difference the program made in students' performance; the social impact on students of being separated from their home school, and so forth. Our guests were very impressed. Soon GATE programs opened in six schools, including Barclay. We were able to hire two GATE teachers, Steve Alpern for science and math and Maryann Moxon for the language arts and social studies. They were great additions to the staff.[30]

Before GATE, and in some cases even after we had GATE, we sometimes reached a point where we did not have the resources for children who were fast moving. I decided that the only way that these children could keep moving was to place them in a private school. I started doing this when John Possidente came to us. He was such a bright little boy! His family lived in Remington. I hired his mother as a school lunch aide. She soon went back to school and became a teacher. Because we weren't challenging John enough, he was constantly in trouble. I knew if I didn't get him into another school I would be tempted to strangle him! I asked his mother about getting him into Boy's Latin. She said they couldn't afford it. So I contacted Boys' Latin and got him a scholarship.

I went to all the meetings that the private schools held, where they described their programs, and I got to know them—Roland Park Country, Gilman, Bryn Mawr. Then they began to send representatives to Barclay to meet and talk with the children. If I recommended a child they would test him. The children I recommended were usually way above the average and they usually were admitted with scholarships. This is another example of something that I just went on and did. I did not ask my regional superintendent or anyone else, "Is it okay?" I decided that the only people who needed to know were the parents. Unless I was doing something detrimental to children, the people downtown did not have to be involved. I felt it was my responsibility to strengthen the child, not the system. However, I also believe that when we strengthen the students the system automatically benefits.

As long as students and their parents leave public school with a good feeling about what they got there, they will have no animosity toward us. Animosity builds up when children stay in public schools, their needs are not met, and they regress—then we create bad feelings. I know that the Department of Education would not agree with me,[31] but I think we make our public system stronger by guiding students toward private school when we cannot meet their needs in the public setting.

In the same way, I developed contacts with the pediatric departments of several city hospitals, the Kennedy-Krieger Institute for learning disabled children, and other institutions whose services a number of our students required. The school system did not have enough psychologists and specialists to screen all the children with handicapping conditions. Rather than keep a family waiting for months or more to have their child tested and given an appropriate referral, I often prevailed upon these institutions to accept Barclay students.

The instructional system for all Barclay students received a big boost from Gil Schiffman and Paul Daniels, faculty members in the Johns Hopkins University's Evening College in the Division of Education.[32] I first met Gil when I was vice principal, and one of my responsibilities had been curriculum. He was teaching at Hopkins and some Barclay teachers were in his classes. They talked to him about Barclay, and he called and asked to visit the school. He used Barclay students as he studied the effectiveness of various teaching methods and tried out new curriculums. He also taught in-service courses for city teachers. Whenever he came to Barclay, he and I would have long conversations about teaching and curriculum. We would see that a certain aspect of instruction wasn't effective and would talk about how we could do it better. Gil would then work out a plan and meet with the staff and help them improve their teaching. Then, through Dea Kline, the director of community relations for Hopkins, I became acquainted with Paul. He also taught courses for teachers. Gil was one of those who wanted me to become principal. He promised me that if I did take the job he and Paul would work with me on teacher training and curriculum. So I held him to that.

At that time (the 1970s) teachers took courses offered through the city, and they complained that many of those courses didn't given them the material they really needed to help them in the classroom. Taking those courses meant hearing the same old platitudes year after year after year. Paul Daniels invited us to get together and decide what courses we wanted. He then wrote them up and sent them to the State Department of Education, which authorized them to be given for the same credit as the city's courses. Then he and Dea Kline pulled strings with Hopkins and arranged for our teachers to take Paul's courses free of charge.

He designed a program that covered such areas as "Reading Through the Content Areas" and "Language Arts Through the Grades." There were also courses on math. Several Barclay teachers earned their Masters degrees by taking these courses. At the same time, Gil—who was a reading specialist—was also working with the teachers. Later on, when we sought to improve upon the city's approach to instruction, we would find ourselves in a major war. But we met no resistance when we were working with Paul and Gil, because we didn't tell anyone what we were doing! We just treated it as our business within our school.

Even though the Barclay staff was generally strong, I did have to handle the problem of incompetent teachers. Some of these teachers just hadn't been taught properly. I could ask the assistant principal or a senior teacher to work with them, and they would try, grow, and become satisfactory teachers. Some I would put in other classes or move them to positions for which they were better suited, and they would start to perform better. But some teachers did not change. They were just there to pick up their paychecks. I would put them on a plan, and when they did not improve, I would have them removed from teaching. They would ask to be sent to another school, and I would say, "If they're not good enough for the children in this school, they're not good enough for children in any school."

One year, after I had been an administrator for awhile, I had seven teachers removed. They took me to the union, but I had the documentation and could show how we had tried to help them and how they had not responded. We always had to think of the children. Some children learn nothing in a whole year being in a class with a teacher who has no idea about how to teach.

Parents are usually quite aware when their children have poor teachers. When a parent would call me with a concern I always said, "Put it in a letter." Parents don't realize how much power they hold. I would often repeat that the power is in the pen. When they put down in black and white what a teacher is doing, or failing to do, that becomes part of the teacher's folder. Having letters from parents was very effective when I recommended the removal of a teacher.

When the Red Wagon parents brought their children to Barclay, in 1975, Baltimore City provided only half-day kindergarten classes. The Red Wagon children had been in an all-day program that was much more advanced than any public school program. When they were tested we knew they needed an all-day kindergarten. In addition, we observed that many students in our prekindergarten had become so socialized and learned so much that they too were ready for more than another half-day program. I met with our kindergarten teachers, Rita Cooper and Jan French, who said that it was impossible for the children to do any real work in the half-day schedule. We also talked with parents. Then we worked out an all day schedule for the fast-moving children. Soon we realized that the slower moving children would also benefit from an all-day program.

To avoid problems with the school system, we said that the children who were enrolled in the morning session could stay late, and the children in the afternoon session could come early. The teachers kept separate roll books for morning and afternoon sessions, and we made the budget adjustments so that we did not need extra funding.

Eventually we presented our case for an all-day kindergarten to the school board. There were some frowns, but we showed what the children could accomplish, and we got it over. We received board approval. That was very important in later years. Other schools that added all-day kindergartens later lost them to budget cuts. We kept ours because it was board-approved.[33] However, our program never was fully funded. I had to look at the budget each year and see where I could find money to sustain the all-day kindergarten classes. One year I gave up my assistant principal; another year I did without the parent liaison position. I sometimes transferred the money from the supplies budget. We lived with these cuts, because we were certain that having a full day of school for the kindergartners was extremely important.

The critics who complain that five-year olds should just be left alone to play, and shouldn't be pushed to learn, are mistaken. That's how we lose children. Even in pre-K, children come wanting to learn. In pre-K they need socialization activities, and they should be learning how to focus on sights and sounds in their environment, using all their senses, beginning to put things into categories. When they reach kindergarten they are ready and eager to work with letters and numbers; many are ready to read; some come already reading.

Watch five-year olds: they want to start putting things together. If we reward their curiosity by teaching them, getting them ready for first-grade, they will become good learners. If we just let them play, we are holding them back. In a good kindergarten program children do have time to play and a period to rest. But they also have a chance to learn, to get the foundation that will help them succeed, not just in school, but in life.

After-school care for the children of working parents was another project we began in the 1980s. Before national attention was called to "Latchkey children," Barclay's working parents could enroll their children in a program that began at the end of school and closed at 5:30 p.m. We served snacks, helped with homework, and had supervised games. We started by having student teachers from local colleges oversee the program. Later, members of the school staff ran it. Sometimes volunteers from local colleges or community groups worked with us. It was no-frills and affordable. We charged two dollars per child per week. Over the years we raised the fee slightly. By the time I retired, parents were paying five dollars. From this money we bought the snacks and paid small stipends to the staff.

Planning and carrying out curriculum changes and new programs required teamwork by the teachers and between them and the parents. Finding times to get together when we could be productive became a challenge. According to the city plan, Mondays and Fridays were set aside for staff meetings. Those are the two worst days in the week. Getting started after the weekend is always hard, and everyone is exhausted by Friday. The meetings were scheduled after school, which meant going home in the dark during the winter. Teachers hated it, and I did too. So we talked about making a "rescheduled week" where we could have one shortened instructional day in which teachers could have time to meet together and plan and coordinate with one another. On this day parents could come in and meet teachers to talk about their own children or PTO matters.

We figured out that by shortening lunch periods each day by 30 minutes, starting the school day 15 minutes early, and extending the school day by 15 minutes, we would not only meet but go beyond the required number of hours per week of instruction. At the same time, we could end the instructional day at noon on Wednesdays and use those afternoons for our meetings. Students in the after-school program would go there at noon. The teachers' union said the plan was acceptable if Barclay teachers voted it in, which they did. We also called a parent meeting to explain the rescheduled week, and the vast majority of parents signed off on it.

When word got around about what we were doing at Barclay, other schools adopted the rescheduled week. For a brief time the whole school system used it. But then teachers were spotted in stores and different places on Wednesday afternoons, and the rescheduled week was outlawed. Not everyone had been serious about using that time for the betterment of the school and the children. We petitioned to keep it, and promised that Barclay teachers would not be shopping at Sears on Wednesdays.

On most issues we had open discussion, and everyone was free to speak his or her mind. But once we had reached a decision, then I enforced it. After all except two members of the staff had agreed on the rescheduled week, I announced to them, "I will not excuse you on a Wednesday. You will have to be deathly ill or dying to be out on a Wednesday. Don't tell me that you have a doctor's appointment on a Wednesday, because I am going to stand beside you while you call and tell him or her you can't take it. Otherwise, you're going to blow it for everyone." So the Barclay staff did not abuse Wednesdays. For the duration of my time as principal, Barclay ran on the rescheduled week. Sometimes we had to put up a fight to keep it, but with parents and staff behind it we always won.

Barclay teamwork got behind "summer packets" when I brought that idea back from a meeting I had attended in St. Mary's County. The packets included one activity a day for children and their families to do during the summer. It was a great way to help the children be mindful of what they had learned during the year. Whether they were on trips or at home, they'd have the packet to help them keep up their skills.

Every teacher sent down materials for their classes, and then a few staff and parent volunteers typed, duplicated, and organized them into packets for each grade. We thought it would be very easy to do, but putting together the first packets was a very big job that boiled down to a few us who stayed up late at night and worked on Saturdays until we got them together. After the first time, we had a model to follow, and we sent home summer packets for many years.

By the mid-1970s the majority of Barclay students was black, yet the school still had a diverse population, including white children and children from a number of other nations. The international students usually had parents who were doing postgraduate work or were teaching at the Johns Hopkins Homewood campus. Because we were one of the few integrated schools, with a really integrated staff. Roland Patterson's desegregation plans in 1973, that turned so many people against him, didn't affect us very much.[34] But they did affect our students' junior high school assignments. That became a total disaster. Most of our children used to go from Barclay's sixth grade to Woodbourne Junior High (now it's called Chinquipin Middle School). The gifted and talented students went to Roland Park Junior High. In either case they rode one bus straight to the school. The few children who came to Barclay from the Hampden area could walk to Robert Poole in their neighborhood. When desegregation started, nearly *all* Barclay students were assigned to Robert Poole. Now all but the Hampden residents had to take three city buses, since school buses were not available.

Why did the school system think they could put a group of children who were mostly black into a school in that all-white area without even meeting with the residents? They would not have tried that with the well-off residents of Roland Park. They wouldn't have tried it with Barclay. They would have met with the community. But they assumed with Hampden that "here's a group of people that we can tell what to do." And they tried to force them to accept our students.[35]

The first day that our children went to Robert Poole, I looked up in the afternoon shortly after dismissal time and the Barclay lobby was packed. The kids had run all the way from there back to us. They had not waited to catch a bus, because they had been threatened and some of them had been beaten by Hampden residents. It wasn't the children doing the beating; it was the parents. When I called to report the problem to the regional office, the phones there were blocked. They knew what had happened. The next week one of the children ended up with a broken jaw. A parent went right into the classroom and broke his jaw.[36]

At this time I was appointed by Mayor Schaefer to a race relations task force in Hampden. He came to the first meeting and talked about the situations that he wanted us to improve, including the school situation. He wanted peace between the schools and among the children. We met several times with another group made up of Hampden leaders and parents from Barclay and from Margaret Brent, whose students were also assigned to Poole. They tried to make Robert Poole safer. They had a bus turn-around put in right by the front door, so the children would not have to go out to the street. And they tried various conflict-resolution strategies. But the situation never really settled. I think it was beyond our control.

The white male principal at Robert Poole in the mid-1970s, Herbert Fendeisen, seemed to detach himself from the problem. He was in the office at Barclay one day when I said to him, "You know what happens when our children come to your school." He said, "Yeah, they beat the hell out of them. Not only the black ones, the white, too." He said this in front of the Barclay secretary, Esther Jeffries, and she could not believe that this was a principal talking in these kinds of braggadocios terms about what his kids were going to do. It was obvious he wasn't going to do anything about it.[37]

After a couple of years of this, and of seeing the parents of fifth graders lie about their addresses or even move away, we said, "we have to get our children out of Robert Poole," and we decided to create a middle school. Beginning around 1980 the school board voted to change junior high schools (grades seven through nine) into middle schools (grades six through eight).[38] So we made our plans with a middle school in mind. We talked to our city council representative, Mary Pat Clarke. She suggested a new school that would draw from five elementary schools in our area—Barclay, Margaret Brent, Abbottston, Coldstream Park, and Montebello.

We had recently worked with these schools when the school board tried to close Abbottston. Children from there would have been sent to the other schools, causing overcrowding and other problems. The five schools set up "The Open Schools Committee," circulated petitions, marched on the Department of Education, and protested until the board backed down and kept Abbottston open. Now the Open Schools group began a middle-school campaign.[39]

Our plan was for a "lower school" to be set up at City College High School. City College had been all-male until the 1960s. After it was renovated and reorganized as a coed school, with a huge expenditure of tax dollars, it remained half-empty.[40] We thought locating a lower school that would draw from our students would be perfect. But the alumni of the school, including Mayor Schaefer, and the principal and many others disagreed. The Open Schools Committee fought hard and long. We filled the school board meetings in droves. But we lost.[41]

The Barclay PTO then sent a delegation to meet with John Crew. The steering committee selected Harwood parents, Darice Claude and Sharon Scott as well as Jo Ann Robinson to speak for Barclay. They presented a plan to pilot a seventh grade at our school in September 1982 and an eighth grade the next fall. The school system could then evaluate our program and decide if we could continue. Dr. Crew agreed.[42]

Barclay had an official capacity to hold around 700 children. This was larger than the total population of our elementary grades, so we had classroom space for a middle school. We also negotiated with the director of the adjoining recreation center to use space there for such classes as music, art, and study hall. Our plan was to move the current sixth graders into the seventh grade, without bringing in new students and to just add one class at a time.

Parents from nearby elementary schools, who also wanted to avoid Robert Poole, pushed to have their children come to Barclay's middle school. Eventually Charles Hancock, who was the assistant superintendent in charge of middle schools, signed an official agreement that grades seven and eight at Barclay would serve only the students already enrolled there. If space became available due to transfers and families moving away, I had the discretionary authority to take in students from outside.

Dr. Crew had stipulated, and the school board had agreed, that our budget would cover the salaries of a full complement of middle-school faculty. We hired new teachers who were trained for middle school but also had experience at the elementary level, and some of our elementary teachers moved up because they also had the middle-school certification. My certification as a principal extended through the middle and secondary grades, but I had a lot to learn, and the staff and I worked diligently to master middle-school philosophy, curriculum, and methodology. Our students did not have the campus that students had in schools that were converted from junior highs. But we worked with the new teachers who helped us set up a science lab and get other materials for the new grades.

To create electives for the students I asked every staff member to write down a second vocation, something they were good at and could teach the children. Evelyn Wallace, Sarah Bazemore, and Margaret Shanklin, three educational assistants, dealt with home economics. The middle-school teachers took on extra projects. Art Nilsen taught shop. Loretta Thornton agreed to teach typing. Cynthia Bossard held art classes. The teachers also set up coach classes. The Homewood Friends helped us acquire typewriters and a sewing machine. In this way we built from within to meet all the requirements of a middle school.

At the end of our second year we began pressing for the evaluation that we had agreed to with Dr. Crew. By then he had retired and Alice Pinderhughes was the superintendent. Some members of her staff and some members of the school board were opposed to a pre-K–eight program at Barclay. I don't know whether they blocked us because we were this bothersome group that had been there before, had asked for other things and now we were knocking at the door again; or whether it was ignorance on their part of how beneficial it could be for the students. Someone suggested to me that it was because we started it. If it had started at the central office it would have been fine. But having to battle just to be evaluated was horrible.

In March 1985 Superintendent Alice Pinderhughes and several members of her staff and three school board commissioners came to Barclay. They observed the middle-school classes at work and heard presentations from parents and staff highlighting the strengths and success of the program. They told us that the school board would decide the program's fate very soon. One morning in April School Commissioner Robert Walker came to see me. A board meeting was scheduled for that night, and he told me that they were going to vote "yes" on a permanent middle school at Barclay. He said I could tell the parents, but that we shouldn't announce it otherwise. I let the parents know, and a large crowd of us went to the board meeting that night, all wearing our Barclay tee-shirts, expecting to celebrate. Instead the superintendent recommended that our middle school be extended for only one more year. The board did not vote. Walker was very upset. He got up and left right away.

I was ready to kill Alice Pinderhughes. I'd never been so angry! At the end of the meeting I rushed up on the stage. (The Board meetings were then held in the auditorium of Coldstream Elementary School.) The parents were right behind me.

Alice was standing there trying to grin. She knew that she had sold us out. I guess I carried on very badly, because she said, "I want my chauffeur to take you home." I would no more have gotten in her chauffeur's car! I wanted to hurt her, I really did. I mean physically. After all we had gone through, this was the final straw. If I had been two feet taller, even one foot, I would have struck her, right there on the stage.

The system had me on its "crazy" list, because I would blurt out what I felt like blurting out when they didn't want to hear it. But actually, my temper tantrums were of two kinds—some were real and some were contrived. There are times when I would act out just to let the people know that I was really super mad. And that usually worked. They would back off, or they would reconsider. But with the real tantrums, when I had just had it, it was hard to control myself. That night, with Alice Pinderhughes, I had a real tantrum.

A few days later a group of us made an appointment and went to Alice's office to talk further about the middle school. We were sent to a meeting room, and while we were sitting there we kept hearing a pounding noise. I finally got up and investigated. Alice had accidentally pulled the knob off the door to the ladies' room, and was locked in. The parents suggested that we leave her there and slide our demands under the door and only let her out after she signed off on our middle school. But I went and told someone, and they got the door opened. What a day!

We battled for almost another year before the board finally granted permanent status to the Barclay Middle School. Their resistance to our requests really didn't make sense. They knew how hard we had tried, through the Open Schools Committee to get a lower school at City College for our children. They knew our children were being really roughed up and beaten up at Robert Poole. But they wouldn't change. Still, it was worth the struggle. Our children were finally able to go to school in peace. Keeping the middle-school students at Barclay was a fantastic idea.[43]

When the school system changed "elementary" from grades K through six to K through five and substituted middle schools beginning at sixth grade for the old junior highs that had previously started at seventh grade, they didn't set up real middle schools. They were just renamed junior highs, and the sixth graders who were sent to them weren't ready. They got lost in the crowd. Many of the teachers were not trained to work with the younger sixth graders. In our pre-K through eight set-up the children knew all the adults in the building and the adults all knew them. They never had to prove who they were. They could still walk to school. Their parents were still close by.

Recently, when Carmen Russo was superintendent, she announced a plan to establish more K–eight schools. Nothing has ever been said, however, about training the principals and teachers and involving the parents and community. Without that preparation the plan could be a disaster. The system cannot improve middle schools by just tacking them on to elementary schools; that will make both schools weak. If they send large numbers of older children into elementary schools without adequate training, preparation, and community involvement, Lord help the elementary students.

We operated as a community—parents, staff, and students accountable to each other. And the school was small enough that, if a problem developed, I could get the whole middle school into the auditorium and say, "This is happening; what are we going to do about it?" We created a school culture in which the middle-school students looked out for the elementary students. Since Barclay was departmentalized in all the grades our middle-school students had an additional advantage. They had already learned how to be accountable for the work of several teachers. They went on through eighth grade, got their work, and then they were ready for senior high school.[44]

Barclay students have done extremely well in senior high. While many schools send only a small percentage of their students to the city-wide schools, some years Barclay has sent as many as 81 percent of its eighth grade class to those schools.[45] And they do well when they get there and go on to successful adult lives. Barclay alumni include numerous college students and college graduates, a Rhodes Scholar, the first woman to coach a male high school basketball team in Baltimore, teachers, professors, a geologist, authors, several individuals active in various aspects of the arts, social workers and others involved in humanitarian work not only in this country but also abroad.

From the time The Red Wagon parents had arrived until we got our middle school, we had accomplished a lot. It was a very exciting time, and we gained a reputation as pioneers. Just recently I ran into a principal who said to me, "Now don't you feel good? A lot of the things that you and your parents had to fight for, the system is trying to put in practice now." And I said, "Not really. Because the system's leaders really don't know what they're doing. They don't take time to study and plan and involve everyone." She said, "Well, that's never going to happen."

It is also disappointing that many of the problems we faced 20 years ago are the *same* problems public schools have today. In the 1980s Mayor Schaefer at least looked into our complaints. When we caused enough of an itch he would try to find out what the trouble was. When school opened in the fall of 1983 he sent members of his cabinet to all the schools, ordering them to report back to him on what they found. The acting secretary of transportation, David Chapin, came to Barclay. We received a copy of his report to the mayor. He said that Barclay was "physically in good condition," the school was well-run, the children were cheerful, we had a "dedicated staff," and a strong, concerned parent group. Then he listed the problems: the budget for materials, supplies, and equipment was too low. Class sizes were "in the target range" but still too large. Enrollment projections came in too late and were too low, so the school was understaffed. Hiring was done too late. "We heard of one teacher who was not told where she would be assigned until two days before school opened," Chapin wrote. He also said that sometimes teachers weren't assigned until after the opening of school. He had asked me for a statement to be sent to the mayor. I said, "Generally the school's doing a good job. There's a greater need for the involvement of principals and teachers in various issues. Those in the trenches need to know what's going on and have a voice. And we must better publicize the good points of the school system."[46]

Almost 20 years later things are the same. In fact, some things have deteriorated. That year was the first time I had gotten a teacher just two days before school opened. Now schools receive teachers in October. When Schaefer was mayor his appointees in the school system and on the school board at least answered calls and letters and would meet with principals, teachers, parents. As time went on the top school authorities talked more and more about our accountability and became less and less accessible and accountable to us. Instead of listening to our problems they ignored what we said. This meant that our battles in the late 1980s and the 1990s would be much harder than those we had waged before.

EIGHT

Principal at Barclay, Part Three: "We Did Not Want a Poor Man's Curriculum"

As the media kept "the crisis in education" in the forefront of public consciousness throughout the 1970s, Gertrude and the steering committee were growing increasingly concerned about the decline in the performance of Barclay students, particularly in the areas of reading and writing. Gertrude blamed the school system's practice of imposing one educational fad after another on teachers and students rather than providing a consistent and cohesive program of instruction. As she later observed with some hyperbole: "We were a system that adopted gimmicks year after year after year to a point that our children did not get any basic skills."[1]

Political and social pressures and chronic under-funding were two chief causes of this herky-jerky approach to curriculum and instruction. As changes initiated by the political and cultural revolutions of the 1960s percolated through the rest of the twentieth century, public education became a battle ground on which multiple and conflicting interest groups clamored for a chance to influence what and how the nation's children would learn. Each group put forward its own specific proposals for change. Organizations such as the National Science Foundation and the National Science Teachers Association pressed for new approaches to teaching science and math. The Rockefeller Foundation and the National Endowment for the Arts supported proposals for more and better instruction in the arts and humanities. The Association of Supervision and Curriculum Development promoted a "world core curriculum" to further the cause of world peace. Author E.D. Hirsch proselytized for "cultural literacy" while historians established the Bradley Commission issuing guidelines for revamping history instruction.[2]

From the arena of business and industry came groups such as the National Committee on Skills of the American Work Force, which advocated preparation in workplace skills for children who were not college-bound. Drug education, character education, citizenship education—all had their lobbyists. When questions were raised about where to target limited funds, "children at risk," children in the "early childhood" years, "gifted children"—every group had its defenders, ready with the rationale for why the students in their category required immediate and special attention. These rationales included instilling in the rising generation a sense of social justice, fostering habits of good citizenship, preparing students for the technological challenges of the future, training a workforce that would be competitive with the labor forces of other nations, nurturing the scientists and other specialists by whose insights and discoveries, the United States would remain first in all ideological, economic, and military contests among the nations of the world.[3]

Further complicating the process of curriculum reform was the matter of determining the effectiveness of any one initiative.[4] At the same time, controversies swirled among educators over methods and standards of teacher training, the content, format and validation of testing, rival traditions and philosophies of the teaching of reading and writing, and the politics and pedagogy of instructional reforms intended to eliminate sexism and racism from the curriculum. From among the welter of findings, warnings, and demands that all the interest groups generated, those who wielded influence over and within local school districts determined what instructional emphases would be followed in their respective bailiwicks. Federal, state, and local governments could shape local curriculum by tying funds to mandates, and establishing state or national standards and tests such as the Maryland School Performance Assessment Program (MSPAP) that Gertrude discusses in this chapter, and the federal No Child Left Behind Act implemented in George W. Bush's administration.

When political winds shifted, so did federal and state programs. Superintendents brought their own instructional and curricular predilections to bear on the districts that they led, and likewise, as they came and went so did the projects that they initiated. By spotlighting a particular commission's report or persuasive educator-personality, the media could encourage school and political leaders to make certain changes. Similarly, when media portrayed an instructional program negatively, they might contribute to the demise of that program.

No matter their quality or effectiveness, the instructional materials needed to implement a given curriculum for tens of thousands of children were costly, as were the expenditures for training the principals and teachers who had to deliver that curriculum to the classroom. As strapped for funds as the Baltimore City public schools always were, the prognosis of even the most highly touted instructional reform was never optimistic. Often the money ran out before the texts, supplies, and training ever reached all the schools. Seldom were funds available when the time came to replace and update the original materials.

Reform from the top rarely connected with the realities faced by principals and teachers every day in their separate schools. Whether the source of the latest reform was a superintendent striving to leave his or her mark on the system's history, or a state or federal government program embodying some version of political idealism, or an academic guru claiming special wisdom and expertise, the fix was almost always too generic. This dilemma fueled demands for yet another reform—"school-based management" (sbm), generally defined as a shift of decision-making authority and responsibility from central office administration to principals and teachers at their respective school sites. In the most extensive version of sbm principals would, within parameters set by the school district, hire their own instructional and support staff, manage their own budgets, and work with faculty to develop a curriculum tailored to the needs of their student body. During the 1980s, Baltimore school officials made halfhearted attempts to initiate sbm in local schools; these efforts had little impact.[5]

In Baltimore, this piecemeal history of reform decimated the coherent city curriculum that had guided Gertrude when she was a teacher in the 1950s. Her colleague, Stanley Curtain—who was vice principal for one of the years that she was counselor at Mordecai Gist, and who went on to become principal of Calloway Elementary School for 18 years—echoed her frustration at how by the 1970s the city school system could no longer "seem to get a handle on curriculum. There was a new text book and a new program every year," he complained.[6]

Bureaucratic reform by mandate made it very difficult to sustain the collegial sharing and planning of the sort that Gertrude eked out for her staff in the rescheduled week, the kind of calibrating of instruction that they undertook through non-gradedness and departmentalization, and the school-community vision and long-term goals that evolved through the steering committee and priorities meetings. Then, in 1983, through a contact she made when Mayor Schaefer appointed her to the board of the fund for Educational Excellence, the Barclay principal became acquainted with the Calvert School. A colleague at the fund, Muriel Berkeley, had children at Calvert and facilitated Gertrude's first visit there. Calvert was a private institution steeped in tradition and offering, in the words of Johns Hopkins University researchers, "a highly structured curricular and instructional program." The antithesis of the always-changing public school system, Calvert promulgated methods and materials that the school's founder and first headmaster, Virgil Hillyer, had instituted in 1899. He insisted on teaching children to read and write before they learned the alphabet; drilled students in phonics; avoided textbooks; and emphasized "classic" children's literature.

Hillyer developed distinctive learning tools, including "the Calvert script," a special and elegant version of cursive writing that children learned in the first grade; a multiplication chart that could be "read in several directions"; and his gracefully composed *A Child's History of the World*. Early in the school's history a rule was established that students must correct their work until it was error free.[7]

The Calvert School admitted students on the basis of their scholastic promise, as determined by the school's own "measures of academic readiness and ability" and their parents' ability to pay the tuition that, by the late 1980s, would reach $8,550 per year. The Calvert student body was therefore comprised almost entirely of the very bright offspring of wealthy families. Since the early 1900s, Calvert had also offered a "home instruction" program. Among its clientele were "children of missionaries, corporate executives stationed abroad, parents in the diplomatic service, children of circus and other acting troupes in transit, children living far from schools and invalid children."[8]

Gertrude had no trouble envisioning Calvert methods and materials in the hands of Barclay teachers and their students and easily persuaded faculty and parents on the school steering committee that a Barclay–Calvert partnership was worth exploring. The allure of such a partnership lay in the "tried and true" nature of an approach that consistently and effectively had been educating children of Baltimore's elite for the better part of a century.

Although school board minutes indicate that curriculum revision in all subject areas had occurred in the Baltimore City schools in the early 1980s, in 1988 the only curriculum guide that Alice Pinderhughes came up with in response to a request from the Barclay Parent–Teacher Organization (PTO) was dated 1973, and finding the books and materials that the curriculum assumed teachers would have proved impossible. By contrast, the Calvert publishing department efficiently supplied every teacher at its North Baltimore facility and every homeschooling family around the world with a curriculum, teaching guides, student workbooks, and all other instructional materials. While the Baltimore public schools were, according to their public relations announcements, hoping one day to "review, revise and reorganize the entire written curriculum pre-K through 12" and to "convey clearly and directly what we believe to be . . . the content, concepts and skills which every child needs to learn . . . ," Calvert School educators and their pupils were confidently following the curriculum that Virgil Hillyer had clearly and directly laid out nearly a hundred years before.

However strongly the private curriculum appealed to her, when Gertrude made her first acquaintance with Calvert School and its headmaster, William Kirk, in the early 1980s, consideration then of a possible private–public partnership was relatively brief and entirely theoretical. Missing from the conversation was the crucial element of a source of money to fund such a partnership. When she revisited the idea in 1988, the president of the second wealthiest philanthropic foundation in Maryland, Robert Embry, who headed the Abell Foundation and also served on the Fund for Educational Excellence with Gertrude, expressed a strong interest in providing that missing element. Embry, an advocate for Baltimore City with a special passion for supporting and strengthening the city's public schools, was on the lookout for creative education projects.[9]

With a likely funding source, a Calvert headmaster willing to work with her— Merrill Hall, William Kirk's successor—the backing of the steering committee, and, once they had visited Calvert, the willingness of Barclay faculty to partner with the private school, Gertrude believed that she had an educational proposition that the authorities of the city school system could not possibly turn down. It would cost the city no money. If students at Barclay flourished with the Calvert curriculum, as she anticipated they would, the Barclay–Calvert project could serve as a prototype for similar projects across Baltimore, and perhaps even beyond the city limits.

In the early spring of 1988, Gertrude and Merrill Hall drafted a formal proposal to phase in Calvert materials and methods at Barclay, beginning with kindergarten and first grade, adding a grade each year for four years. As the first step in seeking school system approval, she submitted the proposal to her district director, Clifton Ball. Excited by the prospect and buoyed by optimism, she anticipated authorization from the city that same spring, looked toward teacher training in the summer, and expected the first Barclay–Calvert classes to begin that fall. As her narrative vividly demonstrates, within weeks the wave of optimism on which she was riding crashed against a bulwark of opposition.

A concatenation of forces created that bulwark, chief among them: the timing of the proposal; suspicion of Bob Embry's motives for supporting the Barclay–Calvert program; the opposition of the newly appointed superintendent, Richard Hunter; Mayor Kurt Schmoke's initial support for Hunter; system-wide resentment of what was perceived to be Barclay's already privileged position; and ultimately a framing of the curriculum issue in racial terms.

In the summer of 1988, when Gertrude and Merrill Hall envisioned their proposal sailing through the school system bureaucracy, the head of that system, Alice Pinderhughes, was on her way out, Mayor Schmoke having requested her resignation. The proposal thus fell prey to the indifference of the lame-duck Pinderhughes administration and the anxieties of an insecure new superintendent, Richard Hunter, who was uncertain of just whom in the city he could trust.[10] It is likely that Hunter and his advisers were quickly warned not to trust the Abell Foundation's Bob Embry. A former president of the City Board of School Commissioners and a close ally of former mayor and now Governor Schaefer,[11] Embry had briefly entertained mayoral ambitions in 1986 but withdrew from the Democratic primary election campaign when polls showed that he could not win. Known for his high energy and penchant for innovative problem-solving, he assumed the presidency of the foundation in 1987 with the expectation that it would "become an agent of change," addressing "problems of public education, human services and community development."[12]

Some within the school system, including Pinderhughes, believed that Embry had designs on the superintendency and interpreted the education projects to which he funneled Abell money as another way that he was trying to run the schools. According to *Sun* reporter Will Englund, Richard Hunter quickly adopted the view that "he needed to show he would not take orders from Mr. Embry." Thus, the possibility of Abell funding that made the Barclay–Calvert proposal viable was also a red flag that provoked opposition.[13]

Mayoral backing of the new superintendent solidified that opposition. By some accounts Hunter arrived in Baltimore with "a constituency of one: Kurt L Schmoke."

In a 1992 interview, Meldon Hollis, who had been appointed school board president by Schmoke, acknowledged that Hunter was not the first choice of the majority of school commissioners. In fact, on their first vote, eight of the nine-member board rejected him. As a good friend of Schmoke, Hollis knew that the mayor wanted Hunter. After some persuasive lobbying the board president was able to satisfy the mayor's wishes.[14]

Schmoke's own recollections stressed the politics of the superintendent's selection. He agreed that the school board initially wanted another candidate, but with only one appointee of his own on the board, the mayor was "skeptical about [the others'] motives."[15] His interview with the board's choice had not gone well; he and that candidate "just didn't connect." In contrast, when he interviewed Hunter he found a person who said that he was ready to go forward with all of the objectives that Schmoke had set out—decentralization, establishing site-based management, and empowering principals.[16]

With his personal imprimatur thus stamped on the new superintendent, Schmoke could be expected to back him in all of his early decisions, and that is exactly what the mayor did. When Barclay advocates tried to force the issue of the Calvert proposal with Hunter, they ran into rejection by not only the school bureaucracy but also the office of the mayor and his political allies, including several influential members of the City Council.[17] The mayor's position held firm from mid-1988 to mid-1989, when Schmoke began to meet with Gertrude. Although during the school year of 1989–1990, he privately pressed Hunter to let Barclay try the Calvert curriculum, the proposal and everyone associated with it hung in limbo.[18]

Finally, the outspokenness of Barclay parents and principal on such issues as funding, senior teachers, and especially, the middle school now redounded unfavorably upon them. Gertrude was known as a principal who insisted on having her way and who had "elite" parents and friends always backing her up. The pro-Barclay editorial stance of the local white-run media only reinforced the resentment of some school system leaders and employees against the school and its principal. Few central administrators—not to mention her fellow principals—were likely to appreciate such media assertions as "Barclay School is a rare gem in the vast wasteland of Baltimore City public schools."[19]

While School #54 was the educational center of the universe for the Barclay community, Richard Hunter's universe of responsibilities was far more extensive. He described the challenges that confronted him when he arrived in Baltimore: 109,000 students in 180 facilities, 35 percent of whom were "performing below grade level in math and reading," and, he declared, "I have accepted the challenge of breaking down the wall that stands between the students and their successes."[20]

From the outset of his administration Hunter stressed his belief that any reform effort should benefit the entire student population and that the superintendent should maintain tight control over the reform process. He initiated "The Nights the Lights Went On," two rounds of community gatherings in all schools across the district in which citizens were invited to identify their priorities for school improvement. "There is no way Baltimoreans, rallied in such a short time with such an inadequate campaign, were going to express common educational goals for their children," commented Mike Bowler. Nonetheless, drawing on impressionistic data compiled from the "Night" meetings, Hunter and his staff developed a five-year improvement plan, *Operation Turnaround*, which he then presented as his public mandate for his decisions. In rejecting the Barclay–Calvert proposal as well as initiatives for change from other sources, Hunter argued that "15,000 parents, teachers, and citizens . . . who spoke their minds [in the Night the Lights Went On meetings] want a more unified school system that will benefit all students."

A wide lacuna separated Hunter's assumptions from those that guided the Barclay community, whose spokesmen insisted that parents could not participate meaningfully in setting system-wide priorities without taking into account the needs of their own individual schools and that the professional educators at the school level should take the lead in determining how best to address those needs.[21] In practical terms the clash of views between the superintendent and advocates for Barclay were summed up when Hunter told a delegation of parents and staff from School #54 that "a school which wants to reduce class sizes and utilizes resources [not available to other schools] creates an exceptionally divisive situation."[22]

Freeing up funds and improving the efficiency of the school system bureaucracy were other goals set by Hunter. In pursuit of them he undertook a personnel reorganization that between 1988 and 1991 eliminated 159 full-time central office positions, reportedly saving four million dollars. In retrospect, he described such downsizing as an example of the "politically dangerous positions" that urban super-intendents were often forced by mayors and school boards to assume. Erasing jobs from the bureaucracy, he observed in a 1997 essay for the journal, *Education and Urban Society*, "alienates the Superintendent from the staff he or she is expected to lead [and] . . . costs him the support of the administrators on whose cooperation he must rely."

Thus it appears that—as happened also with Roland Patterson—not only was the superintendent distrustful in his dealings with such community leaders as Robert Embry, he also felt insecure among his own staff. According to Samuel Banks—who oversaw the teaching of social studies and who in his many years of service to the city schools had seen several superintendents come and go—Hunter also undercut himself by remaining aloof and communicating poorly. "How are you going to get the staff to rally around you, when they haven't been able to get to know you?" asked Banks.[23]

Though the Barclay community was not alone in its frustration with the super-intendent, Gertrude and her allies were singular in their refusal to cut the new school chief any slack. Media pundits, public officials, the school board, and the citizenry at large might have been willing to give Hunter time to acclimate. But with him stand-ing between Barclay and a quarter of a million dollar partnership with a school whose curriculum promised nearly everything that Gertrude had ever dreamed of having for her teachers and students, she saw no reason for patience and did not restrain parents and Barclay friends as they dogged Hunter with letters, petitions, and public protests to allow the Barclay–Calvert program to go forward. Given that Hunter responded to being pressured by becoming stubborn, Barclay's frontal attacks were not the best strategy for gaining his sympathy.

Moreover, the Barclay–Calvert curriculum crashed head-on into the racial politics of curriculum reform. Curriculum lay at the heart of the proposed partnership with Calvert, and curriculum by the last decades of the twentieth century was a volatile issue in many school districts with significantly large black student populations. The declarations of racial pride and celebration of African and African American history that both supported and were augmented by the civil rights and Black Power Movements in the 1960s and 1970s fueled aggressive and impassioned demands by some black parents and educators that schools teach their children about their history and culture.

In Baltimore in the 1970s, high school history teacher, Samuel Banks, had spearheaded a revision of the public schools' social studies curriculum and obtained the position of director of social studies for the school system. He adopted the "multicultural" outlook that was then in the ascendancy among academics who sought to enrich Americans' understanding of their national past by writing and teaching about the whole spectrum of races, cultures, genders, and classes that make up the United States. Bank's curriculum included the history and culture of various ethnic groups, along with substantial treatment of African American history. However, a perception persisted in the black community that the schools were continuing to slight their heritage. Banks maintained that the system's failure to properly train teachers and monitor their use of the curriculum, and not the curriculum itself, was at fault.[24]

By the 1980s, "Afrocentrism"—an ideological attack on the widespread impression that Africans and people of African descent contributed nothing significant to human history—began to eclipse the pluralistic concept of "multiculturalism," which had dominated the social studies curriculum in Baltimore schools. With modern paleontology and archeology on their side, Afrocentrists celebrated the African continent as the birthplace of humankind and pointed to highly advanced ancient African civilizations that "Eurocentric" historians had systematically denigrated or ignored. The narrative constructed by these Afrocentric thinkers provoked disagreement and alarm among establishment scholars, both black and white. Critics warned that in seeking to correct one set of falsehoods and distortions, Afrocentrists were manufacturing yet another flawed and flimsy version of the past that privileged African culture to the point of disregarding the cultural convergences and interactions of peoples that are crucial to understanding the human experience.[25]

These controversies notwithstanding, in many cities across the country, including Portland, Pittsburgh, Washington, DC, and Milwaukee, black parents and teachers were rising up to demand Afrocentric curricula for their children.

Baltimore was no exception. A coalition of black citizens, led by East Baltimore community activist, Hilton Bostic, launched a campaign in the spring of 1990 to bring Afrocentrism to the city public schools. Bostic was convinced that European-based education "has served to even more effectively handicap the intellectual development of African American children than did the earlier system of segregated education."[26]

In response, in the fall of 1990 the school board approved a proposal from Hunter to create a 21-member task force on Afrocentrism.[27] Task force deliberations paralleled deteriorating relations between Hunter and Mayor Schmoke, so about the time that the task force was ready to present its recommendations Hunter was making plans to relocate. Reviewing the recommendations and leading a comprehensive revision of the city curriculum fell to his successor, Walter Amprey. The task was completed three years later, in the fall of 1993.[28]

Afrocentricity emerged as one aspect of the new curriculum but did not pervade it to the extent envisioned by its leading supporters. Nonetheless, Afrocentrism as an ideology had stirred deep feelings among black and white Baltimoreans, as it had among Americans throughout the country. Observers noted the current of anger running through Afrocentrists' attacks on Western civilization. One of the tenets of those attacks was that the Europe-centered version of history was tied up part and parcel with whites' rationalizing of slavery and denying political and social rights to the slaves' descendents. Afrocentrism was also, as Samuel Banks observed, "a bid for intellectual empowerment."[29]

It would be hard to conceive of a socio–political–intellectual climate more alien to the assumptions and content of the Barclay–Calvert proposal than the one shaped by Afrocentric ideas and beliefs. The demographics of Calvert School and the traditional structure of the Calvert curriculum would have inevitably set off alarms among Afrocentric blacks. That children descended from Africa could be nurtured by the same literature and mythology, and history that had nurtured generations of white children and that they could be inspired to excel by the same pedagogy must have been unthinkable for individuals and groups steeped in Afrocentrism.

For her part, Gertrude was generally well versed regarding Afrocentric thought. When she visited her niece and nephew, Joan and Harley Spry, in Philadelphia she accompanied them to the Afrocentric study group to which they belonged and in which one of the foremost proponents of Afrocentric thought, Molefi Asante, was influential. She and the Sprys also attended lectures by Asante at Temple University and had counted him among their guests at a barbeque at their Mount Airy home. After her retirement, Gertrude would travel to Ghana in a group that Asante led. Nonetheless, she was not an adherent of Afrocentrism in the public schools. She preferred that the black community transmit the African heritage to its children in programs and schools apart from the public system. "I'm of the school that says 'Yes every child should know his heritage,'" she stated in our final taping and then added,

> but I don't think that the public schools should develop the history of any one race.
> I think we should celebrate all races. If we teach our children to read well and think
> critically they can learn whatever they need to learn. Give all children a quality edu-
> cation and they can fight for whatever they need.[30]

Woven into much of the discourse on Afrocentrism were implications that not
all dimensions of the human experience would be of value to poor black children and
a tacit denial that a universal culture exists to which all races and nationalities
contribute. Gertrude dismissed this thinking out of hand. She wanted her students to
be equally conversant with African folk traditions, Greek mythology and Italian
opera. She entertained no limits on what or how much knowledge they could master.

While Richard Hunter does not appear to have been an enthusiast of
Afrocentrism,[31] the stress that he placed on the elite clientele of Calvert and his depiction of its program as "a rich man's curriculum" resonated with those who were avidly
attuned to the black ideology. Hunter also charged that Calvert instructional materials were outdated, sexist, and racist—charges that Gertrude vehemently denied and
that she rebuts in her narrative by noting that the Calvert materials were regularly
updated.

While most Calvert materials did include multicultural elements, at the time
that Gertrude was fighting for the right to enter into the partnership with Calvert the
fourth grade history text , *A Child's History of the World*, written by the school's
founder, had not been revised since 1978. Someone examining it and, for that matter other publications such as the Calvert geography text, could have made a case that
they contained race and gender biases. Rather than denying that, advocates would
have done well to acknowledge that they would need to supplement some of the
Calvert materials while remaining focused on those elements of the curriculum that
made it most attractive: its elegant structure, its effective development of basic skills,
the high expectations inherent in all of its requirements.[32]

Also lending credence to Hunter's allegations was the fact that a number of
Barclay spokespersons were white, and that one of the school's staunchest sources
of support—the Charles Village Civic Association (CVCA)—was composed largely
of white and upwardly mobile professionals. Hunter and others transmuted their
involvement into a depiction of Barclay as a school run for and by elite whites, and
Gertrude as a pawn thereof. Those who played on this theme conveniently
overlooked the fact that Barclay was 94 percent black and that over 85 percent of its
students were eligible for the federal free lunch program. The "white elite" image
stuck, and Barclay became a textbook example of the sociological observation that

> For whites in black-led cities to assume a visible role in any education reform
> effort. . . . makes it more likely that the reform initiative will be framed in racial terms;
> such a framing of the issue increases the risk of polarization and sharp resistance.[33]

White journalist Tom Chalkley was one of the first commentators to call attention publicly to the racial divisiveness of the Barclay–Calvert debate. "Viewed simplistically," he wrote, "a black elite—the mayor, Hunter, most of the school board, and some elected officials—have taken stands against the Barclay–Calvert proposal, while a white elite—the *Sun*, the Abell Foundation, and the Calvert School—is identified with the supporters . . . it's . . . important for black supporters of Barclay School . . . to show their faces. The school can't afford to fall victim to a false stereotype."[34]

Among the energetic activists of Charles Village, such stereotyping made no sense. They looked on the neighborhood public school as a critical element in determining their quality of life—not to mention their property values. Even those whites who did not send their children to the public school (or who had no children to send) put a high premium on keeping strong leadership in the school and maintaining effective communication with that leadership and backing the leader when she turned to them for support. They could not understand how their involvement with the school could possibly take on the sinister implications that seemed so clear to some African Americans.

When Schmoke began to support Gertrude on the Calvert issue, R.B. Jones, editor of the black weekly, *The Baltimore Times*, editorialized that the conflict between the mayor and Hunter over Barclay–Calvert was a "battle for control of the Baltimore Public Schools," and depicted Schmoke as playing into the hands of the white power structure. Jones alleged that "the traditional power elites plan to treat the Blacks of Baltimore City the way whites treated Africans in Zimbabwe: Blacks hold political office while the whites retain economic control of the society."[35]

Such rhetoric rallied black support for Hunter while potentially undermining Gertrude's reputation in the black community. As her narrative makes clear, she recognized, resented, and resisted the attempt to label her as "less black" because she worked closely with whites.[36] This controversy that raged between 1988 and 1990 over the Barclay–Calvert proposal posed the most daunting challenges of her career.

* * *

Before the middle-school battle consumed so much of our time and energy, Barclay parents and staff had been looking for ways to improve the curriculum. Joanne Giza, who had two daughters at the school, raised the concern that children did not receive enough instruction in writing. Other parents pointed out gaps in the science curriculum. They were seeing parts of a much bigger problem that had been growing for a long time. We were losing consistency and no longer had the structure that once made the school system strong.

Remember how Mr. Simms took me to task for wanting to retain *one* student at Charles Carroll of Carrollton?[37] Then it was expected that someone in the line of people who were there to support me—the specialists, the supervisors, the assistant principal, and principal—would be able to help that student, and when I didn't seek their help I was at fault, and Mr. Simms held me accountable. By the 1980s that support system no longer existed, and neither did the accountability. There were fewer specialists and supervisors, and they were not always well trained themselves.

When I taught we had a coherent curriculum. When changes were made in it, the system gave us the new information, the instructional materials, and training in how to use them before we had to teach it. By the time I was a principal it was becoming common practice to change curriculum in the middle of the year and have teachers trying to learn it as they were teaching it. Often the supplies they needed did not come until months later. It seemed as if every six months we were given a new pedagogical phrase that was supposed to give teaching a new focus and that was really just the vogue until the next phrase came along. The city curriculum began to unravel, teachers were confused and frustrated, and expectations for students were not clear anymore.

I can't say exactly when this state of affairs began, but it seemed to happen when we started changing superintendents every little while, especially from the time when race started becoming a big issue—when Thomas Sheldon was forced out. Patterson came in after him playing the race card and got in so many tangles that he couldn't concentrate on improving instruction for the children. The system never really recovered from the battles of the Patterson days. Many strong educators retired early or took jobs in other districts. Many parents lost faith in the city schools, and those who could, moved their children to other counties or sent them to private institutions. The general public began to see the Baltimore school system as a lost cause. But, for the sake of the children, we had to prove that such impressions were wrong.

Being on the Fund for Educational Excellence, I had made the acquaintance of Muriel Berkeley whose children attended Calvert, a private school to the north of Barclay. She offered to arrange for me to visit Calvert. When I did, I really got excited. Right away I saw that they had the structure that we were missing. The curriculum was so well ordered. I saw the children's work, and I said, "If our kids could just do one-half of what these children are doing, they would really improve."

I invited Muriel to meet with our steering committee. She was also the education director of the Greater Baltimore Committee (GBC). The GBC was an influential businessmen's organization that had taken a great interest in the public schools. They had an "Adopt a School Program" through which individual businesses supported enrichment programs at selected schools. According to the steering committee minutes for May 11, 1983, "[W]e were joined by Dr. Berkeley [and] discussion turned to the subject of the Calvert School Curriculum. She and Miss Williams described the Calvert School method. We examined samples of the curricular materials. Parents and staff concluded that the possibility of adapting the curriculum to our program is worth further exploration . . ."[38]

A month later we sent a proposal to GBC. Joanne Giza was its main author. She described Barclay as having an enrollment of 625 students who were "reflective of the surrounding community, a community distinguished for its diversity [and including] blacks and whites of varying socio-economic levels." After depicting "Ms. Gertrude Williams" as one who "always extended herself for her students to provide them with the best education possible," Joanne noted that "resources . . . can be stretched only so far":

> Large classes composed of children stretching from one end of the ability spectrum to the other challenge even the finest teachers and administrators . . . [and] prohibit the teachers from expanding adequately on the writing segment of language arts. Though students drill the fundamentals of grammar and work on improving their spelling and increasing their vocabulary, paragraph writing, essay writing, and creative writing are lost.

She made a similar argument about science. She then proposed that GBC assist us in obtaining business or foundation support to adapt Calvert School methods to Barclay's needs.[39]

Nothing came of this proposal, and we were soon caught up in the middle-school issue. But five years later, in January 1988, Robert Embry, President of the Abell Foundation, brought up the possibility of a partnership with Calvert supported by Abell funding. As with Muriel, I had met Bob Embry through the Fund for Educational Excellence. He knew that we were interested in the Calvert curriculum and arranged to meet at Calvert with me and Merrill Hall, the new Calvert head-master.[40] Embry told us that Abell funding would be available if we could convince the city school system to let us use the Calvert curriculum. He stressed that everyone would have to be in agreement.

Merrill Hall then said that he would be willing to consider a partnership with us, but the staffs of the two schools needed to talk, and Barclay parents needed to agree. He visited Barclay, and I visited Calvert again. Then some of the teachers from each school visited the other school. Finally, on May 17, 1988, we met together at Calvert as a large group. We were thinking about focusing on kindergarten through grade four, so the K through four teachers from Barclay went with me to Calvert where we met with Merrill and his K through four teachers. They served us a lovely lunch and then we did a force field analysis of the two schools.

We looked at both schools, their philosophies and expectations, trying to see if they could work together. We listed all the practices and methods that their teachers had seen at Barclay and that our teachers had seen at Calvert. We looked at different aspects of the curriculum—ways of teaching math; ways of approaching reading. We were having social studies; they had history—those kinds of differences. We put a plus sign beside the ones that could work together and a minus beside those that we thought wouldn't work. When we added them all up we had a few minuses but many more pluses.

We at Barclay were drawn to the Calvert curriculum because, unlike the frag-mented curriculum we were following, it is well ordered, and, unlike the tendency to condescend to children and accept less than they are capable of that prevailed all too often in the city school system, Calvert mandates high expectations for all students. The tasks that are given on each grade level are based on what has been taught before. Take writing as an example. As Joanne Giza noted in the proposal that we sent to GBC, the city's approach to instruction in writing seldom reached beyond drills in grammar and vocabulary. And, if the truth be told, those were often inadequate. At Calvert children are taught first how to develop a sentence, then a paragraph, then an essay. They write about simple things that they understand around their home and their school. They learn old-fashioned grammar—that adjectives are used to describe nouns and pronouns, and so forth. In third grade they study mythology (a subject not systematically covered in the city schools), and they love it.

In the Calvert curriculum history lessons begin in fourth grade; not the jumble of "social studies" that we had in the public schools, but real history, history of the world from prehistoric times down to World War II, and then, in fifth grade, American History. In mathematics Calvert follows the same step by step approach, teaching addition, subtraction, multiplication (including the "times tables"), division, basic concepts of algebra, showing how these apply to the world around us. This was a big contrast to city practices where math skills were often presented haphazardly, without laying the necessary foundations.

We also liked how Calvert involved parents in the students' work. Once a month they receive a folder made up of their children's work. They must sign that they have examined it. They meet regularly with the teachers. And we saw the value of the correction time that is built into the Calvert method. It requires students to correct the mistakes they make on their classroom work. Soon they are trying to get the work right the first time. We saw how this would cut down on a lot of the sloppiness that can be seen in students' work nowadays, even at the college level.

Because Calvert students came mostly from wealthy homes, while most Barclay families were middle class and below, our opponents would try to paint Calvert as the rich elite who were using us to validate and promote their curriculum. But from the beginning there was a sense of togetherness. They didn't act like missionaries or condescend to us. There was a really neat feeling between the two schools. The teachers were growing close to one another and were anxious to work together.

We envisioned a four-year partnership, in which the Calvert curriculum would be adapted to Barclay in grades K through four on an incremental basis. We would start with kindergarten and first grade, add second grade the next year, and so on. With funding from Abell we would hire enough teachers to keep class size at no more than 25 children and also employ teaching assistants who would increase the amount of individual attention each child would receive. Abell would also pay for the Calvert instructional materials, the training of teachers to use them, and the salary of a coordinator. The coordinator would come from the Calvert staff and would supervise the training and monitor teachers in the classroom.

I couldn't see any reason why the public school system wouldn't okay this plan. It wouldn't cost the city a penny. Calvert would take care of all the ordering and delivery. All the school system had to do was give us our regular money for teachers' salaries and usual supplies. I was just so sure that it was going to happen. I expected Barclay to open in September 1988 with the Calvert curriculum.

What I didn't realize was that our area director (the position that was once called regional superintendent), Clifton Ball, had no intention of supporting us. I had informed him of the idea of a Barclay–Calvert partnership as soon as Bob Embry mentioned it. He was invited each time we met. When we invited him to the luncheon at Calvert he said he had a time conflict. So we changed the date for him. On the new date we started late, waiting for him. He never came. I said to Merrill, "Cliff is our area director and he needs to give the approval before I move on."

First I sent him a memo. I outlined the conclusions we had reached on May 17 and asked him to respond to questions about matters such as scheduling and the selection of basal readers. He put me off every time I pressed him to answer. May and June went by. If we were going to be ready for the start of school in September we had to get clearance from Cliff. Merrill and I decided that we should try to give him a more detailed account of the plans, so we sat down in early July and wrote a rough draft of a proposal which I delivered to Cliff. I talked to him about the short time we had left and urged him to meet with us. The rest of July went by. Finally he told me he had passed the draft of the proposal on to Edmonia Yates, deputy superintendent in charge of instruction. When I called her she had no idea what I was talking about.[41]

For the first time in years I had planned to take a real vacation—10 days in Disney Land during August. While I was away Cliff scheduled a meeting at Calvert for the day before my expected return. I found out about it when I called back to Baltimore and returned in time to show up at his meeting, which turned out to be nothing. Whatever he had planned for that day, he backed off when I arrived. Anyhow, our chance to start in September was gone.

I have always felt that Alice Pinderhughes should have intervened. She was replaced by Richard Hunter at the end of that summer. But she could have signed off on the Barclay–Calvert partnership before she left. She had known about it, because I had talked to her when the possibility first came up. Then she liked it but said we didn't have the money. Now we had the money, and she still held back. I don't know whether she was game-playing or being pressured from behind the scenes. Whatever the case, she really had nothing to lose.

Thanks to Edmonia Yates the curriculum committee of the school board finally met with Cliff and me in the fall. They instructed him to call a meeting with me and any others who needed to be involved in reaching a decision. The school system then had one curriculum specialist for each area—reading, math, social studies, and so forth. The board wanted their evaluation of the Calvert curriculum. Cliff never called the meeting. By this time I felt betrayed. Clifton Ball had been an excellent area executive officer. I never wanted to miss his administrative meetings, because he always had information for us that we could use. He did a lot for us at Barclay, and we thought he was a friend.

In a letter dated November 22, 1988 Merrill Hall offered to Clifton Ball "the services of myself [and other Calvert staff] to answer any questions, provide any information and speak to any issues which thereby might facilitate . . . the decision making process."[42] Ball did not answer the letter. Throughout December parents and community residents wrote to him. No answer. Just before the winter holiday recess Barclay parents delivered a petition to the school system's headquarters, asking the new superintendent, Richard Hunter, to "immediately approve" our proposal. No answer.[43]

In February 1989—more than a year since I had first spoken to Cliff about a possible Barclay–Calvert partnership—Megan Shook, whose son and daughter attended Barclay, and Karen Olson, former Barclay PTA president, asked at a public school board meeting about the silent treatment we were getting. They spoke at the February 8 board meeting. On February 21, *Baltimore Sun*, reporter, Kathy Lally, wrote about how the school system was denying us this exciting opportunity.[44] Her article showed how idiotic the system was. This brought in everybody. Wherever Superintendent Richard Hunter went and wherever the new mayor, Kurt Schmoke, went, people asked "Why can't they have that program?" It thrust them into answering to everyone, not just us. Kathy Lally really broke the log jam.

Lally had stressed that the partnership would cost the city nothing, and that the Abell Foundation had agreed to fund it. Now that it was a hot issue, Bob Embry became especially careful about clarifying the Abell Foundation's position. Some blacks had begun to distrust him. They believed he was trying to control the school system. A rumor circulated that he was going to use Calvert as a way to take over Barclay, and that this was part of a bigger plan to gain control of the school system. He sent letters to me, Merrill Hall, and the Barclay steering committee stating that "the Abell Foundation has made no commitment to fund the Calvert School–Barclay project." He offered to help us "if you are permitted to proceed . . . to create an application."[45]

This made us angry at the time; it seemed that he was talking out of both sides of his mouth, for he had told Merrill and me that his goal was to better education in Baltimore City and he saw our proposal as one way to do that. Looking back I can see that he had to be cautious. We remained confident that he would fund us, if we could get the proposal through Baltimore City. Embry wasn't our problem. The Baltimore City school system was—especially its new superintendent.

Richard Hunter, who had become superintendent in August 1988, issued a press release on February 24, 1989 stating that the school system had been in constant communication with Barclay about the Calvert proposal. He also claimed that he had visited Calvert. *After* he said that, he showed up at Calvert School unannounced on March 6. We were told by Merrill Hall that he stayed for about 15 minutes. He had some kind of portable phone and kept using it to check with his chauffeur. Finally he said, "I have to go." He observed no classes, really didn't see the school at all, and didn't stay long enough for a real discussion with Merrill.[46]

Hunter called me to bring representatives from Barclay to his office on March 7, the day after he stopped at Calvert. School was out because there was ice on the ground. Driving was treacherous. We—educational assistant Tanya Jackson, who was also a Barclay parent, our PTO president, Pat Straus, community representative, Jo Ann Robinson, the assistant principal, Verna Chase, and I—slid all the way there. When we walked in, his executive assistant, Jerrelle Francois, whispered something to me, like "He really cares for you, Trudy," which made no sense. She took us to a meeting room and after awhile he came in.

He shocked us all by starting out with "I'm tired of hearing about Barclay. Everywhere I go people ask me why I won't let Barclay have this program. I want to tell you something." And he looked at me and said, "Because of all the problems this has caused me, you will never have this curriculum." We were dumbfounded. Finally, Verna, who usually remained quiet, said "Never?" He said, "maybe in a couple of years we can talk about something for Barclay."

We asked a few questions and presented a chart that showed the ways that the Calvert curriculum fit with, and supported, the goals and objectives of the Baltimore City public schools. He was not interested. Finally he said, "Gertrude, you understand my position." "No, I don't," I answered. As the kids would say, we had been "put down" in a very ugly way.[47]

Two days later Hunter announced that he would not approve the use of any Calvert materials or personnel at Barclay ever. He also said that he would not approve *any* project at Barclay unless the Abell Foundation also gave the school system four million dollars to reduce third grade class sizes system-wide.[48] His argument was that if we got the Calvert curriculum then the other children in the city would not have a fair chance. That did not make sense. If Barclay succeeded in using the Calvert program we would help the whole system. It would give them a direction. But he was so angry that he was determined to destroy the whole proposal. In trying to blackmail Abell for four million dollars, he just looked ridiculous. The general reaction was, "What is he talking about?" We said, "He can't get away with this."

The Barclay PTO called its own press conference. The warnings we received about doing this showed how divided the city was becoming over this issue. A prominent city politician told Jo Ann Robinson that the Barclay controversy was going to "tear the city apart" and urged that we avoid having white spokesmen. Hunter was pushing the lie that the white community was trying to take over Barclay for rich white kids.[49]

At the same time Walt Robbins, from the administrators' union, warned me to stay away from public statements. "Hunter's waiting for you to be insubordinate and then he's going to have an excuse to fire you," Robbins predicted. Walt knew that

Hunter had begun to single me out in administrative meetings. I—who almost always sit in the front of every meeting—had started sitting way in the back. Hunter would always spot me, and he would come off the stage and walk up the aisle to where I was and start saying inane things. He would talk about me being a traitor and ask, "What do you do with people who think that they're better than the system?" He had lost all sense of balance and the more people got on him about us the worse he hated what we were doing.

One day Hunter had called and asked me to meet with him, because the mayor was insisting that we had to meet. He came out when the receptionist told him I was there, spoke nicely, took me to his outer office, told me to have a seat and offered me a cup of coffee. After I'd been waiting about 20 minutes, Jerrelle Francois came in and asked why I was there. I told her, and she said, "Oh, Dr. Hunter left 15 minutes ago." He had purposely left me sitting there so he could tell the mayor that he had me over. So when Walt told me, "You're getting ready to get yourself in trouble," I said, "Well, I'm already in trouble."

The Barclay press conference took place in the gymnasium. Pat Straus, the black PTO president, and Jo Ann Robinson read a statement and then took questions. All the newspapers and TV stations were there. A good gathering of parents, staff, and community stood behind Pat. I took care of a little paperwork I had to do at a desk in the opposite corner from where the conference was held. I didn't say anything, but because Walt Robbins had told me to stay away, I was determined to be in the room. For the rest of that school year we were at war.[50]

The Sun kept printing articles and editorials, most of them sympathetic to us. *The Baltimore Afro-American* generally backed Hunter. The pros and cons were debated in letters to the editor in all the papers. Barclay–Calvert was a favorite topic on radio call-in shows. We received letters from all over the city, and beyond, telling us to keep fighting. We also got copies of some of the letters that people had sent to the mayor or the superintendent. Teachers called me from other schools to offer support. They said, "if you can get this through, maybe we can make some changes at our schools." I don't remember any situation ever being as charged as this was. It kept us working day and night, responding to our opponents, keeping our supporters informed, planning our next moves.

One reason that the controversy became so heated is that the mayor had made education the centerpiece of his election campaign. He raised the voters' expectations for school reform. Now here was a reform, and his superintendent was blocking it. The public became very frustrated. They wanted to see improvements in the schools. They didn't want confusion and bickering. Because Schmoke had made education a campaign issue, all the politicians—his supporters and his opponents—had to weigh in. The more they got involved, the more they stirred up the controversy.

Finally, whenever race is interjected into a public debate, that debate is going to become ugly. Richard Hunter convinced many blacks that we were trying to establish in a public school a private program for the white elite in Charles Village. I don't think the issue would have gotten so explosive if Richard Hunter had not been such a divisive person. He went around to the community groups, particularly the black groups, spreading myths about us. Even old friends who usually backed me when I spoke out believed Hunter. Arnett Brown, who was the president of our administrators' union, wrote an op ed article for the *Baltimore Evening Sun* that asked, "Why are we being distracted by groups and individuals who appear to be suggesting that they know better than Dr. Hunter how to improve our schools?" Arnett ended by saying, "Let Dr. Hunter lead."[51]

When I talked to him, Arnett told me that he didn't think Hunter had the ability to deal with the situation that had developed. "That's not our problem," I replied. "We're not going to stop." "I'm not asking you to stop," Arnett said. "But the whole city is upset about this program. If you could just back away for awhile." He knew I wasn't about to back away.

Even Rebecca Carroll, my former supervisor who had liked me as a teacher, stopped me one day in Loehmann's department store, got right up in my face and said, "How dare you do this to a black man!" I answered, "Dr. Carroll, I don't want to hear this! How dare a black man do this to a predominantly black school!" She huffed, "He's not that bad! He's not that bad! You're painting him as bad." I said, "If you'll look and see—he's painting me as an ogre." She went on then, and she never brought it up again.

We had to set the record straight for the Baltimore Teachers Union, when they included Barclay on their list of "experiments" that were being "imposed" on city teachers.[52] After we showed them how the teachers were involved in the planning and were anxious to have the program, Irene Dandridge, the head of the union, apologized. Still, BTU opposed Barclay–Calvert and bought the lie that white parents were trying to take over Barclay and install a private school curriculum for their children.

The black people who were so quick to defend Hunter and say that I was a patsy made me very angry. They questioned my values, and what they said was just untrue. I will never agree that being black requires me to follow every black leader who comes along. Hunter should never have been hired. People who knew about him as superintendent in Richmond, Virginia warned Baltimore not to take him. Our own PTO president, Pat Straus, had lived in Richmond and knew that Hunter was bad news.[53] Whenever he was challenged, Hunter would personalize the issue. He never set out a clear picture of where he wanted to go and where he wanted us to go. He always seemed to be floundering and trying to find his way. It didn't make sense to back him just because he was black.

I also will never agree that every school has to be the same and every child should be given the same program. If the superintendent and school board establish sound and clear goals for the system as a whole, then each school can be designed to reach those goals in the ways that will work best for its particular group of students. Barclay–Calvert made sense to us and I expected that some other communities might take it as a model, but there is no panacea to fit all schools. Every school should have the freedom to identify and implement a model that makes sense to them, under-standing, of course, that whatever that model, they will be held accountable for meeting the goals and standards of the school system.

No community should be made to apologize or feel guilty because they make sure that the needs of their children are fully met. The superintendent should not fight those communities who are well organized. He should make sure that *every* commu-nity is well organized. In the same way that central administrators sent me to Barclay because they saw a need there for someone with my training and experience, the cen-tral office should be able to assess each school's needs and assign a principal and the specialists, supervisors, coordinators who will know how to address those needs.

As for Hunter's claim that I was working for whites and that Barclay was a white school—that was stupid. Part of it was that some of our spokesmen were white. They could speak profoundly and that upset the nerves of those who wanted to discredit us. They resented the white parents. After the group of children who came mostly from Red Wagon had gone on to high school, we had very few white students at Barclay. Even during the time of the Red Wagon group, whites were a small minor-ity. Richard Hunter and Mayor Schmoke had been in the school and they knew that. But Charles Village was white, and Charles Village fought hard for Barclay.

CVCA—the Charles Village Civic Association—had invited Clifton Ball to one of their meetings while he was dodging me. Trudy Bartel was the CVCA president, and after Cliff gave a little talk she asked for questions. People kept asking him about Calvert, and he kept talking out of both sides of his mouth. Nancy Hubble, a promi-nent realtor who rarely got involved in school issues, finally asked, "What's wrong? Why aren't you backing Barclay? I know Barclay and I think they will do well with Calvert." Then Wally Orlinsky, a former City Council president, jumped up and really went after Clifton. That upset Cliff and he had to admit that he had not done what he should have. But he swore he would support us. Of course, that was another dodge.[54] But the fact that Charles Village was our strong ally bothered many admin-istrators in the central office. They used the excuse of race.

Of course, Calvert School was white, and its students came from wealthy fami-lies. Hunter accused me of imposing "a rich man's curriculum" on the poor children at Barclay. I assured him that we did not want a poor man's curriculum. The parents became very angry when he said that. They wanted to know what a rich man should have that a poor man shouldn't have as far as education is concerned. Our PTO President, Pat Straus, put it very well when she said,

> There seems to be some problem about the Calvert curriculum coming from a private school. This puzzles me. I was glad when Baltimore City encouraged student uniforms. I am still interested in this, which is a private school tradition. But why is this idea all right for public school students while a private school curriculum is not? It is good to improve the children's appearance and behavior. But isn't it more important to improve their minds?

She continued:

> We do not understand Dr. Hunter's remark that the Calvert curriculum is not suited
> to "our population." This is a slap in the face to me. "Our" children come to public
> school able to learn as well as children in private school. All children need to receive
> is a strong foundation. The Calvert methods, which are the most important part of
> the proposal, are not tied to race or class.[55]

Hunter claimed that the Calvert curriculum was outdated. It *was* rooted in tradition, and for some people anything that is traditional is outdated. In fact, while pursuing traditional goals, Calvert regularly updated all their instructional materials. Unlike the public schools that have lost their way, Calvert changed without losing sight of its original goals and objectives. Hunter also said the curriculum was racist and sexist, which simply was not true. Another of Hunter's charges was that Calvert was designed for wealthy high achievers. What goal should any curriculum have but to have children become high achievers? We knew that if our students followed this curriculum they *would* achieve at a high level.

The curriculum specialists who were asked by the school board to evaluate the Calvert curriculum agreed with Hunter—at least in public. I had gone through the curriculum with three specialists. They were positive toward it then. Later, under pressure, two of them made a report to the board that was negative. The third specialist refused to participate in the report. The day after they reported, I went to see the other two. One of them told me, "You have to do what you have to do." I said, "No, you don't. You don't have to sell your soul." The second specialist said, "After all, Trudy, there are other curriculums. You're doing all right at Barclay." She meant that it wasn't worth it to fight for the Calvert curriculum. I told her that it was. And I added, "You wait. You're going to get your day!" Several years later when she had become a principal and was having a lot of trouble, she told me, "You put the bad mouth on me." That's the first time anyone ever suggested that I was able to place a jinx on them!

With Hunter, Ball, and the curriculum specialists lined up against us, the school board refused to approve the Barclay–Calvert proposal. Three weeks before they took the final vote I was called to meet with Herman Howard, an assistant superintendent. I asked a parent and a community representative to come with me. Howard brought Cliff Ball, Jerelle Francois, and a new administrator recently hired to be in charge of curriculum, a Dr. Stephens. (She would resign within a matter of months.)[56] Howard also had a stenographer present. First Howard tried to get Pat Straus, the Barclay parent, to say that she didn't care that much about the Calvert curriculum. But she was on the ball and explained why she wanted her children to have that curriculum. Then Howard asked why didn't we take the parts of Calvert that we liked most and just make up "a Barclay curriculum"? We said that would be plagiarism. The meeting fell apart after that. That was on March 23, 1989.[57]

The next school board meeting was April 6. Howard reported on the March 23 meeting. He said that he had offered me other ways in which we could help the children at Barclay and that I was unwilling to go along with them. School board president, Meldon Hollis, asked if the Abell Foundation had agreed to fund class size reductions for the school system. Dr. Hunter said that Abell had expressed no interest in that request, and, therefore, there was no reason for further discussion of our proposal. At the end of the discussion the board voted down the proposal. Our city councilman, Carl Stokes, who was in our corner through the whole battle, was there that night. He saw how we had been railroaded. When Will Englund of the *Sun* talked to me after the meeting I told him that Howard's story was a bunch of "blatant lies."[58]

The board's action fired up people more than ever. We got more letters. They came from all over the state. I'll never forget a letter that I got from a grandmother. She said, "I don't have any children in school but I wish you well because I'm just proud of the fact that someone is willing to stand up and fight for a proper education." The storm kept raging.

School board commissioner, Philip Farfel, set up another meeting between us and Hunter. Six of us from Barclay—teacher Jan French, parent and teaching assistant Tanya Jackson, PTO president Pat Straus, community representative Jo Ann Robinson, and myself—met with Hunter, Farfel, and Francois. In that meeting they told us that we would not be permitted to engage in any special programs that involved foundation funding, though we could ask for support from our own community—as if we had not been working together with that community for years! When we tried to question Dr. Hunter he looked at Jo Ann and said, "I will not talk as long as the tape recorder is here." We looked around for a recording machine and then realized that he was calling her a tape recorder, because she always took detailed notes.[59]

Our city delegates in Annapolis tried to mediate by talking separately with us and then with the mayor. But he supported Hunter, and we wouldn't back down. He heard from a number of our parents at Taxpayers Night in May. While they spoke, we were all there, with the children, in our Barclay shirts, looking at him.

I felt that Mayor Schmoke had really let us down. While he was States Attorney we had had him address our first middle-school graduation. After he became mayor he came back to Barclay for a Reading is Fundamental book distribution. A description of him reading *Green Eggs and Ham* to Barclay students appeared in *Jet* magazine. I had worked in his election campaign. We trooped down to his inauguration with some two hundred children who cheered him. I had all these hopes for him, because he had said he was the education mayor. He knew that the public schools in the city were on a downward spiral, and he promised to bring them up. Now he was clinging to Hunter. He had brought Hunter in, and he was not willing to admit that he had brought in a dud.

Saying he wanted to stay in touch with Baltimore's citizens, Schmoke held community forums. When he announced a forum for our part of the city on June 3, 1989, I signed up to speak after considerable agonizing. Jerelle Francois and others warned me not to. They thought that I was taking the chance of being fired. At first I didn't want to speak. Then I said, "Well, I need to let them know how I feel about what they've done to us. I need to make a last ditch effort and let them know. I was so angry inside. I really was on edge.

When I arrived at the Wyman Park Multi-Purpose Center that Saturday morning the huge meeting area was filling up fast. By the time the forum started, the place was packed. They had many more speakers than there was time for. The person in charge of the speakers' list cut it off after the fifty-second person had signed up.

When my turn came several people had already talked about Barclay, and Schmoke had brushed them off. That made me feel even angrier. I went to the microphone, introduced myself, and heard this great big roar behind me. I went "Oh!" and looked back, because it stunned me. The crowd just roared. The mayor said, "I see your friends are here." Some Barclay staff and parents had come. But the whole crowd—people who had come for many other reasons—was cheering for Barclay.

I started to read the speech I had prepared: "Mayor Schmoke, over thirty years ago I took education as my agenda, as you did when you ran for election. It is a tough and demanding agenda, but it is rewarding." Pretty soon I put down the speech and started talking to him. I told him that our students needed security and stability. They shouldn't have to wait for adults to decide when and how to meet their basic needs. I explained the clear and structured Calvert approach. I said that I was an experienced educator who knew what a curriculum should be and that Barclay teachers also knew what they were looking for. I pointed out that the staff at Calvert was equally experienced. The Barclay–Calvert proposal had been rejected because of myths, I said. I let him know that I was especially angry about the myth that the curriculum is racist. I asked him to uphold my right to be treated fairly.

The crowd roared again. When they quieted the mayor began to ask questions. He asked about various problems in the school system. Then he asked me why I thought I was not being treated fairly. I told him that I had tried to work through the system and had never had a fair hearing. Because speakers were limited to three minutes, one of the mayor's aides started to cut me off. The mayor told me to go on and just snapped at the aide: "I am talking to Miss Williams!" When he had finished his questions Schmoke promised me a fair hearing and said his office would be calling me. At last someone was going to listen to us! I felt better than I had in months.[60]

I know that most people would not have gone on fighting for as long as we did. But I believed that we had the right to adopt the Calvert curriculum. We had demonstrated why we wanted it and why we needed it. We had gone through the whole process. We had talked about it in the steering committee. We had visited Calvert, had joint staff meetings with them. We thought our children could succeed with the Calvert curriculum. Most of all, I guess, I was just darned stubborn. After Hunter said that it was a rich man's curriculum the parents had become very angry, and everyone had gotten stubborn.

We were able to hold out because each person was supportive. When I would reach the point where I was ready to crack, the parents would support me. When the staff got too angry, we would cool them down. When the parents were ready to explode the staff and I would quiet them. Through it all we were determined that we weren't going to turn back.

The mayor's office called me and set an appointment for June 14 at 7:30 a.m. We were meeting before his regular meeting with his cabinet. We talked so long that he was late and had to run. He asked why we wanted the Calvert curriculum. I talked about all of those things that we used to have that were gone and the lack of structure in the city now, the poor quality of the city curriculum, and of teacher training. I explained how Calvert would provide structure and consistency. He asked me a lot about problems in the city and said that very few people seemed willing to come out and say exactly what they thought the problems were.

Schmoke also told me how split the city was because so many blacks believed Hunter, and he had been going to the different black groups and telling them that I was working for the whites. I asked the mayor, "Did you believe him?" He replied that he wanted Hunter to be superintendent if he could be. "You know better," I told him. "You know what Barclay's like."[61] Hunter had convinced Schmoke that he had been meeting and working with us. I told the mayor about our meetings and about the day Hunter took me up to his office and then left the building. I said, "Dr. Hunter just refuses to talk to me." And he said, "Oh, he will."

Mayor Schmoke asked me to cool things down. He promised me that we would get the Calvert program but said that we needed to stop talking about it. He told me that he was going to meet with Hunter and have Hunter begin to work with me. I said to myself, "Okay. He's going to really try to deal with Hunter. And he's not going to get anywhere, because Hunter is just unreasonable." But I promised to go back, quiet Barclay down and give the mayor a chance. I believed that he was our only hope of getting through all of this.[62]

Principal at Barclay, Part Four: In the Spotlight

Kurt Schmoke's belated attention to the Barclay–Calvert issue was only one example of the complicated politics bedeviling the mayor's efforts at school reform. Research on the politics of urban public education demonstrates that mayors who focus on this issue are never unfettered in exercising their authority. They must cope with the heavy constraints of a largely intransigent school system bureaucracy and with powerful interest groups within the city. Political scientist Wilbur Rich has identified "a cartel-like governing entity" that encapsulates big city school systems. Composed of administrators, community activists, and union leaders who are "primarily interested in self-perpetuation," the "cartel" operates on the assumption that no one cares more about the school district's children than its members do, and no one—be he/she the mayor, the most recently appointed superintendent, or some self-appointed critic—is more qualified than they to initiate and oversee any changes that the schools may need. They will block efforts at change that do not originate with them, creating a very low probability of success for mayors who venture into school reforms that reach beyond or in anyway challenge the status quo. Since among cartel members "there is no assumption of permanent tenure for a superintendent," individuals who assume that position, particularly those who are brought in from outside the district, are also working at a disadvantage.[1]

By the time Schmoke had become mayor of Baltimore, a substantial core of career-bureaucrats had long controlled the central administration of the school system, and certain activist bodies had developed a relationship to the system not unlike that of a legislative body's "loyal opposition." Chief among the loyal activists were the Greater Baltimore Committee (GBC), representing business interests, and Baltimoreans United in Leadership Development (BUILD), giving voice to grass-roots elements in the black community—particularly the black churches. Though generally assuming a more adversarial stance, the Baltimore Teachers Union (BTU) was also amenable to working with the system when doing so seemed to be in the best interests of its members. While these organizations may not have held the key to the kind of far-reaching reform that the city school system seemed to call for, their efforts were generally constructive and they had significant political influence.[2]

A multitude of other interest groups also competed for influence in the city schools. While they were not so well healed or well organized as GBC and BUILD, they could—as the Barclay experience illustrates—through testimony at the school board, and other governmental bodies, through petition campaigns and other lobbying and protest mechanisms stir up public opinion and create firestorms over issues that were important to them. These groups included civic organizations with "education committees," such as the National Association for the Advancement of Colored People (NAACP) and the League of Women Voters; parents' groups, including the citywide Parent–Teacher Association (PTA) and its affiliates in individual schools and Parent–Teacher Organizations (PTOs) that, as in the case of Barclay, operated independently; and neighborhood associations and coalitions such as the Barclay School area's Charles Village Civic Association (CVCA) and Greater Homewood Community Corporation (GHCC).

Federal and state governments were yet another force to be reckoned with. Although federal spending on public education had declined from the days of John Kennedy and Lyndon Johnson, compensatory programs such as Title I and federal mandates such as Public Law 94–142, guaranteeing the rights of children with handicapping conditions, meant that reform initiatives in schools receiving funds for these programs had to conform to federal regulations, a requirement that would prove problematic in the Barclay–Calvert effort. Moreover, during Schmoke's tenure as mayor, the Maryland legislature and the State Board of Education exerted intensifying pressures on public school systems, as Maryland instituted a statewide school assessment program, and new state laws linked funding for school districts to the performance of their students as measured by test scores and such criteria as attendance rates.

Thus, however determined Schmoke was to decentralize administrative authority, grant principals more discretionary power and thereby free up educators at each school site to tailor instruction to the needs of their respective student populations, he clearly would have to reckon with entrenched power in many corners. And whatever plans Hunter brought with him, whether or not they coincided with the mayor's goals as closely as Schmoke initially believed, the new superintendent would just as clearly have to comprehend and come to terms with the intricate network of influences bearing from within and without upon the system that he was charged to lead. For them to present a united front within the city thus made much political sense.

At the outset Hunter and Schmoke did seem to be united, and, as the personal choice of the city's first elected black mayor, Hunter enjoyed a warm welcome among Baltimoreans, especially in the black community. Schmoke's willingness—as he later expressed it to Gertrude—"to let the superintendent be the superintendent" drove much of the opposition that the Barclay–Calvert proposal first encountered. If Hunter's stance on Barclay–Calvert had been his only controversial decision, the school chief might well have maintained the backing of the mayor and a large contingent of other Baltimoreans. At least that seems to be the case, if one takes at face value the version of Hunter's sojourn in Baltimore as reported in the *Baltimore Sun* and recalled by Schmoke—a version in which the superintendent repeatedly misread the political culture of Baltimore and mishandled the responsibilities entrusted to him.

In the same period when he was locking horns with Gertrude and the Barclay community, Hunter also rejected an invitation for the city school system to participate in a national project to improve the teaching of science. Sponsored by the American Association for the Advancement of Science (AAAS), it was funded in the amount of $10 million and projected to operate over a period of four years. Opposing the project because it would take participating teachers away from their classrooms 40 days a year and required the hiring of substitutes (that AAAS would pay for), Hunter insisted that "to turn this school system around, we need all of our teachers in class all of the time."

Several months later, he shifted money earmarked for textbook purchases to cover a raise in teachers' salaries. Rebuked for cutting into instructional material that students had to have, he sought a supplemental appropriation for more textbooks. Public trust in him plummeted when the mayor made an unannounced visit to a textbook warehouse and found the shelves bulging with undistributed books.[3]

The mayor once more publicly reprimanded Hunter when the major cultural institutions of the city complained that student field trips to their performances and exhibitions had virtually ceased. Hunter had eliminated the office that coordinated such trips and failed to assign anyone else to be responsible for them. Schmoke intervened in Hunter's domain again in the spring of 1990, declaring wholly inadequate the superintendent's low-key response to a high school student shooting. School safety continued to be an issue as a local television crew demonstrated the ease with which total strangers could circumvent "security" and enter public school buildings.[4]

Hunter's controversial decisions alienated more than the mayor, the media, and the Barclay community. Businessmen involved in GBC had contributed the money that made it possible for the school board to hire Hunter at a salary nearly $40,000 higher than his predecessor's and had assisted him and his family in making the move to Baltimore from North Carolina. Leaders of BUILD had appealed to him to work with their community organization. Yet, Hunter showed little interest in their projects.[5] Both were invested in the Baltimore Commonwealth program that promised preferential hiring opportunities to public school graduates who met certain standards and offered other incentives for completing and doing well in school and going on to college. Hunter cold-shouldered their attempts to involve him in supporting this project. Reflecting a few years after Hunter's departure, Carol Reckling of BUILD remained puzzled by his "non-articulation of a vision for the public school system; the rejection of ideas other than his own; and his reluctance to involve others in the development of new ideas."[6]

Hunter initially remained aloof toward the construction of the school-based management (sbm) system that Schmoke wanted and that GBC, BUILD, and the BTU were in the process of developing, Hunter initially remained aloof, but when BTU incorporated sbm into negotiations for their 1989 contract, he became openly obstructionist. Prodded by Schmoke, he finally compromised with the union, agreeing that BTU might present a "school restructuring proposal" to the school board. According to BTU president Irene Dandridge this represented Hunter's bid to "do as little" [on sbm] as "he could get away with."[7]

Given this problematical record, in the spring of 1990 Schmoke directed the school board to conduct a performance review of Richard Hunter. The mayor did little to hide his desire for the superintendent to depart before the July 31, 1991 expiration of his contract. Hunter, in turn, made clear that he had no intention of leaving early, and he hired a lawyer to press the point. Remembering the carnage created by the involuntary departure of Roland Patterson, Schmoke and his school board reached an *entente* with the superintendent. Hunter would complete his term with the assistance of a deputy superintendent. The board brought in James Edward Andrews Jr., former superintendent of the Montgomery County, Maryland public schools and a professor at the University of Maryland, to handle the everyday operations of the school system, leaving Hunter as (in Schmoke's words) "cheerleader and chief lobbyist for public education in Baltimore."[8]

In December 1990, the Board of School Commissioners voted not to offer Hunter a new contract. Seven months later, on his last day, the departing superintendent called a press conference to lambaste Kurt Schmoke and the school board. While claiming that they had used him as a "scapegoat" for their own failures to make good on Schmoke's promises of school reform, Hunter adopted the language of the Crucifixion, intoning, "It is done. The educational sacrifice has been made. . . . My supporters said to me, 'Hang in there, Doc' . . . I hung in there and, now, it is done."[9]

In his parting remarks Hunter referred to Barclay only once: "If Hunter failed, while conferring with the mayor on every major issue, including the much talked about Barclay decision, then so did Mr. Schmoke." But in every report, analysis, and commentary on Hunter's Baltimore sojourn and departure "the Barclay decision" was viewed as pivotal. Certainly it was the most divisive of the issues that Hunter handled, and it was also the first major decision that confronted him.

However, the Barclay decision does not seem to have been quite what Gertrude assumes in her narrative—the trigger that prompted Schmoke to seek Hunter's resignation. In persuading the mayor that the superintendent's position was unjust and unsound, Gertrude struck a critical blow to Hunter's credibility. But it need not have been a fatal blow. A more discerning and flexible leader might have reassessed the political landscape and adjusted his management style accordingly. The mayor and many others would have applauded such a move. Had Hunter not been the sort of person who, as journalist Will Englund observed, would "rather take a battering than an order," his run-in with the Barclay principal and community might have eventually receded in the public memory. Instead, Hunter generated a succession of new controversies. Each press and TV report of his latest gaffe inevitably rehearsed the story of how he had mishandled Barclay.[10]

Meanwhile Kurt Schmoke had converted from opposition to support for Barclay–Calvert, and the school board approved the project in the spring of 1990, at his behest. By that fall, teachers had been trained, all supplies were delivered, and the unique experiment began. The teachers and students drawn into this project flourished in the next four years.

Barclay–Calvert evoked a mythic aura. In some accounts of the first years of the partnership, learning experiences became magical moments, such as the time when the project curriculum coordinator, Peg Licht took Barclay children to a performance at Calvert School. An actor playing Vincent Van Gogh so captivated them that by the time the play ended and the artist's works were being flashed on a screen, while a "Starry Starry Night" sound track played in the background, they didn't even notice that Calvert students had left to go back to their classrooms. "Our kids just sat there," marveled Licht. When they later got on the bus, they were still so affected that "there wasn't a sound. It was beautiful. . . ." For Licht the early phase of Barclay Calvert was "Camelot. . . . It really was. We were all so keyed up . . . everybody just cared. The children were so excited about everything."[11]

Gertrude's depiction of "Heaven setting up housekeeping right in Barclay School" reflects a similar sense of enchantment and jubilation, while for Merrill Hall "Barclay Calvert was one of the most interesting and challenging pieces of work that I've done in my career. . . . Those [Barclay] children just learned the heck out of that curriculum," he declared. Barclay teachers concurred. While admitting to reservations in the beginning, they soon were celebrating the positive changes they saw in their students and in the whole tone of the school.[12] Johns Hopkins evaluator, Sam Stringfield, later recalled that "For . . . four shining years or so, those kids were writing at levels you rarely see in public education in America, for that matter in private education. . . . If you wanted proof that inner-city kids can do higher-order thinking, Barclay was it."[13]

Stringfield's yearly evaluations had been progressively laudatory. In his fourth year report he concluded that

> Barclay–Calvert students have made academic gains far above those achieved by the preceding Barclay-Pre-Calvert students. The gains have come on two separate norm referenced tests in the area[s] of reading, language arts/writing, and math. The differences are educationally and statistically significant and often dramatic.[14]

All accounts agree that the students' stellar performance owed a great deal to the firm guidance provided by Margaret Licht, known to all as Peg, who in the post of curriculum coordinator trained Barclay teachers and supervised their classroom work. Robert Embry explained the rationale for the coordinator position: Calvert board members "were worried," he recalled, "about risking the reputation of their curriculum."

> They didn't want it misused, and poor results, and they'd get bad publicity. So they agreed [to the partnership] if [Abell] would pay for a full-time Calvert person to be at Barclay to monitor it and make sure it was done right. Gertrude welcomed this, Embry noted.[15]

Despite her skills and dedication, Licht quickly found out that if she wanted to get teachers to respond to her directives she had to have Gertrude's support. "Many times they [the teachers] let me know that I was not in charge," she later remembered. She stressed that Gertrude backed her up "one hundred percent." Teachers validated the description of Licht provided by Gertrude in her narrative. "She [Licht] wouldn't let us deviate. . . . The Calvert way was the only way," recalled Truemella Horne. And they affirmed their great respect for her. "Peg's standards gave us a clear course to follow. Every school should have a coach like her," declared Susan Lattimore, a special education resource teacher. But they remember that they first cooperated with the Barclay–Calvert plan and Licht "because," according to first grade teacher Dorothea Rawlings, "Miss Williams said it was going to be good"; and "because," according to Lattimore, "Miss Williams believed in it so much." Horne declared that "We really wanted to show Miss Williams that we could make it work."[16]

At the end of those four wonderful years the Abell Foundation proffered the funding to continue the program through grade eight, Licht transferred to another city public school to start a new Calvert partnership, and the Barclay program entered a time of difficulties.

Both the halcyon days of high achievement, when Barclay and Calvert Schools were feted in the national media and inundated by visitors from across the country and some foreign nations, and most of the post-1994 period of tension and trouble, occurred while Richard Hunter's successor, Walter Amprey, was superintendent. Amprey, who grew up in Baltimore and attended the city public schools, was an associate superintendent in the neighboring Baltimore County school system when Schmoke persuaded him to apply for the top post in the city system.[17]

Like his predecessors, Amprey struggled mightily with budget allocations from the city and state that badly failed to cover the needs of a highly impoverished and struggling student population. By 1996, he and Schmoke were in court dealing with three separate law suits—one that they filed against the state seeking increased state funding, a countersuit filed by the state against them, and a 12-year-old on-going suit against the city by advocates for disabled students whose needs the city schools had perennially failed to meet.[18] In 1997, the state legislature passed a measure that supplied the city school district with a $254 million increase in funding in exchange for increased state oversight of the city schools. Law makers dismantled the city superintendency and school board, replacing them for the next five years with a new superintendent and board appointed jointly by the governor (Schaefer's successor, Parris Glendening) and the mayor. Thus Amprey was removed to make way for the first joint-appointment, Robert Schiller.

While he was in charge, the relationship between Amprey and Gertrude was strained. In a lengthy letter to him in the spring of 1993, she detailed the kinds of frustrations that she had been dealing with since the beginning of Barclay–Calvert. At the top of her list were staff and budget cuts. She stressed that "the point of seeking community support is not to surplant [*sic*] the tax dollars to which this public school is entitled, but to supplement in those areas where public funding falls short."[19]

When Amprey's budget office erred in its projections for Barclay's 1993–1994 enrollments, cutting the school's city funding by $175,000, Gertrude had to cancel classes in physical education, health, art, and music while she scrounged for basic supplies for the non-Barclay–Calvert classrooms and fended off creditors who were about to repossess the school's main copy machine.

In response to Stringfield's widely publicized and enthusiastic evaluation of Barclay–Calvert's first four years, Amprey did go on record as having an interest in extending the Calvert curriculum to other schools, and he later approved its use at another Baltimore elementary school, Carter G. Woodson. Nonetheless, as Gertrude's discussion of his policies will indicate, Amprey's commitment to the program was lukewarm at best.[20]

In the later years of his administration, Gertrude's problems with Amprey were dwarfed by rising tensions within the program itself. Partnership ties among those overseeing Barclay–Calvert began to fray, as they were tested by internal disagreements and new external challenges, especially a new state testing program. Program expansion beyond the four years of the original proposal also presented new challenges in program oversight. It is hard to judge how much external pressures and lack of system support affected the internal dynamics of the Barclay–Calvert partnership, and how much the wear and tear on that partnership were caused by friction among the partners. Coordinator Peg Licht likened the curriculum reform to a wheel:

> You had these different spokes that made that wheel run smoothly. And if you took away one of them it would begin to bump; if you took away two or three, it would get bumpier and bumpier. There were little things that kept eating at it.[21]

By Gertrude's account, one of the factors that made for some "bumpiness" was the poor working relationship between Licht, the Calvert headmaster, and assistant headmaster on the one hand, and Barclay's Title-I teachers on the other. Perhaps the difficulty was only, as Gertrude viewed it, that the Calvert people did not fully understand the federal mandate for Title I. But from the Calvert vantage point, Gertrude did not hold the two teachers responsible for combining the Barclay–Calvert program with those Title-I mandates to the same instructional standards required of everyone else. From his vantage point at the Abell Foundation, Embry heard from Calvert that the difficulty with the Title-I issue was a matter of Gertrude favoring "her protégés" with lighter teaching loads and not holding them to Calvert standards.

Years later Merrill Hall acknowledged that Calvert staff had little interest in fathoming public school policies, including Title-I regulations. "I'm sure that there were misunderstandings and we could have been viewed as narrow-minded and not understanding" in relation to Title I, he said in 2003. However, he added that the job of Calvert people was to "do Calvert." They were convinced that anything that detracted from one hundred percent implementation of the Calvert curriculum subtracted from what students could accomplish if they received the full Calvert treatment.[22]

For their part, the Title-I teachers, Sandra Brown and Truemella Horne were very conscious of the criticisms leveled against them. "Calvert really felt that Sandra and I were not using the [Calvert] program [correctly] and they really wanted us not to use it at all," recalled Horne. However, the two women were confident that they met the standards of the federal program and conveyed the substance of the private school curriculum to their students. "We were giving the kids a double dose," said Horne. In addition to covering the federal mandate they "broke down the Calvert materials" for the slower learning students. In retrospect, Licht acknowledged that the Title-I argument caught Gertrude in the middle, "trying to appease me and trying to appease" Horne and Brown.[23]

A second source of difficulty was students who transferred into Barclay–Calvert from other schools unprepared for the rigors of the Calvert curriculum. Identifying effective methods for bringing these students up to speed, supplying teachers with the proper training to do so, even providing adequate instructional space for such transfer students caused on-going dissension. For example, Merrill Hall recommended a retired Calvert teacher to direct the first "transition" classes for transfer students. According to Gertrude, that woman "did not like Barclay students." She was replaced by one of the Title-I teachers of whom Hall and others were so critical, and the disagreements continued.[24]

A third dilemma presented itself beginning in 1992, when the Maryland State Department of Education (MSDE) inaugurated the Maryland State Performance Assessment Program (MSPAP), a mandatory battery of tests administered annually in grades three, five, and eight in every school district in the state. Intended to evaluate the quality of instruction in each school, rather than the usual evaluations of individual students, the tests emphasized problem-solving skills and included group exercises in which teams of students attacked a given challenge. The state measured scores for each school against preset standards. tracked schools' performance from year to year, and maintained a list of failing schools that were brought under state supervision. Baltimore City led other school districts in the number of schools placed on that list.

Truemella Horne and Sandra Brown recalled the pressure that the staff were under to prepare students for MSPAP. "We felt very much responsible for making certain the children did well on the MSPAP," Horne said. She added that Calvert instruction alone would not provide the necessary preparation. Brown asserted that they "had to put Calvert a little bit on the side" to prepare for the state test, but their private school partners were not willing to bend their standards. When Barclay teachers expressed the need to spend more time on MSPAP preparations, Hall and others at Calvert reiterated that using their curriculum meant "it has to be done all the way," and if the Barclay staff could not do that, the time to end the partnership had come.[25]

Although Barclay students did well in the first years of MSPAP testing, the school's scores declined sharply in 1997. The next year Barclay was listed among those schools declared by MSDE to be "reconstitution eligible" (RE). Henceforth, the state would have a hand in supervising and monitoring the Barclay instructional program. Both principal and staff at Barclay felt that they should have had some opportunity to appeal the state designation. They could point to substantive mitigating circumstances in the year of the declining scores: a chicken pox epidemic among the children, two teachers out on maternity leave, two other teachers out for personal reasons and illness, and Gertrude's own absence due to brain surgery. "I still look at it as unfair," declared Truemella Horne five years later. It is her perception that "other schools had a couple of years before becoming RE, but Barclay plunged into it the very first year [the scores fell]."[26]

Every Barclay and Calvert educator interviewed for this book sounded the same theme that Gertrude develops in her narrative: MSPAP was an unwelcome distraction. David Clapp, a Barclay–Calvert teacher and eventually Gertrude's successor as principal, declared that "MSPAP definitely derailed Calvert more than anything else, because it was . . . so emphasized and reported in the paper and meant everything— whether your school was getting a certain amount of money, or whether they were going to be taken over by the state."[27]

In numerous ways Calvert and MSPAP methods did not match. Clapp explained that Calvert's "timeline" was not in synch with the state test. Fifth grade students using the Calvert curriculum, for example, were tested by MSPAP on Maryland History before it had been taught to them. Yet another divergence between MSPAP and Calvert was obvious in the MSPAP assumptions about writing. Teachers preparing students for the state tests were advised to not worry a great deal about spelling and syntax but to encourage imaginative word usage with their students. Yet at Barclay, where Peg Licht would countenance no errors in spelling, sentence structure, grammar, or any other element of composition, students were trained to be painstakingly accurate.[28]

A fourth impediment to a continuation of the early Barclay–Calvert harmony was the two-pronged decision, taken in the spring of 1994, to expand the program into the fifth and middle-school grades (six–eight) and to transfer Peg Licht to Carter Woodson Elementary School, where she would coordinate the start-up of a second Calvert–public school project. While neither Gertrude, Hall, nor Embry identified these developments as negatively affecting the partnership, examination of their consequences suggests that the effect was indeed deleterious. They rationalized the removal of Licht from Barclay at least partly by the argument that her expertise lay in the early grades, and she was not certified in intermediate and middle-school education. Additionally, Hall and Embry both noted that, in Hall's words, Licht was "ready for a change." He also stressed that "if they [the Barclay staff] were going to [carry out Calvert instruction] on their own, their teachers would have to become Peg Lichts."[29]

The fact was that no one at hand was fully prepared to guide the program in the higher grades. The Calvert day school did not include middle-school children.[30] Its home schooling department offered a middle-school course of study, but that course had not been translated into a format for classroom teaching. As David Clapp remarked, "the curriculum itself is different at those [intermediate/middle-school grades], where the early stress on basic skills gives way to more emphasis on content." He also noted that the complicated issue of transfer students became even more critical with older children, and questioned "if all the details and all the energy that had been put into the initial implementation was brought to the table in the second phase of implementation."[31]

There is no evidence that this question can be answered in the affirmative. The decision to continue rode on the general feeling that, as Clapp put it, the program "was so successful and things were so positive that there was really no other option but to continue." Merrill Hall maintained that he had expected from the beginning that if the program were successful it would be possible to extend the funding and it would be logical to carry it through all the Barclay grades. Nonetheless, without the kind of precise planning and preparation that made for initial success, without the intensive training for new staff that Licht had heretofore provided, and without her there to be "just adamant" about "this is the way it's going to be done," the program's chances for a long life were compromised.[32]

Absolutely no one was Licht's equal in having the depth of experience with both public school and Calvert school education. No one shared Gertrude's wholehearted enthusiasm for the project as much as she did. Indeed, because Licht was so right for the original position and had so quickly and completely gained Gertrude's confidence, virtually no attention was given to developing a course of training or even to composing a formal job description for the coordinator's post. Licht *was* the Barclay–Calvert Coordinator. The position was undefined apart from her.

Licht's successor, a former Barclay second grade teacher, was neither a Calvert veteran nor experienced in the type of administrative oversight expected of a coordinator. Thus, when Licht left, not only did Gertrude lose a dedicated and expert lieutenant, but also shifted onto her was the responsibility of orienting a novice coordinator; learning the ropes of extending the program to the upper grades; keeping it running smoothly in grades K through four; continuing to manage a staff of over 50 and a student body of over 500, all while operating as a tour guide, public speaker, and media personality. It is doubtful that her critics—those in-house, as well as those at Calvert and the Abell Foundation—fully apprehended the virtually impossible load she was struggling to manage. It's even questionable whether she could admit to herself what overwhelming proportions her agenda had taken on.

In the second year after Licht's departure, at the urging of her Calvert partners, a second coordinator was appointed from the ranks of the Barclay teaching staff, establishing one coordinator for the early grades and one for the upper grades. This second coordinator also did not receive formal training, and now not one but two coordinators were floundering. Gertrude's rapport with these coordinators was never strong. Yet Hall remarked about the two Barclay coordinators, "We thought we had good leaders," and he concluded that "they weren't empowered enough." The ties to other teachers that they brought to the new job handicapped them, he thought. They couldn't maintain the same kinds of friendship they had as colleagues and fulfill their new role as overseers and enforcers.[33]

Lacking clear role expectations; facing mounting tensions over such issues as Title I, transition students, and MSPAP; operating in a fishbowl environment under media scrutiny and among never ending crowds of visitors, the coordinators had no idea how to move the program forward, let alone satisfy Gertrude. They increasingly sought support and direction from Merrill Hall and Muriel Berkeley, whom Hall had assigned as a liaison to work with the Barclay staff.

Hall and his assistant headmaster, Pat Harrison, tried unsuccessfully to engage Gertrude in dialogue about what they saw as a growing failure of Barclay staff to faithfully implement the Calvert program. Hall wrote her a letter, which, as she notes in her narrative, she is certain she did not receive. The letter listed five points of concern: need for improved communication with the curriculum coordinators; alleged administrative inefficiencies on her part in setting up transition classes; assigning instructional space, and making timely evaluations of teachers; personnel who were "not faithfully implementing the Calvert curriculum"; public statements by Gertrude regarding the decline in disciplinary problems and students requiring Title-I services that were in Hall's view exaggerated; and general dissatisfaction on the part of Calvert with her as "instructional leader." Hopkins evaluator Sam Stringfield also expressed disappointment and concern in his last two annual evaluations of Barclay–Calvert, noting that while indicators of student performance were still above the norm, a pattern of decline was setting in, which he attributed to slippage in adherence to Calvert methods.[34]

Throughout this period of conflict and tension Gertrude's lifelong capacity for "compartmentalizing" unpleasant realities and carrying on as if they did not exist—a capacity she first revealed as a public school student in the face of certain manifestations of racism—appears to have been in operation. As long as Hall was cordial in social settings and continued to bring visitors to the school and to boast of Barclay students' achievements, she could remain convinced that their partnership was intact and could fail to hear suggestions to the contrary.

Throughout her professional life, Gertrude had managed to fight her way through even the most tangled of problematic situations, so perhaps she couldn't entertain the possibility that she wouldn't be able to work through whatever tensions had developed with the Calvert leaders. Since she was so revered, commanded so much respect, and carried herself with such authority, criticizing Gertrude was never easy, even under the most relaxed of circumstances. In the strained environment of the last years of Barclay–Calvert, calling any aspect of her leadership into question was extremely painful.

Barclay–Calvert was originally established as a four-year project through which Barclay might internalize the essentials of Calvert methods and materials and, having done so, carry on with those essentials independently of Calvert and presumably without additional private funding. Thus when Calvert ended the partnership in the spring of 1996, Gertrude emphasized that the Barclay community had expected all along to reach a point where they would implement Calvert instruction independently of Calvert. "This is a fitting point for Barclay to assume full responsibility for the program," she declared to the press.[35]

As described by David Clapp, the administration and staff were determined "to grapple with . . . and . . . make [the curriculum their] own." The end result might not be a mirror-image of Calvert, but it would be Barclay's own "self-motivating and self-sufficient program."[36] That is the goal that Gertrude bequeathed to him. It has proved to be much more elusive than she hoped.

Clapp maintained a relationship with the Abell Foundation through which he connected Barclay to the foundation's "Baltimore Curriculum Project," headed by Muriel Berkeley. The roots of the project lay in a 1996 ruling by federal district court judge Marvin Garbis in a case focusing on the city's failure to provide adequate services for children with learning disabilities. The ruling authorized private groups to operate public schools in the city, encouraging them to employ "creative strategies of governance and instruction that will improve academic performance for all students." When the city school district set up an office for New Schools Initiatives and invited proposals, the Abell Foundation contracted to manage four schools, including Barclay.

On the face of it, this was a development that fit well with the tradition of independence and innovation fostered by Gertrude at School #54. It appeared to be even more appropriate when Berkeley introduced "Direct Instruction" (DI) to some Barclay classrooms. She described DI, based on a tightly scripted mode of teaching, as "Calvert to the next power" and promoted it as a viable alternative to Calvert instruction, when Walter Amprey expressed interest in expanding Calvert partnerships in Baltimore, and the Calvert board declined DI, which has acquired substantial factions of promoters and detractors, did not go over well with Barclay teachers. Clapp resigned from Barclay in 2002. His immediate successor, selected by Abell, stayed one year, after which Truemella Horne became principal. She withdrew Barclay from the Abell project and ended DI. Traces of Calvert could still be found at School #54 as late as 2005, in the classrooms of the teachers who pioneered it, but as pressure increased to meet the requirements of the latest state assessment program and the federal No Child Left Behind law to which that program is tailored, the likelihood was slim indeed that Barclay educators would ever return to a Calvert-style instructional model.

Despite such a disappointing denouement, Gertrude's hope that Barclay–Calvert might "point the city schools in a new direction" or at least "raise awareness that there needed to be a change" was not unfounded. By stirring public discourse about school reform and modeling the persistence and courage that achieving such reform entails, she and the Barclay community may have enhanced the chances of other reform advocates. In the mid-1990s a group of parents in the Waverly community began to campaign for a curriculum grounded in the philosophy of experiential education, incorporating into instruction learning opportunities in the community and the larger world. In the first stages of the campaign they consulted with their Barclay neighbors on strategies for overcoming the roadblocks that the bureaucracy would inevitably place in their way. After a protracted struggle they prevailed, and the Stadium School (so-named because originally they hoped to use space in Memorial Stadium when the Orioles moved to new quarters) is flourishing, with a curriculum based on experiential learning, including student explorations beyond the classroom walls. Other groups soon gained an opportunity to start up schools designed under the city's "New Schools Initiative," and, more recently, under the aegis of new state legislation authorizing the development of "charter schools."[37]

Wherever such developments might lead, nothing could rob Gertrude of the sweet satisfaction of having shown the world that Barclay children could not only meet the challenges of the Calvert curriculum but could—and did—excel beyond everyone's expectations, consistently, for four years. However confusing and dispiriting the final years of the Calvert partnership may have been; however predictable and infuriating the incapacity of the city school system to appreciate and facilitate the Barclay–Calvert program, her hard and bravely fought victory over the bureaucrats, and Barclay students' masterful response to the opportunities she won for them, could never be denied. "That's the peace that I have inside," she confided in the spring of 2004. "I know that those children got their chance."

*   *   *

After the June 14, 1989 meeting with Kurt Schmoke I believed that he would find a way for us to get the Calvert curriculum. When I got back to school after that meeting everyone was anxious and wanted to know, "What did he say? Are we going to get the program?" I felt that I had to play cat and mouse. I had been stung before, when Robert Walker had said that Alice was going to sign off on the middle school. I felt like a fool when I got to the board meeting with all those parents, and Alice backed off. Now if the mayor backed off, there I would be with egg on my face again. So I said as much as I thought I could say without coming out and promising that we were going to get the Calvert curriculum. Even though he had been friendly to me, Mayor Schmoke still was not openly in our corner.

I told the staff and the parents that I felt as though he had finally come on to our side and that he was going to help us. Most of them understood when I said, "But I can't say but so much 'til it happens." However, others were really miffed. I understood why. Until my meeting with him, Schmoke certainly had not been supportive of us on the Calvert issue. Why should we trust him now? Everyone had given so much time to Barclay, had worked so hard for the Calvert proposal, backed it at every step. Now here I was hedging and saying that we needed to calm down. They kept questioning me: "Why should we calm down? Why don't we keep battling?" I started making up answers—that we could count on having our class sizes capped and having our staff remain stable and receiving materials and supplies on time. I could have said that the mayor had said, "Just quiet it down and I'll do my part." But I thought I'd better not quote him.

It was a very touchy situation. The mayor saw that no one was backing down, and it had reached a point where he was going to have a split city. Education was supposed to be his top priority, and here the city was about to have an explosion over a matter of education. The newspapers just kept rubbing it in. Schmoke would have been so much more effective if he had brought all the factions together in the beginning, when the conflict started. Instead he dodged and allowed it to reach a dangerous pitch. He was losing face with the white community and with blacks, and he was in the middle. He wanted to run for mayor again, so he knew he had to do something.[38]

For the rest of 1989 the mayor tried over and over again to get Hunter to meet with me, and to work out some way in which he could come out ahead. Hunter just refused. He had Schmoke believing that we were meeting, but he didn't even try to meet. He continued to attack me in administrative meetings. A few of the other principals finally called the mayor and said, "If he has a problem with Trudy why doesn't he go to her school or call her to his office? We go into a meeting, and he sees Trudy, and that's the end of the meeting." Mayor Schmoke called me to ask what was going on. I told him I just wasn't going to any more administrative meetings, because Hunter was acting terrible.

Finally, the mayor told me that he gave Hunter a deadline either to sign the letter to okay our program or submit a letter of resignation. Hunter didn't do either, and that was the last straw for Schmoke. I told him, "Well, now you know what we've been going through." That's when he fired Hunter. It was December, and the *Baltimore Sun* had a cartoon of the mayor serving up Hunter's head on a Christmas platter. I still am labeled by some people as the reason for Hunter's downfall. But he caused his own demise by his lack of vision and his stubbornness.

I have been asked how someone as stubborn as I am can blame Hunter for being stubborn. Usually I got stubborn when I was trying to make a change that would be better for children, and people in positions above me refused to even listen. When I'd gone through all the steps to bring that change to their attention, and these people who should have supported me said "No" without trying to understand what was being asked, that's when I got stubborn. I contrast that with Hunter's kind of stubbornness that came from refusing to see that there was more than one side to an issue. That was just blind stubbornness, and that is what we had to deal with in Hunter.

The agreement for Barclay to adopt the Calvert curriculum was finally signed by Joseph Smith, president of the school board in 1990, and copies were distributed to the superintendent, the mayor, and other central administrators who would have some role in implementing it. Merrill Hall and I also received copies.[39] It covered the points we had listed back in the spring of 1988—introducing the curriculum grade by grade for four years, starting with kindergarten and grade one; class sizes of no more than 25; two adults, a teacher and an assistant, in each class; training for every teacher and assistant; an on-site coordinator; delivery of curriculum-related materials by Calvert; Abell funding channeled through Calvert School for all expenses related to the Calvert curriculum; regular public funding to continue at the usual level.[40] In adopting Calvert, we eliminated departmentalization in the grades that were using the Calvert curriculum. We retained departmentalization in the other grades until they were phased into the Calvert model.

The Barclay–Calvert program began in September 1990. The teachers and assistants had been trained in the summer and knew what was coming. They had their books, materials, and everything they needed by the beginning of August. That was unheard of. We were used to getting materials—*if* we got them—by November. Then the system was likely to change the curriculum late in the fall, and teachers would be scrambling to adjust. Now, our teachers had gone through the training, knew what was expected of them, had a handbook and all of their supplies. They were hepped-up and ready to go.

The Calvert coordinator was Margaret Licht—Peg. She had taught in the public schools at an earlier stage and had been teaching a long while at Calvert. She was really equipped to teach our teachers. Without Peg, the Calvert program would not have been as successful as it was. She believed in the program, was totally focused on it, and understood what it could do for our children. She was determined that Barclay students would perform with the best of the Calvert students, and our children did rise to her expectations. She didn't allow people to say, "This child can't learn." "Yes he can!" she would insist. Then she would put that extra effort in to prove it. We had students who were labeled "special ed" who learned to read and write as well as the other students because of Peg.

She also made sure that the teachers rose along with the students. They had voted "yes" for Calvert; they had been trained in Calvert methods; they knew what had to be done. But it's one thing to *say* we're going to do it and another when we find that doing it means extra time and work. Then the temptation is to complain that the people in charge are demanding too much. In the beginning some teachers did complain about Peg. She had her ways. Her insistence could pluck the teachers' nerves. Sometimes I would have to talk with her. But I saw that Peg knew what she was doing.

My job was to back her and not let the teachers back off. She would not let them leave any gaps in their instruction. If a child's paper was messy or he had left out a word, Peg insisted that he do the paper over. Sometimes the teacher would say, "Why? This looks good compared to the work we used to get." Peg would answer, "It does not meet Calvert standards," and the child would do the paper again. She went into the classrooms every day. If teachers needed help she would teach the lesson to give them a model on which to pattern their teaching. She was magnificent. She made that curriculum work.

Peg as curriculum coordinator functioned the way assistant principals had functioned when I was a teacher. Their main job was to implement the curriculum, monitor the teachers, and help them the way Mrs. Booker Davis had worked with me when I was new at Charles Carroll of Carrollton. Assistant principals in later years were not as well trained as Mrs. Booker Davis, and the system had a way of pulling them from work with the curriculum to go to this meeting and that workshop and involving them with whatever was the latest fad. Since Peg did not work for the Baltimore City public schools and her job description was clear, she had the luxury of concentrating only on the curriculum. That was a big plus for Barclay.

Peg also worked with parents. She got them excited about what was happening in their children's classrooms. They really loved her, because—where so often parents get a call to say, "Your child is in trouble . . ."—Peg would call to say, "Oh, Mary did such a great job today. I wanted to let you know!" Peg was responsible for getting the materials that the teachers needed. She met regularly with me, and once a month we both met with Merrill Hall and Pat Harrison. The assistant headmaster at Calvert, Pat was the liaison between Barclay and Calvert. She mediated if disagreements arose. At our monthly meetings we assessed how the program was going and talked over any problems that were occurring.

Maintaining the federally funded Title-I program while phasing in the Calvert program proved to be a problem. Given our budget constraints, we did not have the luxury of having two sets of teachers—one set to work just with the Calvert program and another set to meet the mandates of the public schools. Being a Title-I school meant that we had to follow federal laws or lose the federal money. That meant that we had some teachers in a dual role.

Sandra Brown and Truemella Horne wore two hats. They were trained as Calvert teachers and were also designated as Title-I specialists in reading and in math. They were both excellent teachers. They were to work with the Title-I students—those who came up with a "severe" ranking on the Comprehensive Test of Basic Skills. Some of these students were in the Calvert classes and others were not part of Calvert at all. Remember that we phased in the Calvert curriculum, one grade at a time.

After the Barclay–Calvert students received instruction in the Calvert curriculum they were taken by Sandra and Truemella for a second experience, using materials and methods mandated by the federal government. They also used the federally man-dated materials and methods with the Title-I children who were not in Calvert. Peg interpreted this as noncooperation with the Calvert program. She did not understand the federal government's requirements. After she, Merrill Hall, Pat Harrison, and I met to discuss this issue it seemed to be resolved, at least for as long as Peg remained coordinator.

The Abell Foundation stayed in close touch with us, mostly through its vice president, Anne LaFarge Culman—known to everyone as Sita. She visited us often and helped in many ways. We found, after about the second year, that the city was short-changing us. Sita brought in an accountant and helped us track our budget. She also provided things that teachers wanted—workshops in the summertime for children, for example. Abell also paid for the Barclay–Calvert students to make trips to Calvert to see the planetarium there and for the "fun day" they would have on the Calvert grounds every spring.

The Calvert program showed the value of having small classes. I have heard the arguments that "in the old days" teachers did fine with 40 or 50 children in a room, and that it's better to spend money on books than on hiring enough teachers to reach individual students. But these aren't the old days. Children today are more anxious, more frustrated. Some are abused physically, mentally, and emotionally. They bring that to school. If they are jammed in with so many tables and chairs in the classroom that they bump each other, they cannot work; some will be ready to fight.

The Calvert agreement capped classes at 25 children, with two adults. The children could move around. The program was set up to meet individual needs. The teacher and educational assistant could give extra help and the extra hug, the extra pat. They had time to notice if a child was having trouble and to send a note to me or to the counselor. With those small classes it was like heaven had come and just set up housekeeping right in the middle of Barclay school.

With the Calvert curriculum, heavy development of language skills begins in kindergarten and is emphasized through first and second grade. We trained our prekindergarten teacher in Calvert methods so that she could prepare her children for the kindergarten curriculum. They learned to use all their senses—seeing, hearing, touching. All of these are part of learning how to read. Reading to the children was also stressed, so that they knew that there's something wonderful on that printed page. By first grade they started keeping lists of the new words they learned each day. The teacher gave dictation, and they wrote down the words they knew in simple sentences. There is a linkage between reading and writing, and the Calvert curriculum develops that linkage.

A typical day for a student in the Barclay–Calvert program began when she shook hands with Peg Licht, who greeted her by name and expected her to return the greeting and look her in the eye—a lesson in etiquette and self-esteem. The child then entered the classroom and corrected her work from the previous day, which the teacher would have waiting for her. Her daily schedule would include phonics, handwriting, reading, and math. Starting in the second half of first grade she would write a composition every week and take a weekly spelling test. She learned to draw inferences, use contextual clues, and all the skills that add up to good reading. Science, history, geography, art, music, and other subjects would be part of her schedule, depending on her grade level and the learning sequence of the curriculum.

The student kept her work in individual folders for writing, reading, and math. At the end of every month she would have a conference with one of the adults working with the program. She would go over the work in her folder and talk about what she was learning and any problems she was having. She took her monthly folders home to have her parents look at them and sign her work. Then she brought the signed folders back to school. At the end of the school year all of her papers were put in a permanent binder that she could keep. Students and parents were enthusiastic about this system. Some parents were so proud of the work they saw in the monthly folder that they wanted to take it to their jobs and show it off, instead of sending it back to school.

The teachers' union claimed that having to review all the folders and insisting that the children make corrections added too much to the teachers' workload. However, each teacher in the program had a class of only 25 students and an educational assistant. With that kind of support they were not overburdened by the folders or the corrections. Besides, the corrections are a part of every teacher's professional duty, whether they are in a Calvert program or not. How do children learn from their mistakes if the teacher does not go over their work and have them correct it? Students learn to take pride in improving their work and striving to make it perfect. The Calvert approach teaches them that education is not easy, but it can be exciting.

As we knew they would be, Barclay children were successful with the Calvert curriculum. From the beginning the program was independently evaluated by Dr. Sam Stringfield and his associates at the Center for the Social Organization of Schools at Johns Hopkins University. By his fourth-year evaluation, which he presented in December 1994, Stringfield found that the Barclay–Calvert students were scoring above local and national norms on the standardized test used by Baltimore City (the Comprehensive Test of Basic Skills). On the standardized test used by most independent schools (the ERB—Educational Research Bureau), our students scored above the norms in writing and in line with the independent schools in other subject areas.

He had also asked the school to administer the Otis-Lennon academic aptitude test. Stringfield reported that according to that instrument our students were "making progress . . . in the ability to integrate new material and absorb new knowledge." He observed that since adopting the Calvert curriculum Barclay had fewer student absences, transfers, and disciplinary removals; fewer students needing Chapter 1 services;[41] and more students eligible for advanced academic work.[42] Transfers went down because, Stringfield said, students' parents "have been less willing than their Barclay–Pre Calvert neighbors to leave the school catchment area; or if they must leave, they have been more willing than their neighbors to make the sacrifices necessary to sustain their students in the Barclay–Calvert program." He was really struck by the decline in Chapter 1 enrollments.[43] The Calvert curriculum was drawing out the abilities and potential of children who had been working at a very low level until they entered this program. It was also benefiting our special education students. Stringfield reported that "during the 1993–1994 school year, the four combined grades of Barclay–Calvert students required fewer LD [learning disabled] services than did the single last Barclay–Pre Calvert grade." He pointed out the economic implications:

> Providing special education services constitutes one of the major drains on school districts' limited budgets. Barclay/Calvert had reduced this expensive demand by more than three quarters. The savings to the Baltimore City Schools are considerable.[44]

Stringfield concluded from the Barclay–Calvert program that "there is nothing wrong with urban students." And that is true.[45] Instead of talking about "at risk" children, we should look at "at risk" curriculums, like the disjointed curriculum that Baltimore City was using then.

Really, it wasn't a curriculum. It was little pieces of this and that latest fad with no real structure or organization. There were "values education" and "character education," for example. Teachers were supposed to teach them in isolation. And there were all these programs to help children have "self-esteem." But values and character and self-esteem grow from being treated with respect, being held to high standards, taking pride in work well done. The Calvert curriculum covers all of that while it teaches the basic subjects in a clear, orderly way.

Another part of "character-education" is how people handle children. My mother used to say, "What you do speaks so loud, I can't hear what you're saying." We can teach character education classes every day, but if the adults in the school say ugly things to the children, if teachers yell "Shut up! Sit down!" that's what the children will learn. The Calvert training supported our belief that every member in the school—student, teacher, custodian, administrator—should give and get respect.

Of course, that rule applied to all the grades, not just those that were phased into the Calvert program. At the same time that we moved ahead with Calvert, the rest of the school still demanded my attention—sometimes in surprising ways. One day in the early 1990s a group of middle-school students came to me. They were in the class of a science teacher who had joined the staff in the middle of the year. He replaced a teacher who went out on sick leave. The students complained that this new teacher, an older man, was saying things that upset them. I told them that I would handle it. Evidently I didn't handle it soon enough.

The next morning a call came through the intercom to the office from another middle-school teacher: "Miss Williams, you need to come up here right away." I went upstairs. When I started down the hall I saw teachers looking in this man's room. I went in the room. There was the teacher sitting at his desk, and the students with homemade banners were marching around him. The banners said things like "Racism Must Go" "Treatment Not Fair"; "Students Will Not Tolerate Unfairness";

"We Refuse to Work in These Conditions." I said, "STOP!" They stopped. I said, "Don't say a word! Just—Come—With—Me!" They filed behind me down the steps. I took them to the far end of the office and said, "Now, tell me, what was all that about?"

They told me that they thought he needed to know how they felt, and that they just couldn't work in his room anymore. I reminded them that I had promised to deal with it, and I let them know that they had gotten themselves in serious trouble. I left them sitting back there and went to my office where I called Sam Billups, who was working as a kind of troubleshooter for Walter Amprey, Richard Hunter's successor.

I told Billups how I wanted to handle this situation. I knew that the students had every right to be angry with this teacher, and I didn't want to suspend them. They were all good students and they had a right to express their feelings—but not this way. I wanted to set up a meeting that every parent had to attend. Any parent who didn't come, that child would be suspended. I wanted to have the parents, students, and the teacher talk through the situation. Billups thought that was a good idea, and said that since the children had protested nonviolently he would back me.

I sent letters home with every student and called each parent. One parent said, "You know what? I helped my daughter make those signs. I thought it was for a Martin Luther King play." Another parent, who was a career military man, was furious with his daughter. I told him not to lay hands on her, just come to the meeting. After he had heard everything, then he could decide about punishment.

Every parent came. We met in the multipurpose room of the Recreation Center. I explained what had happened, and that I thought it was important for the parents to listen to the children and to the teacher. I had talked to the children beforehand and told them that it was one thing to walk around with signs. But now they had a chance to explain why they felt they had to use such drastic means. And how this turned out was going to depend on how they handled themselves.

Those children were good! They had put their little notes together. They spoke to their parents and then they would address the teacher and say, "do you remember the day you did such and such?" He had called them derogatory names, called them stupid, would scratch through their work, even work that was correct, and then force them to write 500 times "the teacher is lord in the classroom, and I am a subject."

I audiotaped that meeting (and wished we still had our video equipment). The parent who was a military officer said, "I am a service man and I always obey. I was extremely angry when I heard that my daughter did something like this. I haven't spoken to her since Miss Williams called. But what I'm hearing is disgraceful. I never had a teacher treat me this way. I know that teachers at Barclay do not act this way." He turned to his daughter and apologized to her, which caused her to start crying. All the parents spoke up. When one of them asked me what was going to happen with this teacher, I told her to ask him what he thought the next step should be. He said, "I quit." He left that day. We wrote lesson plans for that class for the rest of the year and brought in substitutes.

In many schools children would either have gone off in a violent way—probably waited for the teacher after school—or they would have given up. But at Barclay students knew that they were an integral part of the school. We were there to help them develop, not turn them into puppets. As part of their education children should have the right to speak up, but in the right manner. I was very proud of those students and their parents.

Barclay was not immune to the increased violence in Baltimore City and the world in general. We had more problems in the 1980s and 1990s with families where drugs and alcohol were impacting the children. And we had more kids with access to guns. Instead of the additional counselors and social workers that we needed, we had to fight to keep the ones we had, and they were always stretched among several schools. Fortunately the only time a child brought a gun to Barclay our social worker, Gloria Hartley, was on duty.

We had guests in the school, and I was occupied with them. Gloria and another person were on the third floor. As they walked past this sixth grader, a gun dropped out of his locker. They took it and him into a room and after the guests left came to get me. He told me that he was holding it for a friend. It was a *huge* hand gun. I asked him if he was angry with anyone. He wasn't angry. He wasn't planning to use it. It wasn't loaded. When I called his mother, the first thing she said was "Didn't I tell you to throw that away?" Instead of disposing of it herself, she had left it in his hands! She said it was his cousin's or somebody's. That child was expelled, put out of school for the rest of the year.

That was the only real gun. We had children bring in toy guns, but I wouldn't put a child out for a toy gun. I'd threaten him and scare him to death, have the suspension officer meet with him and his parents. Usually that scared them. I only had one child who didn't scare, because his mother kept saying, "It's just a toy gun, and I bought it for him . . ." He finally went out on suspension. So even though we had the new program, we still had to deal with all the old problems.

The next superintendent after Hunter, Walter Amprey, let us know that we may have gotten rid of Hunter, but we weren't going to get rid of him. He was the person in charge and he really didn't want to hear what we had to say. There were times when our money was cut, and he refused to give us what we were entitled to. For example, the 1993–94 school budget was cut by $175,000. That was the equivalent of three and a half teaching positions. Barclay parents and community had to go through another fight before the money was restored, and then we didn't receive all of it. Another time the custodial budget was cut. When parents came and took pictures of me sweeping the floors we got some of that money back.[46]

There were times when Amprey just did not want to accept the Barclay–Calvert agreement on such issues as the number of educational assistants that the city would pay for. "My name's not on that contract," he said. I told him that was why we had the school board president sign and not the superintendent, because superintendents come and go. That just antagonized him more.

There was a consistent resentment toward Barclay because we *dared* to go outside of the system to bring in a program. Whenever we would protest something I would be told, "Trudy, you get so much more." And "Trudy, you can't have everything you want." Like Hunter, Amprey believed we were trying to make elitists out of Barclay's students, and that we didn't have a right to fight for the best for our children. He implied that we were robbing other children. In fact, it cost Baltimore City not one penny for the Barclay–Calvert program while the city kept robbing *us*.[47]

The Calvert program brought many visitors to Barclay, especially after the *Reader's Digest* published an article about me. That sparked other publicity in the national media.[48] Soon educators were coming from all over the country and several parts of the world to learn about Barclay–Calvert. Having all these guests was exciting in the beginning. The teachers put up a big map and put dots on every place from which our visitors came—all over the United States, Japan, Europe, and Australia. I didn't mind sharing what we were learning, and I liked talking about the program with others. But it took a lot of time, and it became more and more of a stress. Media people also came and wanted to write about the program, take pictures, shoot film.[49]

Invitations to speak came in from all over the country. After the American Federation of Teachers produced a video about Barclay, we were asked by AFT president, Albert Shanker, to be spokesmen at various meetings and conferences.[50] I went to Wisconsin where Governor Tommy Thompson and the parents there were really trying to make a change. I was invited to Dover, Delaware by the religious right! A Wal Mart executive in Rogers, Arkansas who had seen me on Dan Rather wanted to send his private jet to carry me to his town. I went, but on a regular plane. I felt like I was in a whirlwind. I enjoyed myself in these different places, but I also felt guilty. I wasn't the one doing all the work. Everyone was responsible for the success of Barclay–Calvert, and especially the teachers and the students. I began to feel like I couldn't keep up. I'm just not famous. I'm just me. All of the publicity took me out of what I am.

When school closed in June 1994 Barclay students from kindergarten through fourth grade were successfully following the Calvert curriculum. The Abell Foundation extended funding for us to carry the program through grade six. Abell had also agreed to back a Calvert partnership with a second Baltimore public school, Carter G. Woodson Elementary, in the Cherry Hill region. Peg Licht, who was not trained to work with the higher grade levels, was appointed to be coordinator of the new program.[51]

We selected a Barclay teacher to replace her, and the following year (1995–96) we added a second coordinator, who also came from the Barclay staff. One of them worked with grades K–four and the other with the fifth and sixth grades. Neither of these individuals proved able to handle the job. Without strong coordinators, Barclay teachers became frustrated. The new coordinators did not provide the same clear, firm direction that Peg had given. Nor did I have the same kind of working relationship with them that I had with Peg.

Old disagreements over the Title-I teachers flared up again. Though he didn't talk to me about it, Merrill continued to be unhappy about those teachers. He thought they were not carrying out the Calvert curriculum. What he didn't understand was that they were required to give extra help to students who tested "severe," and they had to use materials mandated by the federal government for those students. If we didn't follow the federal guidelines we would lose our Title-I funding. He also didn't realize that some of the "severe" students were not involved in the Calvert program at all. They went to the Title-I teachers at a different time than the Calvert students. Apparently he observed one of their classes and became upset that they were not following Calvert practices. If he had asked me about it, I could have explained.

Matters were complicated by students transferring into Barclay from other schools. Some were very far behind. Being a public school, as long as we had space, we had to take in any student who moved into our zone, no matter how he tested. We could not tell him to go elsewhere because our curriculum was too difficult. We had to enroll him and begin to teach him at whatever level he tested. We set up "transition classes" for these students, hoping to prepare them for working with the Calvert curriculum. Some of them needed very rudimentary training and there was disagreement on what form that training should take. Keeping the transition classes staffed was another problem when we were dealing with repeated budget cuts.

A further source of frustration was the new Maryland School Performance Assessment Program (MSPAP). It tested grades three, five, and eight every year. The results came back as a score for the school rather than individual student scores. In some parts of the test the students worked in teams. The first and second years, 1993–1995 we did well. The state superintendent, Nancy Grasmick, had a ceremony where we were one of the schools to receive a cash award for our third and eighth grade scores.[52]

But in 1996–1997 the scores fell. The following year in the fifth and eighth grades the scores slipped just below the "satisfactory" level. In the spring of 1998 the State Department of Education declared us "reconstitution eligible," meaning that if the scores did not improve, the state could make adjustments in the total program, including changes in administration and curriculum.

In my opinion MSPAP was a distraction for every school.[53] Children should be tested on what is taught. This test included questions that were outside the experience of city children. It was like a secret society. Our students could read anything, but they didn't have the experience that the test expected them to have. One little girl told me, "I can read it, but I don't know what they want me to do." The test-taking skills that MSPAP required did not entirely match the skills we stressed with Calvert. Both Calvert and MSPAP required them to read with understanding, but careful writing and correct spelling were not so important for MSPAP. Some questions could be answered by either writing a response or drawing a picture; correct grammar and spelling were not required. Our Calvert-trained students were taught always to be precise in choosing words and using proper grammar and spelling. Our children were also encouraged to read and think critically.

MSPAP was geared to industry, to training children for following explicit instructions and working as part of a team. The test did not reward creative responses and critical thinking. Learning how to take the test was the key. Children who did well on MSPAP were children who were taught the test. Some schools began in September preparing their students, teaching them to give the kinds of answers that MSPAP would ask for.[54]

One rule of MSPAP was that for any child who was absent for the test a zero would be averaged into the school total. We had a chicken pox outbreak in the eighth grade during the '96-'97 test, and all those absent students pulled down our average. One test should not be the standard for judging a school. The importance given to MSPAP was out of proportion. I could see having it serve as *one* aspect of school assessment, but not the only aspect. Poor scores on MSPAP sent the message that the teachers had not done well all year, and that the school was not doing well. Since individual scores were not reported, parents could not know how their children were doing.

Nonetheless, I believed that our children should master MSPAP. It was there, and they should do it. In life they're going to be thrown challenges, and they have to learn to meet them. Merrill Hall agreed. We were sure that the reading, writing, and thinking skills developed by Calvert methods could be used successfully with MSPAP. However, the coordinators after Peg did not seem convinced of this and did not manage to integrate the instruction in MSPAP-taking that the children needed with the Calvert program. This became another point of contention. As the new coordinators sowed confusion, Merrill asked Muriel Berkeley to work as a liaison between the two schools and I asked Jo Ann Robinson to sit in on the meetings with Muriel and the coordinators. But adding these extra voices seemed to just increase the confusion.

Trying to get the coordinators on track, establish effective transition classes, mediate between Calvert and the Title-I teachers, improve MSPAP scores, and handle the daily school routines and crises would have been enough to keep me busy. But I also had to deal with the school system.

Walter Amprey continued to be upset with me. When the results of the first four years of Barclay–Calvert were publicized, he praised the program. He supported the new program at Carter Woodson. But he wanted me to retire. In the spring of 1995 he came by the school one day and asked for "Mother Teresa." He told me that I'd been very fortunate to be at Barclay and to have had so many things that other schools didn't get. Then he said, "I want you to go to another school," and he named the school. When I said, "No," he said, "I don't have to ask you. I can make you go or you will resign." I asked him if he was threatening me, and he didn't answer.

I called Mayor Schmoke and told him about the conversation. When Schmoke called Amprey, the superintendent said he was just joking with me. But soon we learned that he was going to recommend to the school board that I be transferred. The staff and parents organized a rally. Our city councilman, Carl Stokes, came. *The Sun* wrote an article. Parents and neighbors went to the school board meeting where Amprey was expected to make his recommendation. Tanya Jackson and Jo Ann

Robinson spoke to him in the hall just before the meeting. He told them that he had been told that it was the right time for me to go. They assured him that the Barclay community thought otherwise. He did not make the recommendation.

I don't think it was coincidence that this happened at the same time that Bob Embry was expressing displeasure with me. He sent me letters about the drop in MSPAP scores. He had questioned others about my leadership. One of the new coordinators frequently complained about me to Calvert. Bob probably heard about those complaints. For some time I had been hearing from Jo Ann that Calvert and Abell were worried about the program. I thought that Bob was just doing his usual hectoring. Merrill and I had recently gone to lunch and had a good talk, and I felt sure that we were still in agreement. He kept bringing people to see the program and enjoyed showing the children's work.

One June day Bob asked me to meet with him, Merrill, Sita, and Jo Ann at the Abell Foundation Office. The day before Sam, Merrill, and I had gone to Washington, DC to testify at a congressional subcommittee hearing about the effectiveness of the Calvert program. We laughed and talked driving down and back and had a very pleasant day. Now, in this meeting, everything was unpleasant. It was like I had been called to a trial and I didn't know what the trial was about.

They quoted Sam Stringfield that the program was only "sixty percent effective" and blamed me. To this day no one has explained where that "sixty percent" figure came from. They passed a copy of a letter across the table. It was addressed to me from Merrill who said, "And we talked about this." I never received that letter. We hadn't talked about it. He had been bringing visitors to the school, and he and I had attended meetings together. Everything was cordial and we had never talked about that letter. If we had, I wouldn't have been so shocked.

Merrill and the others brought up little things that they could have come to the school and sat down and asked me about at any time. This was like a kangaroo court. I have never been so angry. I didn't hear every thing, because as it went on, I stopped caring what they said. I wasn't going to listen to something that was not true. Something really went out of me that day.

The Barclay–Calvert partnership ended soon after. We received a letter stating that Calvert wished to conclude the partnership at the end of the 1995–1996 school year. We did not challenge or argue with them. I informed the mayor, and he advised us to make a statement. We gave Kathy Lally of the *Sun* a release: "This is a fitting point for Barclay to assume full responsibility for the program." We explained that we would go on using Calvert materials and were going to carry the curriculum into the seventh and eighth grades on our own.

The story that appeared in the paper the next day was a terrible distortion. The headline read, "Maryland Tests Torpedo Successful Program." The article belabored our problems with MSPAP and left the impression that we would no longer use the Calvert curriculum. I demanded that Kathy contact the state superintendent and make clear that we had not blamed MSPAP. When I later spoke with Nancy

Grasmick she said, "Trudy, you must have socked it to Kathy Lally," because she explained that in *no* way had we said anything about the Maryland School Performance Assessment Program. Nonetheless, the damage was done, and the public perception was that Barclay students were no longer going to use the Calvert curriculum.[55]

In the summer of 1996 David Clapp became the coordinator for the Barclay–Calvert Middle School. A product of the Calvert School, as well as Gilman School and Princeton University, David had come to Barclay as a teacher's assistant in October 1992. He was so effective in the classroom that we offered him a teaching position the next year. Now he would coordinate the curriculum. Merrill Hall helped him train the seventh and eighth grade teachers. The Abell Foundation funding carried the program through the seventh grade and purchased materials and supplies and training for the teachers. It would have been well if they had given us one more year. But by that time we weren't hugging cousins anymore.

The middle-school teachers did not completely buy into the Calvert program, and I never felt that they internalized the complete Calvert philosophy. They did not find time to have students maintain individual folders in the complete fashion that they were maintained in the lower grades. Still, they adopted some of the teaching materials and enjoyed the monthly meetings with parents. They came together as a team for those meetings.

We had hoped to show the city schools a new direction to follow. I think we at least gave them awareness that there needed to be a change. But the superintendents and others weren't willing to come and see how the change really happened at Barclay. So they started some weird changes that did not pan out. For instance, they started "privatization" programs that promised to change whole schools all at once, missing how we tried to build carefully, grade by grade.[56]

For those who did look closely at Barclay–Calvert, the program showed the importance of starting skill development with the youngest children. It demonstrated the value of phonics as part of the teaching of reading, along with other strategies. When I was growing up, and when I took my Masters in reading, phonics was one of a number of teaching methods. Evangeline Hall had impressed on us at Cheyney that "when you go into that classroom you use *all* of the techniques." Then phonics fell out of favor, and with the Calvert program it was like we had made a new discovery![57]

The real secret of Barclay–Calvert was consistency—in the structure of the curriculum, in the training and monitoring of teachers, in the routines that the children followed. Yet, the Calvert approach is not for everyone. I believe that schools should work with their communities to find the approach that is best for them. I think Barclay helped pave the way for this to happen. Other schools—like some of the "new schools"—could learn from our having success with the Calvert curriculum, and some have adopted it. They still had to fight, but they had the Barclay example. I think we made other communities aware and willing to take some chances.

The Barclay–Calvert program also did a lot for Calvert School. They received wide recognition and validation. Demonstrating that their curriculum worked well with mostly black, low-income students greatly enhanced their reputation and fund-raising capacity. Our experience in extending the curriculum through the middle-school grades may have contributed to the eventual addition of a middle school to their own school.

I will always remember the closeness, the fighting, and the determination on the part of the Barclay staff, parents, and so many people in the community. They said, "We're going to do it" and stood up and worked on it until we got it. It was just really magnificent. That's the thing that I would hope people would get from our experi-ence: if you believe in something, you just stick to it. It was amazing how the people just pulled together to make sure that these children got a chance.

1 Gertrude devoted half of her life to The Barclay School, where she was assigned vice principal in 1969, promoted to principal in 1973, from which post she retired in 1998. Under her leadership Barclay expanded from offering grades 1–5 and half-day kindergarten to serving students from pre-K through 8 with an all-day kindergarten. From the private collection of Gertrude S. Williams

2 Barclay School Parent Clean-Up Day. From the private collection of Gertrude S. Williams

3 Karen (Whitman) Olson, the first PTA President with whom Gertrude worked as a Barclay Principle, organized Parent Clean-Up Days, and led them by example. Here she varnishes a cupboard in the Art Room. Copyright 2005. Reprinted with permission of the *Baltimore Sun*

4 While predominantly African-American, Barclay students came from a range of diverse backrounds. From the private collection of Gertrude S. Williams

5   While Gertrude was struggling to bring the Calvert Curriculum to students at Barclay, the Johns Hopkins University recognized her stellar leadership by bestowing on her the prestigious University President's Medal. Dr. Steven Muller presented it on May 3, 1990, during a community breakfast at the University

6 Mayor Kurt Schmoke's disillusionment with School Superintendent Richard Hunter and the School Board's consequent decision not to renew Hunter's contract inspired this editorial cartoon in the *Baltimore Sun*. Cartoon by Kal, December 20, 1990, Cartoonists and Writers Syndicate

7   Barclay and Calvert teachers in a training workshop at the Calvert School. From the private collection of Tanya Jackson

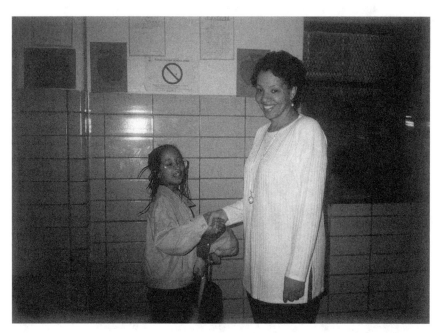

8 At the beginning of each day Barclay–Calvert teachers and students greeted one another with the traditional Calvert hand-shake. Tanya Jackson, a Barclay parent was working as a teaching assistant when this
picture was taken. She would continue on to earn a college degree and become Barclay's pre-Kindergarten
teacher. From the private collection of Tanya Jackson

Barclay School
2900 Barclay Street
Baltimore, Maryland
February 13, 1991

Dear Mayor Schmoke,
    Thank you for helping my
school get the Barclay Calvert
Program. I have been learning
many things in the first grade. I
like writing compositions best because
I can use my own thoughts and
words to write stories and letters.
I love math and reading too!
    Please come to visit us soon
and see why all of us are so
excited about our Barclay - Calvert
Program!
                Love,
            Hanna K.

9   Letter from a Barclay–Calvert student to Mayor Schmoke, penned in the distinctive "Calvert Script" that every Barclay–Calvert student was required to learn. From the private collection of Gertrude S. Williams

10 Student work, meeting the standard of perfection, was displayed in every Barclay–Calvert classroom. Students took great pride in their accomplishments. From the private collections of Tanya Jackson and Gertrude S. Williams

11 Individualized attention from Barclay–Calvert Curriculum Coordinator, Margaret (Peg) Licht. From the private collection of Margaret Licht

12 Among the many volunteers welcomed by Gertrude to Barclay were the Johns Hopkins Women, shown here in the school library, which they rescued from demise when the school lost its librarian due to budget cuts. From left to right: Dea Andersen Kline (the university's community relations director for most of Gertrude's tenure at Barclay), Beth Sykes, Arlene Winchurch, Madelyn Daniels (wife of the late Professor Paul Daniels who also generously contributed his time and expertise working with Barclay faculty and students), Lynn Jones (whose husband, Ross, a university vice president, was also supportive of Barclay), and Esther Bonnet, whose volunteer service at Barclay predates Gertrude's arrival there. From the private collection of Jo Ann O. Robinson

13 Gertrude visiting with Barclay School alumni at a school reunion four years before her retirement. Photograph by the late Joseph Kohl, printed with the permission of Dr. Deborah Kohl

14 Every class prepared a tribute for Gertrude Williams at her retirement, including these kindergartners from the class of Janice French. From the personal collection of Gertrude S. Williams

Unless otherwise noted, all photographs are from the private collection of Gertrude S. Williams

Retirement

In June 1998, Gertrude presided over Barclay commencement exercises. With many hugs, the usual admonitions to students to be true to their best selves, and abundant tears, she let go of the first class to complete the Barclay–Calvert program through grade eight. As those children prepared to enter high school she prepared to retire. Thus the responsibility for appointing a new Barclay principal fell to Superintendent Robert Schiller, who selected David Clapp from among three applicants recommended by a parent-community selection committee who also included Truemella Horne on their short list. After 25 years of Gertrude's high-energy, iconoclastic, devoted leadership, no one in the Barclay-School community could quite imagine how the school would go on without her.

Gertrude had a lot of faith in her replacement, David Clapp, despite his youth and relative lack of administrative experience. He was an alumnus of the Calvert School, which his grandfather and father had also attended, and he shared Gertrude's belief in the efficacy of a Calvert education. "I knew [Calvert] was a special place, even when I was younger," Clapp recalled. "But as I got older . . . I realized the kind of foundation it had laid for me . . ."[1]

After completing an undergraduate degree in economics at Princeton University, Clapp found himself, around the year 1992, searching for work that would be meaningful to him. He had kept in touch with his first grade Calvert teacher, Peg Licht, who suggested that he volunteer at Barclay. At the end of his first day in the school Gertrude asked him if he had enjoyed the day. He recalled saying " 'Yes; it was great; it was a nice experience,' and she said, 'well all right; we'll see you tomorrow then.' That was really it," Clapp reported. "The next day I went on a field trip, and the day after that I came back, and then Miss Williams found a way to get me on the payroll."[2]

He began as an educational assistant and was soon promoted to fourth grade teacher. After Peg Licht's original successors failed to take hold in the coordinator's position, Gertrude appointed David to that role, while also urging him to obtain administrative credentials and giving him increasing responsibilities for leadership in the school.[3] More and more he, along with Truemella Horne whom Gertrude was also mentoring with an eye on her pending retirement, found themselves working with her late into the evening, as she discussed the nuts and bolts, of management issues and problems with which she wrestled every day. She challenged him to think through how he would handle a given situation—taking a leaf from the training procedures of Vic Cord, who more than two decades earlier had drilled Gertrude in such problem solving. Gertrude took Clapp and Horne to administrative meetings and assigned them special projects to work on.[4] "Ordering materials or handling a student issue," were examples that Clapp recalled. And then, he laughed, "she even went so far as to say, 'Okay, I'm going to be out for this day, and now you're in charge' and announcing it to the staff and terrifying me that something was going to go wrong—making sure that I wouldn't get any sleep the night before."[5]

Clapp described his Barclay tutelage as transformative. "There are really no two ways about it," he declared. "She brought me into an entirely different world and gave me the opportunity to succeed in there." Before he walked into Barclay School his sights had been set on finding a path to a lucrative business career, as all of his peers were doing. It was Gertrude who "planted the seed in my head that I should be a teacher, and when I was a teacher that I should be involved in other projects, and when I got involved in other projects that I should think about leading the school. Those concepts never would have developed on their own," Clapp averred. "They were things that needed to be nurtured by someone who I had a lot of respect for and was anxious to please, as well as to learn from and follow."[6]

Clapp inherited both advantages and problems from Gertrude's 25 years as principal. When he assumed that position, he judged the school to be "in good shape." Gertrude had cultivated a "family atmosphere" with "everybody on board for the same ideas, the same goals, the same mission." He was able to tap into that legacy, which provided vital staff and parent support. On the other hand, Clapp described coming up against a rising backlash, resulting from the fact that "Miss Williams . . . had angered some people, stirred up the beehive multiple times within the system to get . . . what she knew she needed for the school. That made it a difficult situation," he reflected, "because I knew there were a lot of people . . . looking to get back at Barclay . . . Barclay was viewed as getting special treatment. . . . And now that Miss Williams was gone school officials in the central administration were going to bring Barclay back to earth . . ."[7]

Clapp cited as an example of this problem school officials' complete refusal to honor the enrollment cap of 25 students per class that had been part of the original Barclay–Calvert agreement with the school board. There had never been total compliance with that cap, but Gertrude had managed to hold the line against major encroachments. When she was still at the helm, once classes reached the 25 limit, children who lived in the Barclay zone were reassigned to schools in bordering zones.

There had always been some resentment on the part of principals and teachers in those schools. According to Clapp, "as soon as I became principal it was like the flood gates opened." Though Gertrude insisted, when commenting on this during our oral interviews, that if Clapp had followed established procedures and alerted the central office in writing as soon as a grade had reached the 25 student cap, he could have avoided overcrowding, the school population went from 440 to 570 in two years. "Even though it went up 130 kids," Clapp lamented, "we were still sending kids out left and right because they didn't live in the zone, trying to make room. If we had kept everyone . . . we'd [have] been above 600, and the school is supposed to be slated for no more than 520." This development was problematic, not only because finding space was difficult, but also because it exacerbated the difficulties with students transferring into Barclay who were not ready for the challenging Calvert curriculum. Furthermore, this swelling of numbers flew in the face of Gertrude's long-held contention that whatever the building capacity, student enrollments should match a school's "program capacity," that is, the optimal number of children the school's program and services can support.

The new principal also felt that central office staff were treating him "like the ugly step child." "If I called facilities or called teacher recruiting or human resources or payroll" he recalled, "it was almost a smug, 'Oh well, you're from Barclay. Don't you know how to solve it? Don't you know how to get that done?' " Clapp's first year, he later remembered, "was an awfully difficult, long, lonely year." He credited Gertrude with getting him through it. "Whether it was crying on the phone to her, or laughing about something that just had become so depressing that it was funny— I don't know where I would have been without her support."

In fact, Gertrude's departure from Barclay did take a gradual course. She maintained a noticable presence for the first two years of her retirement, helping out in the office, substituting in classrooms, advising and encouraging the new administration. According to Clapp "she even knew the stage to slowly wean me off her support." However, Gertrude experienced his growing self-reliance in a somewhat different fashion. She was taken aback when he complained that some Barclay staff were still turning to her when they should have been directing all their questions and requests to him. From that point through the rest of Clapp's tenure, she virtually ended her trips to the school and made a point—whenever she did visit—of calling ahead to ask his permission.

After four years, David Clapp resigned from Barclay to pursue a doctorate in educational leadership. Edward Smith, a principal previously unknown to the community but touted by Bob Embry and the Abell Foundation, was assigned to replace him. He stayed one year. In the fall of 2003 Barclay veteran, Truemella Horne, who had been serving as the school's assistant principal, took the helm.[8] With this regime change Gertrude was welcomed, indeed urged, to resume her visits to the school.

While Gertrude thus stayed in close touch with Horne and other Barclay staff who frequently called for her assistance at the school, she also began to enjoy activities that she had no time for when she was working. She took several trips within the United States, including an extensive train tour to the West Coast, and traveled abroad to Ghana and Brazil. But she did not entirely abjure public school politics, joining a retired educators' association to lobby state and federal governments on such issues as health care benefits. Whatever the enterprises that occupied her in these post-Barclay years, and wherever she might venture, she seemed always to be running into someone who had attended Barclay or sent a child there, who was excited to see her and brimming with memories of their days at School #54. How she continued to hold the admiration and affection of old associates while, still commanding respect, even among those who did not really know her, can be glimpsed in a vignette shared by Barclay teacher Susan Lattimore:

> I was in the room which is off the cafeteria one morning . . . and I heard a voice, and smiled to myself . . . and said "Oh, that sounds like Miss Williams out there." And then I said to myself, "I wish that were Miss Williams." And then I opened the door and it was Miss Williams! And there were children in the cafeteria—it was a big-breakfast scene and they were supposed to be moving to class [and she was moving them along]. I'm sure these children had never seen her before . . . and I think she's smaller now than she was before, but she still commanded that same respect.[9]

*   *   *

In the fall of 1997 I announced that I would retire at the end of that school year. The year before, I had had surgery to remove a brain tumor. It was benign, and I recovered quickly, though five years later, as we were working on this book, my doctor discovered that it was growing back, and I had a second successful surgery. While I was recovering from the first operation, I had a lot of time to think. I really was tired. I knew that it was time for someone to take over the principal's job at Barclay.

I had been working with two staff members, David Clapp and Truemella Horne. David had been an educational assistant, a teacher, and the Calvert curriculum coordinator. Truemella had been at Barclay nearly as long as I and worked for many years as a Title-I teacher, senior teacher, and assistant to the principal. They both became administrative assistants. They were trained in everything about running the school, and I held them accountable for everything, even going to administrative meetings and school board meetings. That spring the regional office initiated a selection process. A committee of parent, community, and faculty representatives interviewed several candidates and recommended three of them. David and Truemella were among their choices. The acting superintendent, Robert Schiller, appointed David as principal. Schiller told me that he had watched David, and he felt that he would make an excellent principal and would work hard to keep up the school.

In the fall of 1998, as David began his first year, the Barclay staff and community invited my family and me to a retirement dinner at the Glass Pavilion on the Johns

Hopkins University campus. Old friends from Charles Carroll of Carrollton and Mordecai Gist came out, and so did many families, students, staff, and community supporters from Barclay. It was great to share memories with them. I could honestly say to everyone that looking at my whole life span so far, I've enjoyed my life in education—in the classroom, out of the classroom, counseling, and as an administrator.

However, as I told Mayor Schmoke, education is a challenging agenda. Being a principal was sometimes really lonely. I could rely on the staff and the steering committee to help set the direction for Barclay. But I was finally left to make decisions that only I could make, and yet I was never the final decision-maker. I had to fight for most of my decisions, and I don't think a person should have to battle as I did for decisions that will help the children. It got to me sometimes.

Stress was a regular part of the job. I used to load some of my stress on my closest friends and supporters. Sometimes going to church helped put things in the right perspective. When I'd go home to Philadelphia I would settle problems around the table with my niece, Joan Spry, and her husband, Harley, who were both teachers. Sometimes the stress would build in me until I couldn't move. Then I'd air it out, holler and scream and go lay people out. One time I completely lost my voice and had to go to a specialist, who told me that the condition was stress-related. He put me on voice rest. My secretary made a sign for my office door: "On Doctor's Orders Do Not Talk To This Woman!"

The Barclay–Calvert battle was exceptionally ugly, and for a long time, even after we won, I was in a permanent state of agitation, ready to jump at anything and anyone. I was just in that fighting mode where I could even turn against friends. I would hope later that they would understand that I didn't mean it. But I'm quite sure that it was hard for them at the time.

My biggest de-stresser was the children. They did so many funny and dear things that I just had to keep laughing. I'd get *so* upset, and I'd say "I'm just *not* going to deal with these thugs out here anymore!" Then I'd think about the kids, and all the other feelings were null and void. One day I was on the second floor, and I was carrying on so, just fussing! One little boy came up and said, "Miss Williams?" I said, "What?" He replied, "Lean down. I have something to tell you." I bent down, and he kissed me right on the cheek. So I had to stop fussing.

I was very fortunate to have the outstanding staff that worked with me at Barclay School. We had our arguments. They didn't always like what I did, and I wasn't always happy with them. But they cared about the children. And if something happened to someone, they were there. When I had personal crises I knew I could count on them.

While I was at Barclay there were four deaths in my immediate family—two of my brothers and both of my parents. My aunt Emma, who lived with us and helped raise me, also died. In the last years of my mother's life I went home to Philadelphia every weekend, and there were times when I had to go to her during the week. In every case I could call on any staff member, and they would take care of the school until I returned. I relied especially on Evelyn Wallace, Truemella Horne, and the late Gwynetta Deans.[10] Sometimes we did not have an assistant principal, and sometimes we did not have a secretary. But everyone was willing to step in and help. The same was true on the few occasions when I was out for surgery or an illness.

On one occasion, when I came back from a three weeks' absence due to surgery, a little boy ran to meet me. After a big hug he said, "You aren't going to leave again, are you?" I promised him I wouldn't, and he looked greatly relieved. I soon realized that Truemella, who acted as teacher in charge, since we didn't then have an assistant principal, and the whole staff had been determined that nothing would go wrong while I was out. They had been tougher on the children than I ever was.

So whenever a family or health crisis did arise, though at first I would get anxious and would say, "Oh, shucks, not now," I knew that the staff and community always came through. So did my friend, Clara Jones. She's been like my family when I'm away from the family.

My actual family has always supported me, and I am proud that three of my nieces and one nephew by marriage have become educators. At first, when I was the only child in my big family who had gone to college, we had some tension. We could be discussing the daily news, or any subject, and if I gave my opinion one of my brothers or sisters would say, "Oh, well, *you* would know. *You* went to college." But that stopped when the next generation came along. I used to talk to them—especially to my sister Lottie's daughter, Joan—about how much I loved school, how I loved teaching. Then Joan decided she would be a teacher, and her husband, Harley Spry, became a teacher, too. Two of my sister Sarah's daughters—Sandra and Carol Jewett, are now teaching. Sandra, who graduated from Boston University, works with autistic children . I have watched her teach, and she's darned good. Carol graduated from Temple University in music. She has a beautiful singing voice and is also trained in library science, which she teaches at the Community College of Philadelphia.

For the younger generations who are taking education as their agenda, I would like to see some changes. Instead of assuming that black students must have a "black curriculum" in order to learn, I would hope that new generations of educators would insist on a strong, traditional curriculum with the same high expectation level for black students as for students of any other race. I do not espouse Afrocentrism, though I do believe that students should learn that the history of black people did not begin when the first slave ships came in. The African heritage is an integral part of human history, and children should master it, just as they should understand what each race and culture has given to make the world rich. The children of today and tomorrow need educators who believe in and are ready to fight for the education of all students—not because of their color or status in life, but because the purpose of all education is to have people become independent and reach their goals in life.

From the time when Alice Pinderhughes was superintendent, the Baltimore school system has been talking about "school-based management" and "shared decision-making." But it's never happened. I would like to see principals and their staffs *really* freed up to manage their own schools, with a fair budget that they could use to get the most for every child in that school. Of course every school would still report to the superintendent and would meet system standards. But a principal and her staff should be able to set up a scheme that works for their students and their families. This seems to be the direction taken by the New Schools Initiative, and I hope it succeeds.[11]

For a school budget to be fair, it shouldn't be based on the number of children in the school, because even if you have half of those children you still need the same facilities and services. The budget should be based on the programs in the school. Those programs should be there because they are meeting the needs of all the children. Funding for the city schools is a disaster. One reason is that schools in the counties, where there is more wealth, receive more than in the cities. This should not be. A change in the state's funding policies is long overdue. The legislature has tinkered with the funding formula for years. But they are not committed to *equal* funding for all children, no matter where they happen to live. Nevertheless, school budgets in the city don't have to be as bad as they are, if the people at the top would understand that before they spend money on anything else they must spend it on the child in the classroom.[12]

I wish that our country would treat educators with the respect that they deserve. Teachers are professionals. They have gone through at least four years of college and most go on to earn higher degrees. Lawmakers and others demand that they perform as professionals. Yet teachers are not paid the salary that is comparable to other professionals.[13] And educators are seldom treated like professionals. More often they are treated as dimwits who must be preached to and talked down to. It's not realistic to ask for professional behavior out of people who are treated with low respect.

The training and supervision of teachers must be upgraded. Few schools of education today offer the rigorous instruction that teachers' colleges such as Cheyney once provided. Nor do school systems support their teachers the way I was supported by a team of supervisors and coordinators when I started teaching in Baltimore. That idea of a whole supervisory team has been thrown away, and it should be brought back. When Dr. Schiller was here he started having retired teachers come back and work with some of the new teachers. That was a good idea, but, but the system could not afford to continue it.[14] Every year promising new teachers leave the system because we have not given them the guidance and support that they need in the beginning. I also believe that the selection of principals and supervisors should be handled differently. They should be chosen because they know what they are doing, and because they will be effective in training and coaching teachers. How many years they have been in the system or who they know in the system shouldn't matter.

I would like to see most of the city's middle schools either torn down or rearranged so that students will not be overwhelmed and lost in these huge spaces. The middle schools and high schools should be small enough, and be staffed well enough, that students receive regular adult guidance, not only from their teachers but from counselors and the principal. Today many middle-school and high-school students don't even know who their principal is, and that's unfair. Young people should have a chance to interact with and feel that they are important to the administration of their school.

Finally, I hope for more leaders at the top of the system who really care about the children in the schools and who treat principals as educational leaders and respect teachers as professionals. Our school system needs leaders who can bring about change with understanding, not by authoritarian tactics.

I left Barclay with a sense of ease, because I felt that I was leaving them the secret of success, what Sam Stringfield described as the "highly demanding, continuously evaluated curriculum and instructional program" that Calvert had shared with us and the "highly reliable implementation techniques" that Peg Licht had trained our teachers to employ, so that now they had the ability to continue to succeed.[15] However, I cannot predict the future of the school. Years of blood, sweat, and tears went into making it a symbol of the right of every child to an excellent education. If the new administrators understand that they must keep fighting for that right, Barclay will thrive. If they fail to understand, Barclay will become just "run of the mill."

Despite all, education is one of the finest professions a person can choose. One can either have a rich life from it, or can become upset by it. I have had a rich life. I've battled. I've gotten on people's nerves. If I could go back and rewrite the script for my life, I would change a few little things. I know that when I get mad I do crazy things, so piece by piece I might make adjustments. But I would make no major changes. I certainly wouldn't want to be in any other community. Whenever people have asked me "How could you stay there that long?" I have said, "This is a pro-education community, and that makes life better." I loved my teaching and my counseling, but all the joys of education came together for me at Barclay.

I didn't become an educator for wealth or glamor. The rewards of taking education as my agenda have come from helping children develop into competent and capable citizens. When I see former Barclay students who have become independent and are being the best that they can be, I feel so good! I look at them using their skills. They are not slick. They are not welfare-minded. They just know their own self-worth. I run into parents who tell me what their child is doing, and they'll say, "And it all started at Barclay." Of course, it didn't *all* start there. But I'm proud that we did our part.

Conclusion

Free, universal public education is a critical element in the democratic way of life to which Americans aspire. The country's public school system has created a population with a level of literacy that ranks at the top of all nations and can be credited with taking the United States to its position as one of the most productive nations in the world.[1] Yet, just as democracy itself has fallen short of securing the blessings of liberty to all Americans, public education has shortchanged the children of the country's most impoverished communities. Among the instruments of this deprivation, three of the most wicked have been state-sanctioned segregation as well as state-tolerated de facto segregation of public schools; school funding formulas that deny children living in poor jurisdictions resources equal to those enjoyed by children in wealthy districts; and what scholar/author Charles Payne has labeled "the doctrine of the ineducability of the children of the urban poor."[2]

These manifestations of injustice profoundly affected the teaching, counseling, and administrative labors of Gertrude Williams. They contradicted the tenets of basic human decency and fairness on which she had been raised, and stirred her ample capacity for righteous indignation. They infused urgency into the mission and purpose behind her training at Cheyney—to nurture "a sturdy self-respect" in all students. And they prompted her to cultivate ties with like-minded allies, as she battled to secure educational opportunities to which she knew her students were entitled.

When Gertrude took up her education agenda in Baltimore in 1949, Maryland school systems, along with those in other border states, all southern states, and some school districts in the northern and western regions of the United States, enforced racial segregation by legal sanctions. Consequently, she was assigned to a school in the "colored" division of the Baltimore education system. Though she and her colleagues at Charles Carroll of Carrollton had to draw on their own ingenuity and personal resources to provide teaching materials their under-funded school lacked, their principals and other instructional supervisors held them to high standards and they in turn taught their students well. For her part, Gertrude's teaching excellence earned her leadership opportunities, as a faculty coordinator in the school and as a demonstration teacher for other parts of the colored district.

Even as the nation embarked upon a mighty, complex, and frequently violent struggle over school desegregation, set off by the 1954 Supreme Court finding that "in the field of public education the doctrine of 'separate but equal' has no place," Gertrude remained in that all-black, unequal setting until 1965. Baltimore school officials nominally complied with desegregation but pursued it with little commitment to equal education for black children. Their laissez faire approach may have spared the city the excesses of massive resistance that occurred in other places, but its main result was that many Baltimore schools remained segregated until 1974, when federal agents forced city authorities, including Baltimore's first black superintendent, Roland Patterson, to seek racially balanced schools through compulsory student and staff assignments. By that time, it was too late to enforce desegregation, because a critical mass of whites had already removed their children from the public schools. As was the case in many places, federal mandates of the 1970s only hastened the exodus of white and black middle-class families to suburban, parochial, and independent schools, leaving in the Baltimore school district a majority black and increasingly impoverished and needy student population.

When Gertrude left Charles Carroll of Carrollton in the mid-1960s to assume a counseling position at Mordecai Gist Elementary School, she observed this transformation, and had to help mediate tensions between children of low-income African American families who began moving into the area and the children of white and black middle-class families who traditionally attended the school.

While she was counselor amidst this transition, she began to demonstrate the capacity for patient listening, the authority to appeal to conscience and the demand for respect that became hallmarks of her career. She also became more conscious of the essential inequalities of segregation. Contrasting the abundant resources she found at Gist with the scarcity that she had known for 15 years at Charles Carroll of Carrollton, Gertrude determined that she would fight to secure a fair share of system resources for any students in her charge.

In 1969 school officials, recognizing Gertrude's capacity for leadership in a changing school milieu, appointed her assistant principal at School #54, Barclay School. Among the parents who welcomed her there, and who within four years successfully advocated her elevation to principal, were a cluster of social activists who believed deeply in not simply desegregation of schools but full integration of the nation's multicultural society. Their presence at Barclay, as at Margaret Brent Elementary a few blocks away, represented a conscious decision to put down roots in the city, cultivate a sense of community within a diverse urban population, and raise their children in an environment where individuals from varying economic backgrounds and cultural, religious, and racial traditions practiced tolerance and mutual respect. The compatibility between their goals and Gertrude's values and beliefs was the wellspring that fed many of the creative and bold endeavors that she has described in her narrative.

Yet, as their children grew and moved on to high school, that activist cohort was not replaced. Some of them maintained their attachment to Barclay, volunteering and lobbying on its behalf even when their offsprings were in college. But the times changed. The reform wave caught by the activist generation had crested and by the 1980s was at low ebb. The next parent generations hurried to place their children's names on private school waiting lists, or moved to other, more socially homogenous areas when their youngsters reached school age.

Even when Barclay student accomplishments were drawing admiring observers from half way around the world, white middle-class families within walking distance of Barclay did not send their children to the school.[3] As a consequence, when Gertrude retired in 1998, Barclay's student population was almost entirely comprised of minorities, and nearly all of them from economically marginal families. By then Baltimore held the distinction of becoming "the most segregated school system in the nation," while "rapid resegregation" was overtaking most large school systems with high minority populations.[4]

In their recent examination of public education in the United States, public policy specialists Jennifer Hochschild and Nathan Scovronick summarized opinion poll data on desegregation:

> Most Americans not only believe that desegregation works, but also claim to believe in the principle behind it. By 1995 fully 96 percent of whites agreed that black and white children should attend the same rather than separate schools (up from half in 1956). Only 12 percent of whites claimed in 1997 that they would object if half of the children in their own child's school were black.

However, when one examines the extent to which whites translated verbal support for desegregation into practice the picture changes dramatically.

> Whites' support for federal government intervention to "see to it that black and white children are allowed to go to the same schools" peaked at only 48 percent in 1966 and declined to 30 percent by 2000.

Hochschild and Scovronick conclude that

> White Americans endorse school desegregation in principle, and believe that it has benefited blacks, the nation as a whole, and arguably whites. They support voluntary measures to achieve it but are not willing to take the necessary actions to make it happen. As one schooling expert put it recently, "Today a bipartisan consensus holds that integrated schools are a good thing but we shouldn't do much of anything to promote them."[5]

Whatever body of research one may choose to credit—that which pronounces school desegregation a failure and enumerates evidence of harm to the students on whom it was imposed, or that which identifies academic and social gains experienced by black and white children who were required to attend school in the same buildings[6]—this most momentous development in the history of American public education did not secure equal opportunity on anywhere near the scale that its architects envisioned. Not only have the nation's poorest children been shunned by the white and black middle classes but the school districts where they have been left behind are in thrall to state funding practices that privilege well-off school systems and leave poorer jurisdictions at an extreme disadvantage, as Hochschild and Scovronick have spelled out:

> Because . . . local taxes fund almost half of school district expenditures [in the United States], districts with expensive houses and correspondingly high rates of return from taxation can raise money relatively easily, while property-poor districts, with children who need more help, have trouble raising money to provide it. As a result, children in affluent (predominantly white) districts receive a better education than do children in poor (disproportionately minority) districts.[7]

Maryland is among the 43 states where litigation over funding inequities has occurred during the past three decades. In the course of Gertrude's career two major law suits challenged the state's funding system. The first was initiated in 1978 and the most recent in 1994. Baltimore was represented in both suits. Gubernatorial commissions, charged with studying funding policy and recommending reform, grew out of each legal proceeding. Several years after state legislators transformed proposals from the first commission into policy, analysts found that the funding disparity between Maryland's poor and wealthy school districts had not only *not* been narrowed but, if present trends continued, would continue to grow wider.[8]

In the wake of the second round of litigation at century's end (in cases known as *Bradford v. Maryland*, 1996 and 2000), the Maryland General Assembly in 2002 "enacted a modern, standards-based finance system . . . to be phased in over six years . . . sending more state funding to high-need districts." Identifying sources of revenue to support the new system triggered rancorous politicking and debate in the 2004 legislative session. Time will tell whether state lawmakers and the citizenry they represent can muster the political will to fully implement this latest attempt at establishing justice.[9]

Resegregation and the resulting poverty of urban public schools shaped the environment in which Gertrude had to pursue her education agenda, stirring her outrage and firing her activism. She was well informed about the financial shortfalls that constantly bedeviled the Baltimore public school system. With her guidance and approval, the Barclay school community joined all the campaigns that city mayors, superintendents, and school boards spearheaded on behalf of fiscal relief. Parents rallied, signed petitions, wrote letters, and testified before state committees and commissions. Simultaneously, however, the Barclay principal called attention to ways in which city leaders weakened their own case for increased state fiscal support.

With some justification, many state lawmakers accused the Baltimore school district of fiscal mismanagement. Their complaints culminated in the 1997 abolition of the mayor-appointed city school board and the establishment of a city–state partnership. Gertrude was rarely surprised when state officials took the city school system to task on funding matters. As her narrative has shown, she routinely questioned Baltimore officials' budget projections, disagreed with their spending priorities, protested allocations that she found to be inadequate, accused City Hall of invoicing procedures that deprived the school of its fair share of materials and supplies, and primed parents and other community allies to challenge publicly the most egregious instances of fiscal irresponsibility on the part of the local school district.

Gertrude did not stop at lobbying and fighting state and local governmental bodies on budget issues. From the days at School 139 when she and a colleague scoured neighborhood factories and returned with carpet remnants for kindergarten children to sit on and shoes at drastically reduced costs for all the children who needed them, through the numerous links she forged between Barclay School and such entities as Johns Hopkins University and the Homewood Friends Meeting, to the crowning Abell Foundation grant for the Barclay–Calvert project, Gertrude proactively supplemented sparse public funding with monies, materials, and services donated by an array of contributors.[10]

In so doing she ignored those commentators who asserted that "throwing money" at public schools will not remedy their deficiencies. She took as a truism that sufficiency of funds is a necessary component of effective education. Any examination of private schools and the wealth that sustains them made this patently obvious. She would heartily agree with fellow-principal Deborah Meier that "What we need [in public education] are strategies for giving to everyone what the rich have always valued." In *Getting What We Ask For*, author-scholar Charles Payne muses "Elite schools are hardly my idea of the best we can do, but . . . treating poor children as we treat rich children looks like a pretty good idea" after all. He imagined what would have happened "had we taken elite upper-middle-class schools as the model for what we wanted in the inner city":

> [W]e would have put students in small schools where they could feel that they matter personally, we would have evaluated teachers with frankly subjective judgments from informed persons, asking those who did not perform to go elsewhere, and we would have given students a level of work that required them to stretch their talents.[11]

The mind-set of certain central administrators—Richard Hunter being the prime example—who expected that she would refrain from empowering parents, cultivating private resources and demanding her students' fair share from public coffers until all schools in the system could enjoy the benefits that she and her allies had secured for the students of Barclay made no sense to her. She was certain, and her parent/community allies, myself among them, agreed, that to hold back or tear down the gains made by a school that was thriving would neither enhance the performance of other schools nor strengthen the school district overall.

Gertrude also countered sweeping and derogatory assumptions about public school students being "at risk"—shorthand in the minds of many who used that term for intellectually limited and socially inferior. "Historically," observed Charles Payne, "the stance of American education toward nonwhite students in particular has been that they can be failed because of their performance or passed in spite of it, but they cannot be taught."[12] Gertrude unequivocally rejected this stance, which was contradicted by every element of her upbringing, professional training, and personal value system.

Growing up in Germantown, Pennsylvania, one of eight children in a family that was always financially strapped, she internalized an ethic of hard work, pride in accomplishment, and faith in education. Not only did the adults who nurtured her push Gertrude to excel in school and to pursue her dream of becoming a college graduate, but also she learned the value of education from their very lives. Her father's certificate from the Manassas Training Institute represented the acquisition of skills upon which Horace Williams could always draw, enabling him to find work when black unemployment rates surged, and even to establish his own contracting business. From her Aunt Emma's experience Gertrude drew another lesson: no matter that her aunt was smart and talented, she would never enjoy the full exercise of her gifts because she lacked formal schooling and the credentials it offered. More than anyone, Mamie Williams, Gertrude's mother, impressed on her daughter the view that education was the avenue of escape from the drudgery of domestic employment and the way to personal fulfillment.

In the public schools of Philadelphia, and especially at Cheyney Teachers College, Gertrude was schooled along the same traditional lines that emphasized thorough attention to detail, a standard of perfection, and a recognition of accomplishment as the only legitimate source of confidence and self-esteem. To a large degree, those same values and assumptions seem to have prevailed in the Baltimore "Colored School District" in the early years of Gertrude's teaching career, where stern curriculum supervisors critiqued every new teacher's lesson plans on a weekly basis; watchful assistant principals coached them on classroom management; and meticulous principals such as George Simms interested themselves in every aspect of their teachers' professional development.

By the time Gertrude had moved from teaching and counseling to the administration of Barclay School, such strongly focused attention on curriculum and instruction within the school system had given way to policies and practices driven by social issues, including desegregation, white flight, black power, and funding inequities. In an increasingly politicized milieu, public school superintendents began to come and go at rapid rates—often in the midst of bitter political warfare and charged racial conflicts. With each new superintendent came new initiatives and mandates to replace those of his/her predecessor.[13]

The impact on classroom instruction was devastating. Baltimore City's curriculum guides grew thicker and less coherent every year. Often the central office had run out of the textbooks and other teaching materials upon which the curriculum was based. By the time of Alice Pinderhughes's superintendency, the curriculum was in such disrepair that copies of the curriculum guides were no longer available for public review. In place of a coherent curriculum and a well-orchestrated regimen of staff-training and supervision, school site staffs were awash in fads and gimmicks. They would no sooner begin to adjust to one innovation when it would be replaced by another. Staffing shortages were also endemic.

From the very first stages of her principalship Gertrude resisted these trends, ignored or refused to entertain directives that she judged to be counterproductive, fought for the staff, equipment, and supplies to which, she was certain, her students were entitled, and insisted on placing effective teaching and high expectations for students at the center of the Barclay agenda. With her gift for forging partnerships and attracting allies, she soon had Johns Hopkins University faculty designing state accredited, Masters level courses specifically for Barclay teachers, with all costs absorbed by Hopkins. Without asking permission, she and her staff instituted a "nongraded" model of instruction, on the premise that each child should be allowed to "learn as fast as he can and as slow as he must."

When ordered by the central bureaucracy to stop nongradedness, she introduced departmentalization—almost unheard of in elementary education, but readily accepted by Barclay staff, students, and parents, who experienced the benefits of having teachers "teach to their strength." Other Barclay innovations—pre-K; all-day kindergarten; the "rescheduled week"; an on-site Gifted and Talented program—signaled Gertrude's determination to deliver an excellent education to every Barclay child. For exceptionally bright students whose needs she could not meet, Gertrude secured private school scholarships, demonstrating her belief that a child's social and economic status ought not determine how far that child can go academically.

It was her belief in the liberating power of a liberal education, as well as her enthusiasm for its discipline and rigor, that drew her to the Calvert curriculum. She thrilled at the vision of Barclay children maturing into adults who would hold their own in any situation, be conversant with all dimensions of life, and make their way in the stream of history not as flotsam but as captains of their own ships, prepared to navigate in all waters. Her vision was not unlike that which African American scholar W.E.B. DuBois laid out in his prophetic work, *The Souls of Black Folk*, in which he invoked a realm beyond the racist world in which talents and intellect determined the company one would keep:

> I sit with Shakespeare and he winces not. Across the color line I move arm in arm
> with Balzac and Dumas, where smiling men and welcoming women glide in gilded
> halls. From out the caves of evening that swing between the strong-limbed earth and
> the tracery of the stars, I summon Aristotle and Aurelius and what soul I will, and

they come all graciously with no scorn nor condescension. So, wed with Truth, I dwell above the Veil.[14]

As Du Bois so sharply challenged the intellectual and cultural hegemony claimed by racist whites in his day, Barclay students' mastery of Calvert methods, materials and discipline offered a striking rebuke to myths of white superiority still prevalent at the end of the twentieth century. Merrill Hall noted how the news media in their coverage of Barclay–Calvert had focused on the personalities of the educators involved and played up the contrasting demographic profiles of the two schools. But what mattered most, Hall emphasized, was "how good the children are, and how well they can perform." "There's nothing wrong with the children," evaluator Sam Stringfield trumpeted. In press conferences, public lectures, and television appearances Peg Licht, Gertrude, the Barclay teachers and—at least once—even Superintendent Walter Amprey echoed him. "This experiment confirms that there's nothing wrong with our kids," Amprey announced after release of the fourth year evaluation:

> Given the right kind of environment, they will do extremely well. What was surprising about [the Barclay–Calvert results] was how quickly kids can do well with the right kind of ingredients.[15]

Why, then, did the magic begin to fade after four years of remarkable success? Hall suggested a kind of law of curriculum reform: "there is a time period of success and then it gets much more difficult." He posited a time frame of four to six years "for bringing improvements into a school . . . and then the school culture begins to shape its own curriculum again." When the object of change is part of a highly bureaucratized system, as is the case with any public school, and the attempted change runs counter to that system, the odds of the change taking permanent root clearly are not good.

As our review of the Barclay–Calvert experience has documented, the public school "culture" inserted itself into the Barclay–Calvert effort in several ways: the need to accommodate increasing numbers of transfer students; MSPAP drawing energy and focus away from Calvert; the incompatibility of aspects of Title I with the private school's requirements. Education historian Ellen Condiffe Lagemann has contended that even the strongest efforts by charitable foundations who spend "untold millions on public school improvement projects . . . are impossible to sustain over time . . . because education systems lack mechanisms to keep those ideas fresh and evolving." The Barclay experience suggests that more than mechanisms are lacking. Bureaucracies produce meager enthusiasm for, and major resistance to, changes that originate beyond their turf.[16] This was amply demonstrated by the singular lack of support for Barclay–Calvert that was available to Gertrude from the school district central office, and the outright opposition to the partnership that she encountered in those quarters.

Whether reflecting on the resistance to change of public school bureaucracies or documenting the malaises that perennially haunt American public education, commentators who focus on the nation's schools have fostered a culture of public school-bashing that is both unfortunate and destructive. By conveying a general impression of confusion among public school leaders, pundits have promoted a view of the nation's schools as dysfunctional. Recurring media reports of failed disciplinary systems, school violence, and drug trafficking on school grounds reinforce images of public schools as places of danger. Certainly, dysfunctions and dangers were part of the public school landscape throughout Gertrude's career, and she faced off with them on numerous occasions. But, as author/educator Mike Rose has so eloquently argued, a "one-dimensional" picture of the country's public school systems that focuses solely on tragedies and failures "misses too much," and is unduly "harsh [and] brittle."[17]

Gertrude resisted this view in the passion that she brought to her job. For all the battles that she waged and all the exasperation that she expressed over school system shortcomings—what Rose sums up as "the daily sorrow of our public schools"—she was also imbued with "the daily joy" of serving in a public school system. Part of what made working with her at Barclay so invigorating for teachers and parents, and so memorable for students, was the vision that she conveyed to everyone of how a good public school should, and could, be exciting, welcoming, and inspiring. Barclay parent, Carol Huppert, once compared Gertrude with an artist who was continually molding and reshaping the instructional program to better challenge and support children's learning and growth. "Every year she adds another creative touch," Huppert marveled. She made public education shine despite its many flaws.[18]

Those who have studied how women handle the job of principal and other positions of influence have found that they bring to their role "a very strong sense of being responsible to the world," as opposed to preoccupation with more individualistic objectives such as career advancement. According to these findings, women principals incorporate into their definition of authority a strong collaborative element. They exercise "power with" rather than "power over" their school communities and seek to replace the usual hierarchy of authority with "an interactive web which balances autonomy and community."[19]

Certainly, Gertrude was driven by a powerful sense of social responsibility. As her college roommate and close friend, Clara Jones, observed, "Her main goal in life has always been to make life better for someone else." She rarely found time for recreation or any form of purely individual pleasure—not only because her job was so demanding, but because she demanded of herself that she—like the servant in her favorite biblical parable—multiply and use her talents for the greater good. Repeatedly she would insist, "I am a servant of the community."

Her collaboration with that community was integral to her authority. She was able to take risks and rebel against the central office because the community "had her back" and in so doing she gained the respect of parents, community activists, and staff. While Gertrude never gave up her autonomy, and in fact often exercised a kind of dictatorial power, she also welcomed, cultivated, and collaborated with an extraordinarily diverse collection of individuals and groups. She was forceful and demanding as a leader but did not impose demands that went against the grain of community experience and sentiment.

Missing from all the media coverage and commentary on the Barclay–Calvert conflict was recognition of how well Gertrude and the Barclay staff and community were prepared for that battle. They had more than a decade of experience in fighting on behalf of the school. From campaigning for program innovations, protesting budget cuts, gaining hard-won approval for a middle school, and similar experiences, the community developed a system of communication and decision-making that was both efficient and democratic.

By conducting priority meetings and serving on the parent–teacher–community steering committee, parents, neighbors, and staff members gained from Gertrude a working knowledge of how the school system was run and the key operators in that system. Between crises the number of people involved with school governance dwindled to very few. But when a struggle ensued those few swelled quickly to a cadre ready to act.

Barclay activists were experts in writing letters, setting up phone trees, circulating petitions, contacting political leaders, talking with reporters. Many of them would never have engaged in such actions if they had not been inspired and primed by Gertrude, who was unique among principals in her willingness to share information with parents, and level with them about the shortcomings of the school system. Even those parents who had experience in the civil rights, feminist, labor, or other movements had not envisioned using that experience on behalf of their children's school, until they came under her influence.

In major confrontations, most especially that over the adoption of the Calvert curriculum, the Barclay troops needed, and got reinforcement from universities, garden clubs, community associations, neighborhood businesses, and other quarters of the community where her vision for public education garnered strong support. A symbol of the community's high regard for Gertrude is the Johns Hopkins University President's Medal, bestowed on her on May 3, 1990 by Hopkins president, Steven Muller, before an assembly of community leaders who gave her a long standing ovation. The President's Medal is usually reserved for "heads of state, diplomats, literary figures and others whom the university president believes have 'achieved unusual distinction.' "[20]

A measure of how deeply the school system's rejection of the Barclay–Calvert proposal stirred public sentiment was the number of individuals outside the Barclay School community who had never met Gertrude, or ever set foot in the school, who rallied in support of the proposal—as happened in the Mayor's Forum, June 3, 1989. No one was more shocked than she by the roaring crowd that greeted her when she rose to address Kurt Schmoke that morning. She had never dreamed that so many strangers felt so strongly about the fight that she and Barclay parents were spearheading on behalf of their children.[21]

Intensive media coverage explains why so many people beyond the borders of the Barclay community learned about the struggle. Her media image—the diminutive, brave woman standing fast against a mean, implacable bureaucracy—garnered great amounts of sympathy. In some versions tiny Gertrude wrestled with multiple dragons, reflecting the popular stereotype of the heroic urban educator.

Beyond such hype, themes of trust, empowerment, and inspiration run through the recollections of those who worked with Gertrude throughout her years at Barclay. Her self-confidence and the clarity of her goals sparked confidence and purposefulness in others. "Part of her way of being in the world was that she was so determined," remembered Karen Olson, the first PTA president in Gertrude's administration. "She was always completely sure of herself and one hundred percent behind whatever we undertook on behalf of the school. . . . She made us feel like we were winning." Describing his Barclay colleague as he knew her nearly two decades after Olson's experience, Calvert Headmaster Merrill Hall exclaimed, "Trudy was such a great ombudsman. She rallied everyone and made everyone feel that there was a real mission."[22]

This kind of intensity in interactions with members of the school community and other allies is another trait of female principals highlighted in the research. According to author Kathleen Hurty:

> [As] women principals went about their work, rather than being casual and routinized [they] gave evidence of emotional energy at work: tending to feelings of children, teachers, parents; expressing anguish over behavior that affected others; generating enthusiasm, showing compassion, and sharing anger and joy . . . [23]

As Gertrude ("Miss Williams" during working hours) moved about Barclay "fussing," joking, hugging, commiserating, or glaring and asking "How dare you!" her abundant reserves of physical and emotional energy insured that life at Barclay was never "casual or routinized."

This dynamic mode of leadership may not be attributable solely to gender, however. Other research points to African American culture as a source for those who would "exercise and create a different sort of power."[24] The influence of Cheyney State and the black college tradition of reaching out to, and taking responsibility in, the larger community must also be taken into account. A comparative study of black and white women college graduates noted the extra sense of responsibility that black women graduates felt "for service and work toward 'uplifting the race.' "[25] The same study also suggests that in remaining single and centering her life around her work, Gertrude exemplifies a trend among women who graduated from college between 1934 and 1969. Black and white women within that cohort—but especially black women—tended "to choose career over family." The authors of this study relate this trend to the importance black women placed on "careers that would raise their status and emancipate them from the domestic work and blocked opportunities that their mothers had known."[26]

General studies of education leadership cite collaboration, creating a sense of community, and frank give and take with community members as qualities that good principals exhibit, irrespective of gender, race, or background. As author, schools-founder, and principal, Deborah Meier, summarized:

> Education depends on relationships between people and nothing [policy-makers] invent in their ivory towers will work If we don't get those right.[27]

Through one means or another, and whatever their demographic profile, all good principals have learned this.

Gertrude sometimes attributed her adeptness in the realm of school, family, and community relationships to her training as a counselor. However, her facility for counseling, as well as her success as a principal, may derive more from her formative years in mostly white Germantown, Pennsylvania. Clark Sulayman's biography of Gertrude's college president, Leslie Pinkney Hill, suggested that Hill's capacity for both exercising influence within African American circles and cultivating strong alliances with whites can be linked to his training in white schools and his early exposure to the dominant culture, at the same time that he developed racial consciousness and pride. In the same manner, as a black child, Gertrude interacted extensively with white children, teachers, neighbors, and her own and family members' employers, but at the same time, through family, church, and eventually Cheyney State, she developed a clear and sturdy African American identity. Gertrude was a person "exposed to two worlds who became wiser because of these dual experiences." They illuminate how she could move so adroitly among the races, cultures, classes, and ideologies of the Barclay community. [28]

A black woman pursuing her education agenda in a period of national history that was rife with racial turmoil, Gertrude honored and drew strength from her African American heritage, while at the same time exerting influence with and through multiracial alliances. Accountable to a poorly managed urban school system where it was not unusual for professional dialogue on pedagogy and curriculum to deteriorate into black–white confrontations over political power and racial identity, she demanded reciprocal accountability from her supervisors, harbored no doubts about her own purpose and beliefs, and was no more fazed by fellow blacks who questioned her race-loyalty than she was by the ignorant and prejudiced whites whom she occasionally had to set straight.

She enforced "respect" as the watchword for all children and adults who came within her purview, as is evident in the recollections of students who attended Barclay school. Dave Possidente, who is white and was enrolled at Barclay from 1970 to 1974 attributed this experience to teaching him "respect for others, not to look at race or beliefs," a lesson that he said in 1994 was still important to his life. A white trio of former students interviewed together in 1994, Zachary Morehouse, Joseph Robinson, and Stefan Rubin, who went through the entire Barclay program from kindergarten through grade eight (1976–1984) agreed that "everybody went along with how Miss Williams wanted the place run" and having "no class lines, no color line" was one aspect of that. Tara Krebs, at Barclay between 1980 and 1991, and also white, believed that she was more "open minded to a lot of different things than I might have been" if she hadn't attended Barclay. Angela Carmichael, an African American student in the years when Gertrude was assistant principal identified "always give respect" as one of her main rules.[29]

Gertrude's approach to teaching such basic values is illustrated by a story from another Barclay alumnus, Brandon Jones. An African American, he attended the school from kindergarten through eighth grade in the class that pioneered the Barclay–Calvert program. He later recalled that in his kindergarten class there was one white girl named Hanna who was "sad a lot. I don't remember exactly what I did," he related,

> but I did something mean to her in the early part of the school year. Miss Williams pulled me into her office . . . and she said, "I want you to sit down with her at lunch; just sit down with her and talk to her." I sat down with her at lunch one day, and we had jello for lunch. And I loved it. I ate it and just looked at my cup, and it was gone. And [Hanna] gave me hers. In Kindergarten that's a big thing. [Later, at nap time when] everyone would sort of get in their own cliques . . . and [Hanna] would be over there by herself . . . I just started to lay down [by her] and we just hung out for a lot of Kindergarten. . . . She was basically my best friend.[30]

Jones also reflected on how "Miss Williams . . . made us feel like we were doing something important, and I guess we were." He avowed that he had "never found any person in my entire life, besides my parents, that's done that much for me and the rest of the kids. She put her entire life into it. . . . She made sure that we tried our best. . . . We just caught that same mentality that she instilled in us."[31]

That countless other students harbor similar feelings about Gertrude, and that she holds an honorary place in the hearts of untold numbers of parents and colleagues evinces the impact that she has had on myriad lives. Pursuing her agenda as a ministry as much as a career, she brought to professional relationships an unusually generous amount of personal care and invested a major share of her life's talents and time in service to the three school communities where she worked over a period of 49 years.

Particularly in the 25 years that she spent at Barclay School, Gertrude transcended, to a remarkable extent, the barriers blocking effective partnerships between schools and communities.[32] She never adopted the mind-set that attributes expertise and understanding to a small coterie of professionals while relegating everyone else to a status of acquiescence and dependency. She was always open to insights and contributions from every segment of the school community and was adept at integrating them harmoniously into that community. Just as curricular and pedagogical initiatives—from nongraded classrooms and all-day kindergarten to the Barclay–Calvert program—grew out of her collaborative interactions with parents and faculty, so did such inventions as school-community priorities meetings, the PTO steering committee, and the parent-produced *Barclay Bugle* operate in organic relationships with all the school's constituencies. They avoided much of the awkward shadow boxing that often occurs when one group or another seeks changes that the rest of the school has not had an opportunity to weigh and comprehend, resulting in a fragmented approach to change at best, destructive conflict among competing groups at worst.

In a similar fashion, linkages between Barclay and such community institutions as the Homewood Friends Meeting, Barclay–Brent Education Corporation, and the Johns Hopkins University began as bonds between Gertrude and individual representatives who were then introduced to and embraced by the school family. These relationships were markedly unconstrained by the mechanical rules and regulations that usually accompany such innovations when they are imposed from outside by central authorities.

Throughout Gertrude's career as principal there was always a notable contrast between the Barclay model of a public school that was "everybody's business" led by a hands-on, self-confident, coalition-building principal and the school system's preferred model of a school and principal falling in line with central office dictates as a matter of course. This contrast grew steadily sharper in the 1990s as Maryland, along with numerous other states, instituted tests such as MSPAP which, if schools were to be judged successful by their standards, required educators to narrow the scope of curriculum and instruction to little more than training children to pass the test— a requirement that was highly detrimental for Barclay–Calvert and generally inimical to the exercise of democratic decision-making at the school site. By the time of her retirement in 1998, enthusiasm among national political leaders for measuring schools by high-stakes tests and standardizing instruction tailored to those tests was swelling. It reached high tide in 2001 when George W. Bush signed the No Child Left Behind Act (NCLB).

Employing the language of excellence, fairness, accountability, and other terms to sell the law to the public, NCLB imposes complicated regulations that require schools to demonstrate "adequate yearly progress" (ayp). Critics insist that ayp criteria are illogical and destructive, demanding impossible gains from students who are already performing at a high level while giving schools strong incentives to "hold back or push out students who are not doing well," since, "as low scoring students disappear, test scores go up."[33] A completely top-down mandate, "NCLB assumes that neither children, their families, their teachers, nor their communities can be trusted to make important decisions about their schools."[34]

Thus, Gertrude's independence and Barclay's example under her leadership, of a school-community that insisted on making important decisions about the direction it would take while holding fast to the belief that all students can reach their full potential when given the opportunity to learn "as fast as they can and as slow as they must," stand out against the present political and educational grain even more than they clashed with prevailing trends of previous times. But just as dissenting opinions in judicial cases can hold the seeds of future reforms and the nonconforming beliefs of one era can serve as touchstones for moral breakthroughs in another, so might the examples set by Gertrude and Barclay serve as guideposts for future school reforms. In light of rebellions against NCLB already in progress in several states, that future might already be arriving.[35]

Whatever their historical impact, Gertrude and those who supported her agenda paid a price for not conforming to the status quo. The more she succeeded in establishing an authentic model of democratic school governance, the more she annoyed bureaucrats and law makers wedded to centralized school management. Whenever she challenged policies and practices that clashed with democratically determined Barclay priorities, she antagonized central managers. Consequently, she and her allies expended large amounts of mental and emotional energy and devoted substantial blocs of time doing battle with authorities who opposed her agenda or were threatened by her leadership style. One must wonder: if the time, determination, and resources that were diverted into those battles could have been channeled into her constructive undertakings, how much more inspiring might the already exciting learning environment at Barclay have become? How many grudges from her earlier battles with the bureaucracy came back to reinforce opposition to the Barclay–Calvert project? What would that partnership have looked like if Gertrude and the two school communities had been able to install it without first enduring two years of bruising, enervating conflict and if they had not been further drained by recurring conflicts over budget short-falls, testing, and Title I? What effect did the scars from those conflicts have on the long-term prospects of the partnership? These questions do not have definitive answers. But they do underscore the difficulties and costs of opposing entrenched, centralized authority such as that which governs American public school systems.

Given her recurring run-ins with central school officials; her networking with independent schools to arrange private schooling for youngsters who she judged would better reach their potential in that environment; and her bold pursuit of the public–private Barclay–Calvert partnership, one might have expected Gertrude to take up the cause of "privatizing" public schools. Advocates of this idea, which has been gaining ground since the 1970s would divert public funds to independent and parochial institutions through such means as tuition vouchers for students transferring from a public system to a private or religious school. Other versions of privatization involve turning management responsibilities for one or more public schools over to a private entity, as was done with several Baltimore schools with unsatisfactory results, when Walter Amprey was superintendent.

Despite claims that privatization stimulates reform in public education by creating "market competition" and arguments that such measures create academic and social opportunities for children from impoverished backgrounds, Gertrude has not been drawn to it. Her purpose in making alliances with private sources was never to press the case against public education, as most voucher proponents do, but to draw on those sources to demonstrate the viability of the public school.

"Williams is building success stories without using one voucher or busing one child," observed Betsy Peoples of *Emerge* magazine after she visited Barclay in the spring of 1998.[36] Gertrude always centered her attention on curriculum and instruction and insisted on having the same expectations for the economically disadvantaged public school student "that you would have if the child was a Rockefeller."[37] In her worldview, education is the keystone of freedom, and the neighborhood public school is the best place for children of all backgrounds, with parents of all religious, political, and ideological persuasions to learn respect for themselves and others and to grow into successful and constructive citizens. "No child is free, no adult is free, unless they are educated," she avers. "If you can't read or understand what you've read you are locked into ignorance and that is only broken through education, a GOOD EDUCATION."[38] This being true, her challenge to public school communities and their leaders is to decide what they need for their children, to "not give up until you get it," and to not give in to the doomsayers who predict the demise of the American public school system. "Don't ever divorce the system," Gertrude Williams admonishes. "Make it work for you."[39]

Notes

Introduction

1. When William Donald Schaefer left his final term unfinished in order to become state governor, Clarence "Du" Burns, an African American and chairman of the City Council, succeeded Schaefer, finished his term, and thus technically became the first black mayor.
2. Sandy Banisky and Ann LoLordo, "Kurt Schmoke Sworn in as 46th Mayor of Baltimore," *Baltimore Sun*, December 11, 1987. Schmoke is quoted in Marion E. Orr, "Black Mayors and Human-Capital Enhancement Policies: A Study of Baltimore," unpublished paper presented at National Conference of Black Political Scientists, March 1991.
3. Michael Ollove, "Schmoke Takes a Sizeable Political Risk by Assuming Responsibility for Schools," *Baltimore Sun*, July 3, 1988.
4. The statistics of poor performance by students in the Baltimore public school system were rehearsed in numerous reports, including the Abell Foundation, "A Growing Inequality, a Report on the Financial Condition of the Baltimore City Public Schools," Baltimore, 1989; Governor's Commission on School Funding, "Report," Baltimore, January 1994; Governor's Commission on School Performance, "The Report of," Annapolis, 1989; Commission for Students at Risk, "Maryland's Challenge," Annapolis, January 1990; Peter L. Szanton, "Baltimore 2000, a Choice of Futures," Baltimore: Morris Goldseker Foundation, 1986. To compare the local education studies with national studies of public education, see U.S. Excellence in Education Commission, "A Nation At Risk," Washington, DC, U.S. Department of Education, 1983; Task Force on Education for Economic Growth, "Action for Excellence," Washington, DC, 1983; Editors of *Education Week*, *Charting a Course for Reform* (Washington, DC: Editorial Projects in Education, 1993).
5. Deborah Meier, *The Power of Their Ideas* (Boston: Beacon Press, 1995) 8.
6. Mike Bowler, "Barclay's Principal Retiring," *Baltimore Sun*, July 22, 1998. The two superintendents to whom he refers were both Schmoke appointees, Richard Hunter, who tried to block the Calvert partnership and his successor, Walter Amprey, who unsuccessfully tried to move Gertrude out of Barclay.
7. I made partial summaries and indexes of the 2001 tapes and other later tapings but have not transcribed them.
8. Valerie Yow, " 'Do I Like Them Too Much?': Effects of the Oral History Interview on the Interviewer and Vice-Versa," *Oral History Review* 24: 1 (Summer 1997) 57–79. Quotation, 76. Karen Fields, "What One Cannot Remember Mistakenly," in *History*

and Memory in African-American Culture, ed. Geneviève Fabre and Robert O'Meally (New York: Oxford University Press, 1994) 150–163. Quotation, 151. In this essay, Fields reflects on the process by which she and her grandmother, Mamie Garvin Fields, composed her grandmother's memoir, *Lemon Swamp and Other Places* (New York: Free Press, 1983).

9. Fields, *Lemon Swamp*, 152.
10. Yow, "Do I Like Them Too Much," 57.
11. Pierre Nora, "Between Memory and History: *Les Lieux de Memoire*," in *History and Memory*, 294.

Chapter One   Beginnings

1. Frederick Miller, "The Black Migration to Philadelphia: A 1924 Profile," in *African Americans in Pennsylvania*, ed. Joe William Trotter Jr. and Eric Ledell Smith (Philadelphia: Pennsylvania Historical and Museum Commission and State University Press, 1997) 289.
2. W.W. Scott, *A History of Orange County Virginia* (Richmond: Everett Waddy Co., 1907) 114. Sarah Bennett Carter, *Orange County in War Time, a Community History*, volume six of Arthur Kyle Davis, ed., *Virginia Communities in War Time* (Richmond: Virginia War History Commission, 1925) 404.
3. W.W. Scott, *History of Orange County*, 134–137.
4. Ibid., 166.
5. The 1880 census recorded Julia as age 24; Caesar as 60; and Grace as 60. The wide age difference between Caesar and Julia is intriguing, all the more so when viewed in light of data from later censuses. See note 44.
6. Scott, *History of Orange County*, 50. The WPA Writers' Program, Virginia, *The Negro in Virginia* (reprint; New York: Arno Press and the New York Times, 1969) 269–270. Emily J. Salmon and Edward D.C. Campbell, *The Hornbook of Virginia History* (Richmond: Library of Virginia, 1994) 53, 98.
7. Scott, *History of Orange County*, 164.
8. Writer's Program, *Negro in Virginia*, 268. Salmon and Campbell, *Hornbook*, 98.
9. Ibid., 164.
10. In 1910, the population had risen slightly with the number of whites recorded as 7,959 and blacks as 5,526. University of Virginia Geospatial and Statistical Data Center, *United States Historical Data Browser* (On Line: University of Virginia, 1998). <http//fisher.lib.virginia.edu/census/>. Accessed January 13, 2004.
11. William A. Link, "Privies, Progressivism, and Public Schools: Health Reform and Education in the Rural South, 1909–1920," *Journal of Southern History* LIV. 4 (November 1988) 628.
12. Writer's Program, *Negro in Virginia*, 326–327.
13. Ibid., 255, 271.
14. Sarah Bennett Carter, "Orange County in War Time," in *Virginia Communities in War Time*, ed. Arthur Kyle Davis (Richmond, Virginia: Virginia War History Commission Ser. 1 v.6, 1926–1927) 414.
15. Writers Program, *Negro in Virginia*, 327, 328.

16. Gertrude knew her grandmother's name as Charlotta. In the census records, it appears as Charlotte.

17. The Mount Holy Baptist Church Clerk and Officers, "Mt. Holy Baptist Church," photocopied excerpt from "Our Father's House, A Look at African-American Churches in Orange County," James Madison Museum, February 1993. Courtesy of the Orange County Historical Society.

18. The Orange County Deed Book recorded the purchase of land in 1890 by Douglas Williams, in collaboration with his brother-in-law, Gilbert Taliaferro. They purchased it from John W. and Susan M. Clark, who, according to the 1889 census were white. In 1900, Douglas bought land from another white couple, James and Emma Clark. In 1877, before Douglas married Margaret Clark, Margaret's mother, Mary S. Clark (identified in the deed as "colored" and a widow) collaborated with her three sons, Robert, William, and Gilbert Taliaferro and her two sons-in-law (Lewis Spotswood and William Hopkins) to purchase land from a white woman identified as Lucy Walker. The Deed Book records a "deed of trust" placed on Douglas's land (September 5, 1908) and indicates a default on the loan (March 26, 1919). It seems possible that Horace could have inherited his father's land but been unable to pay off the lien against it.

19. We were unable to verify the Manassas certificate.

20. The wedding certificate identified Horace as living in La Grangeville, New York and Mamie in East Fishkill. The marriage ceremony occurred in Hopewell Junction, New York, witnessed by Mamie's aunt and uncle, Moses and Mary Wallace. U.S. Census, 1920.

21. *City Directory of the United States, 1902–1935, Philadelphia, Pennsylvania* (Woodbridge, Connecticut: Research Publications Inc.,) Microfilm, Reel 29.

22. Joe Trotter, *The Great Migration in Historical Perspective* (Bloomington: Indiana University Press, 1991).

23. According to V.P. Franklin, in 1930, 33% of Philadelphia's black population (who comprised 12% of the total population) were dependent on public assistance. *The Education of Black Philadelphia* (Philadelphia: University of Pennsylvania Press, 1979) 109.

24. Frederic Miller, "Black Migration," 292, 294. Quotation, 294.

25. Though most migrants crowded into densely populated black areas, Miller does observe that migrants from smaller communities, such as the Williamses tended to settle in areas with mostly white populations. Miller, "Black Migration," 300.

26. Russell Weigley, *Philadelphia a 300-Year History* (New York: W.W. Norton Company, 1982) 492; Frederick M. Miller et al., *Still Philadelphia, a Photographic History, 1890–1940* (Philadelphia, Temple University Press, 1983) 3; Richard R. Wright Jr., *The Negro in Pennsylvania, a Study in Economic History* (New York: Arno Press and the New York Times, 1969 [reprint from 1912]) 65; source of "better class" quotation. Judith Callard, *Germantown, Mount Airy, and Chestnut Hill* (Charleston, South Carolina: Arcadia Publishing, 2003; first edition, 2000).

27. Judith Callard, *Germantown, Mount Airy and Chestnut Hill*, "Slavery Protest," 14; "Johnson House," 37.

28. Such oral history recollections of segregation inform Stephanie Felix, "Committed to Their Own: African American Women Leaders in the YWCA: The YWCA of Germantown, Philadelphia, Pennsylvania, 1870–1970," Ph.D. Dissertation, Temple University, 1999. See also untitled oral history transcript of Jack Jones interviewed by

Lisabeth Holloway and Louise Strawbridge, March 1, 1984, Germantown Historical Society.

29. Felix, "Committed to their Own," 97–98, 100.

30. Population densities in Philadelphia neighborhoods with black residents were calculated by T.J. Woofter Jr. in 1928 in terms of "people per acre": South side, 139; Lower North side, 121; Upper North side, 109; West Philadelphia, 89; Germantown, 79. T.J. Woofter, "Neighborhoods," in *Negro Problems in Cities*, ed. T.J. Woofter, (Greenwood Publishing Group reprint edition, February 1970; originally published 1928) 80. V.P. Franklin documented instances of black families being driven from white neighborhoods in *The Education of Black Philadelphia*, 159.

31. This impression of Germantown as an area that harbored prejudice in many forms but was yet a less harsh environment than one might expect, is conveyed by the grand daughter of William Byrd in whose yard the KKK cross was burned. Louetta Ray Hadley-Riley told German Town Historical Society interviewers that despite evident discrimination, "without romanticizing, most of my memories of growing up in Germantown are happy ones." "I Remember Germantown," *Germantown Crier*, 52.1 (Spring 2002). Gertrude expressed the same sentiment about her Germantown childhood.

32. Clarence Taylor, *Knocking at Our Own Door* (New York: Columbia University Press, 1997) 17–19. Kathryn Morgan, *Children of Strangers: Stories of a Black Family* (Philadelphia: Temple University Press, 1980) 83. Allen B. Ballard, *One More Day's Journey* (New York: McGraw Hill, 1984) 211–213.

33. John Palmer Spencer, "Courage in Cross Fire: Marcus Foster and America's Urban Education Crisis, 1941–1973," Ph.D. Dissertation, New York University, May 2002, 43–44; Franklin, *The Education of Black Philadelphia, passim.*

34. Franklin, *The Education of Black Philadelphia*, 34, 168.

35. W.A. Daniels, "Schools," in *Negro Problems in the Cities*, 183.

36. "[T]here were well over a thousand names on the list of whites eligible for appointment to the elementary schools and over one hundred on the list of blacks. When the two lists were merged . . . [f]or example, the black teacher who was first on the black eligibility list dropped to 390 on the merged list; the one who was number 5 dropped to number 470; the one who was number 11 dropped to number 577. This virtually precluded the possibility that a black teacher would be appointed to a position in the public elementary schools in the near (or distant) future." Franklin, *The Education of Black Philadelphia*, 146.

Gertrude recalled that in the late 1970s, when her niece, Joan Spry, received her teaching degree from Temple and applied for a position in the Philadelphia School system she was offered a position as a permanent substitute, despite high test ranking. When she questioned why she was not given a regular position she was told that the school district was trying to get more white teachers and therefore they were again maintaining two lists.

37. Franklin, *The Education of Black Philadelphia*, 42, 44–48, 169–170; W.A. Daniels, "Schools," in *Negro Problems in the Cities*, 197.

38. See Allan M. Winkler, "The Philadelphia Transit Strike of 1944," *Journal of American History* LIX. 1 (June 1972), 73–88. See Franklin for a summary of racial unrest and black protest in Philadelphia during Gertrude's formative years: an extensive "Don't Buy Where You Can't Work" campaign in the early 1930s; a riot in 1934; an attack by

a white mob on a black child in 1940; black families driven out of white neighborhoods in 1941 and 1942; as well as reports throughout the period in the black press of violent incidents in the public schools. Franklin, *The Education of Black Philadelphia*, 118–119, 159, 169.

39. In 1868, The Joseph E. Hill School for black children was founded in Germantown; it was still operating when Gertrude was growing up.

40. Felix, "Committed to their Own," 139.

41. Karen Fields, "What One Cannot Remember Mistakenly," in *History and Memory in African-American Culture*, ed. Geneviève Fabre and Robert O'Meally (New York: Oxford University Press, 1994) 158.

42. Mary Beth Rogers, *Barbara Jordan, American Hero* (New York: Bantam Books, 1998) 46.

43. Hortense Powdermaker, *After Freedom* (New York: 1939) 299–300; quoted in Clara A. Hardin, "The Negroes of Philadelphia," Ph.D Thesis, Bryn Mawr College, 1945,166.

44. [The County Index of Births includes two slaves named Julia, both born in 1854. The ages recorded for Julia Wallace in census records are not perfectly compatible with this birth date; but the census records are not error-proof. The names and ages of her children and grandchildren are consistent with the family history as passed down to Gertrude. The 1880 census included Ceason [*sic*] Wallace, farm labor, age 60; Julia Wallace, wife, age 24; a son, Nelson, age 6; and two daughters—Charlotte, age 3 and Clora, age 1 month. In the 1900 census Julia did not appear. Caesar appeared, now 80 years old. His wife of 30 years was identified as Emily, age 60! Four children and two grandchildren are living with them: Solomon, 15 years old; Mary, 20 years old; John, age 10; Moses, age 8; the two grandchildren are Gertrude's mother and aunt: Mamie, age 2; Mattie age 5. By 1910, Caesar and Emily had disappeared; he was probably dead; the same could be true for her, though neither was listed in the county Deaths Index. Mattie and Mamie, ages 5 and 8, identified as grandchildren, were living with Julia, recorded as 40 years old. Given the large discrepancy between this age and the birth date of the slave, Julia, this could be another Julia altogether, if the presence of the two grandchildren did not connect her to the Julia listed as Caesar's wife in 1880. Julia was alone, age 68, according to the 1920 census. In the Orange County Birth Record Index, Julia and Caesar appear as the parents of Charlotte, born May 1877; Cora, born May 1880; Moses (listed as white), born June 20, 1893, Sarah born September 1882; Sarah born September 1883 [if this is not a mis-print, the first Sarah must have died]; and Solomon born June 1885. In each of the census records Julia was listed as owning her property. However, no land transactions for her or Caesar appear in the county Deed Book. She died in 1935, leaving a will that divided her estate (not itemized) between "my daughter, Sarah Washington and my granddaughter, Mattie Dance." According to Gertrude, Sarah married and moved to Baltimore; her husband was a chauffeur. Mattie married James Dance, another native of Orange County. They remained there throughout their lives. In the 1920 census they were living with James' parents. Gertrude noted when she read Julia's will that her mother was not included and speculated that perhaps this was because her aunt Mattie had stayed close by and taken care of Julia in her declining years.]

45. [Douglas Williams appears to have been a widower when he married Margaret Clark Williams in 1881. According to the county Marriage Register, his first wife was Rachel Murray, whom he wed in 1873. In the census of 1880, he was listed as one of four siblings living with their mother, Grace Williams. In the 1900 census, Douglas and

Margaret are recorded as the parents of eight children; Gertrude's father, Horace, was number seven. In the 1910 census, three more children and a grandson are listed in Douglas's and Margaret's household. Based on information included in land transactions recorded in the Deed Book, and census information, William Taliaferro appears to have been a brother of Margaret Clark Williams, suggesting that Margaret's mother (Mary Strothers Clark) may have borne children not only by Margaret's black father, John, but by a white member of the Taliaferro family.]

46. [Because the census ages are not always accurate, the exact ages of Horace and Mamie are unclear. The family believed that she was born November 15, 1896. In the 1900 census, her birth date is given as 1897; the 1910 census records her age as 12; and the 1920 census lists her as 21. In the case of Horace, his birth date was April 30, 1896. That tallies with the 1900 census in which his age was recorded as 4 and 1920 where it was reported as 22. In 1910 he was listed as 13, perhaps because the census was taken before his birthday. As noted earlier, documentation is lacking regarding the Williams's residences and travels in the early years of their marriage. According to Gertrude, her oldest sister, Elizabeth [according to the census born in 1915] was born in Philadelphia. She also believes that her parents had already settled in Philadelphia when she was born and that her mother was just staying temporarily with Mattie, because Mattie had been ill. According to her older sister, Lottie, Lottie and Elizabeth, the two oldest children, lived in Virginia until Lottie was 10 and Elizabeth was 14, while the rest of the family resided in Philadelphia.]

47. [Only Margaret's death was recorded in the county Death Index. As reported by William Taliaferro, she died of tuberculosis in 1915. By the 1920 census Emma was living with Horace and Mamie.]

48. [Gertrude is under the impression that her parents returned to Virginia after the New York marriage.]

49. [According to a "History" on the website of Enon Baptist, Adolphus Hobbs was installed as pastor there in 1933 and served in that capacity until his death in 1948. <http://www.enontab.org/aboutenon/history/history2.html>. Accessed April 18, 2004. The church was founded in 1876 by Rev. James D. Brooks, who had been born into slavery in Virginia. Unidentified clipping profiling Rev. Brooks, courtesy of Germantown Historical Society. The church historian, Mrs. Luberta Jean Teagle found that Horace Williams served as a Deacon for 33 years and that Gertrude joined the church "by letter" at age 10. "She participated in Sunday school and Evening Youth Training Activities until she left for college in 1945." Letter to jor from Mrs. Mary E. Hook, Church Clerk and Rev. Dr. Alyn Waller Pastor, Enon Tabernacle Baptist Church, June 2, 2004.]

50. [Exactly what happened with the Duval Street property remains unexplained. The family no longer has the original documentation. However, oral testimony from Jack Jones, an African American who lived with his parents at 219 W. Duval in the same period as Gertrude's childhood, offers a hint about what might have happened. "In those days, whatever the mortgage was, the mortgage could run for a thousand years. Say the mortgage was $2,000. The only way you could reduce that mortgage was, say you wanted to reduce that mortgage by 10%, the only way was to give them $200. . . . {interviewer: "So in other words, you were paying all interest." Jones:} "Paying all interest . . ." Jones interviewed by Holloway and Strawbridge, March 1, 1984, p. 11, Germantown Historical Society.]

51. [The more common label for such church gatherings is "homecoming."]

52. [The farm could have been that of Mattie Dance's in-laws, where according to census records she was living in 1920. It could also have been the property owned by Julia Wallace, Gertrude's great-grandmother Julie, whom Mattie looked after and who willed her property to Mattie and Mattie's aunt Sarah.]

53. [Grace Baptist Church was founded in 1892. Medrika Law, May 17, 2004 phone interview with Mrs. Virginia Ray, Grace Baptist volunteer who was also baptized by Rev. Hughes.]

54. [Gertrude later exhibited this same talent for using her eyes and facial expressions to bring about a change in behavior in a child who was acting up. The church historian, Mrs. Luberta Jean Teagle found that Horace Williams served as a Deacon for 33 years and that Gertrude joined the church "by letter" at age 10. "She participated in Sunday school and Evening Youth Training Activities until she left for college in 1945." Letter to jor from Mrs. Mary E. Hook, Church Clerk and Rev. Dr. Alyn Waller Pastor, Enon Tabernacle Baptist Church, June 2, 2004.]

55. [In her 1945 study of blacks in Philadelphia, Clara Hardin observed that "Masonry has played a very significant part in the social adjustment of its members. . . . Philadelphia Masons enjoy a great deal of prestige because they are men who have been able to meet rigid standards of financial stability, and who must be physically sound. The Masons {as a group} contribute to charities, and support activities for the benefit of their race but . . . it is largely through the individual members who carry the social ideals of Masonry that Philadelphia Negro society has benefited." Hardin, *The Negroes of Philadelphia*, 133. Although Horace Williams may not have been in the same financial bracket as the typical Mason described by Hardin, his induction into the Masonic order indicates his stature as a role model in the community.]

56. [In the early twentieth century, John T. Emlen was the first president of the interracial Armstrong Association that worked to improve education and living conditions for African Americans. See Franklin, *The Education of Black Philadelphia*, 21. Located at Chew and Upsal streets, Emlen School opened in 1927. Edward W. Hocker, *Germantown, 1688–1933* (Germantown, PA: Self-published, 1933).]

57. [Joseph Hill Elementary School was housed in a structure that dated from 1843, according to Franklin, *The Education of Black Philadelphia,* 51. Named for "a pioneer African American educator" it was founded as a school in 1868, the first black school in Germantown. Judith Callard, *Germantown, Mount Airy, and Chestnut Hill* (Charleston, SC: Arcadia Publishing, 2000) 83.]

58. [See, p. 16.]

59. [The absence of black teachers at Emlen was remarked on by David Logan Byrd, the son of black community leader William Byrd. The younger Byrd was born four years before Gertrude and also attended Emlen Elementary and Roosevelt Junior High: "I never saw any Black teachers, except perhaps a substitute. Teachers didn't talk down to us—we were taught like everyone else. There were Irish, Italians, Polish, Blacks at Emlen School." "Interview with David Byrd," *Germantown Crier* (Spring 2002) 31. Byrd's granddaughter, Louetta Ray Hadley-Riley, also recalled that some of our classmates rode in "chauffeur-driven limousines." "I Remember Germantown," *Germantown Crier* (Spring 2002) 33.]

60. [Germantown High School was built at Germantown Avenue and High Street. It opened in 1915. Hocker, 307.]

61. [Franklin reports that "especially before 1945" the academic course of study was preferred by most black senior high students because that course "would guarantee . . . sufficient credits for college admission." He observes that for black students not seeking to go on to college a high school education offered little advantage in the realm of employment. Discrimination by employers and "non-acceptance of Negroes as co-workers by white employees" trumped a black person's high school diploma. Franklin, *The Education of Black Philadelphia*, 168–169.]

62. [Gertrude's senior yearbook pictures 17 black students out of a senior class of 400. Of the 17, 10 are listed as ready for graduation. Of that 10, 6 were in the academic course.]

63. [Jacob N. Gelman was listed in Gertrude's Yearbook as a teacher in "the Commercial Department."]

64. [Garton S. Green appears in the Yearbook as chairman of the History Department.]

65. [Ruth Deane was the wife of George W. Deane, a prominent black realtor, who, according to historian Judith Callard, "owned a good deal of property" in Germantown, and the daughter of Morton Winston who was born into slavery and became the pastor of Mount Zion Baptist Church. Today Mount Zion has the largest Protestant congregation in Germantown. Callard, *Germantown*, 94, 95. Medrika Law telephone interview with Clarice Spain-Pierce, secretary at Mount Zion, June 3, 2004.]

66. [In our conversations, Gertrude noted the substantial age difference between her and Sarah on the one hand, and the rest of their siblings. She did not have precise memories of the degree to which the older children contributed to the family income. She did recall that her sister Lottie had preceded her in working at Penn Fruit and that her brother Charles may have worked with her father when he was still in school. But, as discussed, all three brothers went into the military at very young ages.]

67. [There were two YWCAs in Germantown,—the YWCA of Germantown and the Colored Branch of that institution. During World War I, the national YWCA earmarked special funding for "Colored association work." Black women who were leaders in their community took advantage of that funding and in 1918 founded the Colored Branch of the YWCA of Germantown. Felix, "Committed to Their Own," 48. Clara Hardin singled out the Germantown branch of the YWCA as a valuable community facility. It had an all black membership of 480 in 1941. Hardin, *The Negroes of Philadelphia*, 133.

With regard to the tennis program, Louetta Hadley-Riley recalled that "a group of Black men who were tennis enthusiasts played at the Colored YWCA. They sponsored tennis tournaments each year and since hotels were segregated, the players stated in our homes. One time, we were privileged to have tennis great Althea Gibson stay with us." "I Remember Germantown," *Germantown Crier* (Spring 2002) 32.]

68. [See Allan M. Winkler, "The Philadelphia Transit Strike of 1944," *Journal of American History* LIX. 1 (June 1972) 73–88.]

69. [It was possible for Horace to be drafted since he was 18; Larry was 16. For African Americans, and especially males, the chances for gaining employment as a result of completing high school were much lower than chances that white graduates had. This undoubtedly contributed to the black dropout rate, which was high. See Franklin, *The Education of Black Philadelphia*, 170. He also notes (192) that the absence of black teachers as role models probably also contributed to that rate. See also Hardin, *The Negroes of Philadelphia*, 108.]

Chapter Two   Teacher Training at Cheyney

1. The most comprehensive account of the Cheyney history is Charline Conyers, "History of the Cheyney State Teachers College 1837–1951," Ed.D. Thesis, New York University, 1960. This history also figures prominently in Sulayman Clark's "*Educational Philosophy of Leslie Pinckney Hill: A Profile in Black Educational Leadership, 1904–1951*," Ed.D. Thesis, Harvard University, 1984. Arthur Willis, *Cheyney*, self-published, 1994 includes material on the college up to the 1980s. Both Clark and Willis rely heavily on Conyers. Unless otherwise indicated the information presented here is drawn from her work. Reorganization in 1983 creating the Pennsylvania State System of Education, established the school's present name: Cheyney University of Pennsylvania.

2. Linda Marie Perkins, "Quaker Beneficence and Black Control: The Institute for Colored Youth 1852–1903," in *New Perspective on Black Educational History*, ed. Vincent P. Franklin and James D. Anderson (Boston: G.K. Hall, 1978) 24–27.

3. Ibid., 40. In 1899, the managers reported that ICY alumni staffed 75% of the African American schools in Philadelphia and Camden, New Jersey, while the principals of the two largest black high schools in Philadelphia were trained at ICY.

   When Cheyney was taken over by the state in 1921, the Board of Managers reconstituted themselves as the Richard Humphreys Foundation through which the Quakers could continue to advocate for and provide financial support to the school. The governor appointed a Board of Trustees, that was, in Conyers's words, "predominantly a Quaker Board." See Conyers, "History of the Cheyney State," 262–265.

4. Conyers, "History of the Cheyney State."

5. Like Gertrude, Hill was born in Virginia (albeit 53 years earlier, in 1880) and was one of eight children in a deeply religious family. He attended a segregated public school in Virginia and an integrated public school in New Jersey, where his family migrated when he was 16. Admitted to Harvard in 1899, he earned Bachelors and Masters degrees in education. From 1904 to 1907 he headed the education department at Tuskegee Institute. Over the next six years he directed Manassas Industrial School in his home state. His tenure at Cheyney extended from 1913–1951. While serving as the college president he enrolled in a doctoral program at New York University but never completed it. He was known, nonetheless as "Dr. Hill." He did receive four honorary doctoral degrees. All information on Hill is taken from Clark, unless otherwise stated.

6. In addition to discussion of this issue in Clark and Conyers, see Raymond Wolters, *The New Negro on Campus, Black College Rebellions of the 1920s* (Princeton: Princeton University Press, 1975) 332–339. Also Franklin, *The Education of Black Philadelphia*, 71–73.

7. Hill, "The Future of Our Culture," *Journal of Negro Education*, VI. 1 (January 1937) 7–16. Quotation, 14.

8. Leslie Pinkney Hill Papers, "The Responsibilities of the Young Negro Scholar," 1919. Quoted in Clark, "Educational Philosophy," 181.

9. W.E.B.DuBois, *Crisis*, April 1923, 171. Quoted in Clark, "Educational Philosophy," 118.

10. Clark, "Educational Philosophy," 129.

11. In 1947, Cheyney enrolled its first full-time white student and hired the first full-time white faculty member. Two years later Hill hired a white secretary and a white campus

nurse. According to Clark, Hill viewed these steps as symbolic of the ideal of integration. They did not really alter the black culture of the campus.

12. Leslie Pinkney Hill Papers, "Constructive Services," quoted in Clark, "Educational Philosophy," 211.

13. [Hill and the handful of other African Americans enrolled at Harvard at the turn of the twentieth century were barred from living in college housing and not invited to join the campus social clubs. Nonetheless, his biographer found that Hill passed his Harvard years quite happily. Clark, "Educational Philosophy," 147.]

14. [While sticking to the principle that Cheyney "is frankly devoted . . . to the specific task of developing a professional body of men and women who are trained for service to the Negro race in the school room," Leslie Pinkney Hill also made it clear that "any qualified applicant may be admitted to Cheyney under the rules of the Department of Public Instruction, without regard to race, sex or creed . . ." Hill writing in *The Cheyney Record*, December 1922, quoted by Conyers, "History of the Cheyney State," 266–267.]

15. [For further discussion and examples of intra-race color prejudices see Kathy Russell, Midge Wilson, and Ronald Hall, *The Color Complex, the Politics of Skin Color Among African Americans* (New York: Doubleday, 1992); and Michelle Foster, ed., *Black Teachers on Teaching* (New York: New Press, 1997) xlvii, 119.]

16. [The strict rules for student conduct, especially for female students, appear to have been maintained for later generations. See Mabel Bette Moss' criticism of this aspect of Cheyney as she experienced it as a 1961 graduate, in Michele Foster, *Block Teachers on Teaching* (New York: New Press, 1997) 166–168.]

17. [John Palmer Spencer, "Caught in Crossfire: Marcus Foster and America's Urban Education Crisis, 1941–1973," Ph.D. Dissertation, New York University, May 2002 examines Foster's early life in Philadelphia, describes his student days at Cheyney, where he was an outstanding campus leader, and details his distinguished career as an educator. On November 6, 1973 Foster was fatally shot in Oakland. The Symbionese Liberation Army (SLA) (best known subsequently for the kidnapping of publishing heiress Patty Hearst) claimed responsibility for the "execution." Letters bearing the name and symbol of the SLA were received by police and media, citing as the reason for his assassination Foster's support for what the *New York Times* described as a "program that would have put police officers in the schools, provided special identification cards for students and would have utilized police intelligence in collecting other data on students." The SLA letters denounced the program as "fascist." Earl Caldwell, "Oakland Murder Baffles Police," *New York Times*, November 25, 1973. See also Henry S. Resnick, *Turning on the System: War in the Philadelphia Public Schools* (New York: Pantheon Books, 1970) 129–140, and Marcus A. Foster, *Making Schools Work: Strategies for Changing Education* (Philadelphia: the Westminister Press, 1971).]

18. [During World War II more women students were recruited by Cheyney to help offset the decline in enrollment due to the draft. The women's dorm was not large enough for the increased female population and the women were placed in the men's dorm, Burleigh Hall. After the war, when the men returned, there was no place to move the women in Burleigh. The state leased a property in the village of Cheyney. Described as a "summer villa" that had been turned into a school, it was known as Tanglewood. Whites who lived nearby organized to prevent its use by Cheyney. This white opposition is very likely a major reason the male students did not want to move there. Tanglewood served as a male student residence until a new women's dorm, Yarnall Hall, opened in 1952. Conyers, "History of the Cheyney State," 316.]

19. [Wilson's presidency began in 1968 and concluded in 1981. His memories of being a Cheyney student are quoted in Allen B. Ballard, *One More Day's Journey* (New York: McGraw Hill, 1984) 214–215.]

20. [Girls living in the Quaker's Association for the Care of Coloured Orphans (known as the Shelter) were moved from Philadelphia to Cheyney in 1914. They provided the first student body for the college's "Model School." In 1923, African American boys from the Quaker's Home for Destitute Children were also moved to the Cheyney campus and enrolled in the Model School. Conyers, "History of the Cheyney State," 215–216, 251.]

21. [Evangeline Hall died in December of 1947, during the first semester of Gertrude's junior year. Therefore, she would have supervised the first two or three months of the participation-observation phase of Gertrude's training. Charline Conyers became the director of the laboratory school after Hall's passing. Conyers, "History of the Cheyney State," 354, 357.]

22. [Quoted in Conyers, "History of the Cheyney State," 363.]

23. ["The National Teacher Examinations (NTE) have been in use since 1940 to assess the knowledge of teachers. They were first administered by the American Council on Education and later taken over by the Educational Testing Service." Jerry B. Ayers, Glenda S. Qualls, "Concurrent and Predictive Validity of the National Teacher Examinations," *Journal of Educational Research*, 73.2 (1979) 86.]

Chapter Three   Teacher at Charles Carroll of Carrollton

1. Sidney Hollander Foundation, *Toward Equality* (Hollander Foundation, 1960; second edition, 2003) 5–7. Richard M. Bernard, ed., *Snow Belt Cities* (Bloomington and Indianapolis: Indiana University Press, 1990) 27. See also Karen Olson, "Old West Baltimore: Segregation African-American Culture, and the Struggle for Equality," in *The Baltimore Book: New Views of Local History*, ed. Elizabeth Fee, Linda Shopes, and Linda Zeidman (Philadelphia: Temple University Press, 1991) 61–63 and "Pennsylvania Avenue," *Soul of America.com* <http://www.soulofamerica.com/cityfldr/baltimore16.html>.

2. Hollander Foundation, *Toward Equality*, 5–7. Suzanne Ellery Green Chapelle, *Baltimore, an Illustrated History* (Sun Valley, California: American Historical Press, 2000) 202; Vernon S. Vavrina, "The History of Public Education in the City of Baltimore, 1829–1956, Abstract of a Dissertation" Ph.D. Dissertation Catholic University of America Press, Washington, DC, 1958, 20. Elinor Pancoast et al., "Report of a Study on Desegregation in the Baltimore City Schools" (Baltimore: Maryland Commission on Interracial Problems and Relations, 1956) 5. Karen Olson, "Old West Baltimore,"61.

3. Pancoast et al., "Report of a study on Desegregation," 8. The year of Gertrude's arrival the Baltimore City Public Schools consisted of 173 schools, 4,363 teachers, and a total employee population of 5,257, serving 115,813 students. Vavrina, "The History of Public Education," 24.

4. Quoted in Marilyn Gittell and T. Edward Hollander, *Six Urban School Districts* (New York: Frederick A. Praeger, 1968) 178.

5. Odell Smith, "What's Wrong With Our Schools?" *Baltimore Sun*, June 20, 1948.

6. David Stickle, "Thousands of School Teachers Quit Jobs Because of Low Pay," *Baltimore Sun*, February 15, 1947. Stickle reported that a total of 3,803 Maryland teachers resigned between 1944 and 1947, and since 1939 the total number of resignations in the state teaching force was 9,559. In 1960, the Baltimore Teachers Union (BTU) found "900 classrooms filled by unqualified personnel" in Baltimore City. Diane L. Keely, "Conflict Group Formation: The Development of the Baltimore Teachers Union," Ph.D. Dissertation, Fordham University, 1976, 127.

7. Pancoast et al., "Report of a Study on Desegregation," 8. Nonetheless, white education officials maintained that black teachers were less prepared and less competent than certified whites. Reportedly lower scores on the National Teachers Examination were cited as evidence. Pancourt, 104. Reed Sarrat, *The Ordeal of Desegregation* (New York: Harper and Row, 1966) 113.

8. For other accounts of the supervisory system by other veterans of the Baltimore City Public Schools, see Rebecca E. Carroll, *Snapshots From the Life of an African American Woman* (Baltimore: C.H. Fairfax Co., Inc., 1997) 78–79; and M. Adele Mitzel quoted in Jeanne Saddler, "Why Baltimore Pupils Are At the Bottom," *Sunday Sun*, November 7, 1976. Carroll, an African American, described "a waiting room full of probationary teachers who had come to the Administration Annex on Madison and Lafayette Avenues to have their plans for the week checked." Mitzel, who was not identified by race and who was in 1976 the director of testing for the Maryland State Department of Education, recalled, "When I taught in Baltimore city, we had to have lesson plans, a course of study, and we even had to write out the questions we would ask the children and the expected answers . . ." Gertrude stated with certainty that both the white and colored systems "had quality supervisors who took their directions from the top."

9. National Education Association (NEA), "Baltimore Maryland, Change and Contrast" (Washington, DC: Commission on Professional Rights and Responsibilities, May 1967) 42. For discussion of spending differences between black and white students see also Pancoast et al., "Report of a Study on Desegregation," 6 and Joel A. Carrington, "The Struggle for Desegregation of Baltimore City Public Schools, 1952–1966," Ed.D. Thesis, University of Maryland, 1970, 12.

10. Juan Williams, *Thurgood Marshall, American Revolutionary* (New York: Times Books, 1998) 90–91. See also Leander L. Boykin, "The Status and Trends of Differentials Between White and Negro Teachers' Salaries in the Southern States, 1900–1945," *Journal of Negro Education* (Winter 1949) 40–47; and Michelle Foster, *Black Teachers on Teaching* (New York: New Press, 1997) xl–xli.

11. Boykin, "The Status and Trends of Differentials," 40–47. Vernon S. Vavrina, "Evolving Role of the Superintendent in Baltimore City," *Baltimore Bulletin of Education* XLII.2 (1964–1965) 14.

12. The black students based their entrance request on the fact that no black high school offered the Poly curriculum. M. Dion Thompson, "13 Bright Teens Stood for Many," *Baltimore Sun*, February 28, 2002; Thompson, "Black Alumni Recall Integration of Poly, *Baltimore Sun*, March 1, 2002; Gregory Kane, "Young Poly Integrators Blazed a Trail," *Baltimore Sun*, March 1, 2002; Carrington, "The Struggle for Desegregation," 13–21. Roszel C. Thomsen, "The Integration of Baltimore's Polytechnic Institute: A Reminiscence," *Maryland Historical Magazine* 78 (1983) 235–238. In 1944, Mayor Theodore McKeldin made the first African American appointment to the Board of School Commissioners—"McMechen, George W.F. 1871–1961." *Baltimore Sun*, February 25, 1961.

13. Diane L. Keely, "Conflict Group Formation: The Development of the Baltimore Teachers' Union," (Ph.D. Dissertation, Fordham University, 1976, 79–80. Collective bargaining would not be agreed to until 1976. Ibid., 175–183.

14. The court handed down two rulings, *Brown I* (347 U.S. 483, May 17, 1954), which declared that "in the field of public education the doctrine of 'separate but equal' has no place' "; and *Brown II* (349 U.S. May 31, 1955) which returned the five cases that comprised *Brown v. Board of Education* to their local jurisdictions with the order to proceed "on a racially nondiscriminatory basis with all deliberate speed . . ."

15. Quoted in Reed Sarratt, *The Ordeal of Desegregation, the First Decade* (New York: Harper & Row, 1966) 79.

16. Studies of the 1954 decision include Richard Kluger, *Simple Justice* (New York, 1975) and James T. Patterson, *Brown v. Board of Education, a Civil Rights Milestone and Its Troubled Legacy* (New York: Oxford University Press, 2001). For detailed examination of the desegregation process in Baltimore see Carrington, "The Struggle for Desegregation,"; Samuel L. Banks, "A Descriptive Study of the Baltimore City Board of School Commissioners as an Agent in School Desegregation, 1952–1964," Ed.D. Thesis, George Washington University, 1976; Julia Roberts O'Wesney, "Historical Study of the Progress of Racial Desegregation in the Public Schools of Baltimore, Maryland," Ed.D. Thesis, University of Maryland, 1970; Elinor Pancoast et al., "Report of a Study on Desegregation."

    The strongest resistance to desegregation in Baltimore occurred at Southern High School, the site of several demonstrations by unhappy whites during the 1954–1955 school year. Reginald Fields, " 'Inherently Unequal,' The Supreme Court Ruling That Ended School Desegregation," *Baltimore Sun*, May 16, 2004. In this same *Brown* 50-year anniversary retrospective by *Sun* writers several individuals recall their personal experiences in the immediate aftermath of *Brown*.

    Sources on the generally positive and optimistic assessment of the first phase of desegregation in Baltimore City include: Harry A Bard, "A Baltimorean Reports on Desegregation," *Educational Leadership* (November 1955) 88–96. George C. Grant, "Desegregation in Maryland Since the Supreme Court Decision," *Journal of Negro Education* (Summer 1955) 286. G. James Fleming, "Racial integration in Education to Maryland," *Journal of Negro Education* (Summer 1956) 273–284. Mike Bowler and Laurie Cohen, "The Painful Second Step in School Integration," *The Baltimore Sun*. September 8, 1974. "De Facto Segregation," *Johns Hopkins Magazine*, October 1963, 7.

17. Comparison can be made with the findings of historian William H. Chafe in his study, *Civilities and Civil Rights. Greensboro, North Carolina and the Black Struggle for Freedom* (New York: Oxford University Press, 1981) 8. Typical of Massive Resistance was the avowal of Mississippi Senator James Eastland on the floor of Congress about a month after the Supreme Court ruling that "At no time in the foreseeable future will there be a single racially integrated school in the State of Mississippi. That . . . is something that the white race will not permit under any conditions; and there is not the power of compulsion on the part of the Federal Government to compel it." *Congressional Record* 100, Pt. 1 (July 23, 1954) 11524–11525. In March 1956, 75 members of the House of Representatives (joined later by another 5 congressmen) and 19 senators signed and distributed the "Southern Manifesto" attacking *Brown* and resolving to resist and ultimately reverse the ruling. *Congressional Record* 102, Pt. 1 (March 12, 1956) 4459–4464.

18. School board data indicated that between 1955 and 1961 the percentage of white students in all-white schools went from 50% to 45.6%, while the percentage of black

children in all-black schools dropped from 74.6% to 45.6%. A report prepared by black parents, titled *Seven Years of Desegregation in the Baltimore Public Schools*, countered with drastically different findings. Within their frame of reference 86% of white elementary children were in "white schools" and 92% of African American elementary children were in "black schools" in 1955. By 1961, these percentages remained at 74% of whites in white schools and 83% of blacks in black schools. Carrington, "The Struggle for Desegregation," 56–57; 148, 149.

19. See chapters 4 and 10 in *The Baltimore Book*, ed. Fee, Shopes, and Zeidman, for discussions of residential segregation. W. Edward Orser, *Block Busting in Baltimore* (Lexington: University Press of Kentucky, 2000) examines the role of realtors, speculators, and federal and local housing laws in promoting white flight and impeding desegregation.

20. *Baltimore Sun*, February 12, 1959. Mike Bowler, *The Lessons of Change* (Baltimore: Commissioned by Fund for Educational Excellence, 1991) 5–6. See also Sherry Olson, *Baltimore, the Building of An American City* (Baltimore: Johns Hopkins University Press, 1980) 369–370.

21. Robert L. Crain, *The Politics of School Desegregation* (Chicago: Aldine Publishing Company, 1968) 72–76. Carrington, "The Struggle for Desegregation,"55–78l.

22. Sarratt, *Ordeal of Desegregation*, 352; Jackson quoted in Sarratt, *Ordeal of Desegregation*, 114. Signs of the beginning of resegregation were noted in Sidney Hollander Foundation, *Toward Equality*.

23. Robert L. Crain, *The Politics of School Desegregation*, 78, 79. Mary Gittel and T. Edward Hollander, *Six Urban School Districts* (New York: Frederick A. Praeger, 1968) 180.

24. Brain quoted in *The Baltimore Sun*, March 30, 1962.

25. Citizens' School Advisory Committee, "Studies and Recommendations," three vols., November 1964; "Report of Staff Reactions to the Recommendations of the Citizens School Advisory Committee," January 6, 1966. George Rodgers, three part series on the report, *Baltimore Evening Sun*, November 10, 1964; November 11, 1964; November 12, 1964; and November 13, 1964. Brain left Baltimore the year that the committee reported. His successor, Lawrence Paquin, was not interested in following up on another leaders' agenda. See also, Bowler, *Lessons*, 8 and Gittel and Hollander, *Six Urban School Districts*, 179, 180.

26. T. Anthony Gass, "The Baltimore NAACP During the Civil Rights Movement, 1958–1963," M.A. Thesis, Morgan State University, 2001; Hollander Foundation, "Toward Equality"; Vernon E. Horn, "Integrating Baltimore: Protest and Accommodation, 1945–1963, Masters Thesis, University of Maryland, College Park, 1991; Peter Irons, "Robert Mack Bell v. Maryland," in *The Courage of Their Convictions* (New York: The Free Press, 1988) 131–152; Dennis O'Brien, "Caste of One's Skin," *Baltimore Sun*, November 13, 1994; Gilbert Sandler, "Protests That Changed a City," *Baltimore Sun*, February 14, 1995; Linell Smith, "Four Lives and a Milestone in the Movement," *Baltimore Sun*, August 23 and 24, 1998 (two-part series). Barbara Mills, *"Got My Mind Set On Freedom," Maryland's Story of Black and White Activism, 1663–2000* (Westminster, Maryland: Heritage Books, Inc., 2002).

27. Hollander Foundation, "Toward Equality," 97.

28. [These public housing projects were built in the 1940s for low-income families and reflected the policies of segregation then in effect. Eric Siegel, "A Look at City History," *Baltimore Sun*, December 11, 2003.]

29. [While this account may strike some readers as possibly exaggerated, the impetuous behavior of stalking out of the building is not uncharacteristic of the Gertrude Williams known well by colleagues and friends. As other experiences described in this book show, Gertrude occasionally displayed frustration and anger in rather dramatic ways.]

30. See chapter one, p. 20.

31. [Mabel D. Booker served as vice principal at #139 from 1949 to 1951, when she was appointed as principal of School #126. Board of School Commissioners, *Minutes*, May 3, 1951, 101. *Directory of Personnel, 1949–1950; 1950–1951*, Baltimore City Public Schools.]

32. [Bright is identified as a Supervisor in the Colored Schools in the Baltimore School System's *Directories of Personnel* from 1951–1952 through 1954–1955. She was appointed as principal of School #118 in the fall of 1956. Board of School Commissioners, *Minutes*, October 18, 1956.]

33. [Rochowiak was white and appears in the *Directories of Personnel* as a supervisor from 1961–1962 through 1963–1964. After 1954, when the Colored Schools ceased to exist as a separate division the supervisors were integrated and Gertrude recalled that both black and white supervisors worked with the teachers at #139. Rebecca Carroll described the closing down of the administration building that had housed the Colored Division and the integration of black and white supervisors soon after the *Brown* decision. Carroll, *Snapshots*, 76.]

34. [The minutes of the Board of School Commissioners reported that Gertrude S. Williams "met all requirements for required probationary service" and was "elected as an elementary grade teacher, effective January 15, 1952 at School 139." Baltimore City Board of School Commissioners, *Minutes*, January 24, 1952, 24.]

35. [William Lemmel became Superintendent of Public Instruction in Baltimore City in 1946. He died suddenly in January 1953 while lobbying in the Maryland state capital for improved funding for the Baltimore City teachers' salaries. "Dr. Lemmel, School Head, Dies At 56," *Baltimore Sun*, January 30, 1953.]

36. [The Arena Players, founded in 1953, is a highly regarded black theater company in Baltimore. Sam Wilson, its long-time managing director, was universally recognized as its "driving force." Wilson died in 1996. C.T. Goodman, "Arena Players Ready For Next Act," *Baltimore Sun*, September 15, 2003.]

37. [Baltimore educator Rebecca Carroll noted this aspect of Maryland racism in her autobiography: "Scholarships for four years' graduate study were given to all African Americans whose desire and scholastic average warranted graduate school. In fact, travel and all expenses were paid. . . . No graduate school was too remote or too expensive to keep blacks out of the University of Maryland . . ." Carroll, *Snapshots*, 44–45. At the same time, however, pressure was brought to bear against the segregated professional schools of the university. In fact, the Supreme Court ruling in *Murray v. Maryland* in 1936 was the first in a series of landmark cases in which the NAACP successfully challenged segregation in post-secondary schools. In the 1936 case, argued by NAACP attorneys Charles Hamilton Houston and Thurgood Marshall, African American Donald Gaines Murray was admitted to the University of Maryland Law School. Seeking to avoid more such legal action the state offered prospective black graduate students very handsome scholarships to study anywhere but Maryland. While many blacks took advantage of this ironic beneficence, others continued to

challenge state-sanctioned segregation. In 1950, the Nursing School and the graduate school of sociology were ordered by federal courts to admit black students. The next year the Regents officially abolished professional school segregation and in 1954 desegregation began in all state teachers' colleges. Thus Gertrude was probably among the last of the city's black teachers who were paid to attend graduate school out of state. Hollander Foundation, "Toward Equality," 84–86. Mike Bowler, "Black Students Sent Away," *Baltimore Sun*, May 16, 2004.]

38. [Emmett Albert Betts was Professor of Psychology and Director of the Reading Clinic at Temple University. He earned a doctorate at the University of Iowa in 1931 and taught at Temple from 1945–1954. He authored a number of texts on the teaching of reading. See, e.g., *Foundations of Reading Instruction* (New York: American Book Company, 1946).] Gertrude's summary of his ideas is consonant with what he wrote in this 1946 book, and with an interview he gave in 1982. Roland Jean-Louis and Eugene Provenzo, "An Oral History Interview of Dr. Emmett Albert Betts," *Florida Reading Quarterly* (December 1982), 5–7. Curriculum Vita, "Betts, Emmett," Conwellana-Templana Collection, Temple University Library, n.d. *Who's Who in America*, 1974–1975, 252; *Contemporary Authors*, vol. 33–36, 107.]

39. [Mount Airy is a community near Germantown. See Judith Callard, *Germantown, Mount Airy, and Chestnut Hill* (Charleston, SC: Arcadia Publishing, 2003).]

40. [George E. Simms is identified as principal at 139 in the Baltimore City Public Schools *Directories of Personnel* from 1950–1951 through 1958–1959. He was transferred to School #145 as principal in 1959. Samuel R. Owings had been principal at #110 when he was moved to #139. Board of School Commissioners, *Minutes*, July 15, 1959, p. 137. According to the *Directories* Owings remained at #139 through the spring of 1962.]

41. [Efforts to find a news report of the Owings's boating accident were not successful.]

42. [The way Gertrude revised Taylor's suggestion—turning advice on *not doing* something without telling anyone into encouragement *for doing* something without telling anyone—can be seen as an example of the penchant we all have for hearing what we want to hear. It may also indicate that she reworked Taylor's advice to meet the challenges that she faced in later years.]

43. [A search for records pertaining to this clinic has been inconclusive. Andrew Harrison, Processing Archivist and Fine Arts Coordinator of the Alan Mason Chesney Medical Archives of the Johns Hopkins Hospital reported that a " 'Children's Comprehensive Care Clinic' grew out of a Federal grant that Dr. Robert Cooke, chairman of the Department of Pediatrics at the time, received in 1968/1969 {after Gertrude had left #139} . . . [B]efore that grant, the program did not exist." However, Dr. Cooke did note that his department had "informal relationships" with the public schools in the area of #139 and suggested that "there may have been an earlier forerunner of the clinic but not under that name." Andrew Harrison to Jo Ann Robinson, Email, March 9, 2004.]

44. [The *Directory of Personnel* for 1961–1962 places Gittings at #139 for that year. The school board minutes in November of 1962 report that he was leaving #139 in the fall of 1962 for a promotion to administrative assistant (Board of School Commissioners, *Minutes*, November 15, 1962, 250). Gertrude initially indicated that Gittings remained at #139 between two and four years—an example of how tricky memory can be in pinpointing time periods. Subsequent to his work as an administrative assistant Gittings served as Area Director of Elementary Education and then Assistant Superintendent of Pupil Personnel Services (Board of School Commissioners, December 21, 1967, 581).]

45. [In her autobiography Carroll indicated that she was named as a supervisor after the *Brown* decision, but did not give a specific date. Carroll, *Snapshots*, 76–78. Nor could Gertrude recall specifically when Carroll became her supervisor. Carroll appears as an elementary supervisor in the *Directory* for 1960–1961. The *Directory* for the following three years includes Daniel Rochowiak among the Elementary Supervisors but not Carroll.]

46. [When teachers came from other schools to see a demonstration—a classroom lesson presented by an experienced teacher—substitutes covered their classes, or, in some cases, classes were doubled up and a fellow-teacher would supervise the absent teachers' class along with her own.]

47. [Reginald Watts was transferred from being principal at #135 to being principal at #139 in November 1962. Board of School Commissioners, November 15, 1962, 250.]

Chapter Four   Counselor at Mordecai Gist

1. Brain held the deanship until 1983. The Brain Education Library on the Pullman campus is named for him. <http://www.sulibs.wsu.edu/educ/brain.htm>.

2. *Baltimore News American*, "City's Education System Expands," August 29, 1965.

3. Joel Carrington, "The Struggle for Desegregation of Baltimore City Public Schools, 1952–1970." Ed.D. Thesis, University of Maryland, 1970, 88–92. Mike Bowler, *Lessons of Change* (Baltimore: Fund for Educational Excellence, 1991) 10. Baltimore operated four public high schools with entrance requirements and gender designations. Eastern and Western High Schools were open to girls with the requisite grade point average. High achieving boys could attend either City College or Polytechnic High Schools. The instructional programs at Western and City emphasized the liberal arts and humanities. Eastern and Poly emphasized training in secretarial and business skills in the former case and mathematics and engineering in the latter.

4. Carrington, "The Struggle for Desegregation," 93.

5. "Mrs. Moss Fighting for Negro Principals," *Baltimore Afro-American*, June 10, 1968. Carrington, "The Struggle for Desegregation," 76–77.

6. "Standards Threatened By Slow Students," *Baltimore Sun*, June 5, 1960.

7. Charles A. Glatt and Arliss L. Roaden, "Slums, Suburbs, Schools and Sanctions," *The Maryland Teacher*, September 1967, 30–31, 76–79. For another example of how some educators were viewing the "culturally deprived" child, see Gene C. Fusco, "Preparing the City Child for His School," *School Life*, May 1964.

8. The Baltimore-based report was authored by Dr. Orlando Furno, Director of the Bureau of Research for the school system. The analysis presented here is guided by Carrington, "The Struggle for Desegregation," 94. See also Bowler, *Lessons of Changes* 9.

9. Eugene F. Petty to the Executive Committee, December 15, 1966, Special Collections Department, Langsdale Library, University of Baltimore, GBC Papers II, Box 35, Folder 12.

10. "Schools Operating With Augmented Personnel," *Baltimore Evening Sun*, May 11, 1967; "Union Demands," Ibid. High school teachers seem to have been more attuned to union activism and protest than their colleagues in the elementary schools. With a curriculum organized according to academic disciplines, students who were nearly adults, and a teaching environment where intellectual give and take could be quite robust, high school teachers may have found union membership and activity more congenial than elementary teachers whose work with young children may foster a

professional identity that values nurturing behavior and tends to shy away from political action. That elementary teachers are predominantly female may be another consideration. Many women in this era subscribed to a code of conduct for women that precluded activities that "caused trouble." Women in elementary classrooms may also have interpreted striking as a betrayal of their responsibility for their young students.

11. NEA Commission on Professional Rights and Responsibilities, "Baltimore Maryland, Change and Contrast. The Children and the Public Schools," May 1967.

12. NEA Commission on Professional Rights and Responsibilities, "Baltimore Maryland," 54.

13. Diane L. Keely, "Conflict Group Formation and the Development of the Baltimore Teachers Union," Ph.D. Dissertation, Fordham University, 1976, 175–193.

14. Kay Mills, "Hempstead Praises Work of Dr. Sheldon—Especially In the Area of Community Relations," *Baltimore Evening Sun*, April 5, 1968.

15. For details on the Baltimore riots that occurred in the wake of King's assassination see Jane Motz, "Report on Baltimore Civil Disorders April, 1968" (Middle Atlantic Region American Friends Service Committee, September 6, 1968) and Sono Motoyama, "The Year Baltimore Burned," *City Paper*, April 5, 1995, 14–18. Blacks in Baltimore were also on edge because the competence and honesty of the black director of the first Community Schools program were under attack. The community school concept involved expansion of services provided by public schools and extension of their hours of operation so that the schools would be accessible to all members of their surrounding communities for such purposes as Graduation Equivalency Diploma (GED) classes, food banks, parenting workshops, job counseling, and other social services. "Community School Idea Steaming Ahead," *Baltimore News American*, November 24, 1968.

16. "Funded by the federal government, the Model Schools program aimed at seeing what could be accomplished if enough resources were concentrated in a school to provide one-on-one teaching, tutoring, and extra supplies and books. The program . . . died in the 70's when federal funding was phased out . . ." Bowler, *Lessons of Change*, 12. See also "Model Schools Program," *Baltimore Sun*, February 4, 1968. The Model School idea was similar to what Gertrude would fight for in the Barclay–Calvert program of the 1990s.

17. [Bowler, *Lessons of Change*, 12. According to Bowler, the decentralization efforts of Sheldon failed because he would not incorporate into decentralization plans the "community control" over funding and the hiring and firing of staff that black activists were demanding. Kenneth J. Rabben, "Changes Bring Better Schooling," *Baltimore News American*, August 25, 1968. "1968 Staff Development Conference Report," Maryland State Department of Education, 1969. Edgar Jones, "A Look at the City Schools" (three-part series) *Baltimore Evening Sun*, April 30, May 2, May 9, 1968.]

18. [Motscheidler had been an elementary education supervisor before her appointment as principal of Gist in 1964. The *Directory of School Personnel* for that year does not list an assistant principal at Gist. Stanley Curtain is identified in that role beginning the following year.]

19. [For a discussion of this realtors' practice, see W. Edward Orser, *Block Busting in Baltimore* (Lexington: University Press of Kentucky, 2000) 89.]

20. [Declining enrollment was the stated reason for closing Mordecai Gist in 1982. In 1991 the building was torn down to make room for a housing development. "Finishing Off School No. 69," *Baltimore Sun*, January 10, 1991; Marcia Cohn Buxbaum, Letter to the Editor, *Baltimore Sun*, February 3, 1991; Edward Gunts, "Builder Teams to Show Plans for School Sites," *Baltimore Sun*, May 26, 1991.]

21. [According to the *Directories of School Personnel* for each respective year, Curtain remained at Gist as assistant principal only through the spring of 1966. Edgar Lansey succeeded him in 1967–1968 and Grace Hall succeeded Lansey in Gertrude's last year at Gist, 1968–1969.]

22. [Fallstaff, School #241, was located at Fallstaff Road and Gist Avenue.]

23. [It was customary for someone on the school staff to be assigned responsibility for working with the parent group. While the parents would elect officers from among themselves, they would rely on the staff person to help them in such ways as coordinating meeting times with the school calendar, enlisting the support of faculty in fund-raising activities, and staying abreast of school system policies affecting them and their children.]

24. [While verifying that this episode occurred exactly as Gertrude remembers it has not been possible, the record does indicate that there was a problem with the Fallstaff principal, Margaret Freudenberger, in the middle of the school year, for she was transferred then to Dickey Hill, a predominantly white school. La Verne Reed, a white supervisor, was appointed at the same time to be Fallstaff's principal. Board of School Commissioners, *Minutes*, January 1966, 149.] The proactive, "let's get to the bottom of this problem now" approach that Gertrude attributes to herself is very characteristic of how she later operated as a principal.]

25. [Rival organizations were operating at the time of the strike. While the Baltimore Teachers' Union (BTU) called the strike and simultaneously the Public School Teachers' Association (PSTA), through their national affiliate, the National Education Association (NEA), imposed sanctions. It's indicative of Gertrude's aloofness from school politics at this time that she folded the strike and sanctions together as actions of an unnamed entity, "the union."]

26. [Gertrude received tenure as a counselor in the fall of 1967. Board of School Commissioners, *Minutes*, October 19, 1967, 442.]

27. [In a 1984 study of Baltimore City high school principals, Terry Mobley noted that talented women in the public school system often found mentors who "encouraged and even 'pushed' " them to become administrators. One of his interviewees, Vernon Vavrina, who held various administrative posts in the school system until his retirement in 1975, remarked that in the years that he served the school system, "you didn't apply for anything—you were named by your supervisors." Terry E. Mobley, "History of the Female High School Principal in Baltimore City Public Schools," unpublished essay, Morgan State University Department of History, 1984, 3, 13. Gertrude continued this tradition. As a principal she encouraged teachers to aspire to and prepare for other positions. "She pushed you to go further," Barclay teacher Sandra Brown, emphasized. Her colleague and, as of 2004, Barclay Principal Truemella Horne concurred: "She recognized your talents and pushed and encouraged and toughened you up." Roundtable interview with Barclay teachers by Jo Ann Robinson, December 15, 2003.]

Chapter Five   Becoming Principal at Barclay School

1. Jacques Kelly, "Real Fireworks at Old Ballpark Seared 4th of '44 Into Memory," *Baltimore Sun*, July 5, 1993. Jacques Kelly, "Memory Still Smolders," *Baltimore Sun*, July 4, 1994.

2. Board of School Commissioners, *Minutes*, December 16, 1954, 231–233.

3. Baltimore City Public Schools Division of Research and Development, "Annual Report of Student Body Racial Composition," September 1970.

4. Baltimore City Public School (BCPS) Division of Research and Development, "Iowa Test of Basic Skills, 1971." Barclay third grade students received an overall average score of 2.6 on the 1971 Iowa tests, while the city average was 2.9 and the national average 3.5. The fourth graders' average was 3.6; at the city level was also 3.6 and at the national level 4.5. For fifth grade the Barclay average was 4.5, the city 4.6 and the national 5.5. Sixth graders at Barclay had an average of 5.7; the city 5.6 and the national average was 6.5.

5. As elaborated later in the chapter, this impression of Nitkoski was a strong theme in interviews with teachers who worked under her direction. Interviews by Jo Ann Robinson with Myra Lunsford (by telephone, February 28, 2004), Jennifer Kenney (by telephone, January 25, 2004), Jan French (by Email July 31, 2002), Karen Olson (audiotape, March 27, 2004).

6. Hugh J. Scott, *The Black School Superintendent, Messiah or Scapegoat* (Washington, DC: Howard University Press, 1980) 211, 216. Mike Bowler, "Seattle Wonders, 'Baltimore? And Bust,' " *Baltimore Sun*, August 9, 1971. Bowler observed that the Seattle Central Region for which Patterson was responsible included 7,000 students, about the number of teachers in the Baltimore City school district (which had 190,827 students).

7. Scott, *The Black School Superintendent*, 216. Bowler, "Seattle Educator Picked as Head of City Schools," *Baltimore Sun*, July 15, 1971.

8. Bowler, "Seattle Wonders"; John De Vonge (*Seattle Post Intelligencer Special to the Baltimore News American*), "New School Head Outspoken" *Baltimore News American*, July 16, 1971.

9. Bowler, "Seattle Wonders"; "Patterson Expected," *Baltimore Sun*, September 7, 1971.

10. In the year that Gertrude became Barclay's principal (1973), the school system served 182, 981 children, of which 129,173—slightly more than 70%—were black. Scott, *The Black School Superintedent*, 108.

11. E. Robert Umphrey, taped interviewed by Jo Ann O. Robinson, October 28, 1986. Scott, *The Black School Superintedent*, 10.

12. Baltimore City Public Schools Racial Balance Task Force, "Recommended Plans for the Further Desegregation of the Baltimore City Public Schools, 1974 and Baltimore City Public Schools, "Desegregation Plan Submitted to the Office of Civil Rights of the U.S. Department of Health, Education and Welfare," 1974. The "Introductions" to both of these documents outlined the role of a "broad based task force . . . guaranteeing community input into the development" of the desegregation plan.

On the division of the school district into nine regions see Baltimore City Public Schools, "Reorganization of the Baltimore City Public Schools," 1974. One rationale for this action was that "regional organization provides well-defined procedures by which the views of all segments of society can be considered before decisions involving them are made" (Baltimore City Public Schools, "Reorganization," 6).

13. Scott, *The Black School Superintendent*, 111. Umphrey interview. Bowler, *Lessons of Change* (Baltimore: Fund for Educational Excellence, 1991) 13–14. Bowler's outline of these personnel decisions under the heading of "the Patterson massacre" corroborates Umphrey's description.

14. White's appointment appears in the Minutes of the Board of School Commissioners, August 26, 1971, 440.

15. Umphrey interview. William Donald Schaefer was in his first term of office when Patterson was hired. Schaefer was elected in 1971 and reelected three successive times (1975, 1979, 1983). In his last term, he successfully ran for Maryland governor in 1986. When he assumed that post, the president of the Baltimore City Council, Clarence "Du" Burns, finished out Schaefer's mayoral term.

16. Sue Miller, "Dr. Roland Patterson Will Head Schools," *Evening Sun*, August 9, 1971.

17. Bowler, "Seattle Wonders."

18. "Patterson: Haven't Done Well on Key Issues," *Baltimore News American*, May 19, 1974.

19. Baltimore City Public Schools, "Superintendent's Progress Report," 1974, 5–7; Neal Friedman, "City Hall," *Baltimore Magazine* May 1974, 12–21. Mike Bowler, "Teacher's Gripe is 25th Street," *Baltimore Sun*, March 3, 1974. "Patterson: Haven't Done well on Key Issues," Baltimore *News American*, May 19, 1974.

20. *Adams v. Richardson*, 351 F2d 636 (1971).

21. HEW quoted in "Recommended Plans for the Further Desegregation . . . ," 1.

22. "Patterson: Haven't Done Well on Key Issues," *Baltimore News American*, May 19, 1974.

23. Berkowitz, "Baltimore's Public Schools in a Time of Transition," *Maryland Historical Magazine*, 92. 4 (Winter 1997) 426–430. Bowler, *Lessons of Change*, 14. In stressing the dilemma city authorities faced in the 1970s Berkowitz seems to place the blame solely on the federal government for "impos[ing] mandates . . . without providing the financial means for the localities to fulfill those mandates." He seems to overlook how city leaders tried for the better part of 20 years to duck their responsibility to actually enforce—rather than just rhetorically support—the *Brown* decision. Undoubtedly enforcement would have entailed conflict, but as the histories of such communities as Wilmington, Delaware and Charlotte, North Carolina illustrate, such conflict could have generated positive social, political, and economic growth. See Jennifer Hochschild and Nathan Scovronick, *The American Dream and the Public Schools* (New York: Oxford University Press, 2003) 42.

    In November 1975 the *Sun* reported that for the first blak families were fleeing. "School Figures Indicate Black Flight," *Baltimore Sun*, November 3, 1975.

24. In the words of a news reporter, the allegations against Patterson were that he "shifted funds away from supplies and maintenance to build his own administrative empire" by adding unapproved administrative positions to the budget. Richard Ben Cramer, "Audit Finds School Funds Underspent." The board also charged that Patterson would not accept "criticism and direction" from the board and didn't keep board members adequately informed of his plans and had "failed in the important obligation of maintaining harmonious work relationships" with them. "Text of Resolution Asking Patterson to Resign," *Baltimore Sun*, July 18, 1975.

25. Transcript of meeting of Board of School Commissioners, August 8, 1974, 315–388.

26. Ibid.

27. Ibid. Patterson concurred that he was treated differently than a white superintendent would have been treated. He told the *Baltimore News American*, that, regarding a charge that in his hiring practices he was trying to make the school system a black system, "If I had been a white superintendent, nobody would have said that, and he could have been doing the same thing. People would have examined what he was doing. But,

you see, it's just by virtue of the fact that I'm black that that statement would have been made." ("Patterson: Haven't Done Well On Key Issues," *Baltimore News American*.)

28. Scott, *The Black School Superintendent*, 115 (includes quotation from *Baltimore Sun*). Mimi Waxter, League of Women Voters (LWV) President, to Board of School Commissioners, August 16, 1974, League of Women Voters Archives, Baltimore Chapter.

29. Umphrey interview.

30. Education Committee, Baltimore City League of Women Voters, "Reorganization of Baltimore City Public Schools," Mimeographed report, February 11, 1975. In possession of jor.

31. Scott, *The Black School Superintendent*, 115–116. Although the board's action in calling the dismissal hearing was highly unusual, it can be assumed that the City Solicitor found no unwarranted assumption of authority on the board's part. It is likely that Patterson and his lawyers agreed to the hearing because they were convinced that the board's charges were without substance and they hoped public airing of them would make this clear.

32. "Text of Resolution Asking Patterson to Resign," *Baltimore Sun*, June 30, 1975; "Patterson Told Contract's Over in Board Letter," *Baltimore Sun*, June 30, 1975; "School Hearing Set Today," *Baltimore Sun*, July 2, 1975; "School Hearing Opens," *Baltimore Sun*, July 3, 1975; Bowler, "Patterson, Board Reach Stand Off," *Baltimore Sun*, July 9, 1975; "School Chief is Fired," *Baltimore Sun*, July 18, 1975 (includes "Lies, Tom, Judas" quotation).

33. Bowler, "Patterson, Board Reach a Stand Off."

34. "Patterson Asks $1 Million," *Baltimore Sun*, September 19, 1975; Scott, *The Black School Superintendent*, 117—includes quotations from Judge Young. An audit released a year and half after Patterson was fired found "chaotic procedures for handling supplies and a tangle of inefficiency" in how the Patterson administration handled bus tickets for students and the bookkeeping for a federally funded free and reduced lunch program. Stephen McKerrow, "1975 Audit Shows Tangle in Patterson Era," *Baltimore Evening Sun*, January 11, 1977.

   Patterson's "record of 'bucking the establishment' " helped him land his next job as "community superintendent of District 9" in the Bronx, New York. See Joyce Price, "Patterson's Controversy Seen Asset in New York School District," *Baltimore News American*, December 2, 1977. "Patterson to Head New York School District," *Baltimore Evening Sun*, December 14, 1977. Patterson held that post until he died of cancer in 1982. See Robert Benjamin, "Former School Chief Patterson Dies at 53," *Baltimore Sun*, August 10, 1982.

35. Umphrey interview.

36. [Cord was a seasoned veteran of the school system who had held positions from "after-school demonstration teacher" in 1938 to "Elementary Grades Supervisor in 1951. In the late 1950s she received two successive appointments as an elementary principal and had been appointed "Area Director of Elementary Education in 1963. Board of School Commissioners, *Minutes,* July 8, 1938, 216; June 30, 1949, 189; September 20, 1951, 211; July 15, 1954, 136; June 4, 1959, 76; May 16, 1963, 97.]

37. [Nitkoski had been at Barclay as principal since September 1968. Board of School Commissioners, September 5, 1968, 343. She was the school's fourth principal, following Dorothy Rawlings (1959–1963), Harry Levine (1963–1966), and Edwin Cohen (1966–1968). Nitkoski declined a request to be interviewed for this book.]

38. [Jennifer Kenney, who was a new teacher at Barclay the same year Gertrude became assistant principal, recalled finding Nitkoski "extremely structured and by the book and not into personal relationships. She was aloof and not warm at all," Kenney said. Robinson telephone interview with Kenney, January 25, 2004.]

39. [Lorraine King, a white parent who had three children in Barclay at the time, said of Nitkoski, "I never liked her. She let people step on her. {When she was principal} nobody wanted to volunteer." According to Karen Olson, also white, with a son at Barclay, Nitkoski "was not particularly energetic or likeable {and was} not skillful in working with parents who wanted to be active in the schools—who didn't want to just serve cupcakes." Robinson telephone interview with Lorraine King, April 9, 2004. Robinson audiotape interview with Karen Olson, March 27, 2004.]

40. [Former teachers who were working at Barclay at this time remember that "Whenever problems came up, teachers would go to Miss Williams. . . . .We felt that she was just so much more competent [than Nitkoski]." Myra Lunsford interview. Lunsford, an African American, added that after offering her advice, Gertrude always said, "but you have to go to Ms. Nitkoski. She's the principal." Jennifer Kenney, who is white, remarked, "I never felt that Miss Nitkoski was a person to go to with a problem. Teachers went to Miss Williams." Jennifer Kenney interview.]

41. [More than 30 years later Lorraine King described her meeting with Patterson. "I told Dr. Patterson she [Gertrude] was a wonderful person. She was strict but respectable and very kind." King recalled that the superintendent was "very happy that a volunteer mother came down" to talk to him. "He said," she reported, that "if all the PTA and all the mothers wanted her, he would make her principal." King telephone interview. Other parents were also lobbying on this issue. Richard Cook, who was then Director of Greater Homewood Community Corporation (GHCC), an umbrella organization in the Barclay community that supported numerous neighborhood institutions and associations, remembered being asked to write a letter to the superintendent requesting Gertrude's appointment as principal. Richard Eldridge, a Barclay parent and an English instructor at the Community College of Baltimore, requested the letter. According to Cook, Eldridge was "collecting letters" supporting Gertrude who, he had told Cook, was "active, engaged, and cared intensely about kids and about education." Audiotape interview with Richard and Karen Cook by Jo Ann Robinson, March 20, 2004. Olson interview.]

42. [Teacher Myra Lunsford reported that she and several other staff members (she named Gloria Friend, Gwen Day, Juanita Young, and herself as among them) had gone to Vic Cord to ask "if we could possibly have Gertrude Williams as principal. . . . We were trying to get the best principal for our school," Lunsford recalled, "and Miss Nitkoski had sort of lost grips with what the school was all about." She stressed that this staff request for Gertrude to be promoted was "not undercover." They were open about it and when the full staff finally met, "everyone was in agreement. The teachers at that time really wanted Gertrude." Lunsford interview. While Lunsford herself, and the other staff she named are African Americans, Jennifer Kenney, who is white, confirmed that staff sentiment was unanimous for Gertrude. Kenney interview.]

43. [Helen Nitkoski was granted sabbatical leave for 1973–1974 by the school board on June 21, 1973 and at the same meeting Gertrude was appointed as Barclay principal. Board of School Commissioners, *Minutes*, June 21, 1973, 249, 251. In July 1975, the school board appointed Nitkoski as principal at Brehms Lane Elementary School.

She retired in 1981. Board of School Commissioners, *Minutes*, July 31, 1975, 276; August 20, 1981.]

44. [A *Baltimore Sun* reporter noted that Patterson "minced no words about the status of Negroes in the nation." "New School Head Outspoken," *Baltimore News American*, July 16, 1971. Scott, *The Black School Superintendent*, 216.]

45. [Part of his administrative reorganization included the establishment of "Regional Advisory Councils" of parents (RACs), for each of the nine regions. Each RAC was to send representatives to a "District Advisory Council" (DAC). Baltimore City Public Schools, "Reorganization of the Baltimore City Public Schools," 1974, 22, 98.

As a LWV Education Committee report noted, this aspect of the reorganization never really got off the ground during Patterson's administration. The RAC/DAC model did operate under the superintendents who followed Patterson—John Crew and then Alice Pinderhughes. Education Committee Briefing, "Subject: Reorganization of Baltimore City Public Schools," League of Women Voters, February 11, 1975.]

46. [On the 1974 strike, see Neal Friedman, "City Hall," 12–21. Mike Bowler, "Teacher's Gripe is 25th Street." "Patterson: Haven't Done Well on Key Issues," *News American*, May 19, 1974. Tracie Rozhon, "Schaefer Asks 'What Am I to Do?' " *Baltimore Sun*, February 25, 1974. "Summary of Teacher Issues," *Baltimore Sun*, February 6, 1974. Michael Olesker, "Remembering the Winter of '74," *Baltimore Sun*, October 19, 1982.]

47. "Summary of Teacher Issues," *Baltimore Sun*, February 6, 1974.

48. [Looking back in 2004 at his coverage of the strike, journalist Mike Bowler concluded that "the strike ended bitterly, with nowhere near the gains the teachers had sought. {T}he settlement in 1974 moved a typical teacher on the fourth step of the master's degree pay scale from $9,4000 to $9,910." *Baltimore Sun*, February 15, 2004.]

49. [In all that was written about the Patterson administration no reference has been found to charges that he paid school system bills on a schedule opposed by the mayor or the school board. He was charged with using funds for purposes other than their designated use. The stated charges against him made no reference, either, to his empowerment of parents. That does not mean that these factors were not motives behind the dismissal of Patterson. To openly voice them could have worked against the mayor and board.]

50. [The procedure was a hearing, though it had many of the trappings of a trial.]

51. [Since the hearings took place in July, taking days away from the school did not involve being away when classes were in session.]

52. [Commissioners David E. Sloan and Beryl Williams, both African Americans, went on record in support of Patterson at the end of the hearings. The other seven board members, including two other African Americans, voted to fire him. Mike Bowler, "School Chief is Fired."]

53. [Apparently—as Gertrude remembered it—the document to which Sachs was objecting as having been authored by Patterson was from some other source entirely but had somehow become attached to a document in her file of Patterson materials. No report of this particular episode is recorded in the media coverage of the hearings, but reporter Mike Bowler noted a lack of substance in the charges brought against Patterson. Bowler, "Patterson, Board Reach a Stand off."]

54. [Mike Bowler, "School Chief is Fired."]

55. [In the atmosphere of the Watergate revelations and government surveillance of political radicals such as the Black Panthers and groups resisting the Vietnam War, the possibility

of the existence of such a list and of phone taps is not inconceivable, but has not been corroborated. E. Robert Humphrey also spoke of surveillance, stating that someone bugged the office of Roland Patterson, and that he suspected it was a retired CIA operative who had come to work for the school system. E. Robert Humphrey interview.]

Chapter Six Principal at Barclay, Part One: "Barclay is Everybody's Business"

1. Taped oral interview with Austin Schildwachter by Carenda Pittman, Barclay School 35th Reunion, April 17, 1994; Taped oral interview with Audrey Eastman by Carenda Pittman, Barclay School 35th Reunion; Email to Jo Ann Robinson from Jan French, July 31, 2002.
2. Esther Bonnet interviewed by Jo Ann Robinson, September 3, 1997. Conversation with Mrs. Ellie Johnson and Mrs. Mimi Cooper, St. George's Garden Club, December 13, 2001. See also Isaac Rehert, "Garden Club 'Adopts' Inner City School and Teaches Nature," *Baltimore Morning Sun*, May 17, 1972.
3. Lunsford interview.
4. For a historical description of the area known officially as Hampden-Woodberry, see Bill Harvey, "Hampden-Woodberry: Baltimore's Mill Villages," in *The Baltimore Book. New Views of Local History* ed. Elizabeth Fee, Linda Shopes, and Linda Zeidman (Philadelphia: Temple University Press, 1991) chapter 3. Harvey notes that this part of the city, whose origins centered around employment in textile mills, "did not share a thoroughfare, shopping district, or school with any other neighborhood for most of its history." Consequently, the residents, "native-born, rural white Americans," assumed that "the community belonged to them; it was their own." Harvey, *The Baltimore Book*, 44, 46. Beginning in the 1990's Hampden came under the influence of entrepreneurs who opened trendy shops and restaurants along the community's main avenue, working a remarkable transformation of the area in which the old standoffish culture now coexists with a funky new diversity. See <http://www.hampdenmainstreet.org/history.html>.
5. Studies of the social turmoil of this period include Charles DeBenedetti, *An American Ordeal: The Antiwar Movement of the Vietnam Era* (Syracuse: Syracuse University Press, 1990); Judith Hole and Ellen Levine, *Rebirth of Feminism* (New York: Quadrangle Books, 1973); Kim McQuaid, *The Anxious Years: America in the Vietnam-Watergate Era* (New York: Basic Books, 1992); and James Miller, *"Democracy is in the Streets": From Port Huron to the Siege of Chicago* (Cambridge: Harvard University Press, 1994). With regard specifically to Baltimore: Clinton Macsherry, "Underground Railroaded," *City Paper*, February 15, 1990; Jane Motz, "Report on Baltimore Civil Disorders, April 1968," American Friends Service Committee, Middle Atlantic Region, September 6, 1968; *City Paper*, "The Year Baltimore Burned," April 5–April 12, 1995.
6. Seymour Sarason of Yale University has observed, regarding public school governance and reform, that "The decision-making group is usually small and not representative of all those who will be affected by its decisions." *The Culture of the School and the Problem of Change* (Boston: Allyn and Bacon, 1971) 59–60.
7. To sample Greater Homewood's involvement with the public schools of the area, see its 1970s quarterly newsletter, "Neighbors." The fall 1978 "Back to School issue"

discussed the activities of the Greater Homewood Education Committee, reported on the most recent Charles Village Spring House Tour, through which the Barclay-Brent Education Corporation raised $3,000 for Margaret Brent and Barclay Schools; devoted several detailed paragraphs to describing how the city school budget was determined and the role of the public in that process; and conveyed back-to-school messages from the principals and PTA/PTO presidents of the six public schools in the Greater Homewood area—Robert Poole Junior High, Roland Park Elementary and Junior High, Hampden, Barclay, Medfield, and Margaret Brent Elementaries.

8. Audiotape interview with Richard and Karen Cook by Jo Ann Robinson, March 20, 2004. The Cooks's children attended Margaret Brent Elementary, but through their involvement in the Barclay Brent Education Corporation, described later in this chapter, they also volunteered at Barclay and worked with Gertrude. Audiotape interview with Karen Olson by Jo Ann Robinson, March 27, 2004. Olson's son Chris was already at Barclay when Gertrude arrived there.

9. Laura Scism, "Renovators Get An A. It's Not Just Parents Who Make Barclay-Brent Schools Work," *Baltimore News American*, February 26, 1980. Mike Bowler, " 'Discovery Rooms' Let Children Find Knowledge By Exploring," *Baltimore Sun*, March 15 197?, undated clipping in PTO files.

10. David Rogers, *An Inventory of Educational Improvement Efforts in the New York City Public Schools* (New York: Teachers College Press, 1977), 256–260.

11. The title of this position changed over time. When the nine regions set up by Patterson were reduced by his successor they came to be called districts and the heads of those districts were in some years "directors" rather than superintendents. For purposes of this discussion the references to any regional or district officer is to the position originally labeled regional superintendent.

12. See "A Growing Inequality, A Report on the Financial Condition of the Baltimore City Public Schools," Abell Foundation, January 1989. This report includes historical references that make it germane to the years that Crew was in charge. On Crew's administration see Bowler, *The Lessons of Change*, (Baltimore: Commissioned by Fund for Educational Excellence, 1991) 116–118.

13. In 1990, the National Commission on Testing and Public Policy lamented that "the nation's elementary and secondary students are spending more than 20 million days a year 'simply taking standardized tests.' " Bernard R. Gifford [Commission chairman], *From Gatekeeper to Gateway: Transforming Testing in America* (Boston: Boston College, 1990).

14. Annie Linskey, "Fame for Arts School Grads," *Baltimore Sun*, March 12, 2004. Rashod D. Ollison, "Shakur's Story of Anger and Love: Tupac's Mother Credits Arts School," *Baltimore Sun*, March 11, 2004.

15. The stated purpose of P.L. 94–142 is to assure that all disabled children receive "a free appropriate public education . . . to meet their unique needs." Section 614 (a)(5) stipulates that "The local educational agency . . . will establish . . . an individualized education program for each handicapped child at the beginning of each school year and will then review and, if appropriate, revise its provisions periodically, but not less than annually." *U.S. Statutes at Large* 89 (1975) 775, 786. See also Bowler, *Lessons of Change*.

16. Greater Baltimore Committee, Inc., "Agenda for the Meeting of the Education Subcommittee," September 11, 1975. Barclay PTO Parent/Community Involvement file. On the Crew administration see also Lawrence E. Coleman, "Dr. Crew, the Power on 25th Street," *Metropolitan*, September 1981, 21–24; Robert Benjamin, " 'Report

Card' for Crew," *Baltimore Sun*, September 2, 1982; Benjamin, "Chief of City Schools Will Resign Post Today," *Baltimore Sun*, September 2, 1982; Mike Bowler, "Maybe the Toughest Job In Public Life," *Baltimore Evening Sun*, September 6, 1982.

17. The Pinderhughes appointment was controversial because, although she had taken graduate work she did not hold the doctoral degree that was one of the requirements for the job of superintendent. A special waiver from the state superintendent of education, David Hornbeck permitted her hiring. See Bowler, "Maybe the Toughest Job In Public Life."

18. National Commission on Excellence in Education, *A Nation At Risk* (Washington, DC: U.S. Department of Education, 1983). The commission described an erosion of academic culture in which educators had become permissive, allowing curricula to be watered down while letting students pick and choose "smorgasbord style" among course offerings, many of which lacked rigor. The commission also noted that the most capable college graduates were gravitating to professions that paid better than teaching and enjoyed more status.

19. See Diane Ravitch, *The Schools We Deserve* (New York: Basic Books, 1985) 27 and Mike Rose, *Possible Lives* (New York: Penguin Books, 1996) 4, 24 for discussion of the national penchant for bemoaning the shortcomings of public education. For a brief overview of national reports on education since the 1930s, see Theodore R. Sizer, "A Review and Comment on the National Reports" (Reston, VA: National Association of Secondary School Principals, 1983).

20. *Focus on Individual Success, A Local Imperative* (Baltimore: Baltimore City Public Schools, 1987), mimeographed booklet. I was one of the parents involved in the first round of task forces and it was I who co-chaired the sbm committee. For studies of that experience, see Veronica Donahue DiConti, *Interest Groups and Education Reform* (Lanham, MD:, University Press of America, 1996) chapter 4 and Marion Orr, *Dilemma of Black Social Capital: School Reform in Baltimore, 1986–1998* (Lawrence, KA: University Press of Kansas, 2000) chapter 6.

21. Bowler, *Lessons of Change*.

22. Abell Foundation, "A Growing Inequality." Bowler, *Lessons of change*. Sixteen years later a state commission appointed by then Governor Robert Ehrlich determined that the price tag on achieving funding equity among all school districts over the next five years was $1.3 billion. See p. 214.

23. This research is elaborated later on in the conclusion of this volume, 219–223.

24. [Gertrude and other female principals in Baltimore also had an advantage that female administrators did not have in most other places—a tradition of women in leadership roles in public education. Of all principals and assistant principals in U.S. public schools in 1974, only 15% were women. Yet, in Baltimore in the same period, women held 54% of the principal positions. According to the *Baltimore Evening Sun*, this substantial female representation was "a tradition of sorts rather than a spin-off from the new feminist movement." Patricia A. Schmuck and Jane Schubert, "Women Principals' Views on Sex Equity. Exploring Issues of Integration and Information," in *Women Leading in Education*, ed. Diane M. Dunlap and Patricia Schmuck (New York: State University of New York Press, 1995) 274. Sue Miller, "113 of City's 206 Principals Are Women. Situation Oft Differs in Parts of U.S.," *Baltimore Evening Sun*, May 30, 1972.

25. At regularly designated intervals these children had to be reviewed to determine if the work they were being given was meeting their needs. If not, we would decide what

steps should be taken by the school and the teachers to meet those needs. This process continued until the child was performing satisfactorily. He or she would then be "dismissed," that is, the ARD team would no longer meet with him or her and the parents.

26. [Gertrude generated a list of 14 individuals who served as assistant principals. Except for Mrs. Kavanaugh, who held the position at Barclay from 1975 to 1979, most of Gertrude's assistant principals left after one or two years. The general impression—on which no one is inclined to be quoted—was that she was difficult to work under. On the other hand, many former assistants maintained warm friendships with Gertrude and credited her with training them well. This may not be as contradictory as it sounds: in retrospect and at a distance they could see and appreciate how much she had taught them.

27. [Olson remembers that meeting. "We were relentless," she said of the parents.]

28. [This federal government project was started during the administration of John F. Kennedy by Margaret McNamara, the wife of Kennedy's secretary of defense, Robert McNamara. Through the program the school distributed books three times a year to every child free of charge. The goal was to inspire a love of reading in the children and encourage them to maintain personal libraries at home, made up of books that they had chosen and were free to enjoy on their own. Teachers were enjoined not to require book reports or use the RIF (Reading Is Fundamental) books in any formal way. "Reading Is Fundamental. RIF Across the U.S.A.," (Washington, DC: Reading Is Fundamental Inc., 1986).]

29. [*The Baltimore Sun*, October 14, 1975. For coverage of one mayoral visit to a Barclay RIF distribution—that of Kurt Schmoke—see Sandy Banisky, "Mayor Tells Barclay Pupils How to Do It By the Book," *Baltimore Sun*, February 25, 1989; *Jet Magazine*, "People Are Talking About . . ." March 20, 1989, 55.]

30. [Some of the educational assistants were funded by the federal Title-I program. See, p. 135 this volume. Once Barclay became a Title-I school the city government had to match the number of aides funded by the federal government. These aides could be assigned to the school through the city's Title-I office or the principal could—as Gertrude often did—recruit from the school community.]

31. [In her study of school–family relationships author/educator Sarah Lawrence Lightfoot wrote: "When children see a piece of themselves and their experience in the adults that teach them and feel a sense of constancy between home and school, then they are likely to make a much smoother and productive transition from one to the other." She found that "the presence of parents in the school not only provides more adults to . . . help and support [the] children but also transforms the culture of the school . . . [and] changes the adult perceptions of their roles and relationships . . . [Parents] begin to perceive of the school as belonging to them." *Worlds Apart, Relationships Between Families and Schools* (New York: Basic Books, 1978) 173–175.]

32. [Red Wagon was started in the early 1970s by activist parents. It was housed in the basement of a church about a mile from Barclay and included many children from the Barclay area.]

33. [Usually the city assigned each school nurse to several schools that would see their nurse once or twice a week. But at the time discussed here a nursing shortage meant that some schools had no nurse at all. Homewood Friends Meeting was located on Charles between 31st and 32nd streets.]

34. [The Friends funded the nursing position at Barclay, at $4,500 a year, from 1981 to 1985. They also contributed money for other school items, including a *Physicians'*

Desk Reference for the health suite and several rebuilt typewriters for the middle school. Barclay PTO papers include a voluminous file on the Barclay–Society of Friends relationship. A sampling of items from that file follows. Joseph Kovner, Clerk of the Meeting, Religious Society of Friends, Homewood to Gertrude S. Williams, Principal, October 26, 1981. "Homewood and Barclay School," *Homewood Newsletter*, November 1982, 2. Gertrude S. Williams to Joseph Kovner, Clerk, July 25, 1983. Baltimore Monthly Meeting of the Religious Society of Friends, *Minutes*, Homewood, October 30, 1983. Gertrude S. Williams to Society of Friends, Homewood Division, July 12, 1984. Fay Menaker, "Report on Nursing Services at Barclay for School Year 1983–1984," September 24, 1984. Menaker, "Report on Nursing Services at The Barclay School 1984–85," July 16, 1985. Gertrude S. Williams to Religious Society of Friends, Homewood Meeting, July 20, 1985.]

35. [Initially the summer camp served children from Barclay and Margaret Brent schools; it later included a third elementary school in the area, Dallas Nicholas.]

36. [On Paul Daniels 140–141, chapter seven, this volume. While Barclay was without a school librarian, and before the Hopkins women began their volunteer services to the library, the state Department of Education revoked the library's standing as an accredited school library. The accreditation has been restored thanks to the women's efforts.]

37. [Gertrude's first meeting with the Garden Club occurred in May 1974. She, Helen Nitkoski, and club representatives gathered at Evergreen House (a mansion owned by Johns Hopkins University) to evaluate their environmental education program at Barclay. The minutes of the meeting reported that "the new principal, Miss Gertrude Williams, proved to be delightful and most enthusiastic about her initial experience with cucumber sandwiches!" Notes taken by jor at meeting with Ellie Johnson and Mimi Cooper, Morgan State University Soper Library, December 13, 2001. The Garden Club archives are in the possession of club member Meta P. Barton. See also Isaac Rehert, "Garden Club 'Adopts' Inner City School and Teaches Nature."]

38. [According to Karen and Richard Cook, who were among the early members of BBEC, the mini-proposal program was initiated in response to prompting from an African American parent with a child in Margaret Brent, Loretta Cole. Dick Cook observed that the mini-grant was a "wonderful tool for citizen involvement." It enabled parents "to exert influence" on the schools' curriculum and set up a situation in which teachers and parents could begin dialogues about the school program. "For a very puny sum," observed Cook,—usually $1,000 per school each year—the program "created incredible community school interaction."

    Richard Eldridge, who had spearheaded the campaign to make Gertrude the principal, was also responsible for initiating the Discovery Rooms. He got the idea from a visit to the Smithsonian Institution in Washington, DC Cook interviews.]

39. [Don Schaefer to Ms. Gertrude Williams, April 11, 1984, PTO files. Becky Todd York, "Foundation to Seek Funds for City Schools," *Baltimore News American*, May 16, 1984. The fund was an outgrowth of the 1984 mayoral election in which William Donald Schaefer in seeking reelection promised to improve the quality of the city schools. For the chronology of Schaefer's mayoral campaigns see chapter five, note, p. 247, n15.]

40. [I was among those who designed the steering committee. I chaired it and edited the *Bugle* newsletter in the years covered by Gertrude's narrative. In composing the narrative text from the interviews, I inserted my name when she referred to "You," meaning me. jor.]

41. [The schools' public relations director, Anne O. Emery, was following a directive from the mayor's office calling for "a coordinated approach to all city publications." The editor of *The Bugle* informed Gertrude that parents would not submit to censorship; she informed Emery who stood by her directive. To Miss Gertrude S. Williams from Jo Ann Robinson, October 8, 1980. Memo from Anne O. Emery to Mrs. [*sic*] Gertrude Williams, Principal, October 27, 1980 with attachment: Memo To All Department Heads and Publications Coordinators From Mayor William Donald Schaefer, August 7, 1980. Mary Pat Clarke to Dr. John Crew, Superintendent, November 13, 1980. PTO files.]

42. [For an overview of the federal government's parent-involvement programs, see Michael R. Williams, *Neighborhood Organizing for Urban School Reform* (New York: Teachers College Press, 1989) 86–92.

    After Patterson's reorganization of the system into nine regions, Regional Advisory Councils (RACs) were established. Every SAC was expected to send a representative to the monthly RAC meetings where parents from all the schools in the region could share ideas and information. RACs, in turn sent representatives to a city-wide District Advisory Council, or DAC. Not surprisingly, school systems found that they could use SACS, RACs, and DACs to monitor and keep in hand their parent constituencies by controlling meeting agendas and having a strong administrative presence at all gatherings of the organization. Barclay SAC representatives frequently reported on RAC meetings where more principals and assistant superintendents were present than parents. The same was true of many DAC meetings. For the most part these groups were useful in providing a forum where the disgruntled could let off steam, system functionaries could drum up support for the next school budget or the most recent appeal to the state for more funds, and disseminate useful but carefully controlled information about the district's programs and policies. For a highly critical view of Baltimore's Title-I parent groups that asserts that their "activities were orchestrated by the school administration," see Kenneth K. Wong, *City Choices, Education and Housing* (New York: State University of New York Press, 1990) 93-94. Quote on 94.]

43. [PTO files, "Parent-Staff Crisis, 1982." A retired member of the Barclay teaching staff assured an interviewer in 1994 that "whatever differences that may have occurred {at Barclay} we all worked together." Frances Crosby interviewed by Devin Johnson, April 17, 1994. This same theme ran through other staff interviews.]

44. [The Leonards were affiliated with The Institute for Cultural Affairs, a nonprofit organization that promoted the concept of local communities practicing self-determination. The institute provided facilitators for the first priorities meeting. "Barclay's Priorities. Report from Priorities Meeting, November 14, 1981." "Who Is Responsible for Barclay School? A Report on Priorities Meeting #2, October 17, 1987." PTO files.]

45. [Jo Ann Robinson to Mr. John H. Branch Jr., March 23, 1979. PTO files.]

46. [The night that the school board voted approval for attaching a recreation center to Barclay School, Gertrude, her assistant principal, Joyce Kavanaugh, parent/teacher Jan French, and parent Carol Orrick testified in opposition. The board specified in their vote that "the principal will be free to look at the plans and work with the architect at all stages of construction." Board of School Commissioners, *Minutes*, September 16, 1976. The recreation center put Barclay and GHCC at odds, because the leadership of GHCC lobbied for locating the center there. Interview with Richard and Linda Cook.]

47. [John L. Crew Sr. to Mrs. Jo Ann O. Robinson, June 9, 1980. PTO files. Crew wrote, "I have appreciated and found very helpful the work of parents and citizens associated with each school. Barclay Elementary School is no exception. At the same time I do have some problems in trying to interpret the messages which the Barclay PTO has gotten from the administration of the school . . . I would like to discuss this with you and I will call you in the near future in the hope that I can get an appointment . . ." The letter was copied to the president of the school board, Mark K. Joseph, and Gertrude's regional superintendent, Samuel Sharrow, as well as to Gertrude.]

48. [My memory of the meeting with Dr. Crew conforms with Gertrude's except I do not recall the "so goddamned stubborn" comment. I remember her telling me that she had heard from a third party that he said that later, but not during our meeting. My impression is that he wanted to send a message to her through me and that's why he copied the letter to her and other officials. The PTO files include another letter to me from Crew, dated June 30, 1980. It refers to a letter I sent him on June 18 and reads, in part, "I found the meeting with you and Ms. Williams to be very positive from my point of view . . . I also attempted to explain how difficult it is to have everyone agree on the matter of communications. As you stated about yourself, I, too, believe in forthright approaches and statements . . . {H}owever, . . . this school system is a bit too complex to have every facet sorted in every way so that such forthrightness can honestly be indicated at any given time . . . I said that I would write to Ms. Williams and apologize or indicate that I possibly could have misunderstood her motives, etc. I have written that letter. (I hadn't forgotten it, and your letter to me was much more than a timely reminder.) . . ." Jor.]

49. ["Memo" from Gertrude S. Williams, Principal, to David C. Daneker, Chairman Board of School Commissioners, May 12, 1981 with attachment—"Duties Performed by Senior Teachers—P.S. #054," May 11, 1981. Jo Ann O. Robinson to Mrs. Alice G. Pinderhughes, June 25, 1983. PTO files.]

50. ["Song Sheet," PTO files. Richard Berke, "School Budget Cuts Called 'Out of Tune,' " *Baltimore Evening Sun*, June 23, 1982. Jo Clendenon, "No More Teachers . . . At Barclay Elementary, A Silent Farewell and a Primary Grade Protest," *Baltimore News American*, June 23, 1982. David McQuay, "Parents, Teachers Protest Budget Cut," *Baltimore News American*, June 23, 1982. The student letter printed with Clendenon's article said, "Dear Mayor Schaffer [*sic*], I am in second grade and my name is Sarah. You should do something about lay-offs! You laid off one of my favorite teachers! Would you like to be laid off? I wouldn't and teachers wouldn't either. You could get sick if you had a class with 40 or 50 children! Sincerely, Sarah." McQuay's article noted that the protestors came from all parts of the city. In addition to specific references to Barclay parents he quoted parents from City College, Fallstaff Middle School, and the Baltimore Educational Advisory Council.]

51. [Headquarters for the city school district were located first on 25th Street and later were moved to North Avenue.]

52. [Will Englund, "Tightly Knit Group of Survivors Controls Power' " *The Baltimore Sun*, May 3, 1988.]

53. [Mary Pat Clarke, who began an activist career as director of Greater Homewood Community Corporation (GHCC) in the early 1970s, and was then elected in 1975 and re-elected in 1979 as one of three city council representatives for the district in which Barclay was located and who in 1987 won the first of two terms as City Council

President, recalled the appreciation luncheons: "Gertrude Williams made sure that people were there from all over creation . . . I would never miss—no! *you would not miss that event!* I would see who Gertrude had . . . brought into the fold . . . It was very impressive." Mary Pat Clarke interview with Jo Ann Robinson, September 26, 2003.]

Chapter Seven   Principal at Barclay, Part Two: "To Learn as Fast as They Can and as Slow as They Must"

1. Michael Wentzell and Gwen Ifill, "Schaefer Portrait: Clashing Colors," *Baltimore Evening Sun*, September 2, 1983.
2. William Donald Schaefer's biographer recorded a ten-item list of "Schaefer's Rules." Item number ten pegs Gertrude's use of temper to a tee: "Act out: Most people will back down in the face of outrageous behavior. Don't worry when they accuse you of throwing tantrums. When you're right, you're right. And you're always right." C. Fraser Smith, *William Donald Schaefer* (Baltimore: Johns Hopkins University Press, 1999) 395.
3. Robinson interviews with Margaret Licht, March 3, 2003, and David Clapp, June 10, 2002. Email from Jan French, July 31, 2002.
4. Robinson interview with Evelyn Wallace, February 10, 2004.
5. Teacher Roundtable interview.
6. Michael Wentzel and Gwen Ifill, "Schaefer Portrait: Clashing Colors."
7. Henig et al. *The Color of School Reform. Race, Politics, and the Challenge of Urban Education* (Princeton: Princeton University Press 1999) 52.
8. Sandy Banisky, "No. 1 on the Agenda: Better Schools," *Baltimore Sun*, September 19, 1983.
9. See p. 117.
10. Szanton, *Baltimore 2000, A Choice of Futures* (Baltimore: Morris Goldsecker Foundation, 1986) 12.
11. Jill Jonnes, "Everybody Must Get Stoned: The Origins of Modern Drug Culture in Baltimore," *Maryland Historical Magazine* 91.2 (Summer 1996) 133–155. Ibid. Quotations: "lifestyle" 136; "highly troubled" 143; "It soon reached" 143–144; "when these people," 143.
12. Mike Bowler, "Preschools Enliven Inner-City," *Baltimore Sun*, April 25, 1971. The city school system had long maintained a pre-K program for disabled children, and from 1938 to 1958 offered pre-Ks for "normal" children in several schools. This offering was discontinued in September 1958. "Report of Board of School Commissioners, 1958–1960, 71.

    In 1960, Superintendent George Brain used a Ford Foundation grant to institute pre-K classes for economically disadvantaged children in four schools. "A Brave New World: Pre-K," *Baltimore Sun*, February 7, 1965. Federal funds coming into the system through the Elementary and Secondary Education Act (ESEA) of 1965 made it possible to institute pre-K programs in the inner city. ESEA funded Barclay's program.
13. Howard Libit, "MD. Educators Study Funding for All-Day Kindergarten Plans," *Baltimore Sun*, August 30, 2000. As Gertrude notes, the impetus for the all-day kindergarten came from an influx of well-prepared children who had been in an all-day day

care center that was equivalent to pre-K. However, she soon extended the all-day program to children who did not have this background. It's not clear that the kindergarten teachers were initially as convinced of the wisdom of doing this as she recalls.

14. Szanton, *Baltimore 2000*, 10.

15. Stuart E. Dean, "The Nongraded School," *School Life*, 47. 3 (1964) 19–23.

16. Board of School Commissioners, *Minutes*, Baltimore City Public Schools, April 20, 1961, 114–122. Quotation, 115. Gertrude's use of the term "grade level" indicates that the Barclay version of the nongraded school was not quite the same as that described in 1961.

17. Board of School Commissioners, *Minutes*, April 20, 1961, 121.

18. No reference to formal action phasing out nongraded programs was found in school board minutes. Mike Bowler, "Baltimore Schools Revisited," *Baltimore Sun*, April 25, 26, 27, 28, 29, 30, May 1, May 2, May 3, May 4, 1971.

19. David Clapp interviewed by Jo Ann Robinson, June 10, 2002. Margaret Licht interviewed by Jo Ann Robinson, March 30, 2003. Brandon Jones interviewed by Jo Ann Robinson, June 24, 2002.

20. Darice Claude to "Dear Editor," *Baltimore's Child*, October 1998. Joanne Giza, interviewed by Carrinda Pittman, April 17, 1994; Grenville B. Whitman, "Thank You Baltimore City Public Schools," *Baltimore Evening Sun*, June 27, 1983.

21. Olson interview; Barclay Teacher roundtable interview, December 15, 2003. Wallace interview.

22. Pittman interview of Joanne Giza.

23. [Everyone who was employed or who volunteered at Barclay would agree to this description. Frances Crosby, the school's first pre-K teacher, who began her work there in 1975, observed, "Barclay was always a bustle of activity, that began with the principal, Miss Gertrude Williams. Dull moments at Barclay? Never!" Helen Frances Crosby interviewed by Devin Johnson, April 17, 1994.]

24. [For a historical examination of this legislation, see Julie Roy Jeffrey, *Education for Children of the Poor: A Study of the Origins and Implementation of the Elementary and Secondary Education Act of 1965* (Columbus, OH: Ohio State University Press, 1979).]

25. [One of the aides, Evelyn Wallace, recalled that the "educational assistant" title was important to her because it commanded more respect than "children's aides" and she felt that she and the other aides "worked like teachers." In the 1990s, Gertrude asked Wallace to work as an educational assistant with a first year teacher in the Special Education program. Before coming to Barclay Wallace had worked with middle-school and senior-high-school students at the Venable School, a special facility for children with learning disabilities. "I was honored, to be asked to mentor a new teacher," Wallace asserted. "I feel good about what Miss Williams allowed me to do." Interview with Evelyn Wallace.]

26. Some parents hesitated to fill out the lunch applications because they were suspicious of anything from the federal government, others because they feared the "free lunch" would attach a stigma to their children.

27. [Evelyn Wallace noted how common it was for programs such as the High-I labs to start and then soon be ended. But, she reported, "Miss Williams never closed *her* High-I labs. We continued to work but not under the supervision of {the central administrator who had been in charge of the labs} . . . Miss Williams went on with it and didn't pay anybody any attention." Wallace interview.]

28. [At the school's 35th reunion Mrs. Crosby spoke of "the very warm welcome by the principal and the staff" that she received as the first pre-K teacher. She emphasized the "help and encouragement" that the Kindergarten teachers provided, especially the "insights and materials" she received from Jan French. Frances Helen Crosby interviewed by Devin Johnson, April 17, 1994.]

29. [Among the recommendations for desegregation that were considered in 1974, but never realized, was the creation of seven schools for the gifted. At the time there were 89,000 elementary school students, and the educators preparing the recommendations estimated that 10% of that population would be gifted. Baltimore City Public Schools, "A Committee Report on Desegregation, Elementary, Middle Schools and Junior High Schools," Earl Jones Chairman, May 1974.]

30. We screened students for GATE instruction in reading and/or math and/or science and/or physical education and/or music. The physical education and music teachers offered GATE instruction as part of their teaching assignments. Mrs. Moxon also taught Spanish as a GATE offering. GATE teachers pulled students from the regular classes at different times during the day. At the same time we also had classes to give children who needed special help in reading and/or math skills. So, as a matter of course, students would come and go to their assigned programs. No special attention was called to where they were going. Each child was just following his/her schedule.

31. [By the 1990s, the Baltimore school system sponsored the Baltimore Educational Scholarship Trust {B.E.S.T.} program through which school counselors identified students who might benefit from a private school setting, took those students to visit private schools, and helped their families apply for scholarships and admission. See "About B.E.S.T." www.besttrust.org.]

32. [Daniels was the first full-time faculty member of the University Evening College at Hopkins, serving from 1973 until he retired in 1987. He died in 1997. Schiffman began his career at Hopkins in 1971 when he was appointed Director of the Division of Education. During the presidential administration of Jimmy Carter he became the national director of Right to Read. He retired from Hopkins in 1991 and died in 1995. Email from Dean Ralph Fessler to Jo Ann Robinson, January 23, 2004. "Vita" of Gilbert B. Schiffman, Ed.D. and Announcement from Office of Public Relations Regarding Paul R. Daniels's appointment to University Evening College, August 1, 1973, both in Ferdinand Hamburger Jr. Archives, Johns Hopkins University.]

33. [Reference in school board minutes to this approval has not been found.]

34. [In 1974, there were 13 black and 21 white staff members at Barclay. Baltimore Public Schools, "Desegregation Plan Submitted to the Office of Civil Rights of The U.S. Department of Health, Education and Welfare," 1974, Part IV, 4. This plan called for 4 white teachers to be replaced by black teachers at Barclay, to establish a 50/50 black/white ratio. However Gertrude reports that those transfers were not made and that officials concluded that Barclay already had a sufficiently racially balanced staff.]

35. [In 1954, Robert Poole's student body had been 100% white. By the 1973–1974 school years the student composition had changed slightly, with 8% of the students being black. The desegregation plan called for a 67% black population at the school in the following year. In 1973–1974 Barclay had 88 black and 18 white sixth graders. The school system's plan assigned them to Clifton Park Middle School. Like the proposed transfer of white teachers, this was not implemented. However, unlike that proposed transfer, it was replaced by another proposal that was implemented: sending the

Barclay children to Robert Poole. "Desegregation Plan," Part II, 3, 8. When reviewing the plan for this book Gertrude recalled protesting the Clifton Park assignment because that school had a poor academic reputation at the time.]

36. [Corroboration of these specific incidents has not been found. That school safety was a long-standing issue at Robert Poole is suggested in press reports such as "Poole Problems Aired at Meeting," *Baltimore Sun*, January 24, 1979 and "Black Students At Poole Worry More About Safety Than Math, *Baltimore Evening Sun*, September 27, 1991. Richard Cook, whose children attended Margaret Brent Elementary and who was also a community activist, recalled how he arranged to escort students from the Brent area to and from Poole. He described the white parents with picket signs outside the middle school and said that "tension was incredibly high." He did not doubt that black students arriving or leaving without the protection of an adult would be "terrified." He and his wife Karen also recalled the beating of the son of their black neighbor, Loretta Cole during this period. The young man had been walking in the Hampden area and was attacked by whites. Interview with Richard and Karen Cook, March 20, 2004.]

37. [This conversation took place at the end of the summer, as school was about to open for the second year of desegregation. Jeffries' recall of the exchange had Gertrude saying, "We're sending students to Robert Poole to get an education, but they're not comfortable there"; and Fendeisen replying, "When the {Barclay} kids come back to school the kids at Poole are going to be waiting for them and they're going to beat them up." "I was stunned," said Jeffries, in 2000. "I'm still stunned," she added. "We were waiting for him to {say more}: If you know this is going to happen, what are you prepared to do about it? And I guess we're still waiting," she concluded. Jeffries interview.]

38. [Exploration of the middle-school concept was initiated by Roland Patterson as early as 1973. Memo to "Persons Addressed" From Roland R. Patterson, Superintendent of Public Instruction, Paul L. Vance, Deputy Superintendent for Executive Matters, John L. Crew, Deputy Superintendent, Center for Planning, Research and Evaluation, Subject, Middle School Planning Team, October 10, 1973. In its *Baltimore City Public Schools' Five Year Plan, 1981–1986* (Baltimore: Baltimore City Public Schools, 1981) the school board concluded that "the principal organizational model will be K–5 (elementary), 6–8 (middle), and 9–12 (high schools.) It will not be uncommon, however, to find variations such as a K-8 schools where appropriate." Robert Benjamin, "9th Grade Conversions to Increase," *Baltimore Sun*, February 13, 1982; Joe Nawrozki, "City Ninth Graders May Shift to High Schools, *Baltimore News American*, February 13, 1982; Frank D. Roylance, "Shift to Senior High Status Due for New Ninth Graders," *Baltimore Evening Sun*, February 23, 1982. For a discussion of the transition to middle schools nationwide, see Howard LaFranchi, "Attention Turns to Schools At Middle Level," *Baltimore Sun*, February 10, 1985.]

39. [When school officials decided that because of alleged under-enrollment, Abbottston Elementary, about a mile north east of Barclay, should be closed, they devised a plan that included sending 100 students from there to Barclay and to make room for them by sending Barclay students to Margaret Brent. The balance of the Abbottston students were to go either to Coldstream Park or to Montebello, elementary schools. The five schools involved united under the banner of "The Open Schools Committee." With support from Mary Pat Clarke and Nathan Irby of the City Council and State Delegate Anne Perkins they made the case for keeping Abbottston open. Since they

also had in common dissatisfaction with their respective junior high (soon to be middle school) zones the group stayed together to campaign for a new middle school. "Keynotes," Greater Homewood Community Corporation, May 1980, 5. "New City College Lower School Proposal," April 10, 1981, Open Schools Committee, Barclay PTO files.]

40. [Laura Scism, "Too Few Students Attend City College," *Baltimore News American*, March 1, 1981.]

41. [Superintendent John Crew appointed a task force to examine the Open Schools' middle-school proposal. Open Schools' representatives on the task force walked out before the final report was presented to the school board, calling the task force "a sham" because the proposal for using the City College location was never seriously entertained. The task force recommended against the City College site, accepting school system projections of increased high school enrollment that would soon preclude sharing space with a middle school. Another argument against the City College "lower school" proposal was that major renovations would be required to allow a middle school to operate as a separate unit within the City College facility. In fact, the projected enrollment increase did occur, and the City College building was operating at full capacity within a few years of the Open Schools campaign.

   Memo to Dr. John Crew, Superintendent and Mr. David Daneker, President Board of School Commissioners from Valarie Robinson, Chair and Members, Open Schools Committee, February 27, 1981; Memo from John L. Crew Sr., Superintendent to Board of School Commissioners, March 26, 1981; John L. Crew Sr. to Dr. Joanne [*sic*] Robinson, June 3, 1981; Letter to the Editor, Thomas C. Shaner (president-elect of the Baltimore City College Alumni Association), *Baltimore Sun*, May 3, 1981; John Albert Green Sr., President, PTSA(Parent–Teacher–Student Asociation), City College to Dr. John L. Crew Sr. March 6, 1981; Letter to the Editor, Yvette Pack (City College Student) to *Baltimore Sun*, May 2, 1981; Memo to Dr. Thomas Foster and Members, City College Task Force and John Crew, Superintendent from Mrs. Valarie Robinson, Chair, and Members, Open Schools Committee, November 17, 1981. "Middle School Bid Loses," *Baltimore Sun*, January 8, 1982. The Barclay PTO files include minutes from the Open Schools Committee and the City College Task Force established by John Crew and correspondence generated by both the committee and the task force.]

42. [John L. Crew to Mrs. [*sic*] Gertrude Williams, Principal and Dr. Joanne [*sic*] Robinson, P.T.O. President, April 19, 1982. Robert Benjamin, "Assignment Changes for 7 Schools Okayed," *Baltimore Morning Sun*, April 7, 1982. Benjamin noted that the school board had stipulated when approving seventh grade at Barclay in 1982 and eighth grade in 1983 that "Once the planned renovation of Poole is finished in 1984 Barclay pupils may have to attend Poole." The fact that those renovations were going to limit space in Poole for two years went a long way in convincing Crew and the board to let Barclay pilot its middle school. Because Crew had agreed that the system would evaluate the pilot, Gertrude and her parents downplayed the likelihood of their middle-school students being sent back to Poole and assumed that earning a positive evaluation would insure the continuation of grades seven and eight at Barclay.]

43. [The board approved the Barclay Middle School on April 17, 1986. Board of School Commissioners, *Minutes,* April 17, 1986. The PTO files include parent petitions and letters expressing enthusiasm for and trust in Barclay as a middle-school site. A typical letter: "There is no other school that I would want to send my son at this age other

than Barclay. . . . Let the children remain . . . until the eighth grade, by that time they will be prepared to travel on!" Mrs. Mary Trice, January 22, 1986.]

44. [See Liz Bowie, "City Bids To Recast Middle Schools," *Baltimore Sun*, October 24, 2001. Erika Niedowski, "Board Mulls Cut in Middle School Size," *Baltimore Sun*, February 27, 2002. In April 2003, Carmen Russo as superintendent was replaced by Bonnie Copeland amidst a disastrous financial crisis that has preoccupied school leaders. No more has been reported about the creation of new K–eight schools.]

45. ["City-wide" is the category that includes City College, Western, Polytechnic, and the School for the Arts—schools that admit students from all parts of the city who meet specific admissions criteria, in contrast to "zoned schools" to which all other students are automatically assigned by the school system.]

46. ["Memo," David Chapin to William Donald Schaefer, September 16, 1983. Barclay PTO files.]

Chapter Eight   Principal at Barclay, Part Three: "We Did Not Want a Poor Man's Curriculum"

1. Typical of media reports were Mike Bowler, "It Is Time To Confront the Crisis in Education," and Jeanne E. Saddler, "Why Baltimore Pupils Are At Bottom," both in the *Sunday Sun*, November 7, 1976.

   Gertrude's comment was made during a 1996 interview, CNN, "Democracy in America 1996: My Child, My Fear."

2. Hirsch argued that every member of society needed to acquire the same "core" of knowledge in order to live successfully and developed a curriculum that would impart the historical, literary, scientific, mathematical, and artistic facts that he identified as the essentials of Western culture and published in *Cultural Literacy: What Every American Should Know* (Boston: Houghton Mifflin, 1987). The Bradley Commission was made up of elementary , secondary, college, and university teachers of history. It was formed in 1987 in response to what its members perceived as the waning of their discipline in contrast to the social sciences and new fields, from sex education to computer literacy, that were being taught and required in the nation's schools.

3. *Education Week* whose editors billed it as "the newspaper of record in American education" was started in September 1981 and is a rich source of information on the education reforms put forward from then until the present. For the period covered here, see *From Risk to Renewal, Charting a Course for Reform*, a book of essays edited by *Education Week* editors, highlighting reform efforts. "A Chronology" at the back of the book annotates school reform enterprises across the nation from 1981 to 1992.

4. For an example of the difficulty in measuring effectiveness, see M. William Salganik, "Writing to Read in Baltimore: Expensive Lesson?," *Baltimore Sun*, August 18, 1991.

5. Veronica Donahue DiConti, "School-Based Management Emerges in the Reform Debate: The Case of Baltimore City," in *Interest Groups and Education Reform*, ed. Veronica Donahue DiConti (Lanham, MD: University Press of America, 1996) chapter 4.

6. Telephone interview with Stanley Curtain by Jo Ann Robinson, March 12, 2004.

7. Jane Tinsley Swope, "Calvert and Hillyer," *The Evening Sun*, October 26, 1994. Sam Stringfield, "Fourth Year Evaluation of the Calvert School Program at Barclay School," Johns Hopkins University Center for Social Organization of Schools, 1994.

8. Stringfield regarding admissions standards; Swope regarding home school clientele. In a statement of "Philosophy and Objectives" Calvert spokesmen in the 1990s asserted that "through scholarship and recruitment efforts, Calvert strives to offer an educational opportunity to students of varied ethnic and economic backgrounds." "Calvert School," n.d., Barclay PTO files.

9. On Embry and Abell, see Alex Friend, "The Kingdom and the Power. Inside the Abell Foundation: A Bastion of Wealth and Change," *Warfield's Business Record*, December 18, 1992, 1, 20.

   According to Robert Embry, his first encounter with the idea of using the Calvert curriculum in a public school came in 1986 when he was president of the school board. Alice Pinderhughes asked his opinion about a request from Cathy Pope-Smith, the principal of Federal Hill Elementary School, to use the private curriculum there. That request came to naught with the death of Dr. Pope-Smith. When Embry became president of the Abell Foundation, Calvert officials approached him about the possibility of Abell funds being granted to Calvert. Embry told them that Abell did not fund private institutions except for scholarships for public school children or partnerships with public schools. When the Calvert headmaster and board proved willing to explore such a partnership, Embry identified Gertrude as a principal who might be interested "in a different way of doing things." That Barclay was relatively near Calvert also contributed to making it a likely partnership candidate. Interview by Jo Ann Robinson with Robert Embry, January 29, 2003.

10. On Hunter when he arrived see Will Englund, "The Ordeal of Richard Hunter," *Sun Magazine*, June 3, 1990, 9–12, 16–17.

11. Embry also had been a city councilman, served as Baltimore's first housing commissioner, and worked in Washington for the Carter administration's Department of Housing and Urban Development (HUD). He also chaired the state school board for several years.

12. "About the Foundation. Our History," Abell Foundation web page, <www.abell.org>. Accessed January 18, 2003.

13. Jeffrey H. Henig et al., *The Color of School Reform* (Princeton: Princeton University Press, 1999) 224–225. Henig quotes Pinderhughes: "Embry would have loved to be superintendent or mayor of Baltimore. Now he realizes that neither are [*sic*] possible he is trying to do what he can." Will Englund, "The Ordeal of Richard Hunter," 16.

14. Jennifer Joy-Marie Beaumont, "Factors Contributing to Involuntary Superintendency Turnover in Urban Public School Systems," Ph.D. Thesis, University of Maryland Baltimore County, 1993, 102. Hunter had reportedly been "quietly courted" by some members of the search committee seeking a permanent replacement for John Crew. Hunter—then superintendent of the Richmond, Virginia schools—denied that he was a candidate for the Baltimore post. "Two Dropped Out Over Publicity," *Baltimore Sun*, December 19, 1982.

   According to both Beaumont and Englund, Hunter stirred controversy in both of his previous appointments. In Richmond he had been at odds with a mayor who, reportedly, he had demoted when that mayor had been a school principal. Hunter left the Dayton, Ohio school system shortly after having taken the superintendent's job there. He attributed his departure to a desire to join the faculty at the University of North Carolina. Officials in Dayton refused to discuss their view of his departure.

15. School board commissioners are appointed for three year terms on a staggered basis. Eight of Schaefer's appointees still had time to serve, giving Schmoke just one representative of his new administration.

16. Rejecting a candidate picked by board member hold-overs from his predecessors' administrations was not the only way in which politics influenced the new mayor's decisions about education. Removing Alice Pinderhughes as superintendent was purely political. What mattered was not her plans for the school system (which appeared to differ not at all from Schmoke's) but that she had been close to William Donald Schaefer and Du Burns and that the new mayor wanted to have his own superintendent.

17. Despite the opposition of many of their colleagues, the City Council representatives from the Second District, where Barclay was located, sided with Gertrude and the Barclay community. They (Anthony Ambridge, Carl Stokes, and the late Jacqueline McLean) were joined in their support of the proposed private–public partnership by council president, Mary Pat Clarke.

18. Typical of the mayor's response to appeals from Barclay supporters was a letter dated March 30, 1989 in which he wrote: "The Board of School Commissioners and I support Dr. Hunter's response to the [Barclay–Calvert] proposal. Dr. Hunter has made a curriculum decision based on his best professional educational judgment. . . . [H]is response to the Barclay proposal was based upon a series of specific educational reservations which unfortunately were not communicated in a timely way by others in the school system." Kurt Schmoke to Mr. David Buchholz, March 30, 1989. Copy in PTO files.

19. *Sun* editorial, "Dr. No," March 11, 1989.

20. Richard C. Hunter, "The Big City Superintendent: Up Against An Urban Wall", *The School Administrator*, May 1990, 8–11. Hunter declined an invitation to discuss his experience in Baltimore for this book. Email from Jo Ann O. Robinson to Dr. Hunter, January 15, 2004; Email to Jo Ann from Richard Hunter, January 22, 2004.

21. Jo Ann Robinson, "Stifling Stewardship in the City Schools," *Baltimore Sun*, May 6, 1989.

22. Notes from meeting of May 18, 1989 between Hunter and Barclay delegation, PTO files. Barclay advocates insisted that the school district "should not stifle the initiative of the stronger schools but [should] sustain them while finding ways to empower the weaker ones. . . . What does the [school system] administration seek to equalize and make consistent?" we asked. In light of the impoverishment of the school system, Barclayites concluded that "when poverty is equalized the result is equal mediocrity at best. Uniform inferiority is the more likely outcome." Robinson, "Stifling Stewardship."

23. Richard C. Hunter, "The Mayor Versus the School Superintendent," *Education and Urban Society*, 29.2 (February 1997) 217–232. Quotation, 223. Banks quoted in Will Englund, "Hunter's Hard Lessons," *Sun Magazine*, June 3, 1990, 16.

24. Banks put up a vigorous fight to obtain the post of director of the social studies curriculum. His opponents questioned his competence, though there is a subtext in the debates on the school board that indicates that the opposition was really resisting Banks's commitment to integrating black history and culture into the curriculum. In support of his efforts Banks assembled an advisory committee of prominent historians

from Morgan State University, Howard University, and Atlanta University. Board of School Commissioners, *Minutes*, December 3, 1970, 837–840; August 6, 1970, 471–477; September 3, 1970, 530–560; November 1970, 802–806; December 3, 1970, 817–818; January 21, 1971, 22–23; February 25, 1972, 60–63; April 27, 1972, 180–181. The League of Women Voters listed the university scholars supporting Banks in "Program, Local Education, 1970." Gloria Marrow, a teacher and administrator who worked closely with Banks, discussed his dissatisfaction with teacher-training in an interview with Jo Ann Robinson, April 7, 2004.

For descriptions and discussion of multiculturalism, see Jennifer Hoschschild and Nathan Scovronick, *The American Dream and the Public Schools* (New York: Oxford University Press, 2003) 170–176. Also James A. Banks and Cherry A. McGee Banks, eds., *Handbook of Research on Multicultural Education* (New York: Simon and Schuster Macmillan, 1995).

25. To sample the debate among academics, see Molefe Kete Asante and Diane Ravitch, "Multiculturalism: An Exchange," *The American Scholar* (Spring 1991) 267–276.

26. Jay Merwin, "African American Curriculum Eyed for City Schools," *Baltimore Evening Sun*, April 18, 1990. Merwin, "Schools Should Teach Black Heritage, City Councilmen Told," *Baltimore Evening Sun*, June 14, 1990. Bostic quoted in Glenn McNatt, "Debate Over 'Afro-Centric' Curriculum Misses the Point, *Baltimore Evening Sun*, July 3, 1990.

27. Board of School Commissioners, *Minutes*, September 13, 1990.

28. "Working Drafts" for all grade levels of the new curriculum were printed in 1993. The "Introduction" to the curriculum describes it as based on both "multicultural education [that] affirms diversity . . . challenges racism and discrimination . . . and stereotypic thinking . . . promotes pride, dignity and self esteem . . . furthers the cause of social justice." The Afrocentric section of the fifth grade curriculum presented the Afrocentric version of ancient Egypt (called "Kemet"). The "infusion" was presented with no indication that parts of it are matters of controversy. Curriculum Guide For the Fifth Grade Teacher," Baltimore City Public Schools, 1993, 3, 14, 15, 16–29. A cursory review of curriculum guides in use in Baltimore City in 2004 leaves the impression that emphasis on Afrocentrism has waned and multicultural themes are again in the ascendancy. This impression is based on Baltimore City Public School System, Office of Social Studies, "2001–2002 Curriculum Documents" for grades one, two, three, and four.

29. See the *Newsweek* issue on Afrocentrism and Englund's "Backers, Skeptics" for references to desperation and anger. Asante "500 Years" quotation is in *Newsweek*, 42. Samuel Banks, "Why Do We Need an Afrocentric Curriculum?," *Evening Sun*, July 23, 1990. Along with Banks, other African Americans in Baltimore who expressed reservations about Afrocentrism included two black columnists for *The Evening Sun*. Gregory P. Kane questioned whether an Afrocentric curriculum would be as motivating and inspiring to black students as its proponents claimed. He also observed that "two plus two is still four, and fractions and decimals have to be mastered no matter what is centric in a curriculum." Glenn McNatt speculated that "the current debate of the 'Afro-centric' curriculum is just another diversion from what really ails the schools." He pointed out that adding African materials to the instructional program was so much cheaper than "to really turn the schools around [which]would cost millions." Kane, "What If They Gave An 'Afro-centric' Party and Nobody Came?,"

Evening Sun, April 23, 1990. McNatt, "Debate Over Afrocentric Curriculum Misses the Point," *Evening Sun*, July 3, 1990.

30. Audiotaped conversation between Jo Ann Robinson and Gertrude Williams, January 20, 2004.

31. Hunter's public comments on curriculum stressed the need for a complete overhaul and employed such adjectives as "multi-cultural" and "multi-ethnic." See Hunter quoted by Mike Bowler, *The Lessons of Change* (Baltimore: Commissioned by Fund for Educational Excellence, 1991) 22 and in minutes of the Board of School Commissioners, March 16, 1989, 5–6. Pressure from Bostic and other community leaders, including members of the City Council, help account for his appointment of the Afrocentric task force. Interestingly, one of the most enthusiastic City Council advocates of Afrocentrism, Carl Stokes, was also a stalwart backer of Gertrude and the Barclay–Calvert proposal. He recalled in 2004 that his goal was "the inclusion of the contributions and perspectives of Black culture" and that he hoped a "modified Calvert curriculum" would also meet that goal. Email from "Carl" to Jo Ann Robinson, March 24, 2004.

32. The Johns Hopkins evaluators of the Barclay–Calvert program noted that "the reading program is a mixture of 'children's classics' and phonics. Several of the choices of books to be read by Calvert students have not changed in a half century, and today's students still seem to enjoy them. Consistent with this 'don't change until you are convinced that the new thing is better for your students' approach is the school's history curriculum. In fourth grade the school uses Hailers [*sic*] *Child's History of the World*. The first edition was published during the first quarter of this century, and much of the content hasn't changed." Sam Stringfield, "Fourth Year Evaluation of the Calvert School Program at Barclay," 1994. As that assessment was being prepared, a Morgan State University historian was completing a revision of the Calvert history text, removing dated terminology, inserting material based on current research, particularly updating and expanding the text's coverage of Africa. See Virgil M. Hillyer, *A Child's History of the World*, revised in 1994 by Suzanne Ellery Greene Chapelle (Baltimore: Calvert School).

33. Henig et al., *The Color of School Reform*, 277.

34. Tom Chalkley, "Educated Mess," *City Paper*, May 26, 1989, 8–9, Quotation, 9.

35. R.B. Jones, "On the Realside: Hunter and Schmoke (Part II)," *Baltimore Times*, April 2–8, 1990. After the controversy died down and Hunter left Baltimore, Jones visited Barclay and wrote a glowing account of how the school was flourishing under the curriculum and partnership that he had denounced as racist and elitist. R.B. Jones, "People Who Make Things Happen, Gertrude Williams," *Baltimore Times*, December 4–10, 1995.

36. See Henig et al., *The Color of School Reform*, 20 for discussion of blacks labeling other blacks "less black" to discourage interracial alliances.

37. The term "retain" is commonly used by educators when referring to the practice of keeping a student in the same grade for more than one year.

38. Barclay PTO Steering Committee, *Minutes*, May 11, 1983, PTO files.

39. [To Muriel Berkeley from Joanne Giza and Jo Ann Robinson, June 15, 1983. PTO files: Barclay–Calvert, History/Chronology. Merrill Hall had become headmaster in 1983. When Gertrude first visited Calvert in the early 1980s, William Kirk directed the school.]

40. [Merrill Hall had become headmaster in 1983. When Gertrude first visited Calvert in the early 1980s, William Kirk directed the school.]

41. [In a 2004 telephone interview, Dr. Yates recalled the phone call she had received from Gertrude asking "why I had not presented the proposal to the school board. 'What proposal?' I asked. She told me that I should have received the proposal about the Calvert curriculum from Clifton Ball. 'I will have to see about this,' I said. I don't remember whether Miss Williams or I called Clifton Ball, but one of us did and about 4 or 5 in the same afternoon of the day she called me here came Clifton Ball with the proposal. 'I had it and I told her [Gertrude] I had it,' he said." Asked if she believed that Ball had been sitting on the proposal, she replied with a definite "yes." Phone interview with Dr. Edmonia Yates, by Jo Ann Robinson, March 28, 2004.

    Attached to the proposal was a memo from Ball to Yates, dated August 12, 1988. In the memo, Ball described the proposed "Barclay School/Calvert School Project" and reported that "after listening to a discussion of the program and briefly looking at the scope and sequence, the educational specialists discussed the relatedness of the Calvert curriculum to the Baltimore City Scope and Sequence of Skills. Additionally, they supported Barclay's pursuit of this project." Photocopy of memo from Clifton Ball to Edmonia Yates, August 12, 1988, PTO files. Ball's assertion that the curriculum specialists supported the project is noteworthy, since they later reversed themselves. See, p. 171, this volume. In response to a query about the length of time involved between Gertrude's handing him the proposal and his handing it off to Yates, Clifton Ball wrote, "I have no recollection of the lapse of time between Miss Williams' first submission of the proposal to me and when I first responded to it. Further, I cannot recall when the proposal was shared with others." Clifton B. Ball to Dr. Jo Ann O. Robinson, March 9, 2004.]

42. [Merrill S. Hall to Dr. Clifton Ball, November 22, 1988. PTO files: Barclay–Calvert History/Chronology.]

43. [Carol B. Elder to Mr. Clifton Ball, December 9, 1988; Paula Eisenrich to Dr. Edonia [*sic*] Yates, December 12, 1988; Megan Shook to Mr. Clifton Ball, December 14, 1988; Karen Olson to Mr. Clifton Ball, December 20, 1988; Kathy Beck to Mr. Clifton Ball, December 20, 1988; Petition to Dr. Hunter, December 21, 1988; Megan Shook to Richard Hunter, January 16, 1989. PTO files: Barclay–Calvert History/Chronology.]

44. [Karen Olson, "Testimony to the Baltimore City School Board," February 9, 1989. PTO files: Barclay–Calvert History/Chronology. Kathy Lally, "Barclay Parents Say Innovations in Learning Prove Lesson in Futility," *Baltimore Sun*, February 21, 1989.]

45. [Robert C. Embry Jr. to Ms. Jo Ann Robinson, March 6, 1989. Barclay PTO files: Abell Foundation.

    Embry recalled that the foundation did not "want it to look like we had gone behind the school system and were doing something without their approval, because they were claiming that was the case and that this was our thing and not the school's thing . . . that we were trying to impose a white man's curriculum on black kids . . . We wanted to make sure that it {was seen} as a school initiative rather than our initiative." Robinson interview of Embry, January 29, 2004.]

46. ["Chronology of the Proposed Barclay–Calvert Partnership," n.d. [c. 1989]. Barclay PTO files: Barclay–Calvert History/Chronology. Merrill Hall confirmed his description of Hunter's visit in an interview with Jo Ann Robinson on September 5, 2003.]

47. [The only record that remains of the March 7, 1989 meeting with Dr. Hunter is the chart that the steering committee had prepared: "Baltimore City Public

Schools—Barclay School/Calvert School Partnership: Complementary Goals & Priorities," PTO files.]

48. [Will Englund, "Hunter Turns Back Barclay On Calvert School Program," *Baltimore Sun*, March 10, 1989. Suzanne P. Kelly, "Hunter Asks Abell Fund to Pay for Class-Size Cuts," *Baltimore Evening Sun*, March 10, 1989.]

49. [Mary Pat Clarke is the politician to whom Gertrude refers. When asked if she recalled that conversation, Clarke did not remember calling me but with regard to the comment about "tearing the city apart" she indicated that she had felt that was possible at the time. Interview by Robinson of Mary Pat Clarke, September 26, 2003.]

50. [Will Englund, "Barclay School Parents Ask School Board to Reject Hunter's Decision on Curriculum," *Baltimore Sun*, March 14, 1989. Suzanne P. Kelly, "Hunter's Barclay Refusal Attacked," *Baltimore Evening Sun*, March 14, 1989.]

51. [Arnett J. Brown Jr., "Let Hunter Lead," *Baltimore Evening Sun*, March 16, 1989. The following appeared in the press between March 15 and March 28. This is a sample of the reports and comments that flooded the local media from late February 1989 through the summer of 1990. Will Englund, "Barclay Says Barclay Plan Needs Airing," *Baltimore Sun*, March 15, 1989; Suzanne P. Kelly, "Barclay Issue Leadership Test for School Administration," *Baltimore Evening Sun*, March 15, 1989; Editorial, "Hunter in Wonderland," *Baltimore Evening Sun*, March 16, 1989; Suzanne P. Kelly, "Barclay Proposal Vote is Deferred," *Baltimore Evening Sun*, March 17, 1989; Will Englund, "Barclay Parents Call School Action Unfair," *Baltimore Sun*, March 17, 1989. Letters to the Editor from Elizabeth Kirk Weller, R.W. Fairbanks, E.M. Walker, *Baltimore Sun*, March 17, 1989; editorial, "One for All," *Baltimore Afro-American*, March 18, 1989; Delfield S. Yoes III, "The Barclay School Issue: An Administrative Challenge," *Baltimore Afro-American*, March 18, 1989; Will Englund, "Rebuffs By Hunter Leave School Parents, Charities Unsure of Role," *Baltimore Sun*, March 20, 1989; Letters to the Editor: Howard Bluth, Susan E. Mannion, Mary O. Styrt, *Baltimore Sun*, March 20, 1989; Letter to Editor, Robert W. Baker, *Baltimore Sun*, March 21, 1989; Richard W. Smith, "The Parents Wanted a Good School," *Baltimore Sun*, March 23, 1989; Suzanne P. Kelly, "Embry, Hunter Discuss Abell Aid, Barclay," *Baltimore Evening Sun*, March 23, 1989; Suzanne P. Kelly, "City Schools Reviewing Adoption of Projects, Their Efficacy," *Baltimore Evening Sun*, March 24, 1989; Letters to the Editor: Harry E. Bennett Jr., *Baltimore Evening Sun*, March 24, 1989; Paul H. Belz, *Baltimore Sun*, March 25, 1989; Marta Garriott, Mary E. Stuart, *Baltimore Sun*, March 27, 1989; Darrell T. Belton, *Baltimore Evening Sun*, March 27, 1989; Ida Mae Johnson, *Baltimore Sun*, March 28, 1989.]

52. [Irene B. Dandridge and Loretta Johnson to Dear Colleague, March 10, 1993; Karen Olson to Irene Dandridge and Loretta Johnson, April 27, 1993; cover letter for petition from Barclay parents stating that "It does no seem fair or necessary for the Teachers Union to disseminate untrue and negative information" about the Barclay–Calvert project. Barclay PTO files.]

53. [Pat Straus had called attention to an editorial in the Richmond press that began, "Remember Richard Hunter? He was the superintendent who did so much damage to Richmond's public schools. Now, as superintendent in Baltimore, he's evidently well on his way to doing the same thing there . . ." *Richmond News Leader*, June 20, 1989.]

54. [In "Notes From February 15, 1989 Meeting of the Charles Village Civic Association," appended to the Barclay PTO Press release of March 13, 1989, Ball was reported to

have "told the meeting that he has had the concerns about the Calvert/Barclay project which were raised by curriculum supervisors answered, that he has pulled each supervisor's piece together for his review report, which has been completed. This report, he said, gave a positive recommendation on the project on the basis of the Superintendent's priorities." Attachment II, Barclay Parent–Teacher Organization/Barclay Community Council Joint Press Conference, Monday, March 13, 1989, PTO files.

While his foot-dragging and circumlocutions on the Barclay–Calvert proposal implied a lack of enthusiasm and contributed in a major way to preventing Gertrude from implementing it according to her timetable, Clifton Ball did not go on record in opposition to it at the time, nor in retrospect has he expressed disagreement to it, deeming it "educational reform on uncharted ground." Clifton Ball to Dear Dr. Robinson, February 24, 2004.

An observation by Edmonia Yates may help put Ball's actions in context. "There were," said Yates, "three elementary school district directors [including Clifton Ball]. This triumverate was advocating whatever [education innovation] was in vogue at the time . . . Since they were in charge they felt that principals should come to them [for guidance on school improvement] and they wondered why [Gertrude] had not done so." Yates Phone interview. Pressured by Gertrude and at the same time vested in the "triumvirate's" antipathy to reform efforts originating outside of their realm, Ball could have been conflicted to the point of indecision, and his position would only get worse as other factions and forces—from the superintendent and school board to the Barclay parents and the Charles Village Civic Association—pressed him to take a stand.]

55. [Barclay Parent–Teacher Organization/Barclay Community Council Joint Press Conference, Monday, March 13, 1989. PTO files.]

56. [The minutes taken by the stenographer identify everyone by title: Ball, Executive Director, Northern District; Francois, Executive Assistant to the Superintendent, Herman Howard, Special Assistant to the Superintendent; Dorothy C. Stephens, Special Assistant to the Superintendent. "Meeting to Discuss Barclay/Calvert Project Proposal," Thursday, March 23, 1989. PTO files.]

57. [According to the *Minutes*, Straus reiterated several times that "she trusts Ms. Williams' judgment as the administrator of her school and supports the teachers in this effort to make the school better and to provide a better education for the children." Herman Howard hammered at the theme that Baltimore city schools curriculum specialists had found the Calvert curriculum to be "unacceptable" but the system was willing to work with Barclay on some other approach. Dorothy Stephens was the person who suggested "that Barclay come up with a document that does not supplant the BCPS curriculum. The curriculum could be enriched by components of the Calvert curriculum." The Barclay spokesmen asked if Calvert staff would be involved. When Howard replied "we would not be involving Calvert staff," the representatives from Barclay are quoted as saying, "We would be plagiarizing by taking parts of Calvert's curriculum." The Barclay contingent also repeatedly protested the ultimatum that Richard Hunter had announced, requiring the Abell Foundation to fund the lowering of class size in all city school third grades as a condition of Barclay being authorized to accept funding from Abell. "Meeting to Discuss Barclay/Calvert," March 23, 1989.]

58. [Board of School Commissioners, *Minutes*, April 6, 1989, 3–11. Howard's actual words were that Barclay representatives had made "no modifications" to their proposal and there was "no recommendation from the community" for alternative ways of

improving the instructional program at Barclay. Will Englund, "Baltimore School Board Flatly Turns Down Barclay Plan," *Baltimore Sun*, April 7, 1989. Carl Stokes did not remember specific details of that school board meeting, but he stated in a 2004 interview that "what I do remember squares with Miss Williams' memory. I recall that the Board voted down the proposal and I thought Barclay had not been treated fairly." Telephone interview of Stokes by Jo Ann Robinson, February 25, 2004.]

59. [Detailed notes from that meeting of May 18, 1989 are in the PTO files. Hunter's comment on note-taking is rendered as "I'm trying to say things but I can't say with a tape recorder. I don't want to create more divisiveness . . ." Gertrude is quoted as talking at length about the ways the Barclay community has supported the system and concluding that theme by saying to Hunter, "We're one of your children. We're not fighting the daddy. We're here to support the program." Among comments on the controversy is one attributed to Hunter: "It's hard to put it aside. I've been beat over the head with it every day. I get it from both sides . . ." He also offered that "We would like to work with you to develop approaches to enhance education of children at Barclay and system-wide," but gave no specific data on how he planned to do that. "May 18, 1989 200 E. North Avenue Office of the Superintendent," notes in PTO files, recorded by Jo Ann Robinson.]

60. [In addition to the hearty support evinced by the crowd that probably contained 300 or 400 people, the mayor may have been predisposed to give Gertrude a sympathetic hearing by notes he had received before the forum. A member of his staff, who was also a neighbor and parent of a former Barclay student had given him a two-page handwritten memo indicating how well respected Gertrude was in the Barclay community and telling the mayor that "Barclay folks . . . believe that you have been misinformed about the details of the {Barclay–Calvert} proposal." Donna Keck, to Mr. Mayor: Re: "Barclay School/Wyman Park Community Forum," June 1, 1989. Dea Andersen Kline also wrote to the mayor in her capacity as Hopkins Director of Community Affairs. Expressing regret that she would be out of town on the day of the forum, she enclosed unspecified "background material" about the proposal. The material was probably summaries and replies to critics prepared by the PTO Steering Committee. Dea to Dear Kurt, May 23, 1989. Copies of both communications are in the PTO files. Looking back 14 years later, Schmoke did not recall specific appeals from Barclay supporters, but he remembered that he "got a lot of information from people," including Gertrude, parents, and "especially Mary Pat Clarke," the president of the City Council at that time. Schmoke interview by Robinson.

Clarke has said about Gertrude's directly and publicly addressing the mayor that "she gave him a way out. He was suffering politically. Everybody was backed into their corner. Gertrude went in front of the world and asked him to help. So he could justify that he was moved by this and had some second thoughts." Robinson interview with Clarke, September 26, 2003.]

61. [In later recollection, Schmoke said he knew "indirectly" about the racial charges but no one brought such charges to him. He felt that the charges "didn't gain any traction" because he and the president of the City Council, Mary Pat Clarke, were together in supporting Barclay–Calvert. Schmoke interview by Robinson. In offering this assessment the former mayor ignored the period when he backed Hunter in opposition to the proposal.]

62. [Schmoke did not specifically remember telling Gertrude to quiet things down, but he said, "it sounds like something I would say." Schmoke interview by Robinson.]

Chapter Nine   Principal at Barclay,
Part Four: In the Spotlight

1. Wilbur C. Rich, *Black Mayors and School Politics, the Failure of Reform in Detroit, Gary and Newark* (New York: Garland Publishing Company, 1996) 5–8.
2. The objectives and methods of BUILD, GBC, and BTU are examined in Jennifer Joy-Marie Beaumont, "Factors Contributing to Involuntary Superintendency Turnover in Urban Public School Systems," Ph.D. Dissertation, University of Maryland, Baltimore County, 1993, chapter V and Veronica Donahue DiConti, *Interest Groups and Education Reform* (Lanham, MD: University Press of America, Inc., 1996) chapter 4.
3. Brian Sullam, "Schmoke Beginning to Use Intangible Powers of Office," *Sun*, November 20, 1989. Beaumont, "Factors Contributing to Involuntary Superintendency," 108–109. Beaumont reports that school officials explained the undistributed books as materials that were out of date. Schmoke later recalled none of the explanations given to him to have been satisfactory. Schmoke interview by Robinson.
4. Will Englund, "Schmoke's Patience With School System Leadership is Running Out," *Sun*, December 2, 1989. Will Englund, "Hunter Relinquishes Roles to Mayor," *Sun*, January 7, 1990. Patrick Gilbert and Jay Merwin, "Schmoke Rips Hunter—Again," *Evening Sun*, March 3, 1990; Brian Sullivan and Rafael Alvarez, "Schmoke Faults Hunter Inaction on Safety Breach," *Sun*, March 8, 1990. Beaumont, "Factors Contributing to Involuntary Superintendency," 111–112.
5. Beaumont, "Factors Contributing to Involuntary Superintendency," 94, 95, 103. At the time of her retirement, Alice Pinderhughes was earning an annual salary of $85,300. Hunter was brought in at $125,000. Beaumont, "Factors Contributing to Involuntary Superintendency," 94.
6. Beaumont, "Factors Contributing to Involuntary Superintendency," Reckling critique, 103. DiConti, *Interest Groups*, 134–137.
7. DiConti, *Interest Groups*, 150. This author also details how the sbm initiative of Pinderhughes had been shelved.
8. Will Englund, "Mayor Wants Hunter Out, Sources Say," *Sun*, March 20, 1990; Kathy Lally, "Mayor Consults School Board About Hunter," *Sun*, April 1, 1990; Jay Merwin, "Hunter Facing Performance Review," *Evening Sun*, March 21, 1990; Kathy Lally, "Schmoke Says School Chief Will Keep Job," *Sun*, April 12, 1990; Editorial, "Schmoke's Gamble," *Evening Sun*, April 12, 1990; Frank A. DeFilippo, "State of the City, State of the Mayor," *Evening Sun*, April 26, 1990; Untitled Notice of the appointment of Andrews as deputy superintendent of Baltimore public schools, *Education Week*, May 16, 1990, 3; Will Englund, "Hunter's Hard Lessons," *Sun Magazine*, June 3, 1990. Schmoke quoted in Lally, "Schmoke Says School Chief Will Keep Job," April 12, 1990.
9. Mark Bomster, "Board Votes Against Superintendent," *Evening Sun*, December 21, 1990; Michael A. Fletcher and Mark Bomster, "Handling of Hunter Case is Assailed," *Evening Sun*, December 21, 1990; Barry Rascover, "Schmoke Shucks Hunter From Schools," *Sun*, December 23, 1990; Editorial, "Schmoke Under Fire," *Evening Sun*, December 24, 1990; Mark Bomster, "Hunter Exits With Blast at Schmoke," *Evening Sun*, July 31, 1991; "Text From Dr. Richard C. Hunter's Final July 31 Press Conference as Baltimore's City School Superintendent," *Baltimore Afro-American*,

August 3, 1991. The *Afro-American* did not include the italics; these appear in a typescript version of the speech, a copy of which is in the PTO files.

Looking back six years after he left Baltimore, Hunter presented his account presented his account of his years in the city. He decried mayoral meddling in public school governance and enumerated the ways in which he believed Schmoke had undermined him. First by making himself a prominent spokesman on education, the mayor, Hunter alleged, drew attention and respect away from the superintendent. Moreover, as Hunter saw it, the mayor had positioned himself to benefit whether school reform efforts succeeded or failed. If they were successful, Schmoke would take the credit. If not, he would (and, Hunter claimed did) blame the superintendent. Second, Hunter reported that the mayor often determined where and when he must be present on any given day "This usurpation of my work calendar extended to other areas as well," he wrote. Third, he complained that Schmoke lacked expertise in education policy and practice and was prone to advocate "initiatives . . . [that]made little educational sense." As the professional educator, Hunter explained, he was "compelled to oppose" such initiatives, making himself politically vulnerable Richard C. Hunter, "The Mayor Versus the Superintendent: Political Incursions," *Education and Urban Society* 29.2 (1997) 217–232.

10. Kurt Schmoke concurred with this analysis in the January 2003 interview. The Barclay controversy, he said, "wasn't the nail in the coffin but it was a contributing factor" in Hunter's decline and fall. Schmoke interview by Robinson, January 14, 2003. Examples of reportage on other issues that also rehashed the Barclay controversy include Englund, "Schmoke's Patience With School System Leadership is Running Out,"; Englund, "Hunter Relinquishes Roles to Mayor," Gilbert and Merwin, "Schmoke Rips Hunter—Again,"; Sullivan and Alvarez, "Schmoke Faults Hunter Inaction on Safety Breach."

11. Licht interview.

12. Roundtable interview.

13. Quoted in Mike Bowler, "A 'Distressing' Time On City School Board," *Baltimore Sun*, August 25, 2004.

14. Sam Stringfield, "Fourth Year Evaluation of the Calvert School Program at Barclay School," Center for the Social Organization of Schools, Johns Hopkins University, 1994, 15.

15. Robinson interview with Embry. Licht was a graduate of Hollins College with an MA in Education from Goucher College. She taught in the city public schools from 1959 to 1969, when she began her career at Calvert. Robinson interview with Licht.

16. Teachers' roundtable interview.

17. As he had in the case of Hunter, Schmoke turned thumbs down on candidates recommended by others—this time the teachers' union and several city interest groups—and pushed to have Amprey hired.

18. Baltimore had previously joined with other poorly funded school districts in a law suit against the state (*Hornbeck v. Somerset County Board of Education*, 1980, 1983). The state circuit court found that "a child in the wealthiest subdivision has approximately twice the amount spent on his education as a child in the poorest subdivision" and called the "present system of financing . . . unconstitutional." However, on appeal that finding was overturned on the grounds that school funding was a legislative, not a judicial matter. In 1989 an Abell Foundation report, "A Growing Inequality," demonstrated that the gap between rich and poor counties had "increased markedly," a trend

that was still in progress in 2001 when two separate study commissions—the government-appointed Commission on Education, Finance, Equity, and Excellence (the Thornton Commission) and a nonprofit advocacy group, the New Maryland Education Coalition, endorsed augmentation of state funding for schools. In 2002, the state legislature enacted a new school finance system, tied to a system of school district accountability. The legislation did not include funding sources and whether the Thornton reform could be funded was a matter of hot debate.

19. Gertrude S. Williams to Dr. Walter Amprey, April 28, 1993. Copy in PTO files.

20. Amprey questioned that funding would be available for further expansion, and pointed out that the Calvert curriculum was "protected and copyrighted." Additional partnerships would have to be "their call," he declared, referring to Calvert. For their part, the administrators and trustees of Calvert School were chary of forging further into public school territory. Guaranteeing faithful implementation of their program was too daunting. "We have a lot of our reputation tied up in the success of this program," Merrill Hall explained. He added, "We don't think we want to see a number of schools failing at it." Amprey and Hall quoted in "A Public Offering of the Calvert Curriculum?," *The American School Board Journal*, December 1995, 20. Calvert programs do operate in other public schools in Washington, DC, Florida, Georgia, and Brazil. Robinson interview with Hall.

21. Margaret Licht interviewed by Jo Ann Robinson, March 31, 2003.

22. Interview with Hall. See pp. 176, 190, 197 in Gertrude's narrative for discussion of this conflict over Title I.

23. Robinson interview with Embry. Robinson interview with Hall. Horne and Brown in Roundtable interview. Robinson interview with Licht.

    At the same time that Gertrude had to mediate between Calvert and Barclay Title-I teachers, she also had to deal with challenges from the school officials in the local Title-I office who were hostile to the Calvert program. See unsigned "Summary Report—School #054, Technical Assistant Visit," December 6, 1990, Division of Compensatory Education; and memo from Gertude S.Williams to Herman A Howard et al., "Request for Information," December 19, 1990.

24. In his "Fourth Year Evaluation of the Calvert School Program at Barclay School," Sam Stringfield observed that "a typical Baltimore City School District student who transfers into Barclay in the second, third, fourth, or fifth grade finds himself or herself at least one year behind his/her same-grade Barclay classmates. In language arts/writing, the gap will probably be two years . . . [T]ransfers in . . . create several problems. The incoming students are likely to be far behind in all academic areas. This can severely threaten a child's self-image and place him even further 'at risk' than when he came to Barclay." Center for the Social Organization of Schools, Johns Hopkins University, Baltimore, Maryland, 1994, 224–225.

25. Roundtable interview.

26. Roundtable interview. Ronald A. Peiffer, Deputy State Superintendent for Academic Policy in the MSDE, has stipulated that "very, very few appeals [of RE decisions] were made and only one or two were successful." He cited the example of a school whose population and staff changed drastically "when a housing project had been demolished since the last testing." It was therefore unfair to pin an RE designation based on the performance of the previous population on the new population and staff. Although "not surprised to hear the reactions of staff about a second chance, there were no second chances," Peiffer insisted. Peiffer Emails to "Dear Mrs. Robinson," April 28 and April 29, 2004.

27. Interview of David Clapp by Jo Ann Robinson, June 10, 2002. Participants in the Faculty roundtable interview at Barclay, December 15, 2003 echoed Clapp's opinion.
28. Interview with Clapp. Clapp noted that Barclay eighth grade students (after the Barclay–Calvert program had extended into middle school) usually scored above the city average. This is documented in the "composite index of scores for Baltimore middle schools over the past seven years under the Maryland School Performance Assessment Program," published in the *Baltimore Sun*, January 29, 2002. Only in 1997 and 2002 did their scores slip below the city average. They remained below the state average, however. Barclay roundtable interview. Workshop advice quoted in Mike Bowler, "Looking for Better Way, Teachers Engage in Never Ending-Learning," *Baltimore Sun*, March 21, 1999.
29. Robinson interviews with Embry and Hall.
30. A Middle School at Calvert was inaugurated in the spring of 2002.
31. Clapp interview. Clapp's views were echoed in the Roundtable interview with other Barclay staff.
32. Clapp and Hall interviews.
33. Hall interview.
34. Hall interview. To "Trudy" from Merrill Hall, n.d. (Spring 1995), copy PTO files. (when I was asked to participate in the meeting that Gertrude describes later where this letter was discussed with her by the Calvert leaders and Bob Embry, a copy of it was shared with me. While he did not remember that particular meeting, Embry later recalled a deterioration in the relationship between Calvert leaders and Gertrude. The former, according to Embry, were disturbed by what they saw as lapses in her management of the school—reportedly allowing teachers to come in late, questionable administration of certain tests, permitting sloppy implementation of the Calvert curriculum). Robinson interview with Embry. Stringfield, Fifth and Sixth Year Evaluations.
35. Gertrude S. Williams, "RELEASE: 'A New Phase of Curriculum Reform,' an Announcement From the Principal and School Improvement Team of the Barclay School," March 1, 1996. PTO files.
36. Clapp interview.
37. Citizens Planning and Housing Commission, "Notes From New Schools Meeting," April 25, 1996; Jean Thompson, "City School Initiative Considered," *Baltimore Sun*, June 10, 1996; Marilyn McCraven, "Plenty of Ideas to Reinvent Schools," *Baltimore Sun*, November 6, 1996. Liz Bowie, "Schools Sell Themselves," *Baltimore Sun*, June 14, 2002. Baltimore Area Grantmakers, "ABAG Education Affinity Group . . . New Schools Initiative: Looking Toward the Future," meeting announcement, January 22, 2002. <http://www.abagmd.or/calendar2445/calendar>. Doug Donovan and Laura Loho, "City to Push for Charter Schools," *Baltimore Sun*, May 2, 2005; Laura Loh, "5 Charter Schools' Funding Uncertain," *Baltimore Sun*, February 20, 2005.
38. [Schmoke later said that he tried to give Hunter a chance to demonstrate a "policy basis" for opposing Barclay–Calvert. When Hunter proved incapable of doing this the mayor began to back Gertrude. "What she was arguing for made sense," he declared. He recalled arguing to Hunter that "it wasn't like we couldn't reverse it if it didn't work out. Why not try it?" Schmoke concluded that Hunter saw the Barclay–Calvert project as "a threat to his control" of the school system. Schmoke interview by Robinson.
    In retrospect, what stood out for the former mayor was the backing he gave Gertrude from the late spring of 1989 on—backing that was critical to the launching

of the Barclay–Calvert project. When he was interviewed for a 1995 *Phi Delta Kappan* article Schmoke claimed "the Calvert–Barclay experiment" as his "most unqualified success" with regard to education. Similarly in his interview with Robinson in 2003 he stressed how he had come out in support of Gertrude, with no reference to his original opposition to her proposal. Mark F. Goldberg, "Education in Baltimore. An Interview with Mayor Kurt Schmoke," *Phi Delta Kappan* (November 1995) 234–235. Quotation, 236. Schmoke interview by Robinson.

39. [The agreement was in the form of a letter on Abell Foundation letterhead: Robert C. Embry Jr. to Mr. Joseph L. Smith, President, Baltimore City Board of School Commissioners, May 16, 1990; copy in PTO files. As the funding source, Abell was technically the author of the proposal.]

40. [The original grant, dated April 23, 1990, was in the amount of $500,000.00, of which $499,999.96 was spent. It was issued "to cover the cost of books, teacher training, full-time consultant {coordinator, Peg Licht}, and salaries for teacher aides to integrate the Calvert School curriculum into Barclay Elementary School's K–4th grades over four years."

   In April 1994, a second grant in the amount of $691,738.00 was issued "for continuation and expansion of the Calvert School program at Barclay . . . over four years to encompass grades K–8." From that grant, $686,188.93 was spent. Abell Foundation "Grants-Alpha List," 1/29/03, courtesy of Sita Culman.]

41. [The federal program for compensatory education has undergone several name changes. The term Title I was used for it from 1965 to 1981. Chapter 1 was the nomenclature from 1981 to 1994 when Title I came back into use. The transition from Chapter to Title had not taken place when Stringfield published his fourth year report in 1994. See Robert C. Johnston, "By Any Other Name, Chapter 1 Program Will Still Aid Poor Children," *Education Week*, October 12, 1994.]

42. [Sam Stringfield, "Fourth Year Evaluation of the Calvert School Program at Barclay School."]

43. [Stringfield Fourth Year Report, 16–17. These signs of success with the Chapter-1 students are especially interesting in light of the conflict between the Barclay Chapter-1 teachers and the Calvert staff. The teachers' contention that they were working effectively with the students seems to be borne out by Stringfield's findings. But the findings also lend credence to Merrill Hall's contention that once the Chapter-1 teachers had fewer students needing Chapter-1 services, those teachers should have been available for other assignments. He and Peg Licht both indicated that the teachers resisted such additional assignments.]

44. [Stringfield Fourth Year Report, 18. Barclay teacher Susan Lattimore confirmed that Calvert methods worked well with the dyslexic children that she taught. Roundtable interview.]

45. [Peg Licht reported that at a meeting of the Calvert Board of Directors, headmaster Merrill Hall had distributed folders of Barclay students and folders of Calvert students, with all names removed. He asked the board members whether they could tell which came from Barclay and which from Calvert. They could not. Robinson interview with Licht. Hall repeated this story in his interview.]

46. [Gary Gately, "Angry Parents Assail Barclay School Underfunding," *Sun*, January 6, 1994. Editorial, "Making Barclay Kids Suffer," *The Evening Sun*, January 10, 1994. The floor-sweeping was reported in "A Better Idea," *The Economist*, December 2, 1995, 3.]

47. [Private Abell funds covered all aspects of the Barclay–Calvert program and Gertrude's disagreements with the public sector concerned funding that Barclay was entitled to as a public school. The Barclay response to this charge was that the school district should "not stifle the initiative of the stronger schools but [should] sustain them while finding ways to empower the weaker ones . . . What does the [school system] administration seek to equalize and make consistent?," we asked. In light of the impoverishment of the school system, Barclayites concluded that "when poverty is equalized the result is equal mediocrity at best. Uniform inferiority is the more likely outcome." Jo Ann Robinson, "Stifling Stewardship in the City Schools," *Baltimore Sun*, May 6, 1989."

    Evaluator Sam Stringfield noted that "the entire four-year Abell Foundation grant has supplied less money per student at Barclay than is the annual difference in per child funding between a Baltimore City and suburban Baltimore County school." "Fourth Year Evaluation," 4.]

48. ["The Woman Who Battled the Bureaucrats," *Reader's Digest*, December 1993, 142–149; "Borrowing from the Basics," *Education Week*, April 20, 1994, 32; "A Better Idea." *The Economist*, December 2, 1995, 3; "Shakespeare vs. Spiderman," *U.S. News and World Report*, April 1, 1996, 61; "The Power of One" (tribute to Gertrude Williams), Mobil Corporation advertisement, *New York Times*, April 11, 1996; "The Learning Principal," *Emerge*, May 1998, 52–55. There were also national television appearances—on *ABC Weekend News*, December 23, 1995; *CBS Evening News*, March 27, 1996; and *CBS This Morning*, April 10, 1996. In addition writers included the Barclay story in their books: Veronica Donahue DiConti, *Interest Groups*, chapter four; Marion Orr, *Black Social Capital: The Politics of School Reform in Baltimore, 1986–1998*, University Press of Kansas, 1997, passim; Charles J. Sykes, *Dumbing Down Our Kids* (New York: St. Martin's Press, 1995) 275–279; John Kasich, *Courage is Contagious* (New York: Doubleday, 1998) 141–155.]

49. [Referring to the large numbers of visitors that were attracted by Barclay–Calvert, Calvert Headmaster Merrill Hall judged that "for our teachers to be viewed as leaders in instruction was good. It showed they were masters, what they were doing was important, and we were proud enough to show them off." He added that the magnitude of the visitor-phenomenon made school leaders "a little frantic" and it was a challenge "to manage that influx." Hall interview.

    Illustrating Hall's observation about the visitors' effect on teachers, Dorothea Rawlings told of having Gertrude call up to her room on the intercom late on a Friday afternoon to say that a visitor, who turned out to be a reporter, was coming up to observe her class. "You know we had it 'goin' on' at Barclay, when we could accept a visiting reporter on a Friday afternoon!" she declared. She added, "It was good for the children to read good things about themselves" and proudly noted that Gertrude's confidence in sending visitors to classes at any time showed that "Miss Williams felt that her teachers were doing exactly what her teachers should be doing." Roundtable interview.]

50. [American Federation of Teachers, "Learning To Reach the Stars," 1966. Albert Shankar wrote about Barclay in the weekly column, "Where We Stand," carried as an advertisement in the *Sunday New York Times*. Shankar, "A Baltimore Success Story," *New York Times*, August 20, 1995.]

51. [Robert Embry later observed that despite all the publicity that the Barclay–Calvert partnership received, the Abell Foundation received no calls from other Baltimore

public schools asking to have a similar partnership with Calvert. He did not remember specifically how the grant to Woodson came about.]

52. [Mary Maushard, "Schools Get Cash Awards From MD," *Sun*, November 27, 1996.]

53. [After the administration of George W. Bush succeeded in getting "The No Child Left Behind Act" through Congress, the Maryland State Department of Education (MSDE) announced that MSPAP would be replaced with new tests that would meet the requirements of the federal law. Mike Bowler, "Maryland School Test is Dropped," *Sun*, April 25, 2002. Prior to that announcement, opposition to MSPAP on the part of several school districts had been rising. Howard Libit, "Montgomery Schools Ask That MSPAP Be Suspended," *Sun*, February 8, 2002. Editorial, "Bye-bye, MSPAP," *Sun*, March 6, 2002.]

54. [Incidents arose where teachers were charged with coaching students for the test using exact test questions. See "Learning a Hard Lesson," *Sun*, January 13, 1997; " 'Improbable Gains' Lost," *Sun*, January 26, 1997. "Teachers to Appeal Proposed Suspension," *Sun*, February 5, 2002.]

55. ["RELEASE: A New Phase of Curriculum Reform: An Announcement From the Principal and School Improvement Team of the Barclay School," March 1, 1996, PTO files. Kathy Lally, "Maryland Tests Torpedo Successful Program," *Baltimore Sun*, March 2, 1996. Gertrude S. Williams, Jo Ann O. Robinson, "MSPAP Didn't Torpedo Program," Letter to the Editor, *Baltimore Sun*, March 9, 1996. Despite the frustration that everyone felt with MSPAP, no one from Barclay–Calvert had ever publicly spoken against the testing program.]

56. [In 1992, Walter Amprey forged a partnership between the Baltimore school system and Education Alternatives, Inc., a private company based in Minnesota offering the "Tesseract" program that was established in nine Baltimore schools. It promised to improve instruction and student performance as well as streamline the schools' budgets. This venture proved to be a disappointment and was ended in 1995. "Professional Service Agreement Between Baltimore City Public Schools and Education Alternatives, Inc.," 1992; "Minn. Firm To Run 9 City Public Schools," *Sun*, June 10, 1992; American Federation of Teachers, "Research Report: The Private Management of Public Schools, an Analysis of the EAI Experience in Baltimore," n.d. (1993?); "School Board Urges Mayor to Drop EAI," *Sun*, November 22, 1995; "Quick End to EAI Experiments," *Sun* Editorial, November 24, 1995; "After EAI," *Sun* Editorial, December 5, 1995.]

57. [The School Board embraced the teaching of phonics in their end-of-century master plan. Liz Bowie, "School Board To Require Phonics," *Sun*, January 31, 1998. This put them ahead of the national pro-phonics wave that developed in 2000. Mike Bowler, "Phonics Teaching Gets Top Grade," *Sun*, April 14, 2000; Kathleen Kennedy Manzo, "Reading Panel Urges Phonics for All in K-6," *Education Week*, April 19, 2000.]

Chapter Ten   Retirement

1. David Clapp interviewed by Jo Ann Robinson, June 10, 2002.

2. Ibid.

3. Clapp earned a Masters degree in elementary education and obtained certification in administration, both from Johns Hopkins.

4. Gertrude mentored Horne and Clapp together. Both became candidates for the principalship when she retired and both were recommended to Schiller by the faculty–parent–community selection committee.

5. Ibid.

6. Ibid.

7. Ibid. Clapp's perceptions of a vengeful spirit directed from the central administration to Barclay were shared by other members of the Barclay staff. Truemella Horne recalled that at the start of his time as principal "it was really rough for David. . . . There would be things not done because someone would say 'you're not going to get that any-more . . .' " Susan Lattimore sounded a similar note. "Miss Williams was such a mav-erick and stepped on so many toes. There was resentment about the class size cap. A lot of resentment came from the central office." Ignoring the cap on class size was "a way to get back."

8. Horne began working at Barclay in February of 1974 as a third grade teacher. Over the years she taught every elementary grade, worked as a Title-I reading teacher, directed the High Intensity Reading Lab, coordinated the Calvert program in the elementary grades, and served as an assistant principal. Roundtable interview.

9. Roundtable interview.

10. [Deans was a teacher's assistant who became very close to Gertrude. Her death in the 1980s was hard on Gertrude and the entire school community.]

11. [Germs of the school-based management concept appeared in earlier administrations, particularly those of William Lemmel (1946–1953), the first superintendent that Gertrude served under, and George Brain (1960–1964). The idea gained new currency in Baltimore while John Crew was superintendent (1975–1982), but Pinderhughes was the first superintendent to embrace it as an administrative priority.]

12. [In addition to the 1997 city–state partnership arrangement for administering the city schools the governor of Maryland, Parris Glendening, appointed a blue-ribbon com-mission to examine and make recommendations for closing the gap between poorly funded and well-funded school districts. The Thornton Commission—so known for its chairman, Howard University Professor Alvin Thornton—worked for two years and reported back in 2001. The commission found that meeting the needs of children in high poverty areas, where large numbers of students require special education and/or many other special services, calls for nearly twice as much funding as is needed in more financially well-off jurisdictions. The commission boldly declared that to achieve equi-table funding in every school district the state needed to add to current school funding a total $1.3 billion over a five-year period, with a major share of that amount targeted for the poorest school districts. In the spring of 2002, the Maryland General Assembly passed an historic new school funding bill embracing the Thornton recommendations but not identifying the means of funding them. To date the governor and state legisla-tors have been wrestling ever since over how to fund the new law. Christopher N. Maher, "Maryland Must Find Funds for Educational Equality," *Baltimore Sun*, February 28, 2002. Howard Libit, "Finding Funds for Education Is Next Hurdle," *Baltimore Sun*, April 8, 2002. "Education Aid flies On Political Wings," *Baltimore Sun*, April 9, 2002. Michael Dresser and Alec Macgillis, "Governor Accused of Reneging On School Aid," *Baltimore Sun*, February 28, 2003. "The Kids Can't Wait," *NEA Today*, April 2004.]

13. [The Research Department of the American Federation of Teachers reported that as of 1998 "salaries in other white collar occupations remain high compared to teachers." Citing $39,347 as the average teacher salary that year, the AFT researchers found that attorneys on average in the same period earned $71,530; engineers $64, 489; account-ants $45,919. The National Center for Education Statistics, a federal agency, reported a similar gap between teachers and other professions in the 1990s. "Survey & Analysis

of Teacher Salary Trends 1998," AFT Department of Research. <http://www.aft.org/research/survey/national.htm> "Teacher Salaries—Are They Competitive?," National Center for Education Statistics. <http://nces.ed.gov/pubs03/web/93450.asp>.

Salary disparities among teachers are also problematic. The Baltimore-based advocacy organization, Advocates for Children and Youth, published a study in the summer of 2003 reporting that public school teachers working in "high-poverty schools" in Baltimore County and Baltimore City were paid several thousand dollars less than their counterparts in wealthier schools. Mike Bowler, "Taking from the Poorer Schools," *Baltimore Sun*, June 8, 2003.]

14. [While Schiller was superintendent Baltimore City school board chairman, Tyson Tildon, initiated the REACT program (Retired Educators Advocating Change for Tomorrow) under which retirees were assigned to city schools. The practice continued through the next two administrations (Robert Booker, 1998–2000, and Carmen Russo, 2000–June 2003). Russo left the school district in debt to the tune of $58 million. Extensive hiring of retirees as "academic coaches" was one of the items identified by auditors as encouraging the buildup of the massive deficit. The coaches were among several hundred system employees to be laid off by Russo's replacement, Bonnie Copeland. "Retired Teachers Return," *Baltimore Sun*, January 17, 1998. Claudia Diamond, "Layoff of Aides Will Hurt City Kindegarteners," *Baltimore Sun*, December 4, 2003. Liz Bowie, "Warnings Lined Road to Disaster," *Baltimore Sun*, April 4, 2004. Sam Stringfield, "Adding Up Causes, Cures," *Baltimore Sun*, March 25, 2004.]

15. [Quotations from Stringfield's Fourth Year Evaluation.]

Conclusion

1. Deborah W. Meier, *untitled* contribution to "Saving Public Education," *The Nation*, February 17, 1997, 23–24.
2. For a discussion of *de jure* segregation, sanctioned by law, and de facto segregation, supported by custom, see Jennifer Hochschild and Nathan Scovronick, *The American Dream and the Public Schools* (New York: Oxford University Press, 2003) 31–36. For an overview of school funding policies and practices, Hochschild and Scovronick, *The American Dream*, chapter 3, and Jonathan Kozol, *Savage Inequalities* (New York: Perennial Books, 1992). For elaboration on "the doctrine of ineducability . . ." see Charles Payne, *Getting What We Ask For* (Westport,CN: Greenwood Press, 1984) 5.
3. Through community associations such as the Charles Village Civic Association and Greater Homewood Community Corporation these later parent cohorts did provide some fund-raising and volunteer energy for the public schools, while sending their own offspring to private institutions.
4. Mike Bowler, "City's Schools Lead U.S. in Segregation," *Baltimore Sun*, August 11, 2002.
5. Hochschild and Scovronick, *The American Dream*, 43–44. The authors note various reasons offered by white parents for avoiding inner city public schools: a fear that mixing with poor black children will be educationally harmful to their offspring; the desire to keep their children in a privileged environment; unwillingness to have their children bear any of the pressure of social change involved in desegregation. Though not noted by the authors, the statistic that indicates that white parents do not object to having half of their child's school mates be black needs to be placed in the context of cities

such as Baltimore where most schools are three-quarters to entirely black. Few white parents are willing to place their children in schools where they would be so drastically in the minority, though most probably would think that it was fine if black children were the ones to be outnumbered in an interracial setting.

6. For a review of the positive and negative research findings on desegregation see Hochschild and Scovronick, *The American Dream*, chapter 2.

7. Ibid.

8. The first commission was headed by and named for former U.S. Attorney General, Benjamin Civiletti. Abell Foundation, "A Growing Inequality," January 1989, 23. See chapter 3 in Hochschild and Scovronick (*The American Dream*) for an overview of finance reform efforts around the nation. On page 59 they explain the difficult politics of such reform: "At almost any acceptable standard of educational quality, students in poor districts require some support from taxpayers outside their district" The majority of these students are usually black or Hispanic and revenue sources for reform "are disproportionately available" in districts that are mostly white. "Thus for a community of interest to develop on matters of education funding, not only class and district lines, but often racial or ethnic lines as well, have to be crossed. Politically that can be hard to do."

9. Politician and political scientist, Alvin Thornton, led and gave his name to the second commission. Advocacy Center for Children's Educational Success With Standards (ACCESS), "Finance Litigation," Maryland, April 18, 2002 <http://www.accessednetwork.org/litigation/lit_md.html>.

10. Not explored in our taped conversations but a matter of common knowledge within Barclay School were the generous amounts of money that Gertrude contributed out of her own personal resources to assist individual families and to purchase materials for the school. As is true of many public school teachers, Barclay teachers also supplemented classroom supplies with dollars from modest salaries.

11. Meier, "Saving Public Education," 97–98. Payne, *Getting What We Ask For*, 187.

12. Payne, *Getting What We Ask For*, 151.

13. In the course of 80 years—from 1866, when the first public school superintendent was appointed in Baltimore city, to 1946, when David Weglein reached the legal retirement age, after leading the school system for 21 years—nine individuals held that position. The first superintendent under whom Gertrude served, William Lemmel, held the post for seven years 1946–1953, his tenure cut short by death. Across the remaining 42 years of Gertrude's career thirteen superintendents came and went (counting interim appointees).

14. W.E.B. DuBois, *The Souls of Black Folk* (New York: Modern Library: 1996; originally published 1903) 109–110.

15. Hall interview. Gary Gately, "More Schools May Get Calvert as Partner," *Baltimore Sun*, December 3, 1993. As discussed earlier Amprey soon backed away from trying to implement more Calvert programs beyond those at Barclay and Carter Woodson.

16. Hall interview. Lagemann paraphrased in Catherine Gewertz, "Foundations Ponder Their Impact on Schools", *Education Week*, November 15, 2000, 10. The same idea was expressed by a staff member at the Abell Foundation who did not want to be quoted, but who perceived a "honeymoon pattern" of about four years in the various school reform projects supported by the foundation.

17. Mike Rose, *Possible Lives, the Promise of Public Education in America* (New York: Penguin Books, 1996) 4. This book, Deborah Meier's *Power of Their Ideas*, and

The American Dream by Hochschild and Sovronick provide well-argued and occasionally stirring antidotes to the negative accounts that dominate public discourse on public education in the United States.

18. Informal conversation of Jo Ann Robinson with Carol Huppert in the 1970s, recalled to Huppert, in telephone conversation, May 13, 2004. While not remembering the conversation Huppert concurred with the sentiment expressed.

19. Andra Makler, "Courage, Conviction and Social Education," in ed. Margaret Smith Crocco and O.L. Davis Jr., *Bending the Future to Their Will, Civic Women, Social Education, and Democracy* (New York: Rowman and Littlefield, 1999) 258—source of "responsibility to the world." Kathleen S. Hurty, "Women Principals—Leading With Power," in *Women Leading in Education*, ed. Diane M. Dunlap and Patricia A. Schmuck (New York: State University of New York Press, 1995) 380–405; "power with," 338; "interactive web," 394.

20. Dea Andersen Kline, the Director of Community Affairs for Hopkins, was instrumental in arranging the presentation. The citation that accompanied the medal described Gertrude as "Teacher, counselor, principal; standard-bearer of excellence; exemplar of public education at its best . . ." Kathy Lally, "Hopkins Honors Barclay School's Embattled Principal," *Baltimore* Sun, May 4, 1990; "Recognition," *Evening Sun*, May 4, 1990; "Citation Read by Steven Muller in Awarding Gertrude Susan Williams The President's Medal," copy in PTO files. The description of those who usually receive the medal appeared in an article about a later recipient, state delegate Pete Rawlings, who is now deceased: "Top Honor Is Given to Rawlings," *Baltimore Sun*, June 3, 2003.

Richard Hunter was present when Muller honored Getrude but left quickly after the presentation. That same evening the Board of School Commissioners met. Commissioner Doris Johnson, who had also been present at the morning gathering at Hopkins, announced the award. Standing tall, Getrude strode the full length of the table behind which the superintendent and commissioners sat, personally displaying the medal to each one of them.

21. A reader has pointed out that this demonstration of popular support could be *against* the school system as much as it was *for* Gertrude. Nonetheless, her fervor and courage are likely to have touched numerous supporters who came from that angle.

22. Interview of Karen Olson by Jo Ann Robinson, March 27, 2004. Interview of Merrill Hall by Jo Ann Robinson, September 5, 2003.

23. Hurty, "Women Principals," in *Women Leading in Education*, 386.

24. Ibid, 381. Referring to Sharon Welch, *A Feminist Ethic of Risk* (Minneapolis: Fortress Press, 1990).

25. This tradition among African American college graduates (whether or not they attended black schools) appears to have survived into the present. In their examination of 80,000 graduates of highly selective colleges and universities in the United States in the last half of the twentieth century, William G. Bowen and Derek Bok wrote: "Particularly striking is the high degree of commitment to community and social service organizations by those African Americans with advanced degrees." They reported that 33% of blacks with doctorates held leadership positions in community and service organizations as compared with 6% of whites with doctorates. *The Shape of the River: Long-Term Consequences of Considering Race in College and University Admissions* (Princeton, N.J: Princeton University Press, 1998) 167.

26. Joyce Antler and Sari Knopp Biklen, *Changing Education. Women as Radicals and Conservators* (New York: State University of New York, 1990) 193, 197.

27. Deborah W. Meier, in symposium on "Saving Public Education," 23. Examples of the general research include Sandra L. Christenson and Susan M. Sheridan, *Schools and Families* (New York: Guilford Press, 2001); Michael Fullan, *Changing Forces, Probing the Depths of Educational Reform* (London: The Falmer Press, 1993); Sara Lawrence Lightfoot, *Worlds Apart. Relationships Between Families and Schools* (New York: Basic Books, 1978); and Seymour B. Sarason, *The Culture of the School and the Problem of Change* (Boston: Allyn and Bacon, Inc., 1971).

28. Sulayman Clark, "Educational Philosophy of Leslie Pinkney Hill: A Profile in Black Educaional Leadership, 1904–1951," Ed.D. Thesis, Harvard University, June 1984, 236. Clark refers to Charles V. Willie, who is the source of the "exposed to two worlds" quotation. Charles V. Willie, "Theory of Liberation Leadership," *Journal of Negro History* (Fall 1983), 1–7; Quotation, 7.

29. Dave Possidente interviewed by Devin Johnson, April 17, 1994. Zachary Morehouse, Joseph Robinson, and Stefan Rubin interviewed by Devin Johnson, April 17, 1994. Tara Krebs interviewed by Georretta McMillan, April 17, 1994. Angela Carmichael, interviewed by Syreeta Byrd, April 17, 1994. All tapes are in the possession of Jo Ann Robinson.

30. Robinson interview with Brandon Jones.

31. Ibid.

32. These barriers are identified and examined in an interesting study set in Baltimore by Howell S. Baum, *Community Action for School Reform* (Albany: State University Press of New York, 2003).

33. Linda Darling-Hammond, "From 'Separate But Equal' To 'No Child Left Behind': the Collision of New Standards and Old Inequalities," in *Many Children Left Behind,* ed. Deborah Meier and George Ward (Boston: Beacon Press, 2004) 19, 9. Some critics charge that proponents of NCLB are purposely setting up as many public schools as possible for failure as part of their agenda to privatize American education. Alfie Kohn, "NCLB and the Effort to Privatize Public Education," in *Many Children Left Behind*, 79–97.

34. Deborah Meier, "NCLB and Democracy," in *Many Children Left Behind*, 71.

35. The state legislatures of Utah and Virginia have voted against any compliance with NCLB. The National Education Association also opposes it in its present form. Ibid., x. Other examples of opposition are noted in Sara Neufeld, "Teacher Aims Campaign to Revise No Child Left Behind," *Baltimore Sun*, March 1, 2005 and "State Legislatures Call for Changes to Bush's No Child Left Behind Law," *Baltimore Sun*, February 24, 2005.

36. Betsy Peoples, "The Learning Principal," *Emerge* , May 1998, 52–55; Quote, 52.

37. Gertrude quoted in John Kasich, *Courage is Contagious* (New York: Doubleday, 1998) 145.

38. Gertrude quoted in Anita Durel, "The Barclay School Makes the Grade," *Baltimore's Child*, March 1995, 10–11, 13; Quote 11.

39. Gertrude quoted in Marego Athans, "Black Group Seeks Ways to Improve Education," *Baltimore Sun,* September 8, 1996.

Bibliography

Manuscript Sources

Baltimore City Archives.
Barclay School Parent–Teacher Organization Files.
Enoch Pratt Free Library, Maryland Room.
Special Collections Department, Langsdale Library, University of Baltimore.

Interviews

Interviews by J. Robinson

Barclay School Faculty Roundtable Interview December 15, 2003 with Brown, Sandra V.; Horne, Truemella M.; Jackson, Tanya J.; Lattimore, Susan; Rawlings, Dorothea A.
Bonnet, Esther, September 3, 1997.
Clapp, David, June 10, 2002.
Clarke, Mary Pat, September 26, 2003.
Cook, Karen and Cook, Richard, March 20, 2004.
Curtain, Stanley, by telephone March 12, 2004.
Embry, Robert, January 29, 2003.
Hall, Merrill, September 5, 2003.
Huppert, Carol, May 13, 2004.
Jeffries, Esther, April 28, 2004.
Johnson, Ellie and Cooper, Mimi, December 13, 2001.
Jones, Brandon, June 24, 2002.
Kenney, Jennifer, by telephone January 25, 2004.
King, Lorraine by telephone April 9, 2004.
Licht, Margaret, March 31, 2003.
Lunsford, Myra by telephone February 28, 2004.
Marrow, Gloria, April 7, 2004.
Olson, Karen, March 27, 2004.
Pinderhughes, Alice, July 14, 1983.
Schmoke, Kurt by telephone January 14, 2003.
Stokes, Carl by telephone September 12, 2004.
Umphrey, Robert, October 28, 1986.
Wallace, Evelyn, February 10, 2004.
Yates, Edmonia by telephone March 28, 2004.

Student Conducted Interviews at Celebration of 35th Anniversary of Barclay's Opening, April 19, 1994

Interview by Syreeta Byrd

Carmichael, Angela.

Interviews by Devin Johnson

Crosby, Frances.
Possidente, David.
Group interview with Morehouse, Zachary; Robinson, Joseph; Rubin, Stefan.

Interview by Georetta McMillan

Krebs, Tara.

Interviews by Carrenda Pittman

Eastman, Audrey.
Giza, Joanne.
Schildwater, Austin.

Other Interviews

Jones, Jack, interviewed by Lisabeth Holloway and Louise Strawbridge Germantown Historical Society, March 1, 1984.
Ray, Virginia, telephone interview by Medrika Law, May 17, 2004.
Spain-Pierce, Clarice, telephone interview by Medrika Law.

Government Publications

Federal

Adams v. Richardson 351F636 (1971).
National Commission on Excellence in Education.
A Nation at Risk. Washington, DC: Department of Education, 1983.
PL 94–142 *U.S. Statutes at Large* 89 (1975).
PL 107–110 *U.S. Statutes at Large* 115 (2002).
U.S. Census, 1880, 1900, 1910, 1920, 1930.

State of Maryland

Commission on Interracial Problems and Relations, "Report." Baltimore, 1956.
Commission for Students at Risk, "Maryland's Challenge." Annapolis, January 1990.
Governor's Commission on School Funding, "Report." Annapolis, January 1994.
Governor's Commission on School Performance, "Report." Annapolis, 1989.
Hornbeck v. Somerset County Board of Education 295md597, 458 A 2d 758 (1983).

City of Baltimore

Bradford v. Maryland State Board of Education NO 9434 0058/CE 189672 (Circuit Court of Baltimore City, October 18, 1996).
Bradford v. Maryland State Board of Education NO 9434 0058/CE 189672 (Circuit Court of Baltimore City, June 30, 2000).
"Desegregation Plan Submitted to Office of Civil Rights," U.S. Department of Health, Education and Welfare. Baltimore City Public Schools, 1974.

Orange County, Virginia

Deed Book.
Index of Births and Deaths.
Marriage Registry.

Newspapers

Baltimore Afro-American. June 10, 1968; March 18, May 6, 1989; January 21, August 3, 1991.
Baltimore's Child. March 1995; October 1998.
Baltimore Evening Sun. June 14, 1965; March 11, 1967; April 5, 30, May 2, 9, 1968; August 9, 1971; May 30, 1972; November 7, 1976; January 11, 1977; February 23, September 6, 1982; June 27, September 2, 1983; March 1, 3, 10, 14, 15, 16, 17, 18, 21, 23, 1989; April 12, 18, 23, 26; May 4; June 14; July 3; December 21, 24, 1990; January 10, October 26, 1994.
Baltimore News American. August 29, 1965; April 30, May 2, 9, August 25, November 24, 1968; July 16, 1971; May 19, 1974; December 2, 1977; February 26, 1980; March 1, 1981; June 23, February 13, 1982; May 16, 1984.
Baltimore Sun. February 15, 1947; June 20, 1948; January 30, 1953; June 5, 1960; March 30, 1962; February 7, 1965; February 4, 1968; April 25, through May 4, July 15, August 9, September 7, 1971; February 6, 25, March 3, June 2, September 8, 1974; June 30, July 2, 3, 9, 18, September 11, 19, November 14, 1975; November 6, 1976; December 14, 1977; January 24, 1979; January 8, August 10, September 2, October 19, December 19, 1982; September 19, 1983; December 11, 1987; May 3, July 3, 1988; February 21, 25, March 3,4, 5, 10, 11, 14, 15, 17, 20, 21, 23, 24, 25, 27, April 7, May 6, 1989; January 7, March 8, 20, April 1, 12, May 5, 16, December 23, 1990; February 3, May 26, July 31, August 18, September 27, 1991; June 10, 1992; July 5, September 19, December 3, 1993; January 6, 10, July 4, November 13, 1994; February 14, November 24, December 5, 1995; March 2, 9, June 10, September 8, November 9, 27, 1996; January 10, 26, 1997; January 17, 31, July 23, August 24, 1998; March 21, 1999; August 30, 2000; October 24, 2001; January 29, February 5, 8 27, 28, March 1, 6, April 8, 9, 14, 25, June 14, August 11, 30, 2002; February 28, June 3,8, September 15, December 4, 11, 2003; March 11, 12, 25, April 4, May 16, August 25, 2004. February 24, March 1, 2005.
Baltimore Times. April 2–8, 1990; December 4–10, 1995.
City Paper. May 26, 1989; February 15, 1990; April 5, 1995.
Education Week. October 12, 1994; April 19, November 15, 2000.
New York Times. November 8, 9, 25, 1973; August 20, 1995; April 11, 1996; December 28, 2002.

Richmond News Leader. June 20, 1989.
Warfield's Business Review. December 18, 1992.

Articles and Chapters about Gertrude Williams

Bowler, Mike. "Barclay's Principal Retiring," *Baltimore Sun* (July 22, 1998).
Edmunds, Lavinia. "The Woman Who Battled the Bureaucrats," *Reader's Digest* (December 1993) 142–146.
Janofsky, Michael. "Private School Curriculum Brings Public School Improvement," *New York Times* (February 22, 1995) B7.
Kasich, John. "Demanding Excellence," *Courage Is Contagious* (New York: Doubleday, 1998) 141–155.
Lally, Kathy. "Hopkins Honors Barclay School's Embattled Principal," *Baltimore Sun* (May 4, 1990).
Lawton, Millicent. "Borrowing From the Basics," *Education Week* (April 20, 1994) 32–33.
Leo, John. "Shakespeare vs Spiderman," *U.S. News and World Report* (April 1, 1996) 61.
Natale, Jo Anna. "Write This Down," *The American School Board Journal* (December 1995) 16–20.
Peoples, Betsy. "The Learning Principal," *Emerge* (May 1998) 53–55.
"School Reform, A Better Idea," *The Economist* (December 2, 1995) 23–24.
Sykes, Charles J. "Scenes From the Front. Barclay," *Dumbing Down Our Kids* (New York: St. Martin's Press, 1995) 275–279.

Selected Journal and Magazine Articles

Berkowitz, Edward. "Baltimore's Public Schools in a Time of Transition," *Maryland Historical Magazine* 92 no. 4 (Winter 1997) 413–432.
Fields, Karen. "What One Cannot Remember Mistakenly," *History and Memory in African American Culture*, Geneviève Fabre and Robert O'Meally, eds. (New York: Oxford University Press, 1994) 150–163.
Goldberg, Mark F. "Education in Baltimore," *Phi Delta Kappan* (November 1995) 234–235.
Hadley-Riley, Louetta Ray. "I Remember Germantown," *Germantown Crier* 52 no. 1 (Spring 2002) 32–33.
Harvey, Bill. "Hampden-Woodberry: Baltimore's Mill Villages," *The Baltimore Book. New Views of Local History*, Elizabeth Fee, Linda Shopes, and Linda Zeidman, eds. (Philadelphia: Temple University Press, 1991).
Hunter, Richard C. "The Mayor Versus the School Superintendent," *Education and Urban Society* 29 no. 2 (February 1997) 217–232.
Jonnes, Jill. "Everybody Must Get Stoned: The Origins of Modern Drug Culture in Baltimore," *Maryland Historical Magazine* 91 no. 2 (Summer 1996) 133–155.
Miller, Frederick. "The Black Migration to Philadelphia: A 1924 Profile," *African Americans in Pennsylvania*. Joe William Trotter Jr. and Eric Ledell Smith, eds.

(Philadelphia: Pennsylvania Historical and Museum Commission and State University Press, 1997).

Vavrina, Vernon S. "Evolving Role of Superintendency in Baltimore City," *Baltimore Bulletin of Education* XLLII (1964–1965) 3–15.

Theses and Dissertations

Banks, Samuel. "A Descriptive Study of the Baltimore City Board of School Commissioners as an Agent in School Desegregation, 1953–1964." Ed.D. Dissertation, Georgetown University, 1976.

Beaumont, Jennifer Joy-Marie. "Factors Contributing to Involuntary Superintendency Turnover in Urban Public School Systems." Ph.D. Dissertation, University of Maryland Baltimore County, 1993.

Carrington, Joel. "The Struggle for Desegregation of Baltimore City Public Schools, 1952–1966." Ed.D. Dissertation, University of Maryland, 1970.

Clark, Sulayman. "Educational Philosophy of Leslie Pinckney Hill: A Profile in Black Educational Leadership, 1904–1951." Ed.D. Dissertation, Harvard University, 1960.

Conyers, Charline. "History of the Cheyney State Teachers College 1837–1851." Ed.D. Dissertation, New York University, 1960.

Felix, Stephanie. "Committed to Their Own: African American Leaders in the YWCA: The YWCA of Germantown, Philadelphia Pennsylvania, 1870–1970." Ph.D. Dissertation, Temple University, 1999.

Gass, T. Anthony. "The Baltimore NAACP During the Civil Rights Movement, 1958–1963." M.A. Thesis, Morgan State University, 2001.

Horn, Vernon E. "Integrating Baltimore: Protest and Accommodation: 1945–1963." M.S. Thesis, University of Maryland, College Park, 1991.

Keeley, Diane L. "Conflict Group Formation: The Development of the Baltimore Teachers' Union." Ph.D. Dissertation, Fordham University, 1976.

Mobley, Terry E. "History of the Female High School Principal in Baltimore City Public Schools." Unpublished essay, Morgan State University Department of History, 1984.

O'Wesney, Julia Roberts. "Historical Study of the Progress of Racial Desegregation in The Public Schools of Baltimore, Maryland." Ed.D Dissertation, University of Maryland, 1970.

Spencer, John Palmer. "Courage in Cross Fire: Marcus Foster and America's Urban Education Crisis, 1941–1973." Ph.D. Dissertation, New York University, 2002.

Vavrina, Vernon S. "The History of Public Education in the City of Baltimore, 1829–1956." Abstract of Ph.D. Dissertation (Washington, DC: Catholic University of America Press, 1958).

Books, Selected Titles

A Growing Inequality: A Report on the Financial Condition of the Baltimore City Public Schools (Baltimore: Abell Foundation, 1989).

Antler, Joyce and Sari Knopp Biklen. *Changing Education. Women as Radicals and Conservators* (New York: State University Press of New York, 1990).

Baum, Howell S. *Community Action for School Reform* (Albany, NY: State University of New York Press, 2003).

Bowler, Mike. *Lessons of Change. Baltimore Schools in the Modern Era* (Baltimore: Fund for Educational Excellence, 1991).

Callard, Judith. *Germantown, Mt. Airy and Chestnut Hill* (Philadelphia: Arcadia Publishing, 2000).

Crain, Robert L. *The Politics of School Desegregation* (Chicago: Aldine Publishing Company, 1968).

DiConti, Veronica Donahue. *Interest Groups and Education Reform* (Lanham, MD: University Press of America, 1996).

Dunlap, Diane M. and Patricia Schmuck, eds., *Women Leading in Education* (New York: State University of New York Press, 1995).

Editors of *Education Week. From Risk to Renewal: Charting a Course for Reform* (Washington, DC: Editorial Projects in Education, 1983).

Franklin, Vincent P. *The Education of Black Philadelphia* (Philadelphia: University of Pennsylvania Press, 1979).

Gittel, Marilyn and Edward Hollander. *Six Urban School Districts* (New York: Frederick Praeger, 1968).

Goodlad, John I. and Robert H. Anderson. *The Nongraded Elementary School* (New York: Teachers College Press, revised edition, 1987).

Henig, Jeffrey R. et al. *The Color of School Reform. Race, Politics, and the Challenge of Urban Education* (Princeton: Princeton University Press).

Hochschild, Jennifer and Nathan Scovronick. *The American Dream and the Public Schools* (New York: Oxford University Press, 2003).

Jeffrey, Julie Roy. *Education for Children of the Poor: A Study of the Origins and Implementation of the Elementary and Secondary Education Act of 1965* (Columbus, OH: Ohio State University Press, 1979).

Meier, Deborah. *The Power of Their Ideas* (Boston: Beacon Press, 1995).

Meier, Deborah and George Ward. *Many Children Left Behind* (Boston: Beacon Press, 2004).

Orr, Marion. *Black Social Capital: The Politics of School Reform in Baltimore, 1986–1998* (Lawrence: University Press of Kansas, 1999).

Orser, Edward. *Block Busting in Baltimore* (Lexington, KY: University Press of Kentucky, 2000).

Payne, Charles. *Getting What We Ask For* (Westport, CT: Greenwood Press, 1984).

Rich, Wilbur C. *Black Mayors and School Politics, the Failure of Reform in Gary, Detroit, and Newark* (New York: Garland Press, 1996).

Rose, Mike. *Possible Lives* (New York: Penguin Books, 1996).

Sarason, Seymour B. *The Culture of the School and the Problem of Change* (Boston: Allyn and Bacon, Inc., 1971).

Scott, Hugh J. *The Black School Superintendent, Messiah or Scapegoat* (Washington, DC: Howard University Press, 1980).

Scott, W.W. *A History of Orange County Virginia* (Richmond VA: Everett Waddy Co., 1907).

Sidney Hollander Foundation. *Toward Equality* (Baltimore: Hollander Foundation, second edition, 2003).

Szanton, Peter L. *Baltimore 2000, A Choice of Futures* (Baltimore: Morris Goldseker Foundation, 1986).

Index